Shakespeare

David Bevington

**Goldentree Bibliographies
in Language & Literature**

Shakespeare

GOLDENTREE BIBLIOGRAPHIES

In Language and Literature
under the series editorship of
O. B. Hardison, Jr.

Shakespeare

compiled by

David Bevington

University of Chicago

AHM Publishing Corporation
Arlington Heights, Illinois 60004

Copyright © 1978

AHM PUBLISHING CORPORATION

All rights reserved

ISBN: 0-88295-555-1, paper
ISBN: 0-88295-556-X, cloth

Library of Congress Card Number: 76-5220

PRINTED IN THE UNITED STATES OF AMERICA
738

For Philip

Contents

CONTENTS

CONTENTS

CONTENTS

CONTENTS

CONTENTS

CONTENTS

Preface

In preparing this selective bibliography, I have attempted to provide the names of various books and articles that cannot safely be ignored by anyone intending to survey the current state of Shakespearean criticism and contribute something to our further understanding of Shakespeare. In other words, I have focused on the following single criterion: What critical studies should be familiar to the student or scholar who undertakes an essay or dissertation on any particular Shakespearean topic?

The volume is thus offered as a guide to the field, by topic and genre as well as by individual play or poem. The process of selection involves a subjective element, to be sure, since my views on the usefulness of any particular item are apt to vary at times from those of some other compiler. The criterion of relevance to the current study of Shakespeare does, on the other hand, afford some steadiness of perspective. It argues in favor of recent work so long as it is insightful in some way, while it militates against scholarship that is fifty years or more out of date unless it has managed to say something genuinely memorable. Believing much scholarship and criticism of the twentieth century to be progressive in character, I have permitted some early works to retire discreetly from view when their contributions have been subsumed by later studies. The historical record of shifting tastes and methods in the study of Shakespeare is of course an interesting subject in its own right, and I have included many older items under "The History of Shakespeare Criticism." Otherwise, the focus of this volume is on the present state of Shakespeare studies.

Most items, then, except for those dealing with the history of Shakespeare criticism, will be seen to date from 1930 onwards. This early cutoff date is by no means absolute, however, and does not exclude the work of A. C. Bradley, C. T. Onions, C. F. Tucker Brooke, E. E. Stoll, and others. The final cutoff date is February of 1977.

I have included many items with which I disagree, and some that I consider downright misleading, so long as they are a significant part of today's debate on the understanding of Shakespeare. I have tried to exclude items that seem to me to say nothing new, or that deal with matters of overly specialized interest (this embraces a great many notes, readings of particular lines, reviews of particular productions, book reviews, and the like), or that deal unhelpfully with "crank" issues such as the so-called authorship controversy. I have included studies written in some foreign languages, notably German and French, bearing in mind the problems of availability and usefulness. Thus, I have not included any articles written in Japanese, for instance, because so few readers would be able to use such items. Works in English by Japanese authors, on the other hand, receive due consideration. I should confess that I have not been able to read carefully all the items examined, nor can I imagine that any compiler of a Shakespeare bibliography today would be able or willing to do so. I have, notwithstanding, attempted at least to examine every item included here (as well as many not included) in order to be able to classify the item properly and gain some impression of its quality.

Because that quality varies considerably from item to item, and because the coverage of this volume is designed to provide as broad as possible a perspective of differing viewpoints, I have used asterisks (*) to mark those items that seem to me most nearly indispensable. Here the subjective element is particularly acute, and I would not have the reader suppose these markings to indicate anything more than a partial (that is, both biased and incomplete) listing of my own critical tastes. I know that I have missed, through inattentiveness, a number of items deserving better recognition, and apologize to those who have been unintentionally slighted. No system of preferential markings for so large a project can hope to be accurate and consistent, and can be defended only as a set of personal recommendations from one inadequate mortal to another.

Cross-referencing is an important feature of this volume. In order to save space, I have listed general works under the appropriate general category (Shakespearean tragedy, for example) and have then cross listed the item by number under the various individual plays or other topics it treats. What this means is that an important general study often appears under the individual works only as a number, too easily overlooked by the reader who sees before him the authors and titles of various studies devoted solely to a particular work. The reader should remember that the most significant treatments of an individual work may well be found elsewhere in the bibliography, as indicated by the cross-referenced numbers. Some items are so manifestly significant that I have repeated the entry, but have had to limit this practice severely in the interests of saving space.

Cross-referencing is also necessary because of the inevitable overlap between categories in this classified bibliography. In order to keep individual lists down to a manageable size, and to offer as specific guidance as possible, I have subdivided the field of Shakespearean studies into a large number of individual units. The user of this book will quickly observe, however, that no hard and fast line can be drawn between general studies of *Hamlet* and studies of the character of Hamlet, or between Shakespeare's thought and his imagery, or between pastoral plays and romantic comedies. I hope the reader will adopt a mistrustful attitude toward the categorizing nature of this bibliography and will range freely in related topics, aided by cross-referenced numbers.

Annotation is used sparingly in this bibliography. I have annotated only those items in which the titles seem to me to require further explanation as to subject and intention. These annotations are not intended to be judgmental. In general, I have preferred to rely on full titles and on the topical organization of this book as a means of informing the reader whether an item is likely to be of use.

I have attempted to respect the desire of scholars and critics to be known by the professional names they use in print—W. W. Greg, M. C. Bradbrook, E. M. W. Tillyard, J. A. Bryant, Jr., Jeanne Addison Roberts, Frank Kermode, Barbara K. Lewalski, M. Channing Linthicum—rather than reducing this colorful variety to a standard format. Most such critics are sufficiently prolific to pose no hazard for the user of the library card catalogue. Where a critic has used a variety of forms in print, on the other hand, I have employed one form of the name throughout to avoid inconsistency and confusion.

I have made some effort to provide up-to-date information on reprinted editions of books once out of print, as an aid to anyone wishing to obtain a copy for personal use or to order it for the library. Dates of reprinted editions are not always easy to discover, however, and are omitted when the information was unavailable to me.

I wish to thank the staffs of the various libraries where I have compiled and checked this bibliography, especially the Folger Shakespeare Library, the Library of Congress, the University of Chicago Library, the Newberry Library, Northwestern University Library, Duke University Library, the Library of the University of Illinois at Urbana, and the Library of the University of North Carolina at Chapel Hill. I have been personally assisted in checking some otherwise inaccessible items by David Kastan of Dartmouth College and by his able graduate assistant, Ellen Duke. Professor Kastan has also given me invaluable criticism on the bibliography as a whole. So has my wife, Peggy. My daughter Kate helped me alphabetize the index. Professor William Gibson of Idaho State University was kind enough to let me examine relevant portions of the 1974 PMLA International Bibliography prior to its publication, and Professor Harrison Meserole of Pennsylvania State University similarly sent me advance proofs of his 1975 Annotated World Shakespeare Bibliography prepared for *Shakespeare Quarterly*. To all, my warmest thanks.

I, or the publisher, will be most grateful to receive notice of any errors or important omissions in the volume, in anticipation of future printings or editions.

Abbreviations

AI	American Imago
AR	Antioch Review
ArlQ	Arlington Quarterly
BFLS	Bulletin de la Faculté des Lettres de Strasbourg
BJA	British Journal of Aesthetics (London)
BJRL	Bulletin of the John Rylands Library
BSUF	Ball State University Forum
BuR	Bucknell Review
BUSE	Boston University Studies in English
CahiersE	Cahiers Elisabéthains
CE	College English
CentR	Centennial Review (Mich. State U.)
CL	Comparative Literature
CLAJ	College Language Association Journal (Morgan State Coll., Baltimore)
ClioW	Clio: An Interdisciplinary Journal of Literature, History, and the Philosophy of History (U. of Wisconsin, Parkside)
CLS	Comparative Literature Studies (U. of Illinois, Urbana)
CollL	College Literature
CompD	Comparative Drama
ContempR	Contemporary Review (London)
	Costerus: Essays in English and American Language and Literature (Amsterdam)
CQ	Cambridge Quarterly
CR	Critical Review (Melbourne; Sydney)
CritQ	Critical Quarterly
CUF	Columbia University Forum
Daedalus	(Proceedings of the American Academy of Arts and Sciences)
	Discourse: A Review of the Liberal Arts (Concordia Coll.)
DR	Dalhousie Review
DUJ	Durham University Journal
E&S	Essays and Studies by Members of the English Association
EA	Études Anglaises
EIC	Essays in Criticism (Oxford)
EIE	English Institute Essays
EJ	English Journal
ELH	Journal of English Literary History

ELN	English Language Notes (U. of Colorado)
ELR	English Literary Renaissance
EM	English Miscellany (Rome)
ES	English Studies. A Journal of English Letters and Philology (Amsterdam)
	Essays in Literature (Western Illinois U.)
ETJ	Educational Theatre Journal
EUQ	Emory University Quarterly
Genre	(U. of Illinois at Chicago Circle)
HAB	Humanities Association Bulletin (Canada)
HLQ	Huntington Library Quarterly
HSL	Hartford Studies in Literature
HudR	Hudson Review
JAAC	Journal of Aesthetics and Art Criticism
JEGP	Journal of English and Germanic Philology
JGE	Journal of General Education
JHI	Journal of the History of Ideas
JWCI	Journal of the Warburg and Courtauld Institute
KR	Kenyon Review
L&P	Literature and Psychology (U. of Hartford and Fairleigh Dickinson U.)
Lang&S	Language and Style
LC	Library Chronicle (U. of Pennsylvania)
LeedsSE	Leeds Studies in English
LFQ	Literature/Film Quarterly
M&L	Music and Letters (London)
MD	Modern Drama
MichA	Michigan Academician [Supersedes PMASAL]
MLN	Modern Language Notes
MLQ	Modern Language Quarterly
MLR	Modern Language Review
MP	Modern Philology
MQR	Michigan Quarterly Review
MuK	Maske und Kothurn (Graz-Wien)
N&Q	Notes and Queries
NDQ	North Dakota Quarterly
Neophil	Neophilologus (Groningen)
NLH	New Literary History (U. of Virginia)
NM	Neuphilologische Mitteilungen
NS	Die Neueren Sprachen
OL	Orbis Litterarum
Palaestra	(Berlin)
PBA	Proceedings of the British Academy
PBSA	Papers of the Bibliographical Society of America
PLL	Papers on Language and Literature
PLPLS-LHS	Proceedings of the Leeds Philosophical and Literary Society, Literary and Historical Section
PMASAL	Papers of the Michigan Academy of Science, Arts, and Letters [Superseded by MichA]

ABBREVIATIONS

PMLA	Publications of the Modern Language Association of America
PP	Philologica Pragensia
PQ	Philological Quarterly
PR	Partisan Review
PsyQ	Psychoanalytic Quarterly
PsyR	Psychoanalytic Review
PTRSC	Proceedings and Transactions of the Royal Society of Canada
QQ	Queen's Quarterly (Ottawa)
QR	Quarterly Review (London)
REL	Review of English Literature (London)
RenD	Renaissance Drama
RenP	Renaissance Papers
RenQ	Renaissance Quarterly
RES	Review of English Studies
Rice U. Studies	Rice University Studies
RIP	Rice Institute Pamphlets
RMS	Renaissance and Modern Studies (U. of Nottingham)
RNL	Review of National Literatures
RORD	Research Opportunities in Renaissance Drama
RS	Research Studies (Washington State U.)
SAB	South Atlantic Bulletin
SAQ	South Atlantic Quarterly
SB	Studies in Bibliography: Papers of the Bibliographical Society of the University of Virginia
SEL	Studies in English Literature, 1500–1900
ShAB	Shakespeare Association Bulletin
ShakS	Shakespeare Studies (U. of Cincinnati and others)
ShN	Shakespeare Newsletter
SHR	Southern Humanities Review
ShS	Shakespeare Survey
ShStud	Shakespeare Studies (Japan)
SJ	Shakespeare-Jahrbuch
SJH	Shakespeare-Jahrbuch (Heidelberg)
SJW	Shakespeare-Jahrbuch (Weimar)
SLitI	Studies in the Literary Imagination (Georgia State College)
SN	Studia Neophilologica
SoQ	Southern Quarterly (U. of Southern Mississippi)
SoR	Southern Review (Louisiana State U.)
SP	Studies in Philology
SQ	Shakespeare Quarterly
SR	Sewanee Review
SRO	Shakespearean Research and Opportunities
TDR	Tulane Drama Review, and subsequently The Drama Review
	Theoria: A Journal of Studies in the Arts, Humanities, and Social Sciences (Natal)
Thoth	(Department of English, Syracuse U.)

Thought	(Fordham U.)
ThR	Theatre Research
ThS	Theatre Survey (American Society for Theatre Research)
TLS	Times Literary Supplement (London)
TN	Theatre Notebook
TSE	Tulane Studies in English
TSL	Tennessee Studies in Literature
TSLL	Texas Studies in Literature and Language [Supersedes UTSE]
UCPE	U. of California Publications in English
UCSLL	U. of Colorado Studies in Language and Literature
UKCR	U. of Kansas City Review [Superseded by UR]
UMSE	U. of Mississippi Studies in English
UR	University Review [Supersedes UKCR]
UTQ	U. of Toronto Quarterly
UTSE	U. of Texas Studies in English [Superseded by TSLL]
VQR	Virginia Quarterly Review
WHR	Western Humanities Review
YR	Yale Review
ZAA	Zeitschrift für Anglistik und Amerikanistik (East Berlin)

Other abbreviations:

comp., comps.	compiler, compilers
ed., eds.	editor, editors, *or* edition
enl.	enlarged
n.d.	no date
n.s.	new series
orig.	originally
pub.	published
rev.	revised
rpt.	reprinted
trans.	translated
U.P.	University Press
vol., vols.	volume, volumes

Part I
General

The Study of Shakespeare

Bibliographies

General Bibliographies

See also **104.**

1 *Abstracts of English Studies.* Published by the National Council of Teachers of English. Boulder, Colo., 1958–.

2 *Annual Bibliography of English Language and Literature.* (Title varies.) Compiled by Members of the Modern Humanities Research Association. Cambridge, Eng.: Bowes & Bowes, 1921 (for 1920)–.

3 *Bibliographie internationale de l'Humanisme et de la Renaissance.* Geneva: Librairie Droz, 1966 (for 1965)–. An annual bibliography.

4 GREG, W. W. *A Bibliography of the English Printed Drama to the Restoration.* 4 vols. London: Printed for the Bibliographical Society at the Oxford U.P., 1939–59.

5 HARBAGE, Alfred. *Annals of English Drama, 975–1700.* Rev. S. SCHOEN-BAUM. Philadelphia: U. of Pennsylvania P.; London: Methuen, 1964.

6 POLLARD, Alfred W., and G. R. REDGRAVE, comps. *A Short-Title Catalogue of Books Printed in England, Scotland, and Ireland . . . 1475–1640.* London: The Bibliographical Society, 1926. Rev. and enl., New York: Index Committee of the Modern Language Association, 1972–.

7 STRATMAN, Carl J. *Bibliography of English Printed Tragedy, 1565–1900.* London: Feffer & Simons, 1964; Carbondale: Southern Illinois U.P., 1966.

8 WATSON, George, ed. *The New Cambridge Bibliography of English Literature.* 4 vols. Cambridge: Cambridge U.P., 1974.

1

Shakespeare Bibliographies

For specialized bibliographies dealing with Bibliography and Textual Criticism, Shakespeare and the Stage, Studies in Shakespeare's Chronology, Sources, Shakespeare's Life, The Tragedies, Music, The Sonnets, *Hamlet,* and others, see the following: **116, 178, 182, 384, 426, 615, 768, 1542, 1575, 2029, 2612, 2619, 2621, 3512,** and **4534.** For further information on bibliographies of Shakespeare, see Louis MARDER, "A Bibliography of Shakespearean Bibliographies." *ShN* 12 (1962):24–25.

9 BARTLETT, Henrietta C. *Mr. William Shakespeare: Original and Early Editions of His Quartos and Folios.* New Haven: Yale U.P., 1922.

10 BARTLETT, Henrietta C., and Alfred W. POLLARD. *A Census of Shakespeare's Plays in Quarto, 1594–1709.* Rev. ed., New Haven: Yale U.P., 1939.

11 BERMAN, Ronald. *A Reader's Guide to Shakespeare's Plays.* Glenview, Ill.: Scott, Foresman, 1965. Rev. ed., 1973.*

12 Bibliothèque Nationale. *Catalogue des Ouvrages de William Shakespeare.* Paris: Imprimerie Nationale, 1948.

13 Birmingham Shakespeare Library. *A Shakespeare Bibliography: The Catalogue of the Birmingham Shakespeare Library.* 7 vols. London: Mansell, 1971.

14 British Museum. *Shakespeare: An Excerpt from the General Catalogue of Printed Books in the British Museum.* London: Trustees of the British Museum, 1964.

15 EBISCH, Walther, in collaboration with Levin L. SCHÜCKING. *A Shakespeare Bibliography.* Oxford: Clarendon, 1931. *Supplement for the Years 1930–1935.* Oxford: Clarendon, 1937.*

16 ELLIS-FERMOR, Una. "English and American Shakespeare Studies 1937–1952." *Anglia* 71 (1952):1–49.

17 Folger Shakespeare Library. *Catalog of the Shakespeare Collection.* 2 vols. Boston: G. K. Hall, 1972.

18 FOLSOM, Michael B. *Shakespeare: A Marxist Bibliography.* New York: American Institute for Marxist Studies, 1965.

19 FORD, H. L. *Shakespeare 1700–1740: A Collation of the Editions and Separate Plays.* Oxford: Oxford U.P., 1935.

20 JAGGARD, William. *Shakespeare Bibliography: A Dictionary of Every Known Issue of the Writings of Our National Poet and of Recorded Opinion Thereon in the English Language.* Stratford-on-Avon: Shakespeare Press, 1911. Rpt., New York: Ungar, 1959.

21 LAVIN, J. A. "Shakespeare: Bibliographical Spectrum." *RNL* 3.2 (1972):163–84.

22 MCMANAWAY, James G., and Jeanne Addison ROBERTS. *A Selective Bibliography of Shakespeare: Editions, Textual Studies, Commentary.* Charlottesville: U.P. of Virginia for the Folger Shakespeare Library, 1975.*

23 PAYNE, Waveney R. N. *A Shakespeare Bibliography.* London: Library Association, 1969.

24 SHAW, A. Capel. *An Index to the Shakespeare Memorial Library.* Birmingham: Percival Jones, 1900.

25 SMITH, Gordon Ross. *A Classified Shakespeare Bibliography, 1936–1958.* University Park: Pennsylvania State U.P., 1963.*

26 TANNENBAUM, Samuel A., ed. *A Concise Bibliography.* New York: For the editor, 1940–50. Separate bibliographical volumes for *The Merchant of Venice, Macbeth, King Lear, Othello, Romeo and Juliet, Troilus and Cressida, Sir Thomas More,* and the Sonnets.

27 THIMM, Franz. *Shakspeariana from 1564 to 1864: An Account of the Shakespearian Literature of England, Germany, France, and Other European Countries during Three Centuries, with Bibliographical Introductions.* London: Franz Thimm, 1865. Rev. ed., 1872.

28 VELZ, John W. *Shakespeare and the Classical Tradition: A Critical Guide to Commentary, 1660–1960.* Minneapolis: U. of Minnesota P., 1968.

29 WELLS, Stanley. *Shakespeare: A Reading Guide.* London: Oxford U.P., 1969. 2nd ed., 1970.

30 WELLS, Stanley, ed. *Shakespeare: Select Bibliographical Guides.* London: Oxford U.P., 1973.*

Periodicals and Annual Bibliographies

Many of the following periodicals include an annual bibliography useful to the student of Shakespeare.

31 *Publications of the Modern Language Association of America (PMLA).* New York, 1884/85–. Contains annual bibliography of modern literatures beginning with vol. 37 (1922).

32 *Research Opportunities in Renaissance Drama (RORD).* Evanston, Ill., 1956–.

33 *The Shakespeare Association Bulletin (ShAB).* New York: Shakespeare Association of America, 1924–49. Superseded by *Shakespeare Quarterly.* (See item 36 below.) Contains annual bibliography.

34 *Shakespeare Jahrbuch (SJ). Jahrbuch der Deutschen Shakespeare-Gesellschaft.* Vols. 1–99. Berlin: G. Reimer and subsequently Heidelberg: Quelle & Meyer, 1865–1964. Since 1965, *Shakespeare Jahrbuch* has been published simultaneously as two separate journals: one in Heidelberg, West Germany *(SJH)* by Quelle & Meyer, and one in Weimar, East Germany *(SJW)* by Herman Böhlaus, vol. 101 (1965)–. Each contains an annual bibliography.

35 *Shakespeare Newsletter (ShN).* New York and subsequently Chicago, 1951–. Contains occasional bibliographies on special topics, such as Shakespeare on Film, Shakespeare's Life, etc.

36 *Shakespeare Quarterly (SQ).* New York: Shakespeare Association of America, 1950–72; Washington, D.C.: Folger Shakespeare Library, 1972–. Contains annual bibliography. *Cumulative Index* to vols. 1–15 compiled by Martin SEYMOUR-SMITH. New York and London: AMS, 1969.

37 *Shakespeare Studies (ShakS).* Cincinnati, and subsequently Nashville and Columbia, S.C., 1965–.

38 *Shakespeare Survey (ShS).* Cambridge: Cambridge U.P., 1948–. Contains annual review articles on twentieth-century scholarship.

39 *Shakespearean Research and Opportunities (SRO).* (Originally entitled *Shakespearean Research Opportunities.*) Riverside, Calif., and subsequently New York, 1965–. Since 1967 contains an annual selective annotated bibliography of Shakespeare in relation to Renaissance intellectual contexts, mainly the latter.

40 *Studies in English Literature (SEL).* Houston: Rice U., 1961–. The spring issue of each volume is devoted to Elizabethan and Jacobean drama and contains a review article on recent studies.

41 *Studies in Philology (SP).* Chapel Hill: U. of North Carolina P., 1906–. Vols. 15 through 66 (1918–69) contain annual Renaissance bibliography, discontinued since 1969.

42 *The Year's Work in English Studies (YWES).* London: for the English Association by the Oxford U.P., 1921–. Contains an annual survey and evaluation of works on Shakespeare among other authors. Rpt. of vols. 1–32 (1921–53), New York: AMS.

Handbooks, Study Guides, Companions to Shakespeare

43 BATE, John. *How to Find Out about Shakespeare.* Oxford and New York: Pergamon, 1968.

44 BERGERON, David M. *Shakespeare: A Study and Research Guide.* New York: St. Martin's, 1975.

45 CHARNEY, Maurice. *How to Read Shakespeare.* New York: McGraw-Hill, 1971.

46 CLARK, Sandra, and T. H. LONG. *The New Century Shakespeare Handbook.* Englewood Cliffs, N.J.: Prentice-Hall, 1974.

47 FRYE, Roland Mushat. *Shakespeare: The Art of the Dramatist.* Boston: Houghton Mifflin, 1970.

48 GRACE, William J. *Approaching Shakespeare.* New York: Basic Books, 1964.

49 HALLIDAY, F. E. *A Shakespeare Companion, 1550–1950.* London: Duckworth, 1952. 2nd ed., *A Shakespeare Companion, 1564–1964.* Harmondsworth: Penguin; London: Duckworth; New York: Schocken, 1964.

50 HARBAGE, Alfred. *William Shakespeare: A Reader's Guide.* New York: Noonday and Farrar, Straus; Toronto: Ambassador, 1963. Rpt., New York: Octagon, 1971.*

51 HOLZKNECHT, Karl J. *The Backgrounds of Shakespeare's Plays.* New York: American Book, 1950.

52 KLEIN, David. *The Living Shakespeare.* New York: Cyrco, 1976. An introduction to the major works.

53 MARDER, Louis. "Shakespeare Handbooks: A Survey 1887–1975." *ShN* 25 (1975):40–41.

54 MAY, Robin. *Who's Who in Shakespeare? The Man, The Times, The Works.* London: Elm Tree, 1972; New York: Taplinger, 1973; Newton Abbot, Eng.: David & Charles, 1974.

55 MUIR, Kenneth, and S. SCHOENBAUM, eds. *A New Companion to Shakespeare Studies.* Cambridge: Cambridge U.P., 1971.* In part this is an updated revision of Harley GRANVILLE-BARKER and G. B. HARRISON, eds., *A Companion to Shakespeare Studies.* Cambridge: Cambridge U.P.; New York: Macmillan, 1934. The earlier volume remains available and is not entirely superseded.

56 SPENCER, T. J. B., ed. *Shakespeare: A Celebration, 1564–1964.* Harmondsworth and Baltimore: Penguin, 1964.

57 ZESMER, David M. *Guide to Shakespeare.* New York: Barnes & Noble, 1976.

Dictionaries, Concordances, and Other Reference Works

See also **529, 1530,** and **1534–35.**

58 ABBOTT, E. A. *A Shakespearian Grammar.* 3rd ed., London: Macmillan, 1870. Rpt., New York: Haskell House; Gloucester, Mass.: P. Smith; New York: Dover, 1966.*

59 BARTLETT, John. *A Complete Concordance or Verbal Index to Words, Phrases, and Passages in the Dramatic Works of Shakespeare.* London: Macmillan, 1894. Rpt., 1953.

60 BROWNING, D. C., comp. *Everyman's Dictionary of Shakespeare Quotations.* London: Dent; New York: Dutton, 1953. Rev. ed., 1961.

61 CAMPBELL, Oscar James, and Edward G. QUINN, eds. *The Reader's Encyclopedia of Shakespeare.* New York: Crowell, 1966.*

62 CHAMBERS, E. K. *William Shakespeare: A Study of Facts and Problems.* 2 vols. Oxford: Clarendon, 1930.* An abbreviated version in one volume, *A Short Life of Shakespeare, with the Sources,* edited by Charles WILLIAMS, appeared in 1933.

63 DOBSON, E. J. *English Pronunciation, 1500–1700.* 2 vols. 2nd ed., Oxford: Clarendon, 1968.

64 DONOW, Herbert S. *A Concordance to the Sonnet Sequences of Daniel, Drayton, Shakespeare, Sidney, and Spenser.* Carbondale: Southern Illinois U.P., 1969.

65 ENGSTROM, J. Eric. *Coins in Shakespeare: A Numismatic Guide.* Hanover: Dartmouth College Museum, 1964.

66 FALCONER, Alexander Frederick. *A Glossary of Shakespeare's Sea and Naval Terms Including Gunnery.* London: Constable; New York: Ungar, 1965.

67 FRANZ, Wilhelm. *Shakespeare-Grammatik.* 3rd ed., Heidelberg: Winters, 1924.*

68 IRVINE, Theodora. *A Pronouncing Dictionary of Shakespearean Proper Names.* New York: Barnes & Noble, 1944.

69 KÖKERITZ, Helge. *Shakespeare's Names: A Pronouncing Dictionary.* New Haven: Yale U.P., 1959.

70 KÖKERITZ, Helge. *Shakespeare's Pronunciation.* New Haven: Yale U.P.; London: Oxford U.P., 1953.*

71 MACKAY, Charles. *Glossary of Obscure Words and Phrases in the Writings of Shakespeare and His Contemporaries.* London: Low, Marston, Searle, & Rivington, 1887.

72 MARTIN, Michael Rheta, and Richard C. HARRIER. *The Concise Encyclopedic Guide to Shakespeare.* New York: Horizon, 1971.

73 NARES, Robert. *A Glossary . . . [of] Shakespeare and His Contemporaries.* 2 vols. London: Triphook, 1822. New ed. by James O. HALLIWELL and Thomas WRIGHT. London: J. R. Smith, 1859. Rev. ed., 1888. Rpt., Detroit: Gale Research, 1966.

74 ONIONS, C. T. *A Shakespeare Glossary.* Oxford: Clarendon, 1911. 2nd ed., 1919.*

75 *Oxford Shakespeare Concordances.* Oxford: Clarendon, 1969–. A separate volume for each individual play.

76 PARTRIDGE, Eric. *Shakespeare's Bawdy.* London: Routledge & K. Paul, 1947. Rev. popular ed., New York: Dutton, 1955. Rev. and enl., London: Routledge & K. Paul, 1969.*

77 QUENNELL, Peter, and Hamish JOHNSON. *Who's Who in Shakespeare.* London: Weidenfeld & Nicolson; New York: Morrow, 1973.

78 SCHMIDT, Alexander. *Shakespeare-Lexicon.* 2 vols. Rev. and enl. by Gregor SARRAZIN. 5th ed., Berlin: de Gruyter, 1962. Rpt., New York: Blom, 1968.*

79 SPEVACK, Marvin. *A Complete and Systematic Concordance to the Works of Shakespeare.* 6 vols. Hildesheim: Olms, 1968–70. This work is available in a one-volume abridgement as *The Harvard Concordance to Shakespeare.* Cambridge, Mass.: Harvard U.P., 1973.*

80 STEVENSON, Burton, comp. *The Home Book of Shakespeare Quotations.* London and New York: Scribner's, 1937.

81 STEVENSON, Burton, comp. *The Standard Book of Shakespeare Quotations.* New York: Funk & Wagnalls, 1953.

82 STOKES, Francis Griffin. *A Dictionary of the Characters and Proper Names in the Works of Shakespeare.* London: Harrap, 1924.

83 SUGDEN, Edward H. *A Topographical Dictionary to the Works of Shakespeare and His Fellow Dramatists.* Manchester: U. of Manchester P.; London and New York: Longmans, Green, 1925.

84 THOMSON, W. H. *Shakespeare's Characters: A Historical Dictionary.* Altrincham: Sherratt; New York: British Book Centre, 1951.

Modern Editions of Shakespeare's Sources

See also **3897.**

85 BOSWELL-STONE, W. G., ed. *Shakespeare's Holinshed: The Chronicle and the Historical Plays Compared.* London and New York: Longmans, Green, 1896. 2nd ed., London: Chatto & Windus; New York, Duffield, 1907. Rpt., New York: Blom, 1966.

86 BROOKE, C. F. Tucker, ed. *Shakespeare's Plutarch.* 2 vols. New York: Duffield; London: Chatto & Windus, 1909. Rpt., New York: Haskell House, 1966.

87 BULLOUGH, Geoffrey, ed. *Narrative and Dramatic Sources of Shakespeare.* 8 vols. London: Routledge & K. Paul; New York: Columbia U.P., 1957–75.*

88 CAMPBELL, Lily B., ed. *The Mirror for Magistrates.* Cambridge: Cambridge U.P., 1938. New York: Barnes & Noble, 1970.* *Parts Added to the Mirror for Magistrates* by John HIGGINS and Thomas BLENERHASSET. Cambridge: Cambridge U.P., 1946.

89 GRIFFIN, Alice S., ed. *The Sources of Ten Shakespearean Plays.* New York: Crowell, 1966.

90 HOSLEY, Richard, ed. *Shakespeare's Holinshed.* New York: Putnam's, 1968.*

91 NICOLL, Allardyce, and Josephine NICOLL, eds. *Holinshed's Chronicle, As Used in Shakespeare's Plays.* Everyman's Library. London and Toronto: Dent; New York: Dutton, 1927.

92 ROUSE, W. H. D., ed. *Shakespeare's Ovid, Being Arthur Golding's Translation of the Metamorphoses.* London: De la More, 1904. Rpt., Carbondale: Southern Illinois U.P., 1961; New York: Norton, 1966.*

93 SATIN, Joseph, ed. *Shakespeare and His Sources.* Boston: Houghton Mifflin, 1966.

94 SCHANZER, Ernest, ed. *Shakespeare's Appian: A Selection from the Tudor Translation of Appian's "Civil Wars."* Liverpool: Liverpool U.P., 1956.

95 SPENCER, T. J. B., ed. *Elizabethan Love Stories.* Harmondsworth and Baltimore: Penguin, 1968.

96 SPENCER, T. J. B., ed. *Shakespeare's Plutarch.* Harmondsworth and Baltimore: Penguin, 1964.*

Commentary on Shakespeare and His Sources

See also **1471–72, 1591–94, 1655, 1666, 1828, 1871, 2014,** and **2168.**

97 ARTHOS, John. "Shakespeare and the Ancient World." *MQR* 10 (1971):149–63.

98 BARROLL, J. Leeds, ed. "Shakespeare's Other Ovid: A Reproduction of Commentary on Metamorphoses I–IV." *ShakS* 3 (1968 for 1967):173–256.

99 BLUESTONE, Max. *From Story to Stage: The Dramatic Adaptation of Prose Fiction in the Period of Shakespeare and His Contemporaries.* The Hague and Paris: Mouton, 1974.*

100 BOAS, Frederick S. "Aspects of Classical Legend and History in Shakespeare." *PBA* 29 (1944 for 1943):107–32.

101 BORINSKI, Ludwig. "The Origin of the Euphuistic Novel and Its Significance for Shakespeare." In **1117.**

102 BROOKE, Nicholas. "Marlowe as Provocative Agent in Shakespeare's Early Plays." *ShS* 14 (1961):34–44.

103 BROOKS, Harold F. "Marlowe and Early Shakespeare." *Christopher Marlowe.* Ed. Brian MORRIS. London: Benn, 1968.

104 BROWN, Huntington. "The Classical Tradition in English Literature: A Bibliography." *Harvard Studies and Notes in Philology and Literature* 18 (1935):7–46. See especially pp. 31–34 on Shakespeare.

105 BUSH, Douglas. "Classical Myth in Shakespeare's Plays." In **1131.**

106 CAIRNCROSS, Andrew S. "Shakespeare and Ariosto: *Much Ado About Nothing, King Lear,* and *Othello."* RenQ 29 (1976):178–82.

107 CARTER, Thomas. *Shakespeare and Holy Scripture.* New York: AMS, 1970. Orig. pub. New York, 1905.

108 CLEMEN, Wolfgang. "Shakespeare and Marlowe." In **1151.**

109 COGHILL, Nevill. "Shakespeare's Reading in Chaucer." In **1131.**

110 COHEN, Eileen Z. "The Visible Solemnity: Ceremony and Order in Shakespeare and Hooker." *TSLL* 12 (1970):181–95.

111 COLEMAN, Hamilton. *Shakespeare and the Bible.* New York: Vantage, 1955.

112 CORMICAN, L. A. "Medieval Idiom in Shakespeare: (1) Shakespeare and the Liturgy; (2) Shakespeare and the Medieval Ethic." *Scrutiny* 17 (1950–51):186–202, 298–317.

113 COULTER, Cornelia C. "The Plautine Tradition in Shakespeare." *JEGP* 19 (1920):66–83.

114 ELLRODT, Robert. "Self-Consciousness in Montaigne and Shakespeare." *ShS* 28 (1975):37–50.

115 GESNER, Carol. *Shakespeare and the Greek Romance: A Study of Origins.* See **1645.***

116 GUTTMAN, Selma. *The Foreign Sources of Shakespeare's Works: An Annotated Bibliography of the Commentary Written on This Subject between 1904 and 1940, Together with Lists of Certain Translations Available to Shakespeare.* New York: King's Crown, 1947. Rpt., New York: Octagon.

117 HARMON, Alice. "How Great Was Shakespeare's Debt to Montaigne?" *PMLA* 57 (1942):988–1008.

118 HARRISON, T. P., Jr. "Shakespeare and Montemayor's *Diana."* UTSE 6 (1926):72–120.

119 HART, Alfred. *Shakespeare and the Homilies.* Melbourne: Melbourne U.P., in association with the Oxford U.P., 1934. Rpt., New York: AMS, Octagon.*

120 HODGEN, Margaret T. "Montaigne and Shakespeare Again." *HLQ* 16 (1952): 23–42.

121 HONIGMANN, E. A. J. "Shakespeare's Plutarch." *SQ* 10 (1959):25–33.

122 HOSLEY, Richard. "The Formal Influence of Plautus and Terence." *Elizabethan Theatre.* Eds. John Russell BROWN and Bernard HARRIS. Stratford-upon-Avon Studies 9. London: Arnold, 1966.

123 HUNTER, G. K. "Shakespeare's Reading." In **55.**

124 KAUFMANN, R. J. "The Seneca Perspective and the Shakespearean Poetic." *CompD* 1 (1967):182–98.

125 KERMODE, Frank. "On Shakespeare's Learning." *BJRL* 48 (1965):207–26. Rpt. in **1223.** Also published separately by the Wesleyan U. Center for Advanced Studies, Middletown, Conn., 1964.

126 KLOSE, Dietrich. "Shakespeare und Ovid." *SJH* (1968):72–93.

THE STUDY OF SHAKESPEARE

127 LIVERMORE, Ann. "Shakespeare and St. Augustine." *QR* 303 (1965):181–93.

128 MARTIN, L. C. "Shakespeare, Lucretius, and the Commonplaces." *RES* 21 (1945):174–82.

129 MILWARD, Peter. *Shakespeare's Religious Background.* Bloomington and London: Indiana U.P.; Tokyo: Hokuseido P., 1973.

130 MINCOFF, Marco. "Shakespeare and Lyly." *ShS* 14 (1961):15–24.

131 MUIR, Kenneth. *Shakespeare's Sources.* 2 vols. London: Methuen; New York: Hillary House, 1957. Rpt. with appendices, 1961.*

132 NOBLE, Richmond. *Shakespeare's Biblical Knowledge and Use of the Book of Common Prayer.* London: Society for Promoting Christian Knowledge; New York: Macmillan, 1935. Rpt., New York: Octagon.*

133 OAKESHOTT, Walter. "Shakespeare and Plutarch." In **1139.**

134 POTTS, Abbie Findlay. *Shakespeare and "The Faerie Queene."* Ithaca: Cornell U.P., 1958.

135 PRAZ, Mario. "Shakespeare's Italy." *ShS* 7 (1954):95–106.

136 PROUTY, Charles Tyler. "Some Observations on Shakespeare's Sources." *SJ* 96 (1960):64–77.

137 RIBNER, Irving. "Marlowe and Shakespeare." *SQ* 15.2 (1964):41–53. Also in **1153.**

138 ROBERTSON, J. M. *Montaigne and Shakspere.* London: London U.P., 1897. 2nd ed., London: A. & C. Black, 1909.

139 ROOT, Robert Kilburn. *Classical Mythology in Shakespeare.* New York: Holt, 1903.

140 ROSTON, Murray. "Shakespeare and the Biblical Drama." *Biblical Drama in England, from the Middle Ages to the Present Day.* Evanston, Ill.: Northwestern U.P., 1968.

141 SANDERS, Norman. "The Comedy of Greene and Shakespeare." In **1582.**

142 SHACKFORD, Martha Hale. *Plutarch in Renaissance England with Special Reference to Shakespeare.* Wellesley, Mass. (?), 1929.

143 SHAPIRO, I. A. "Shakespeare and Mundy." *ShS* 14 (1961):25–33.

144 SIMPSON, Percy. "Shakespeare's Use of Latin Authors." In **1250.**

145 SIMS, James H. *Dramatic Uses of Biblical Allusions in Marlowe and Shakespeare.* Gainesville: U. of Florida P., 1966.

146 SOELLNER, Rolf. "Shakespeare, Aristotle, Plato, and the Soul." *SJH* (1968): 56–71.

147 TAYLOR, George Coffin. *Shakspere's Debt to Montaigne.* Cambridge, Mass.: Harvard U.P.; London: Oxford U.P., 1925.

148 THALER, Alwin. *Shakespeare and Sir Philip Sidney: The Influence of "The Defense of Poesy."* Cambridge. Mass.: Harvard U.P., 1947. Rpt., New York: Russell & Russell, 1967.

149 THOMSON, J. A. K. *Shakespeare and the Classics.* London: Allen & Unwin, 1952.*

150 THORNDIKE, Ashley H. *The Influence of Beaumont and Fletcher on Shakespeare.* Worcester, Mass.: Oliver B. Wood, 1901. Rpt., New York: AMS, 1966.

151 TYNAN, Joseph L. "The Influence of Greene on Shakspere's Early Romance." *PMLA* 27 (1912):246–64.

152 WATKINS, W. B. C. *Shakespeare and Spenser.* See **1447.**

153 WEIMANN, Robert. *Shakespeare und der Tradition des Volkstheaters.* Berlin: Henschelverlag, 1967.*

154 WHITAKER, Virgil K. *Shakespeare's Use of Learning: An Inquiry into the Growth of His Mind and Art.* San Marino, Calif.: Huntington Library, 1953.*

155 WILSON, F. P. *Marlowe and the Early Shakespeare.* Oxford: Clarendon, 1953.*

156 WILSON, F. P. "Shakespeare's Reading." *ShS* 3 (1950):14–21. Rpt. in **1272.**

Shakespeare's Life

Studies in Biography

See also **1474** and **4538.**

157 ADAMS, Joseph Quincy. *A Life of William Shakespeare.* Boston: Houghton Mifflin, 1923.

158 AKRIGG, G. P. V. *Shakespeare and the Earl of Southampton.* London: Hamilton; Cambridge, Mass.: Harvard U.P., 1968.

159 AKRIGG, G. P. V. "Something More About Shakespeare's Patron." *SQ* 28 (1977):65–72.

160 BALDWIN, T. W. *William Shakespeare's Petty School.* Urbana: U. of Illinois P., 1943.

161 BALDWIN, T. W. *William Shakspere's Small Latine & Lesse Greeke.* 2 vols. Urbana: U. of Illinois P., 1944.

162 BENTLEY, Gerald Eades. *Shakespeare: A Biographical Handbook.* New Haven: Yale U.P., 1961.*

163 BROOKE, C. F. Tucker. *Shakespeare of Stratford.* New Haven: Yale U.P., London: Oxford U.P., 1926.

164 CHAMBERS, E. K. *Sources for a Biography of Shakespeare.* Oxford: Clarendon, 1946.

165 CHAMBERS, E. K. *William Shakespeare: A Study of Facts and Problems.* See **62.**

166 DE GROOT, John Henry. *The Shakespeares and "The Old Faith."* New York: King's Crown, 1946. Rpt., Freeport, N.Y.: Books for Libraries P., 1968.

167 ECCLES, Mark. *Shakespeare in Warwickshire.* Madison: U. of Wisconsin P., 1961.

168 FRIPP, Edgar I. *Shakespeare's Stratford.* London: Oxford U.P., 1928.

169 FRYE, Roland Mushat. *Shakespeare's Life and Times: A Pictorial Record.* Princeton: Princeton U.P., 1967.

170 HALLIDAY, F. E. *The Life of Shakespeare.* London: Duckworth, 1961; Baltimore: Penguin, 1963.

171 HALLIDAY, F. E. *Shakespeare: A Pictorial Biography.* London: Thames & Hudson; New York: Viking, 1956. Rev. ed., 1964.

172 HARBAGE, Alfred. *Conceptions of Shakespeare.* Cambridge, Mass.: Harvard U.P., 1966.

173 HOTSON, Leslie. *I, William Shakespeare, Do Appoint Thomas Russell, Esquire* . . . London: Cape, 1937; New York: Oxford U.P., 1938.

174 HOTSON, Leslie. *Mr. W. H.* London: Hart-Davis; New York: Knopf, 1964.

175 HOTSON, Leslie. *Shakespeare Versus Shallow.* London: Nonesuch; Boston: Little, Brown, 1931.

176 LEE, Sidney. *A Life of William Shakespeare.* New York and London: Macmillan, 1898. Rev. ed., 1915.

177 LEWIS, B. Roland. *The Shakespeare Documents: Facsimiles, Transliterations, Translations, and Commentary.* Stanford: Stanford U.P.; London: Oxford U.P., 1940.

178 MARDER, Louis. "Shakespearean Biography: A Bibliography." *ShN* 11 (1961): 20–21.

179 MUTSCHMANN, Heinrich, and Karl P. WENTERSDORF. *Shakespeare and Catholicism.* New York: Sheed & Ward, 1952.

180 SCHOENBAUM, S. *Shakespeare's Lives.* Oxford: Clarendon; New York: Oxford U.P., 1970.*

181 SCHOENBAUM, S. *William Shakespeare: A Documentary Life.* Oxford: Oxford U.P. in association with the Scolar P., 1975.* *A Compact Documentary Life* has been announced for 1977.

182 SISSON, Charles J. "Studies in the Life and Environment of Shakespeare since 1900." *ShS* 3 (1950):1–12.

183 SMART, John Semple. *Shakespeare: Truth and Tradition.* London: Arnold, 1928. Rpt., Oxford: Clarendon, 1966.

184 STOPES, C. C. *Shakespeare's Family.* London: Elliot Stock, 1901.

185 STOPES, C. C. *Shakespeare's Warwickshire Contemporaries.* Stratford-upon-Avon: Shakespeare Head P., 1907. An earlier version appeared in 1897.

186 WALLACE, Charles William. *Shakespeare and His London Associates, As Revealed by Recently Discovered Documents.* Lincoln: U. of Nebraska P., 1910.

187 WRIGHT, Louis B., and Elaine W. FOWLER. *A Visual Guide to Shakespeare's Life and Times.* New York: Washington Square P., 1975.

Shakespeare's Life and Artistic Achievement

188 ALEXANDER, Peter. *Shakespeare's Life and Art.* London: Nisbet, 1939. Rev. ed., New York: New York U.P., 1961.*

189 BROWN, Ivor. *Shakespeare.* London: Collins; Garden City, N.Y.: Doubleday, 1949.

190 FRIPP, Edgar I. *Shakespeare, Man and Artist.* 2 vols. London: Oxford U.P., 1938.*

191 QUENNELL, Peter. *Shakespeare: A Biography.* Cleveland and New York: World, 1963; Harmondsworth: Penguin, 1969.

192 REESE, M. M. *Shakespeare: His World and His Work.* London: Arnold; New York: St. Martin's, 1953.

193 ROWSE, A. L. *William Shakespeare: A Biography.* London: Macmillan; New York: Harper & Row, 1963.

194 SPENCER, Hazelton. *The Art and Life of William Shakespeare.* New York: Harcourt, Brace, 1940. Rpt., New York: Barnes & Noble, 1970.

195 WILSON, J. Dover. *The Essential Shakespeare.* Cambridge: Cambridge U.P., 1932.

The Authorship Controversy

On the question of the authenticity and scope of the Shakespearean canon, see "Plays of Doubtful or Composite Authorship" at the end of this volume. See also **172.**

196 CHURCHILL, R. C. *Shakespeare and His Betters: A History and a Criticism of the Attempts Which Have Been Made to Prove that Shakespeare's Works Were Written by Others.* London: Reinhardt, 1958.

197 FRIEDMAN, William F., and Elizebeth S. FRIEDMAN. *The Shakespearean Ciphers Examined.* Cambridge: Cambridge U.P., 1957.

198 GIBSON, H. N. *The Shakespeare Claimants: A Critical Survey of the Four Principal Theories Concerning the Authorship of the Shakespearean Plays.* London: Methuen; New York: Barnes & Noble, 1962.

199 LEVIN, Harry, in collaboration with G. Blakemore EVANS. "Shakespeare as Shakespeare." *Harvard Magazine* 77 (February 1975). Rpt. in **1233.**

200 MCMICHAEL, George, and Edgar M. GLENN, eds. *Shakespeare and His Rivals: A Casebook on the Authorship Controversy.* New York: Odyssey, 1962.

201 WADSWORTH, Frank W. *The Poacher from Stratford: A Partial Account of the Controversy over the Authorship of Shakespeare's Plays.* Berkeley and Los Angeles: U. of California P., 1958.

The Social, Political, and Intellectual Background

General Studies

See also **169.**

202 ASHLEY, Maurice. *Life in Stuart England.* London: Batsford; New York: Putnam's, 1964.

203 BROWN, Ivor. *Shakespeare and His World.* New York: Walck, 1965.

204 BROWN, Ivor. *Shakespeare in His Time.* Edinburgh: Nelson, 1960.

205 FORD, Boris, ed. *The Age of Shakespeare.* Vol. 2 of The Pelican Guide to English Literature. Harmondsworth and Baltimore: Penguin, 1955. Rev. eds., 1956 and 1960.

206 HARRISON, G. B. *An Elizabethan Journal . . . 1591–94.* London: Constable, 1928. *A Second Elizabethan Journal . . . 1595–98.* London: Constable, 1931. *A Last Elizabethan Journal . . . 1599–1603.* London: Constable, 1933. Three vols. published jointly as *The Elizabethan Journals.* London: Routledge, 1938. Rpt., Ann Arbor: U. of Michigan P., 1955; Gloucester, Mass.: P. Smith, 1965; Garden City, N.Y.: Doubleday, 1965.

207 HARRISON, G. B. *A Jacobean Journal . . . 1603–06.* London: Routledge, 1941. *A Second Jacobean Journal . . . 1607–10.* Ann Arbor: U. of Michigan P., 1958.

208 HUIZINGA, Johan. *The Waning of the Middle Ages.* London: Arnold, 1924. Rpt., Baltimore: Penguin, 1955.

209 HURSTFIELD, Joel. "The Historical and Social Background." In **55.**

210 HUSSEY, Maurice. *The World of Shakespeare and His Contemporaries: A Visual Approach.* New York: Viking, Studio Books, 1972.

211 JOSEPH, Bertram L. *Shakespeare's Eden: The Commonwealth of England 1558–1629.* London: Blandford, 1971.

212 KINNEY, Arthur F., ed. *Elizabethan Backgrounds: Historical Documents of the Age of Elizabeth I.* Hamden, Conn.: Archon, 1975.

213 LEE, Sidney, and C. T. ONIONS, eds. *Shakespeare's England: An Account of the Life and Manners of His Age.* 2 vols. Oxford: Clarendon, 1916.

214 MCMANAWAY, James G., special ed. "Shakespeare and England." *RNL* 3.2 (1972):1–197.

215 *Shakespeare Survey* 17 (1964). Devoted to "Shakespeare in His Own Age."*

216 SMITH, Lacey Baldwin. *The Elizabethan World.* Boston: Houghton Mifflin, 1966.

217 SMITH, Lacey Baldwin. *The Horizon Book of the Elizabethan World.* New York: American Heritage, book trade distribution by Houghton Mifflin, 1967.

218 STEVENSON, David Lloyd, ed. *The Elizabethan Age.* Greenwich, Conn.: Fawcett, 1967.

219 WILLIAMS, Penry. *Life in Tudor England.* London: Batsford; New York: Putnam's, 1964.

220 WILSON, J. Dover, ed. *Life in Shakespeare's England.* Cambridge: Cambridge U.P., 1911. 2nd ed., 1926. Harmondsworth and Baltimore: Penguin, 1964. New York: Barnes & Noble, 1969.

221 WRIGHT, Louis B., and Virginia A. LA MAR, eds. *Life and Letters in Tudor and Stuart England: First Series.* Ithaca: for the Folger Shakespeare Library by the Cornell U.P., 1958. A Collection of the first twelve Folger Booklets on Tudor and Stuart Civilization. Rpt., Charlottesville: U.P. of Virginia.

The Social and Economic Background

222 BERGERON, David M. *English Civic Pageantry, 1558–1642.* Columbia: U. of South Carolina P.; London: Arnold, 1971.

223 BERLIN, Normand. *The Base String: The Underworld in Elizabethan Drama.* Rutherford, N.J.: Fairleigh Dickinson U.P., 1968.

224 BORNSTEIN, Diane. *Mirrors of Courtesy.* Hamden, Conn.: Archon, 1975.

225 BRADBROOK, M. C. "Shakespeare and the Structure of Tudor Society." *RNL* 3.2 (1972):90–105.

226 BRADFORD, Gamaliel. *Elizabethan Women.* Ed. Harold Ogden WHITE. Boston: Houghton Mifflin, 1936.

227 BUXTON, John. *Elizabethan Taste.* London: Macmillan, 1963.

228 BYRNE, Muriel St. Clare. *Elizabethan Life in Town and Country.* London: Methuen, 1925; Boston and New York: Houghton Mifflin, 1926. 7th rev. ed., 1954.

229 CAMDEN, Carroll. *The Elizabethan Woman.* Houston: Elsevier, 1952. Rev. ed., Mamaroneck, N.Y.: P. Appel, 1975.

230 CAMPBELL, Mildred. *The English Yeoman under Elizabeth and the Early Stuarts.* New Haven: Yale U.P.; London: Oxford U.P., 1942. Rpt., London: Merlin, 1967.

231 CASPARI, Fritz. *Humanism and the Social Order in Tudor England.* Chicago: U. of Chicago P., 1954.*

232 CLARKSON, Paul S., and Clyde T. WARREN. *The Law of Property in Shakespeare and the Elizabethan Drama.* Baltimore: The Johns Hopkins P., 1942. Rpt. with corrections, New York: Gordian, 1968.

233 CURTIS, Mark H. *Oxford and Cambridge in Transition, 1558–1642: An Essay on Changing Relations Between the English Universities and English Society.* Oxford: Clarendon, 1959.

234 DODD, A. H. *Elizabethan England.* London: Batsford; New York: Putnam's, 1961. Rpt., 1973.

235 EDELEN, Georges, ed. *The Description of England* by William HARRISON. Ithaca: for the Folger Shakespeare Library by the Cornell U.P., 1968.*

236 EINSTEIN, Lewis. *Tudor Ideals.* New York: Harcourt, Brace, 1921. Rpt., New York: Russell & Russell.*

237 HOLMES, Martin. *Elizabethan London.* London: Cassell; New York: Praeger, 1969.

238 HURSTFIELD, Joel. "The Elizabethan People in the Age of Shakespeare." In **1170.**

239 JUDGES, A. V., ed. *The Elizabethan Underworld.* London: Routledge; New York: Dutton, 1930. Rpt., London: Routledge & K. Paul, 1965.

240 KELSO, Ruth. *Doctrine for the Lady of the Renaissance.* Urbana: U. of Illinois P., 1956.

241 KELSO, Ruth. *The Doctrine of the English Gentleman in the Sixteenth Century.* Urbana: U. of Illinois P., 1929.

242 KETTLE, Arnold, ed. *Shakespeare in a Changing World: Essays on His Times and His Plays.* See **1148.**

243 KNIGHTS, L. C. *Drama and Society in the Age of Jonson.* London: Chatto & Windus, 1937. Rpt., New York: Norton, 1968.*

244 MCPEEK, James A. S. *The Black Book of Knaves and Unthrifts in Shakespeare and Other Renaissance Authors.* Storrs: U. of Connecticut P., 1969.*

245 MELCHIORI, Giorgio. "Shakespeare and the New Economics of His Time." *RNL* 3.2 (1972):123–37.

246 NICHOLS, John, ed. *The Progresses and Public Processions of Queen Elizabeth.* 3 vols. London: printed for the editor, 1788–1805. Rpt., New York: AMS, Burt Franklin.

247 NICHOLS, John, ed. *The Progresses, Processions, and Magnificent Festivities of King James the First.* 4 vols. London: J. B. Nichols, 1828. Rpt., New York: AMS, Burt Franklin.

248 PEARSON, Lu Emily. *Elizabethans at Home.* Stanford: Stanford U.P., 1957.

249 PENROSE, Boies. *Travel and Discovery in the Renaissance, 1420–1620.* Cambridge, Mass.: Harvard U.P., 1955.*

250 ROWSE, A. L. *The England of Elizabeth: The Structure of Society.* London: Macmillan, 1950; New York: Macmillan, 1951.

251 SIMON, Joan. *Education and Society in Tudor England.* Cambridge: Cambridge U.P., 1966.

252 STONE, Lawrence. *The Crisis of the Aristocracy, 1558–1641.* Oxford: Oxford U.P., 1965. Abridged ed., 1967.*

253 STONE, Lawrence. *Family and Fortune: Studies in Aristocratic Finance in the Sixteenth and Seventeenth Centuries.* Oxford: Clarendon, 1973.

254 STOW, John. *A Survey of London.* Ed. Charles Lethbridge KINGSFORD. 2 vols. Oxford: Clarendon, 1908. Rpt., 1971.*

255 TAWNEY, R. H. *Religion and the Rise of Capitalism.* London: Murray; New York: Harcourt, Brace, 1926. Rpt., New York: American Library, 1954; Gloucester: P. Smith, 1962.*

256 WEIMANN, Robert. *Drama und Wirklichkeit in der Shakespearezeit.* Halle/Salle: Niemeyer, 1958.

257 WILSON, F. P. "Illustrations of Social Life." In 4 parts. *ShS* 11 (1958):98–99; 12 (1959):107–08; 13 (1960):106–10; and 15 (1962):125–29.

258 WILSON, F. P. *The Plague in Shakespeare's London.* Oxford: Clarendon, 1927. Rev. ed., 1963.

259 WITHINGTON, Robert. *English Pageantry: An Historical Outline.* 2 vols. Cambridge, Mass.: Harvard U.P., 1918–20. Rpt., New York: Blom, 1963.

260 WRIGHT, Louis B. *Middle-Class Culture in Elizabethan England.* Chapel Hill: U. of North Carolina P., 1935. Reissued, Ithaca: for the Folger Shakespeare Library by the Cornell U.P., 1958.

The Political Background

See also **1451–53** and **1494.**

261 AKRIGG, G. P. V. *Jacobean Pageant; or, The Court of King James I.* Cambridge, Mass.: Harvard U.P., 1963.

262 ASHLEY, Maurice. *England in the Seventeenth Century (1603–1714).* Harmondsworth and Baltimore: Penguin, 1952. Rev. ed., 1958.

263 BINDOFF, S. T. *Tudor England.* Harmondsworth and Baltimore: Penguin, 1950.

264 BINDOFF, S. T., et al., eds. *Elizabethan Government and Society: Essays Presented to Sir John Neale.* London: Athlone Press of the U. of London, 1961.*

265 BLACK, John B. *The Reign of Elizabeth, 1558–1603.* The Oxford History of England, vol. 8. 2nd ed., Oxford: Clarendon, 1959.*

266 CROWSON, P. S. *Tudor Foreign Policy.* New York: St. Martin's; London: Macmillan, 1973.

267 DAVIES, Godfrey. *The Early Stuarts, 1603–1660.* The Oxford History of England, vol. 9. 2nd ed., Oxford: Clarendon, 1959.*

268 ELTON, G. R. *England under the Tudors.* London: Methuen; New York: Barnes & Noble, 1955.

269 ELTON, G. R. *The Tudor Revolution in Government.* Cambridge: Cambridge U.P., 1953, 1959.

270 HILL, Christopher. *The Century of Revolution, 1603–1714.* London and Edinburgh: Nelson; New York: Norton, 1961.*

271 HURSTFIELD, Joel. *Elizabeth I and the Unity of England.* London: English U.P., 1960. Rpt., New York: Harper & Row, 1969.

272 HURSTFIELD, Joel. "The Politics of Corruption in Shakespeare's England." *ShS* 28 (1975):15–28.

273 HURSTFIELD, Joel, ed. *The Tudors.* London: Sidgwick & Jackson, 1973.

274 JOHNSON, Paul. *Elizabeth I.* New York: Holt, Rinehart & Winston, 1974.

275 LACEY, Robert. *Robert, Earl of Essex: An Elizabethan Icarus.* London: Weidenfeld & Nicolson, 1971.

276 MACCAFFREY, Wallace T. *The Shaping of the Elizabethan Regime.* Princeton: Princeton U.P., 1968.*

277 MACCAFFREY, Wallace T., ed. *The History of the Most Renowned and Victorious Princess Elizabeth, Late Queen of England,* by William CAMDEN. Selected chapters. Chicago: U. of Chicago P., 1970.

278 MCELWEE, William. *The Wisest Fool in Christendom: The Reign of King James I and VI.* London: Faber & Faber, 1958.

279 MATTINGLEY, Garrett. *The Armada.* Boston: Houghton Mifflin, 1959.*

280 NEALE, John E. *Elizabeth I and Her Parliaments.* 2 vols. London: Cape; New York: St. Martin's, 1953–57. Rpt., New York: Norton, 1966.

281 NEALE, John E. *The Elizabethan House of Commons.* London: Cape, 1949; New Haven: Yale U.P., 1950.

282 NEALE, John E. *Queen Elizabeth I.* London: Cape; New York: Harcourt, Brace, 1934. Rpt., New York: Doubleday, 1957.*

283 PRAZ, Mario. "Machiavelli and the Elizabethans." *PBA* 14 (1930 for 1928): 49–97.

284 RAAB, Felix. *The English Face of Machiavelli: A Changing Interpretation, 1500–1700.* London: Routledge & K. Paul; Toronto: U. of Toronto P., 1964.

285 READ, Conyers. *Lord Burghley and Queen Elizabeth.* London: Cape; New York: Knopf, 1960.

286 READ, Conyers. *Mr. Secretary Cecil and Queen Elizabeth.* London: Cape; New York: Knopf, 1955.

287 READ, Conyers. *Mr. Secretary Walsingham and the Policy of Queen Elizabeth.* 3 vols. Oxford: Clarendon; Cambridge, Mass.: Harvard U.P., 1925.

288 READ, Conyers. *The Tudors: Personalities and Practical Politics in Sixteenth-Century England.* London: Oxford U.P.; New York: Holt, 1936. Rpt., Freeport, N.Y.: Books for Libraries P., 1968.

289 RUSSELL, Conrad. *The Crisis of Parliaments: English History, 1509–1660.* London: Oxford U.P., 1971.

290 STRACHEY, Lytton. *Elizabeth and Essex.* London: Chatto & Windus; New York: C. Gaige and Harcourt, Brace, 1928.

291 TREVELYAN, G. M. *England under the Stuarts.* London: Methuen; New York: Barnes & Noble, 1965. First pub., 1904.*

292 WILLIAMS, C. H. *The Making of the Tudor Despotism.* New York: Russell & Russell, 1928. Rev. ed., 1935.

Religious Controversy

See also **601, 1428, 1435–36,** and **2986.**

293 COLLINSON, Patrick. *The Elizabethan Puritan Movement.* Berkeley and Los Angeles: U. of California P., 1967.

294 COLLINSON, Patrick. "Towards a Broader Understanding of the Early Dissenting Tradition." *The Dissenting Tradition. Essays for Leland H. Carlson.* Eds. C. Robert COLE and Michael E. MOODY. Athens: Ohio U.P., 1975.

295 DANIELS, R. Balfour. "Shakspere and the Puritans." *ShAB* 13 (1938):40–53.

296 DAVIES, Horton. *Worship and Theology in England: From Cranmer to Hooker, 1534–1603.* Princeton: Princeton U.P., 1970.*

297 EMERSON, Everett H. *English Puritanism from John Hooper to John Milton.* Durham, N.C.: Duke U.P., 1968.

298 FISCH, Harold. "Shakespeare and the Puritan Dynamic." *ShS* 27 (1974):81–92. On Shylock, Angelo, and Malvolio.

299 FRYE, Roland Mushat. *Shakespeare and Christian Doctrine.** See **1421.**

300 HAUGAARD, William P. *Elizabeth and the English Reformation: The Struggle for a Stable Settlement of Religion.* Cambridge: Cambridge U.P., 1968.*

301 KNAPPEN, M. M. *Tudor Puritanism: A Chapter in the History of Idealism.* Chicago: U. of Chicago P., 1939.*

302 MCGRATH, Patrick. *Papists and Puritans under Elizabeth I.* New York: Walker, 1967.

303 ZEEVELD, W. Gordon. *Foundations of Tudor Policy.* Cambridge, Mass.: Harvard U.P., 1948; London: Methuen, 1969.*

The Intellectual Background

See also **1494, 1504, 1508, 2538, 3258, 3574–75, 3600,** and **4485.**

304 ALLEN, Don Cameron. *Mysteriously Meant; The Rediscovery of Pagan Symbolism and Allegorical Interpretation in the Renaissance.* Baltimore and London: The Johns Hopkins P., 1970.*

305 ALLEN, Don Cameron. *The Star-Crossed Renaissance: The Quarrel about Astrology and Its Influence in England.* Durham, N.C.: Duke U.P., 1941. Rpt., New York: Octagon.

306 BABB, Lawrence. *The Elizabethan Malady: A Study of Melancholia in English Literature from 1580 to 1642.* East Lansing: Michigan State College P., 1951.*

307 BAKER, Herschel. *The Image of Man: A Study of the Idea of Human Dignity in Classical Antiquity, the Middle Ages, and the Renaissance.* Cambridge, Mass.: Harvard U.P., 1961. First published as *The Dignity of Man: Studies in the Persistence of an Idea* in 1947.*

308 BAKER, Herschel. *The Wars of Truth: Studies in the Decay of Christian Humanism in the Earlier Seventeenth Century.* Cambridge, Mass.: Harvard U.P., 1952.

309 BAMBOROUGH, J. B. *The Little World of Man.* London and New York: Longmans, Green, 1952.

310 BARKAN, Leonard. *Nature's Work of Art: The Human Body as Image of the World.* New Haven: Yale U.P., 1975.*

311 BUCKLEY, George T. *Atheism in the English Renaissance.* Chicago: U. of Chicago P., 1932.

312 BUSH, Douglas. *The Renaissance and English Humanism.* Toronto: U. of Toronto P., 1939.*

313 CASSIRER, Ernst. *The Platonic Renaissance in England.* Trans. James E. PETTEGROVE. Austin: U. of Texas P., 1953.

314 CHARLTON, Kenneth. *Education in Renaissance England.* London: Routledge & K. Paul; Toronto: U. of Toronto P., 1965.

315 CRAIG, Hardin. *The Enchanted Glass: The Elizabethan Mind in Literature.* New York: Oxford U.P., 1936. Rpt., Oxford: Blackwell, 1950, 1966; Westport, Conn.: Greenwood, 1975.

316 CRUTTWELL, Patrick. *The Shakespearean Moment and Its Place in the Poetry of the Seventeenth Century.* London: Chatto & Windus, 1954; New York: Columbia U.P., 1970.*

317 EINSTEIN, Lewis. *The Italian Renaissance in England.* New York: Columbia U.P.; London: Macmillan, 1902. Rpt., New York: Burt Franklin, 1962.

318 ELTON, William R. "Shakespeare and the Thought of His Age." In **55.**

319 FERGUSON, Arthur B. *The Articulate Citizen and the English Renaissance.* Durham, N.C.: Duke U.P., 1965.

320 HAYDN, Hiram. *The Counter-Renaissance.* New York: Scribner's, 1950; Grove, 1960. Rpt., Gloucester, Mass.: P. Smith.*

321 HENINGER, S. K., Jr. *A Handbook of Renaissance Meteorology, with Particular Reference to Elizabethan and Jacobean Literature.* Durham, N.C.: Duke U.P., 1960. Rpt., Westport, Conn.: Greenwood, 1968.*

322 HENINGER, S. K., Jr. *Touches of Sweet Harmony: Pythagorean Cosmology and Renaissance Poetics.* San Marino, Calif.: Huntington Library, 1974.

323 JOHNSON, Francis R. *Astronomical Thought in Renaissance England: A Study of the English Scientific Writings from 1500 to 1645.* Baltimore: The Johns Hopkins P.; London: Oxford U.P., 1937.

324 KOCHER, Paul H. *Science and Religion in Elizabethan England.* San Marino, Calif.: Huntington Library, 1953.*

325 LEVER, J. W. "Shakespeare and the Ideas of His Time." *ShS* 29 (1976):79–92.

326 LEVIN, Harry. *The Myth of the Golden Age in the Renaissance.* Bloomington: Indiana U.P., 1969.*

327 LEVY, F. J. *Tudor Historical Thought.* San Marino, Calif.: Huntington Library, 1967.

328 LOVEJOY, Arthur O. *The Great Chain of Being: A Study of the History of an Idea.* Cambridge, Mass.: Harvard U.P., 1936.*

329 MCLEAN, Antonia. *Humanism and the Rise of Science in Tudor England.* London: Heinemann, 1972.

330 MAZZEO, Joseph Anthony. *Renaissance and Revolution: The Remaking of European Thought.* New York: Pantheon, 1965.*

331 NICOLSON, Marjorie. "The 'New Astronomy' and English Literary Imagination." *SP* 32 (1935):428–62.

332 OVERHOLSER, Winfred. "Shakespeare's Psychiatry—And After." *SQ* 10 (1959):335–52.

333 POPKIN, Richard H. *The History of Scepticism from Erasmus to Descartes.* Assen: Van Gorcum, 1960. Rev. ed., New York: Humanities P., 1964.

334 QUINONES, Ricardo J. *The Renaissance Discovery of Time.* Cambridge, Mass.: Harvard U.P., 1972.*

335 SEEBOHM, Frederic. *The Oxford Reformers: John Colet, Erasmus, and Thomas More.* London: Longmans, Green, 1887; London: Dent; New York: Dutton, 1914. Rpt., New York: AMS, 1971.

336 SEIGEL, Jerrold E. *Rhetoric and Philosophy in Renaissance Humanism: The Union of Eloquence and Wisdom, Petrarch to Valla.* Princeton: Princeton U.P., 1968.

337 SMITH, Warren D. "The Elizabethan Rejection of Judicial Astrology and Shakespeare's Practice." *SQ* 9 (1958):159–76.

338 SOELLNER, Rolf. *Shakespeare's Patterns of Self-Knowledge.* See **1443.**

339 SPENCER, Theodore. *Shakespeare and the Nature of Man.* New York: Macmillan, 1942. 2nd ed., 1949. Rpt., New York: Collier; London: Collier-Macmillan, 1966.*

340 TILLYARD, E. M. W. *The Elizabethan World Picture.* London: Chatto & Windus, 1943; New York: Macmillan, 1944. Rpt., New York: Random House.*

341 WATSON, Curtis Brown. *Shakespeare and the Renaissance Concept of Honor.** See **1499.**

342 WEST, Robert H. "Elizabethan Belief in Spirits and Witchcraft." In **1157.**

343 WEST, Robert H. *The Invisible World: A Study of Pneumatology in Elizabethan Drama.* Athens: U. of Georgia P., 1939. Rpt., New York: Octagon.*

344 WHITAKER, Virgil K. *Shakespeare's Use of Learning.* See **154.**

345 WILLEY, Basil. *The Seventeenth-Century Background: Studies in the Thought of the Age in Relation to Poetry and Religion.* London: Chatto & Windus, 1934. Rpt., New York: Columbia U.P., 1942, 1958; Garden City, N.Y.: Doubleday Anchor, 1953.*

346 WILSON, F. P. *Elizabethan and Jacobean.* Oxford: Clarendon, 1945.*

Collected Editions

347 ALEXANDER, Peter, ed. *William Shakespeare: The Complete Works.* London and Glasgow: Collins, 1951; New York: Random House, 1952.

348 BARNET, Sylvan, gen. ed. *The Complete Signet Classic Shakespeare.* New York: Harcourt Brace Jovanovich, 1972. Issued earlier in separate paperback editions by individual editors, 1963–68.

349 BROOKE, C. F. Tucker, ed. *The Shakespeare Apocrypha.* Oxford: Clarendon, 1918. The plays in this collection are currently being reedited by G. Richard PROUDFOOT.

350 BROOKS, Harold F., and Harold JENKINS, gen. eds. *The New Arden Shakespeare.* London: Methuen; Cambridge, Mass.: Harvard U.P.; New York: Random House, Vintage Books, 1951–. Previously edited at various times by W. J. CRAIG, R. H. CASE, and Una ELLIS-FERMOR, 1899–.

351 CLARK, William George, William Aldis WRIGHT, and John GLOVER, eds. *The Cambridge Shakespeare.* 9 vols. Cambridge: Cambridge U.P., 1863–66. 2nd ed., 1867; 3rd ed., 1891–93. The text only was published in one volume in 1864 as *The Globe Shakespeare.* Rpt., New York: AMS, 1970.

352 CRAIG, Hardin, ed. *The Complete Works of Shakespeare.* Chicago and Glenview: Scott, Foresman, 1951. Rev. ed. by David BEVINGTON, 1973.

353 EVANS, G. Blakemore, textual ed. *The Riverside Shakespeare.* Boston: Houghton Mifflin, 1974.

354 FURNESS, Horace H., ed. *A New Variorum Edition of Shakespeare.* Philadelphia: Lippincott, 1871–. Rpt., New York: Dover. Various plays are currently being reedited or newly edited under the auspices of the Modern Language Association of America.

355 GREG, W. W., and Charlton HINMAN, eds. *Shakespeare Quarto Facsimiles.* London: Shakespeare Association and Sidgwick & Jackson, 1939–52. Oxford: Clarendon, 1957–.

356 HARBAGE, Alfred, gen. ed. *William Shakespeare: The Complete Works.* The Pelican Shakespeare. Baltimore: Penguin, 1969. Thirty-eight titles issued in paperback, by separate editors, 1956–67.

357 HARRISON, G. B., ed. *Shakespeare: The Complete Works.* New York: Harcourt, Brace, 1948.

358 HINMAN, Charlton, ed. *The Norton Facsimile: The First Folio of Shakespeare.* New York: Norton, 1968.

359 HOUGHTON, R. E. C., ed. *The New Clarendon Shakespeare.* Oxford: Clarendon, 1938–.

360 KITTREDGE, George Lyman, ed. *The Complete Works of Shakespeare.* Boston: Ginn, 1936. Rev. ed. by Irving RIBNER, 1971.

361 SISSON, Charles J., ed. *William Shakespeare: The Complete Works.* London: Odhams, 1954.

362 SPENCER, T. J. B., gen. ed. *The New Penguin Shakespeare.* Harmondsworth and Baltimore: Penguin, 1967–. Individual paperback editions.

363 WILSON, J. Dover, Arthur QUILLER-COUCH, and others, eds. *The Works of Shakespeare.* The New Cambridge Shakespeare. Cambridge: Cambridge U.P., 1921–. Individual volumes.

Textual Criticism

Early Printers; Shakespeare's Quartos and Folios

See also **358, 426, 2399, 2400–02, 2405–06, 2414–16, 2781, 2785, 2810, 2821, 2826, 2851, 3005–08, 3010, 3020–22, 3371, 3638, 3669, 3671, 3673, 3829, 3853, 3928–29, 3932–37, 3972–73, 3975–77, 4047, 4059, 4227, 4232, 4244, 4254, 4272–74, 4665, 4668, and 4671.**

364 ALDEN, Raymond Macdonald. "The Punctuation of Shakespeare's Printers." *PMLA* 39 (1924):557–80.

365 ARBER, Edward, ed. *A Transcript of the Registers of the Company of Stationers of London: 1554–1640 A.D.* 5 vols. London: Privately printed, 1875–77. Rpt., Gloucester, Mass.: P. Smith, 1950.

366 BENNETT, H. S. *English Books and Readers, 1558 to 1603, Being a Study in the History of the Book Trade in the Reign of Elizabeth I.* Cambridge: Cambridge U.P., 1965.

367 BROWN, Arthur. "The Printing of Books." *ShS* 17 (1964):205–13.

368 BURKHART, Robert E. *Shakespeare's Bad Quartos: Deliberate Abridgements Designed for Performance by a Reduced Cast.* The Hague: Mouton, 1975.*

369 CAIRNCROSS, Andrew S. "Shakespeare and the 'Staying Entries.' " In **1169.**

370 CRAIG, Hardin. *A New Look at Shakespeare's Quartos.* Stanford: Stanford U.P., 1961. Rpt., New York: AMS.

371 GREG, W. W. *The Shakespeare First Folio: Its Bibliographical and Textual History.* Oxford: Clarendon, 1955.*

372 GREG, W. W., and E. BOSWELL, eds. *Records of the Court of the Stationers' Company, 1576 to 1602, from Register B.* London: Bibliographical Society, 1930. See also **378.**

373 HART, Alfred. *Stolne and Surreptitious Copies: A Comparative Study of Shakespeare's Bad Quartos.* Melbourne: Melbourne U.P.; London: Oxford U.P., 1942.

374 HINMAN, Charlton. *The Printing and Proof-Reading of the First Folio of Shakespeare.* 2 vols. Oxford: Clarendon, 1963.*

375 HONIGMANN, E. A. J. "Re-enter the Stage Direction: Shakespeare and Some Contemporaries." *ShS* 29 (1976):117–26.

376 HOWARD-HILL, T. H. *Ralph Crane and Some Shakespeare First Folio Comedies.* Charlottesville: U.P. of Virginia, 1972.

377 JACKSON, MacD. P. "Punctuation and the Compositors of Shakespeare's *Sonnets,* 1609." *Library,* 5th ser. 30 (1975):1–24.

378 JACKSON, William A., ed. *Records of the Court of the Stationers' Company, 1602 to 1640.* London: Bibliographical Society, 1957. From Court-Book C. See also **372.**

379 JEWKES, Wilfred T. *Act Division in Elizabethan and Jacobean Plays, 1583–1616.* Hamden, Conn.: Shoe String, 1958.

380 KABLE, William S. "Compositor B, the Pavier Quartos, and Copy Spellings." *SB* 21 (1968):131–61.

381 KIRSCHBAUM, Leo. *Shakespeare and the Stationers.* Columbus: Ohio State U.P., 1955.

382 NOSWORTHY, J. M. *Shakespeare's Occasional Plays: Their Origin and Transmission.* London: Arnold; New York: Barnes & Noble, 1965.*

383 POLLARD, Alfred W. *Shakespeare's Fight with the Pirates and the Problem of the Transmission of His Text.* Rev. ed., Cambridge: Cambridge U.P., 1937.*

384 POLLARD, Alfred W. *Shakespeare's Folios and Quartos: A Study in the Bibliography of Shakespeare's Plays, 1594–1685.* London: Methuen, 1909. Rpt., New York: Cooper Square.*

385 SHAKESPEARE, William. *Shakespeare's Poems: A Facsimile of the Earliest Editions.* New Haven: Yale U.P., 1964.

386 SHROEDER, John W. *The Great Folio of 1623: Shakespeare's Plays in the Printing House.* Hamden, Conn.: Shoe String, 1956.

387 SIMPSON, Percy. *Proof-Reading in the Sixteenth, Seventeenth, and Eighteenth Centuries.* London: Oxford U.P., 1935. Reviewed by W. W. GREG. "From Manuscript to Print." *RES* 13 (1937):190–205.

388 THOMAS, Sidney. "The Myth of the Authorized Shakespeare Quartos." *SQ* 27 (1976):186–92.

389 WALKER, Alice. *Textual Problems of the First Folio: "Richard III," "King Lear," "Troilus and Cressida," "2 Henry IV," "Hamlet," "Othello."* Cambridge: Cambridge U.P., 1953.

390 WALTON, J. K. *The Quarto Copy for the First Folio of Shakespeare.* Dublin: Dublin U.P., 1971.

Shakespeare's Seventeenth- and Eighteenth-Century Editors

391 BLACK, Matthew W., and M. A. SHAABER. *Shakespeare's Seventeenth-Century Editors, 1632–1685.* New York: Modern Language Association; London: Oxford U.P., 1937.

392 BROWN, Arthur. *Edmond Malone and English Scholarship.* London: H. K. Lewis for University College, 1963.

393 CAPELL, Edward. *Notes and Various Readings to Shakespeare.* 3 vols. London, 1779. Rpt., New York: Burt Franklin, 1970.

394 DAWSON, Giles E. "Warburton, Hanmer, and the 1745 Edition of Shakespeare." *SB* 2 (1949–50):35–48.

395 DIXON, P. "Pope's Shakespeare." *JEGP* 63 (1964):191–203.

396 EASTMAN, Arthur M. "The Texts from which Johnson Printed His Shakespeare." *JEGP* 49 (1950):182–91.

397 EDDY, Donald D. "Samuel Johnson's Editions of Shakespeare (1765)." *PBSA* 56 (1962):428–44.

398 FORD, H. L. *Shakespeare, 1700–1740: A Collation of the Editions and Separate Plays, with Some Account of T. Johnson and R. Walker.* Oxford: Oxford U.P., 1935. Rpt., New York: Blom.

399 HART, John A. "Pope as Scholar-Editor." *SB* 23 (1970):45–59.

400 JACKSON, Alfred. "Rowe's Edition of Shakespeare." *Library,* 4th ser. 10 (1930): 455–73.

401 MCKERROW, Ronald B. "The Treatment of Shakespeare's Text by His Earlier Editors, 1709–1768." *PBA* 19 (1934 for 1933):89–122. Rpt. in **1116.**

402 SCHOLES, Robert E. "Dr. Johnson and the Bibliographical Criticism of Shakespeare." *SQ* 11 (1960):163–71.

403 SHERBO, Arthur. *Samuel Johnson, Editor of Shakespeare.* Urbana: U. of Illinois P., 1956.

404 SHERBO, Arthur. "Warburton and the 1745 *Shakespeare.*" *JEGP* 51 (1952): 71–82.

405 WALKER, Alice. "Edward Capell and His Edition of Shakespeare." *PBA* 46 (1961 for 1960):131–45. Rpt. in **1116.**

Editorial Problems: Bibliography and Textual Criticism

See also **62, 2414–15, 2814, 2821, 2826,** and **3673.**

406 ALEXANDER, Peter. "Restoring Shakespeare: The Modern Editor's Task." *ShS* 5 (1952):1–9.

407 BLACK, Matthew W. "Problems in the Editing of Shakespeare: Interpretation." *EIE 1947* (1948):117–36.

408 BOWERS, Fredson. *Bibliography and Textual Criticism.* Oxford: Clarendon, 1964.*

409 BOWERS, Fredson. *On Editing Shakespeare and the Elizabethan Dramatists.* Philadelphia: U. of Pennsylvania Library, 1955. Rpt. with additions, as *On Editing Shakespeare.* Charlottesville: U.P. of Virginia, 1966.*

410 BOWERS, Fredson. *Principles of Bibliographical Description.* Princeton: Princeton U.P., 1949.

411 BOWERS, Fredson. *Textual and Literary Criticism.* Cambridge: Cambridge U.P., 1959.*

412 BOWERS, Fredson. "What Shakespeare Wrote." *SJ* 98 (1962):24–50. Rpt. in **409** and **1163.**

413 BROWN, Arthur. " 'The Great Variety of Readers.' " *ShS* 18 (1965):11–22.

414 BROWN, John Russell. "The Rationale of Old-Spelling Editions of the Plays of Shakespeare and His Contemporaries." *SB* 13 (1960):49–67. Reply by Arthur BROWN in *SB* 13 (1960):69–76.

415 DORAN, Madeleine. "An Evaluation of Evidence in Shakespearean Textual Criticism." *EIE 1941* (1942):95–114.

416 EVANS, G. Blakemore. "Shakespeare's Text: Approaches and Problems." In **55.**

417 FOGEL, Ephim G. "Electronic Computers and Elizabethan Texts." *SB* 15 (1962):15–31.

418 GASKELL, Philip. *A New Introduction to Bibliography.* New York and Oxford: Clarendon, 1972.*

419 GREG, W. W. *Collected Papers.* Ed. J. C. MAXWELL. Oxford: Clarendon, 1966.

420 GREG, W. W. *The Editorial Problem in Shakespeare: A Survey of the Foundations of the Text.* 3rd ed., Oxford: Clarendon, 1954.*

421 GREG, W. W. "Principles of Emendation in Shakespeare." *PBA* 14 (1929 for 1928):147–216.

422 HINMAN, Charlton. "Shakespeare's Text—Then, Now, and Tomorrow." *ShS* 18 (1965):23–33.

423 HINMAN, Charlton. "Shakespearian Textual Studies: Seven More Years." In **1151.** Responded to by Fredson BOWERS, "Seven or More Years?" in the same volume.

424 HONIGMANN, E. A. J. *The Stability of Shakespeare's Text.* London: Arnold; Lincoln: U. of Nebraska P., 1965.

425 HOSLEY, Richard, Richard KNOWLES, and Ruth MCGUGAN. *Shakespeare Variorum Handbook: A Manual of Editorial Practice.* New York: Modern Language Association, 1971.

426 HOWARD-HILL, T. H. *Shakespearian Bibliography and Textual Criticism: A Bibliography.* Oxford: Clarendon, 1971.

427 JACKSON, William A. *Bibliography and Literary Studies.* Berkeley and Los Angeles: U. of California, 1962.

428 LEECH, Clifford. "On Editing One's First Play." *SB* 23 (1970):61–70.

429 MCKENZIE, D. F. "Printers of the Mind: Some Notes on Bibliographical Theories and Printing-House Practices." *SB* 22 (1969):1–75.

430 MCKERROW, Ronald B. *An Introduction to Bibliography for Literary Students.* Oxford: Clarendon, 1927. 2nd ed., 1928.

431 MCKERROW, Ronald B. *Prolegomena for the Oxford Shakespeare.* Oxford: Clarendon, 1939.

432 MCMANAWAY, James G. *Studies in Shakespeare, Bibliography, and Theater.* New York: Shakespeare Association of America, 1969.

433 SHAABER, M. A. "Problems in the Editing of Shakespeare: Text." *EIE 1947* (1948):97–116.

434 *Shakespeare Survey* 5 (1952). Much of this issue is devoted to textual criticism.*

435 SISSON, Charles J. *New Readings in Shakespeare.* 2 vols. Cambridge: Cambridge U.P., 1956. Rpt., London: Dawsons, 1961.

436 THORPE, James. *Principles of Textual Criticism.* San Marino, Calif.: Huntington Library, 1972.

437 THORPE, James, and Claude M. SIMPSON, Jr. *The Task of the Editor.* Los Angeles: William Andrews Clark Memorial Library, 1969.

438 TURNER, Robert K., Jr. "Analytical Bibliography and Shakespeare's Text." *MP* 62 (1964):51–58.

439 WALKER, Alice. "Compositor Determination and Other Problems in Shakespearian Texts." *SB* 7 (1955):3–15.

440 WALKER, Alice. "Principles of Annotation: Some Suggestions for Editors of Shakespeare." *SB* 9 (1957):95–105.

441 WALKER, Alice. "Some Editorial Principles (with Special Reference to *Henry V*)." *SB* 8 (1956):95–111.

442 WALLER, Frederick O. "The Use of Linguistic Criteria in Determining the Copy and Dates for Shakespeare's Plays." In **1156.**

443 WILLIAMS, Philip. "New Approaches to Textual Problems in Shakespeare." *SB* 8 (1956):3–14.

444 WILSON, F. P. *Shakespeare and the New Bibliography.* Rev. and ed. Helen GARDNER. Oxford: Clarendon, 1970.

445 WILSON, J. Dover. "The New Way with Shakespeare's Texts: An Introduction for Lay Readers." In four parts. *ShS* 7 (1954):48–56; 8 (1955):81–99; 9 (1956): 69–80; and 11 (1958):78–88.

Style and Language

Studies in Language and Rhetoric

See also **316, 336, 346, 1291, 1357, 1596, 2125, 2369, 2969–70, 3189, 3195, 3198, 3211, 3820–21, 3918, 4035–36, 4366–67,** and **4509.**

446 AUERBACH, Erich. "The Weary Prince." *Mimesis: The Representation of Reality in Western Literature.* Trans. Willard R. TRASK. Princeton: Princeton U.P., 1953. Rpt., Garden City, N.Y.: Doubleday, 1957.*

447 BARTON, Anne. "Shakespeare and the Limits of Language." *ShS* 24 (1971): 19–30.

448 BENNETT, Paul E. "The Statistical Measurement of a Stylistic Trait in *Julius Caesar* and *As You Like It.*" *SQ* 8 (1957):33–50.

449 BOYCE, Benjamin. "The Stoic *Consolatio* and Shakespeare." *PMLA* 64 (1949): 771–80.

450 BRADBROOK, M. C. "Fifty Years of the Criticism of Shakespeare's Style: A Retrospect." *ShS* 7 (1954):1–11.

451 BYRNE, Muriel St. Clare. "The Foundations of Elizabethan Language." *ShS* 17 (1964):223–39.*

452 CHARNEY, Maurice. *Style in "Hamlet."* See **2628.**

453 COLIE, Rosalie L. *Paradoxia Epidemica: The Renaissance Tradition of Paradox.* Princeton: Princeton U.P., 1966.*

454 CUSACK, Bridget. "Shakespeare and the Tune of the Time." *ShS* 23 (1970): 1–12. On Shakespeare's dramatic use of shifting linguistic conditions of his time.

455 DANSON, Lawrence. *Tragic Alphabet: Shakespeare's Drama of Language.* See **1931.**

456 DORAN, Madeleine. "The Idea of Excellence in Shakespeare." *SQ* 27 (1976): 133–49. On hyperbole and the rhetoric of praise.

457 DORAN, Madeleine. *Shakespeare's Dramatic Language.* Madison: U. of Wisconsin P., 1976.

458 EHRL, Charlotte. *Sprachstil und Charakter bei Shakespeare.* Heidelberg: Quelle & Meyer, 1957.

459 ELTON, Oliver. "Style in Shakespeare." *PBA* 22 (1937 for 1936):69–95.

460 EVANS, B. Ifor. *The Language of Shakespeare's Plays.* 3rd. ed., London: Methuen, 1964.

461 FOAKES, R. A. "Contrasts and Connections: Some Notes on Style in Shakespeare's Comedies and Tragedies." *SJ* 90 (1954):69–81.

462 FRANZ, Wilhelm. *Die Sprache Shakespeares in Vers und Prosa, unter Berücksichtigung des amerikanischen Entwicklungsgeschichtlich dargestellt.* Halle/Salle: Niemeyer, 1939.

463 GERSTNER-HIRZEL, Arthur. *The Economy of Action and Word in Shakespeare's Plays.* Bern: Francke, 1957. Rpt., New York: AMS.

464 HALLIDAY, F. E. *The Poetry of Shakespeare's Plays.* London: Duckworth, 1954; New York: Barnes & Noble, 1964.

465 HAWKES, Terence. *Shakespeare's Talking Animals: Language and Drama in Society.* London: Arnold; Totowa, N.J.: Rowman & Littlefield, 1973.

466 HIBBARD, G. R. "Words, Action, and Artistic Economy." *ShS* 23 (1970): 49–58.

467 HOWELL, Wilbur Samuel. *Logic and Rhetoric in England, 1500–1700.* Princeton: Princeton U.P., 1956.

468 HULME, Hilda M. *Explorations in Shakespeare's Language.* London: Longmans, Green, 1962; New York: Barnes & Noble, 1963.*

469 HULME, Hilda M. "Shakespeare's Language." In **1170.**

470 HULME, Hilda M. *Yours That Read Him: An Introduction to Shakespeare's Language.* London: Ginn, 1972.

471 JESPERSEN, Otto. "Shakespeare and the Language of Poetry." *Growth and Structure of the English Language.* Leipzig: Teubner; New York: G. E. Stechert, 1905. 9th ed., rev., 1938. Rpt., Oxford: Blackwell, 1943.*

472 KAUFMANN, R. J. "The Seneca Perspective and the Shakespearean Poetic." *CompD* 1 (1967):182–98.

473 KENNEDY, Milton Boone. *The Oration in Shakespeare.* Chapel Hill: U. of North Carolina P., 1942.

474 LANHAM, Richard A. *The Motives of Eloquence: Literary Rhetoric in the Renaissance.* New Haven and London: Yale U.P., 1976. Contains chapters on the Sonnets, *Venus and Adonis, The Rape of Lucrece, Hamlet,* and the Henriad.*

475 MCALINDON, T. *Shakespeare and Decorum.* London: Macmillan; New York: Barnes & Noble, 1973.*

476 MCDONALD, Charles Osborne. *The Rhetoric of Tragedy: Form in Stuart Drama.* Amherst: U. of Massachusetts P., 1966.

477 MAHOOD, M. M. "Unblotted Lines: Shakespeare at Work." *PBA* 58 (1974 for 1972):163–76. On Shakespeare's loose ends, false starts, anomalies, etc.

478 MIRIAM JOSEPH, Sister. *Shakespeare's Use of the Arts of Language.* New York: Columbia U.P., 1947. Rpt., New York: Hafner, 1966. Rpt. in part as *Rhetoric in Shakespeare's Time.* New York: Harcourt, Brace, & World, 1962.*

479 MUIR, Kenneth. "Shakespeare and Rhetoric." *SJ* 90 (1954):49–68.

480 MUIR, Kenneth. "A Trick of Style and Some Implications." *ShakS* 6 (1972 for 1970):305–10.

481 OYAMA, Toshiko. *Shakespeare's World of Words.* Tokyo: Shinozaki-Shorin, 1975.

482 PRIOR, Moody E. *The Language of Tragedy.* New York: Columbia U.P., 1947. Rpt., Gloucester, Mass.: P. Smith, 1964; Bloomington: Indiana U.P., 1966.

483 QUIRK, Randolph. "Shakespeare and the English Language." In **55.**

484 RANSOM, John Crowe. "On Shakespeare's Language." *SR* 55 (1947):181–98.

485 REPLOGLE, Carol. "Shakespeare's Salutations: A Study in Stylistic Etiquette." *SP* 70 (1973):172–86.

486 SCHANZER, Ernest. "Atavism and Anticipation in Shakespeare's Style." *EIC* 7 (1957):242–56.

487 *Shakespeare-Jahrbuch* 90 (1954). Issue devoted largely to style.

488 *Shakespeare Survey* 7 (1954) and 23 (1970). Issues devoted largely to style and language.*

489 SUTHERLAND, James. "How the Characters Talk." In **1170.**

490 SUTHERLAND, James. "The Language of the Last Plays." In **1138.**

491 VICKERS, Brian. "Shakespeare's Use of Rhetoric." In **55.**

492 VISWANATHAN, S. " 'Illeism With a Difference' in Certain Middle Plays of Shakespeare." *SQ* 20 (1969):407–15. On characters referring to themselves in the third person.

493 WALDO, Tommy Ruth. *Musical Terms as Rhetoric: The Complexity of Shakespeare's Dramatic Style.* Salzburg: Institut für Englische Sprache und Literatur, 1974.

494 WILLCOCK, Gladys D. "Shakespeare and Elizabethan English." *ShS* 7 (1954): 12–24.

495 WILLCOCK, Gladys D. "Shakespeare and Rhetoric." *E&S* 29 (1944 for 1943): 50–61.

496 WILLCOCK, Gladys D. *Shakespeare as a Critic of Language.* London: for the Shakespeare Association by Oxford U.P., 1934.*

Prosody: Versification, Metrics, Punctuation

See also **364, 377, 2358, 4525, 4527,** and **4567.**

497 ALEXANDER, Peter. "Shakespeare's Punctuation." *PBA* 31 (1946 for 1945): 61–84.

498 BAYFIELD, M. A. *A Study of Shakespeare's Versification.* Cambridge: Cambridge U.P., 1920.

499 FLATTER, Richard. *Shakespeare's Producing Hand: A Study of His Marks of Expression to be Found in the First Folio.* London and Melbourne: Heinemann; New York: Norton, 1948.

500 HIBBARD, G. R. " 'The Forced Gait of a Shuffling Nag.' " In **1151.**

501 HOWARTH, Herbert. "Metre and Emphasis: A Conservative Note." In **1167.**

502 MCKENZIE, D. F. "Shakespearian Punctuation—A New Beginning." *RES,* n.s. 10 (1959):361–70.

503 NESS, Frederic W. *The Use of Rhyme in Shakespeare's Plays.* New Haven: Yale U.P.; London: Oxford U.P., 1941.

504 PARTRIDGE, A. C. *Orthography in Shakespeare and Elizabethan Drama: A Study of Colloquial Contractions, Elision, Prosody, and Punctuation.* London: Arnold; Lincoln: U. of Nebraska P., 1964.

505 SIMPSON, Percy. "Shakespeare's Versification: A Study of Development." In **1250.**

506 SIPE, Dorothy L. *Shakespeare's Metrics.* New Haven and London: Yale U.P., 1968.

Shakespeare's Prose

See also **3628.**

507 BARISH, Jonas A. *Ben Jonson and the Language of Prose Comedy.* Cambridge, Mass.: Harvard U.P., 1960, pp. 23–40.*

508 BARISH, Jonas A. "Continuities and Discontinuities in Shakespearian Prose." In **1151.**

509 BORINSKI, Ludwig. "Shakespeare's Comic Prose." *ShS* 8 (1955):57–68.

510 BURRIS, Quincy Guy. " 'Soft! Here Follows Prose'—*Twelfth Night* II, v, 154." *SQ* 2 (1951):233–39.

511 CRANE, Milton. *Shakespeare's Prose.* Chicago: U. of Chicago P., 1951.*

512 NEWELL, Alex. "Early Modern English Idiom in a Prose Passage from *King Lear.*" In **1613.**

513 SALMON, Vivian. "Elizabethan Colloquial English in the Falstaff Plays." *LeedsSE,* n.s. 1 (1967):37–70.

514 VICKERS, Brian. *The Artistry of Shakespeare's Prose.* London: Methuen; New York: Barnes & Noble, 1968.*

Grammar and Idiom

See also **2243, 3815, 4062,** and **4521.**

515 ABBOTT, E. A. *A Shakespearian Grammar.* See **58.***

516 BURTON, Dolores M. *Shakespeare's Grammatical Style: A Computer-Assisted Analysis of "Richard II" and "Antony and Cleopatra."* Austin and London: U. of Texas P., 1973.

517 BYRNE, Sister St. Geraldine. *Shakespeare's Use of the Pronoun of Address: Its Significance in Characterization and Motivation.* Washington, D.C.: Catholic U. of America, 1936. Rpt., New York: Haskell House, 1970.

518 ECCLES, Mark. "Shakespeare's Use of *Look How* and Similar Idioms." *JEGP* 42 (1943):386–400.

519 FRANZ, Wilhelm. *Shakespeare-Grammatik.* See **67.***

520 GILLETT, Peter J. "Me, U and Non-U: Class Connotations of Two Shakespearean Idioms." *SQ* 25 (1974):297–309.

521 JOHNSON, Judith A. "Second Person Pronouns in Shakespeare's Tragedies." *MichA* 8 (1975):151–56.

522 KAKIETEK, Piotr. *"May* and *Might* in Shakespeare's English." *Linguistics* 64 (1970):26–35.

523 MULHOLLAND, Joan. *"Thou* and *You* in Shakespeare: A Study in the Second Person Pronoun." *ES* 48 (1967):34–43.

524 SMITHERS, G. V. "Guide-Lines for Interpreting the Uses of the Suffix '*-ed*' in Shakespeare's English." *ShS* 23 (1970):27–37.

525 TAYLOR, Estelle W. "Shakespeare's Use of 'S' Endings of the Verb *To Do* and *To Have* in the First Folio." *CLAJ* 16 (1972):214–31.

526 WILLIAMS, Charles. "The Use of the Second Person in *Twelfth Night." English* 9 (1953):125–28.

Vocabulary and Wordplay

See also **63, 66, 69–71, 73, 1931, 2641, 3182, 3186–87, 3191, 3216, 3244, 3820, 3823, 3916, 4042, 4063,** and **4528.**

527 BLAND, D. S. "Shakespeare and the 'Ordinary' Word." *ShS* 4 (1951):49–55.

528 COLMAN, E. A. M. *The Dramatic Use of Bawdy in Shakespeare.* London: Longman, 1974.

529 EKWALL, Eilert. *Shakspere's Vocabulary: Its Etymological Elements.* Uppsala: Uppsala U.P., 1903. Rpt., New York: AMS, 1966.

530 EMPSON, William. *The Structure of Complex Words.* London: Chatto & Windus; New York: New Directions, 1951. 2nd ed., 1964.*

29

531 GOVE, Philip B. "Shakespeare's Language in Today's Dictionary." *TSLL* 7 (1965):127–36.

532 GRIVELET, Michel. "Shakespeare as 'Corrupter of Words.'" *ShS* 16 (1963): 70–76.

533 HALE, J. R. "The True Shakespearean Blank." *SQ* 19 (1968):33–40. On the use of "blank" in archery and gunnery.

534 HART, Alfred. "The Growth of Shakespeare's Vocabulary." *RES* 19 (1943): 242–54.

535 HART, Alfred. "Vocabularies of Shakespeare's Plays." *RES* 19 (1943):128–40.

536 HENKE, James T. *Renaissance Dramatic Bawdry (Exclusive of Shakespeare): An Annotated Glossary and Critical Essays.* 2 vols. Salzburg: Institut für Englische Sprache und Literatur, 1974.

537 HUDSON, Kenneth. "Shakespeare's Use of Colloquial Language." *ShS* 23 (1970):39–48.

538 JORGENSEN, Paul A. *Redeeming Shakespeare's Words.* Berkeley and Los Angeles: U. of California P., 1962.*

539 JORGENSEN, Paul A. "Shakespeare's Dark Vocabulary." In **1120.**

540 LEVIN, Harry. "Shakespeare's Nomenclature." In **1127.**

541 MAHOOD, M. M. *Shakespeare's Wordplay.* London: Methuen, 1957.*

542 MUIR, Kenneth. "The Uncomic Pun." *Cambridge Journal* 3 (1950):472–85.

543 ONIONS, C. T. *A Shakespeare Glossary.* See **74.***

544 PAFFORD, J. H. P. "Words Used Only Once in Shakespeare." *N&Q* 203 (1958): 237–38.

545 PARTRIDGE, Eric. *Shakespeare's Bawdy.* See **76.***

546 SALMON, Vivian. "Some Functions of Shakespearian Word-Formation." *ShS* 23 (1970):13–26.

547 SCHÄFER, Jürgen. *Shakespeares Stil: Germanisches und romanisches Vokabular.* Frankfurt: Athenäum, 1973.

548 SCHMIDT, Alexander. *Shakespeare-Lexicon.* See **78.***

549 SPEVACK, Marvin. "Shakespeare's English: The Core Vocabulary." *RNL* 3.2 (1972):106–22.

550 WEIMANN, Robert. "Shakespeare's Wordplay: Popular Origins and Theatrical Functions." In **1151.**

551 WILSON, F. P. "Shakespeare and the Diction of Common Life." *PBA* 27 (1942 for 1941):167–97. Corrected and expanded in **1272.***

Imagery

For studies of imagery in individual plays or groups of plays, see **1238, 1256, 1358, 1532, 1827, 2039, 2122, 2147, 2153, 2353, 2355, 2357, 2359–61, 2640, 2644–45, 2700, 2791, 2855, 2860, 2968, 2973, 2993, 3183, 3190, 3192–93, 3196, 3356, 3361, 3631, 3814, 3822, 3909, 3911, 3913, 3915, 3919–21, 3923–24, 4037–40, 4098, 4255, 4369, 4583, 4638, 4647, 4663,** and **4672.**

552 ARMSTRONG, Edward A. *Shakespeare's Imagination.* See **1352.***

553 BERRY, Francis. *The Shakespeare Inset: Word and Picture.* See **1277.***

554 CLEMEN, Wolfgang. *The Development of Shakespeare's Imagery.* Cambridge, Mass.: Harvard U.P.; London: Methuen, 1951. First pub. in German in 1936.*

555 DOEBLER, John. *Shakespeare's Speaking Pictures: Studies in Iconic Imagery.* Albuquerque: U. of New Mexico P., 1974.*

556 DOWNER, Alan S. "The Life of Our Design: The Function of Imagery in the Poetic Drama." *HudR* 2 (1949):242–63.

557 ELLIS-FERMOR, Una. *Some Recent Research in Shakespeare's Imagery.* London: for the Shakespeare Association by Oxford U.P., 1937. Rpt., Folcroft, Pa.: Folcroft, 1975.

558 EWBANK, Inga-Stina. " 'More Pregnantly Than Words': Some Uses and Limitations of Visual Symbolism." *ShS* 24 (1971):13–18.

559 FISCH, Harold. "Shakespeare and 'The Theatre of the World.' " In **1146.** On the trope of the world as a stage.

560 FOAKES, R. A. "Suggestions for a New Approach to Shakespeare's Imagery." *ShS* 5 (1952):81–92.

561 HANKINS, John E. *Shakespeare's Derived Imagery.* Lawrence: U. of Kansas P., 1953. Rpt., New York: Octagon.

562 HOBDAY, C. H. "Why the Sweets Melted: A Study in Shakespeare's Imagery." *SQ* 16 (1965):3–17.

563 JACKSON, James L. "Shakespeare's Dog-and-Sugar Imagery and the Friendship Tradition." *SQ* 1 (1950):260–63.

564 JOHNSON, Francis R. "Shakespearian Imagery and Senecan Imitation." In **1154.**

565 KIROV, Todor T. "The First Step of a Giant." *SJW* 104 (1968):109–40. On Shakespeare's early imagery.

566 KNIGHTS, L. C. "Shakespeare's Imagery." In **1140.**

567 KOLBE, F. C. *Shakespeare's Way: A Psychological Study.* London: Sheed & Ward, 1930. A study of iterative imagery.

568 LAWLOR, John. "Mind and Hand: Some Reflections on the Study of Shakespeare's Imagery." *SQ* 8 (1957):179–93.

569 LEWIS, Anthony J. "The Dog, Lion, and Wolf in Shakespeare's Descriptions of Night." *MLR* 66 (1971):1–10.

570 LYONS, Clifford. "Stage Imagery in Shakespeare's Plays." In **1144.**

571 MEHL, Dieter. "Visual and Rhetorical Imagery in Shakespeare's Plays." *E&S,* n.s. 25 (1972):83–100.

572 MOROZOV, Mikhail M. "The Individualization of Shakespeare's Characters through Imagery." *ShS* 2 (1949):83–106.

573 MUIR, Kenneth. "Shakespeare's Imagery—Then and Now." *ShS* 18 (1965): 46–57. Rpt., rev., in **1238.**

574 PETERSON, Douglas L. "Tempest-Tossed Barks and Their Helmsmen in Several of Shakespeare's Plays." *Costerus* 9 (1973):79–107.

575 RODRIGUES, Linda A. M. "The Latticework of Imagery." *Main Currents of Modern Thought* 32.1 (Sept.–Oct. 1975):24–28.

576 ROTHENBERG, Alan B. "Infantile Fantasies in Shakespearean Metaphor: I. The Fear of Being Smothered; II. Scopophilia and Fears of Ocular Rape and Castration." *PsyR* 60 (1973):205–22, 533–56.

577 SPURGEON, Caroline F. E. *Leading Motives in the Imagery of Shakespeare's Tragedies.* London: for the Shakespeare Association by Oxford U.P., 1930. Rpt., New York: Haskell House.

578 SPURGEON, Caroline F. E. *Shakespeare's Imagery and What It Tells Us.* Cambridge: Cambridge U.P., 1935; New York: Macmillan, 1936. Rpt., Boston: Beacon, 1958.*

579 SPURGEON, Caroline F. E. "Shakespeare's Iterative Imagery." *PBA* 17 (1932 for 1931):147–78. Rpt. in **1152.**

580 STEADMAN, John M. "Iconography and Methodology in Renaissance Dramatic Study: Some Caveats." *SRO* 7–8 (1972–74):39–52.

581 WEIMANN, Robert. "Shakespeare and the Study of Metaphor." *NLH* 6 (1974): 149–67.*

582 WEISS, Samuel A. " 'Solid,' " 'Sullied,' and Mutability: A Study in Imagery." *SQ* 10 (1959):219–27.

583 WENTERSDORF, Karl P. "Imagery as a Criterion of Authenticity: A Reconsideration of the Problem." *SQ* 23 (1972):231–59.

584 YODER, Audrey. *Animal Analogy in Shakespeare's Character Portrayal.* New York: King's Crown; London: Oxford U.P., 1947.

Proverbs

See also **2633, 2752, 3181,** and **3818.**

585 LEVER, Katherine. "Proverbs and *Sententiae* in the Plays of Shakespeare." *ShAB* 13 (1938):173–83, 224–39.

586 SMITH, Charles G. *Shakespeare's Proverb Lore.* See **1538.**

587 TILLEY, Morris Palmer. *A Dictionary of the Proverbs in England in the Sixteenth and Seventeenth Centuries.* Ann Arbor: U. of Michigan P., 1950.

588 WILSON, F. P. "The Proverbial Wisdom of Shakespeare." In **1272.**

Shakespeare and His Stage

Reference Works

See also **246–47** and **645.**

589 BENTLEY, Gerald Eades. *The Jacobean and Caroline Stage.* 7 vols. Oxford: Clarendon, 1941–68.*

590 CHAMBERS, E. K. *The Elizabethan Stage.* 4 vols. Oxford: Clarendon, 1923.*

591 CUNNINGHAM, Peter. *Extracts from the Accounts of the Revels at Court, in the Reigns of Queen Elizabeth and King James I, from the Original Office Books of the Masters and Yeomen.* London: Shakespeare Society, 1842. Rpt., New York: AMS.

592 FEUILLERAT, Albert, ed. *Documents Relating to the Office of the Revels in the Time of Queen Elizabeth.* Louvain: Uystpruyst, 1908.

593 FOAKES, R. A., ed. *The Henslowe Papers: The Diary, Theatre Papers, and Bear Garden Papers.* In full and in facsimile. Bound 3 vols. in 2. London: Scolar, 1976.*

594 FOAKES, R. A., and R. T. RICKERT, eds. *Henslowe's Diary.* Cambridge: Cambridge U.P., 1961.

595 GILDERSLEEVE, Virginia Crocheron. *Government Regulation of the Elizabethan Drama.* New York: Columbia U.P., 1908. Rpt., New York: Burt Franklin, 1961.

596 GREG, W. W., ed. *Dramatic Documents from the Elizabethan Playhouses: Stage Plots; Actors' Parts; Prompt Books.* 2 vols. Oxford: Clarendon, 1931.*

597 GREG, W. W., ed. *Henslowe Papers, Being Documents Supplementary to Henslowe's Diary.* London: Bullen, 1907.

598 GREG, W. W., ed. *Henslowe's Diary.* 2 vols. London: Bullen, 1904.

599 SORLIEN, Robert Parker, ed. *The Diary of John Manningham of the Middle Temple, 1602–1603.* Hanover: U.P. of New England for the U. of Rhode Island, 1976.

600 STEELE, Mary Susan. *Plays and Masques at Court During the Reigns of Elizabeth, James, and Charles.* New Haven: Yale U.P.; London: Oxford U.P., 1926.

601 THOMPSON, Elbert N. S. *The Controversy Between the Puritans and the Stage.* New Haven: Yale U.P.; New York: Holt, 1903. Rpt., New York: Russell & Russell, 1966.

General Studies

See also **690, 705, 781,** and **1272.**

602 BARROLL, J. Leeds, Alexander LEGGATT, Richard HOSLEY, and Alvin B. KERNAN. *The Revels History of Drama in English, Vol. III, 1576–1613.* Gen. eds. Clifford LEECH and T. W. CRAIK. London: Methuen; New York: Barnes & Noble, 1975.

603 BECKERMAN, Bernard. *Shakespeare at the Globe, 1599–1609.* New York: Macmillan, 1962.*

604 BENTLEY, Gerald Eades, ed. *The Seventeenth-Century Stage: A Collection of Critical Essays.* Chicago: U. of Chicago P., 1968.*

605 BENTLEY, Gerald Eades. *Shakespeare and His Theatre.* Lincoln: U. of Nebraska P., 1964.

606 BROWN, Ivor. *How Shakespeare Spent the Day.* London: Bodley Head, 1965.

607 GALLOWAY, David, ed. *The Elizabethan Theatre.* Papers given at International Conferences on Elizabethan Theatre held at the U. of Waterloo. 3 vols. Toronto: Macmillan of Canada; Hamden, Conn.: Archon, 1969–73.* See also **610.**

608 GURR, Andrew. *The Shakespearean Stage, 1574–1642.* Cambridge: Cambridge U.P., 1970.*

609 HARRISON, G. B. *Elizabethan Plays and Players.* London: Routledge, 1940; Ann Arbor: U. of Michigan P., 1956, 1961.

610 HIBBARD, G. R., ed. *The Elizabethan Theatre IV and V.* Papers given at International Conferences on Elizabethan Theatre held at the U. of Waterloo. A continuation of the series begun by David GALLOWAY; see **607** above. 2 vols. to date. Toronto: Macmillan of Canada; Hamden, Conn.: Archon, 1974–75 and to be continued.*

611 JACQUOT, Jean, ed., in collaboration with Elie KONIGSON and Marcel OD-DON. *Le Lieu théâtral à la Renaissance: Colloque de Royaumont, 22–27 Mars 1963.* Paris: Centre national de la recherche scientifique, 1964.

612 KERNODLE, George R. *From Art to Theatre: Form and Convention in the Renaissance.* Chicago: U. of Chicago P., 1944.*

613 KING, T. J. *Shakespearean Staging, 1599–1642.* Cambridge, Mass.: Harvard U.P., 1971.*

614 KLEIN, David. *Milestones to Shakespeare: A Study of the Dramatic Forms and Pageantry That Were the Prelude to Shakespeare.* New York: Twayne, 1970.

615 KOLIN, Philip C., and R. O. WYATT, II. "A Bibliography of Scholarship on the Elizabethan Stage since Chambers." *RORD* 15–16 (1972–73):33–59.

616 LAWRENCE, W. J. *Pre-Restoration Stage Studies.* Cambridge, Mass.: Harvard U.P.; London: Oxford U.P., 1927. Rpt., New York: Blom.

617 NICOLL, Allardyce. "Studies in the Elizabethan Stage since 1900." *ShS* 1 (1948): 1–16.

618 PROUTY, Charles Tyler, ed. *Studies in the Elizabethan Theatre.* Hamden, Conn.: Shoe String, 1961.

619 Shakespeare Association. *A Series of Papers on Shakespeare and the Theatre . . . by Members of the Shakespeare Association.* London: for the Shakespeare Association by Oxford U.P., 1927.

620 *Shakespeare Survey* 1 (1948); 2 (1949); and 12 (1959). These issues are largely devoted to Shakespeare's stage, Shakespearean production, and the Elizabethan theater.*

621 SMITH, Warren D. *Shakespeare's Playhouse Practice: A Handbook.* Hanover: U.P. of New England for the U. of Rhode Island, 1975.

622 SOUTHERN, Richard. *The Staging of Plays before Shakespeare.* London: Faber & Faber; New York: Theatre Arts Books, 1973.

623 THORNDIKE, Ashley H. *Shakespeare's Theatre.* New York: Macmillan, 1916.

624 WICKHAM, Glynne. *Shakespeare's Dramatic Heritage.* London: Routledge & K. Paul, 1969.

Acting Companies, Players, and Playwrights

See also **368, 589–90, 609, 656, 1519,** and **2743.**

625 ARMSTRONG, William A. "Actors and Theatres." *ShS* 17 (1964):191–204.

626 ARMSTRONG, William A. "Shakespeare and the Acting of Edward Alleyn." *ShS* 7 (1954):82–89.

627 BALDWIN, T. W. *The Organization and Personnel of the Shakespearean Company.* Princeton: Princeton U.P., 1927. Rpt., New York: Russell & Russell.

628 BENTLEY, Gerald Eades. *The Profession of Dramatist in Shakespeare's Time, 1590–1642.* Princeton: Princeton U.P., 1971.*

629 BETHELL, S. L. "Shakespeare's Actors." *RES,* n.s. 1 (1950):193–205.

630 BRADBROOK, M. C. *The Rise of the Common Player: A Study of Actor and Society in Shakespeare's England.* London: Chatto & Windus; Cambridge, Mass.: Harvard U.P., 1962.

631 BROWN, Ivor. *Shakespeare and the Actors.* London: Bodley Head, 1970; New York: Coward, 1971.

632 DAVID, Richard. "Shakespeare and the Players." *PBA* 47 (1962 for 1961): 139–59. Rpt. in **1116.**

633 DAVIES, W. Robertson. *Shakespeare's Boy Actors.* London: Dent, 1939.

634 FELVER, Charles S. *Robert Armin, Shakespeare's Fool: A Biographical Essay.* Kent, Ohio: Kent State U., 1961.

635 FOAKES, R. A. "The Profession of Playwright." In **1582.**

636 HARBAGE, Alfred. "The Role of the Shakespearean Producer." *SJ* 91 (1955): 161–73.

637 HARRISON, G. B. "Shakespeare's Actors." In **619.**

638 HILLEBRAND, Harold Newcomb. *The Child Actors: A Chapter in Elizabethan Stage History.* Urbana: U. of Illinois P., 1926. On child actors, see also Michael SHAPIRO. "Toward a Reappraisal of the Children's Troupes." *Theatre Survey* 13.2 (1972):1–19; and Michael SHAPIRO. "Audience vs. Dramatist in Jonson's *Epicoene* and Other Plays of the Children's Troupes." *ELR* 3 (1973):400–17.

639 HODGES, C. Walter. *Shakespeare and the Players.* London: Benn, 1948. 2nd ed., New York: Coward, 1970.

640 HOLMES, Martin. *Shakespeare and His Players.* London: Murray; New York: Scribner's, 1972.

641 JAMIESON, Michael. "Shakespeare's Celibate Stage: The Problem of Accommodation to the Boy-Actress in *As You Like It, Antony and Cleopatra,* and *The Winter's Tale.*" In **1134.** Rpt. in **604.**

642 KLEIN, David. "Did Shakespeare Produce His Own Plays?" *MLR* 57 (1962): 556–60.

643 MCMILLIN, Scott. "Casting for Pembroke's Men: the *Henry VI* Quartos and *The Taming of A Shrew.*" *SQ* 23 (1972):141–59.

644 MURRAY, John Tucker. *English Dramatic Companies, 1558–1642*. 2 vols. London: Constable; Boston and New York: Houghton Mifflin, 1910. Rpt., New York: Russell & Russell, 1963.

645 NUNGEZER, Edwin. *A Dictionary of Actors and of Other Persons Associated with the Public Representation of Plays in England before 1642*. New Haven: Yale U.P.; London: Oxford U.P., 1929. Rpt., Westport, Conn.: Greenwood; St. Clair Shores, Mich.: Scholarly P.*

646 PINCISS, G. M. "Shakespeare, Her Majesty's Players, and Pembroke's Men." *ShS* 27 (1974):129–36.

647 RINGLER, William A., Jr. "The Number of Actors in Shakespeare's Early Plays." In **604.**

648 STOPES, C. C. *Burbage and Shakespeare's Stage*. London: Moring, 1913.

Elizabethan Acting

See also **589–90, 602,** and **641.**

649 BROWN, John Russell. "On the Acting of Shakespeare's Plays." In **604.**

650 DOWNER, Alan S. "Prolegomenon to a Study of Elizabethan Acting." *MuK* 10 (1964):625–36.

651 DOWNER, Alan S. "The Tudor Actor: A Taste of His Quality." *TN* 5 (1951): 76–81.

652 FOAKES, R. A. "The Player's Passion: Some Notes on Elizabethan Psychology and Acting." *E&S,* n.s. 7 (1954):62–77.

653 GURR, Andrew. "Elizabethan Action." *SP* 63 (1966):144–56.

654 GURR, Andrew. "Who Strutted and Bellowed?" *ShS* 16 (1963):95–102.

655 HARBAGE, Alfred. "Elizabethan Acting." *PMLA* 54 (1939):685–708. Rpt. in **909.**

656 JENSEN, Ejner J. "The Style of the Boy Actors." *CompD* 2 (1968):100–14.

657 JOSEPH, Bertram L. *Elizabethan Acting*. 2nd ed., London: Oxford U.P., 1964.*

658 JOSEPH, Bertram L. "The Age of Shakespeare." In **769.**

659 KLEIN, David. "Elizabethan Acting." *PMLA* 71 (1956):280–82. A reply to **662.**

660 MARKER, Lise-Lone. "Nature and Decorum in the Theory of Elizabethan Acting." In **607,** vol. 1 (1969 for 1968).

661 MOWAT, Barbara A. "The Beckoning Ghost: Stage-Gesture in Shakespeare." *RenP 1970* (1971):41–54.

662 ROSENBERG, Marvin. "Elizabethan Actors: Men or Marionettes?" *PMLA* 69 (1954):915–27. Rpt. in **604.***

663 SELTZER, Daniel. "The Actors and Staging." In **55.***

664 SELTZER, Daniel. "Elizabethan Acting in *Othello.*" *SQ* 10 (1959):201–10.

Public Playhouses

See also **602, 613,** and **4031.**

665 ADAMS, John Cranford. *The Globe Playhouse: Its Design and Equipment.* Cambridge, Mass.: Harvard U.P., 1942; London: Oxford U.P., 1943. Rev. ed., New York: Barnes & Noble, 1961.

666 ADAMS, Joseph Quincy. *Shakespearean Playhouses.* Boston: Houghton Mifflin, 1917. Rpt., Gloucester, Mass.: P. Smith, 1960.

667 BALD, R. C. "The Entrance to the Elizabethan Theater." *SQ* 3 (1952):17–20.

668 BERNHEIMER, Richard. "Another Globe Theatre." *SQ* 9 (1958):19–29.

669 BERRY, Herbert. "Americans in the Playhouses." *ShakS* 9 (1976):31–44. A survey of American scholarly studies of Elizabethan playhouses.

670 BERRY, Herbert. "Dr. Fludd's Engravings and Their Beholders." *ShakS* 3 (1968 for 1967):11–21.

671 CARSON, Neil. "The Staircases of the Frame: New Light on the Structure of the Globe." *ShS* 29 (1976):127–31.

672 FISHER, Sidney. *The Theatre, The Curtain, and the Globe.* Montreal: McGill U. Library, 1964.

673 FORREST, G. Topham. "The Architecture of the First Globe Theatre." *The Site of the Globe Playhouse, Southwark.* Published by arrangement with the London County Council. 2nd ed., London: Hodder & Stoughton, 1924.

674 HODGES, C. Walter. *The Globe Restored: A Study of the Elizabethan Theatre.* London: Benn, 1953. 2nd ed., London: Oxford U.P.; New York: Coward-McCann, 1968. New York: Norton, 1973.*

675 HODGES, C. Walter. *Shakespeare's Second Globe: The Missing Monument.* London: Oxford U.P., 1973.*

676 HOOK, Lucyle. "The Curtain." *SQ* 13 (1962):499–504.

677 HOSLEY, Richard. "An Approach to the Elizabethan Stage." *RenD (A Report on Research Opportunities)* 6 (1963):72–78.

678 HOSLEY, Richard. "The Discovery-Space in Shakespeare's Globe." *ShS* 12 (1959):35–46. Rpt. in **604.***

679 HOSLEY, Richard. "The Gallery over the Stage in the Public Playhouse of Shakespeare's Time." *SQ* 8 (1957):15–31.*

680 HOSLEY, Richard. "The Origins of the Shakespearian Playhouse." *SQ* 15.2 (1964):29–39. Also in **1153.***

681 HOSLEY, Richard. "The Origins of the So-Called Elizabethan Multiple Stage." *TDR* 12.2 (1968):28–50.

682 HOSLEY, Richard. "The Playhouse and the Stage." In **55.**

683 HOSLEY, Richard. "Shakespeare's Use of a Gallery over the Stage." *ShS* 10 (1957):77–89.*

684 HOSLEY, Richard. "Shakespearian Stage Curtains: Then and Now." *CE* 25 (1964):488–92.

685 HOSLEY, Richard. "The Staging of the Monument Scenes in *Antony and Cleopatra.*" *LC* 30 (1964):62–71.

686 HOSLEY, Richard. "Was There a Music-Room in Shakespeare's Globe?" *ShS* 13 (1960):113–23.*

687 HOTSON, Leslie. *Shakespeare's Wooden O.* London: Hart-Davis, 1959.

688 KING, T. J. "The Stage in the Time of Shakespeare: A Survey of Major Scholarship." *RenD,* n.s. 4 (1971):199–235.

689 LATTER, D. A. "Sight-Lines in a Conjectural Reconstruction of an Elizabethan Playhouse." *ShS* 28 (1975):125–35.

690 LAWRENCE, W. J. *The Elizabethan Playhouse and Other Studies.* Stratford-upon-Avon: Shakespeare Head; Philadelphia: Lippincott, 1912. 2nd ser., 1913. Rpt., New York: Russell & Russell, 1963.

691 LAWRENCE, W. J. *The Physical Conditions of the Elizabethan Public Playhouse.* Cambridge, Mass.: Harvard U.P.; London: Oxford U.P., 1927. Rpt., New York: Cooper Square.

692 NAGLER, A. M. *Shakespeare's Stage.* Trans. R. MANHEIM. New Haven: Yale U.P., 1958.

693 REYNOLDS, George F. *On Shakespeare's Stage.* Ed. Richard K. KNAUB. Boulder: U. of Colorado P., 1967.

694 REYNOLDS, George F. *The Staging of Elizabethan Plays at the Red Bull Theater, 1605–1625.* New York: Modern Language Association; London: Oxford U.P., 1940.

695 RHODES, Ernest L. "Cleopatra's 'Monument' and the Gallery in Fludd's *Theatrum Orbi.*" *RenP 1971* (1972):41–48.

696 RHODES, Ernest L. *Henslowe's Rose: The Stage and Staging.* Lexington: U. of Kentucky P., 1976.

697 ROWAN, D. F. "The English Playhouse: 1595–1630." *RenD,* n.s. 4 (1971): 37–51.

698 SCOUTEN, A. H. "Some Assumptions behind Accounts of the Elizabethan Stage." *On Stage and Off.* Ed. John W. EHRSTINE, et al. Seattle: Washington State U.P., 1968.

699 SHAPIRO, I. A. "An Original Drawing of the Globe Theatre." *ShS* 2 (1949): 21–23.

700 SHAPIRO, I. A. "The Bankside Theatres: Early Engravings." *ShS* 1 (1948): 25–37.

701 SHAPIRO, I. A. "Robert Fludd's Stage-Illustration." *ShakS* 2 (1967 for 1966): 192–209.

702 SISSON, Charles J. *The Boar's Head Theatre: An Inn-Yard Theatre of the Elizabethan Age.* Ed. Stanley WELLS. London, Boston: Routledge & K. Paul, 1972.

703 SMITH, Irwin. *Shakespeare's Globe Playhouse: A Modern Reconstruction.* New York: Scribner's, 1956.

704 SOUTHERN, Richard. "On Reconstructing a Practicable Elizabethan Public Playhouse." *ShS* 12 (1959):22–34.

705 WICKHAM, Glynne. *Early English Stages, 1300–1660.* 2 vols., with vol. 2 in two parts. London: Routledge & K. Paul; New York: Columbia U.P., 1959–72. A third volume has been announced.*

706 YATES, Frances A. "Fludd's Memory Theatre and the Globe Theatre." *The Art of Memory.* Chicago: U. of Chicago P., 1966.

707 YATES, Frances A. "The Stage in Robert Fludd's Memory System." *ShakS* 3 (1968 for 1967):138–66.

708 YATES, Frances A. *Theatre of the World.* London: Routledge & K. Paul; Chicago: U. of Chicago P., 1969.

Private Playhouses

See also **602** and **669.**

709 ADAMS, Joseph Quincy. "The Conventual Buildings of Blackfriars, London, and the Playhouses Constructed Therein." *SP* 14 (1917):64–87.

710 ARMSTRONG, William A. *The Elizabethan Private Theatres: Facts and Problems.* London: Society for Theatre Research, 1958.*

711 BENTLEY, Gerald Eades. "Shakespeare and the Blackfriars Theatre." *ShS* 1 (1948):38–50. Rpt. in **605.***

712 BERRY, Herbert. "The Stage and Boxes at Blackfriars." *SP* 63 (1966):163–86.

713 HOSLEY, Richard. "A Reconstruction of the Second Blackfriars." In **607,** vol. 1 (1969 for 1968).*

714 HOSLEY, Richard. "Three Renaissance English Indoor Playhouses." *ELR* 3 (1973):166–82.*

715 ISAACS, J. *Production and Stage Management at the Blackfriars Theatre.* London: for the Shakespeare Association by Oxford U.P., 1933.

716 LAVIN, J. A. "Shakespeare and the Second Blackfriars." In **607,** vol. 3 (1973 for 1970).

717 SMITH, Irwin. *Shakespeare's Blackfriars Playhouse: Its History and Its Design.* New York: New York U.P., 1964.

Shakespeare's Stagecraft

See also **663, 1217–18, 1286, 1304, 1311, 1331, 1601, 2137, 4268,** and **4323.**

718 ADAMS, John Cranford. "The Original Staging of *King Lear.*" In **1154.**

719 BRADBROOK, M. C. *Elizabethan Stage Conditions: A Study of Their Place in the Interpretation of Shakespeare's Plays.* Cambridge: Cambridge U.P., 1932. Rpt., Hamden, Conn.: Archon, 1962.

720 CAMPBELL, Lily B. *Scenes and Machines on the English Stage during the Renaissance: A Classical Revival.* Cambridge: Cambridge U.P., 1923. Rpt., New York: Barnes & Noble, 1960.

721 CHILDS, Herbert E. "On the Elizabethan Staging of *Hamlet.*" *SQ* 13 (1962): 463–74.

722 HART, Alfred. "The Time Allotted for Representation of Elizabethan and Jacobean Plays." *RES* 8 (1932):395–413. Rpt. in **119.**

723 HOSLEY, Richard. "The Staging of Desdemona's Bed." *SQ* 14 (1963):57–65.

724 JOSEPH, Bertram L. "The Elizabethan Stage and the Art of Elizabethan Drama." *SJ* 91 (1955):145–60.

725 KLEIN, David. "Time Allotted for an Elizabethan Performance." *SQ* 18 (1967): 434–38.

726 LINTHICUM, M. Channing. *Costume in the Drama of Shakespeare and His Contemporaries.* Oxford: Clarendon, 1936.

727 MCDOWELL, John H. "Conventions of Medieval Art in Shakespearian Staging." *JEGP* 47 (1948):215–29.

728 NICOLL, Allardyce. "Passing over the Stage." *ShS* 12 (1959):47–55.

729 NOSWORTHY, J. M. *"Macbeth* at the Globe." *Library,* 5th ser. 2 (1947): 108–18.

730 REYNOLDS, George F. *"Hamlet* at the Globe." *ShS* 9 (1956):49–53.

731 REYNOLDS, George F. "Two Conventions of the Open Stage (As Illustrated in *King Lear?*)." *PQ* 41 (1962):82–95. Also in **1174.**

732 ROSENBERG, Marvin. "Public Night Performances in Shakespeare's Time." *TN* 8 (1954):44–45.

733 ROSS, Lawrence J. "The Use of a 'Fit-Up' Booth in *Othello."* *SQ* 12 (1961): 359–70.

734 SAUNDERS, J. W. "Staging at the Globe, 1599–1613." *SQ* 11 (1960):401–25. Rpt. in **604.**

735 SAUNDERS, J. W. "Vaulting the Rails." *ShS* 7 (1954):69–81.

736 SELTZER, Daniel. "The Staging of the Last Plays." In **1599.**

737 SHAW, Irwin. "Their Exits and Reentrances." *SQ* 18 (1967):7–16.

738 SHIRLEY, Frances Ann. *Shakespeare's Use of Off-Stage Sounds.* Lincoln: U. of Nebraska P., 1963.

739 SMITH, Hal H. "Some Principles of Elizabethan Stage Costume." *JWCI* 25 (1962):240–57.

740 SMITH, Irwin. " 'Gates' on Shakespeare's Stage." *SQ* 7 (1956):159–76.

741 SMITH, Warren D. "The Elizabethan Stage and Shakespeare's Entrance Announcements." *SQ* 4 (1953):405–10.

742 SMITH, Warren D. "Evidence of Scaffolding on Shakespeare's Stage." *RES,* n.s. 2 (1951):22–29.

743 SMITH, Warren D. "New Light on Stage Directions in Shakespeare." *SP* 47 (1950):173–81.

744 SMITH, Warren D. "Stage Business in Shakespeare's Dialogue." *SQ* 4 (1953): 311–16.

745 SMITH, Warren D. "Stage Setting in Shakespeare's Dialogue." *MP* 50 (1952): 32–35.

746 SOENS, A. L. "Cudgels and Rapiers: The Staging of the Edgar-Oswald Fight in *Lear."* *ShakS* 5 (1970 for 1969):149–58.

747 STYAN, J. L. *Shakespeare's Stagecraft.* Cambridge: Cambridge U.P., 1967.*

748 VENEZKY, Alice S. *Pageantry on the Shakespearean Stage.* Boston: Twayne, 1951.*

749 WEINER, Albert B. "Elizabethan Interior and Aloft Scenes: A Speculative Essay." *ThS* 2 (1961):15–34.

750 WRIGHT, Louis B. "Stage Duelling in the Elizabethan Theatre." *MLR* 22 (1927):265–75.

The Audience

See also **1423**.

751 ARMSTRONG, William A. "The Audience of the Elizabethan Private Theatres." *RES*, n.s. 10 (1959):234–49. Rpt. in **604**.*

752 BENNETT, H. S. "Shakespeare's Audience." *PBA* 30 (1945 for 1944):73–86. Rpt. in **1116**.*

753 BENNETT, H. S. "Shakespeare's Stage and Audience." *Neophil* 33 (1949):40–51.

754 BRADLEY, A. C. "Shakespeare's Theatre and Audience." In **1185**.

755 BRIDGES, Robert. *The Influence of the Audience: Considerations Preliminary to the Psychological Analysis of Shakespeare's Characters.* Garden City, N.Y.: Doubleday, 1926.

756 BYRNE, Muriel St. Clare. "Shakespeare's Audience." In **619**.

757 COOK, Ann Jennalie. "The Audience of Shakespeare's Plays: A Reconsideration." *ShakS* 7 (1974):283–305.*

758 HARBAGE, Alfred. *Shakespeare's Audience.* New York: Columbia U.P.; London: Oxford U.P., 1941.*

759 HOLMES, Martin. *Shakespeare's Public: The Touchstone of His Genius.* London: Murray, 1960.

760 PRIOR, Moody E. "The Elizabethan Audience and the Plays of Shakespeare." *MP* 49 (1951):101–23.

The History of Shakespearean Production on Stage and in Film

General Studies

See also **432, 631, 909, 933, 939, 949, 1559, 2095, 2611, 2616, 2620, 2623–24, 3180, 3347, 3352, 3519, 3810, 3971, 4179, 4225,** and **4317**.

761 BROWN, John Russell. "Theater Research and the Criticism of Shakespeare and His Contemporaries." *SQ* 13 (1962):451–61. Argues that stage history illuminates our understanding of the plays.

762 BYRNE, Muriel St. Clare. *A Pictorial History of Shakespearean Production in England, 1576–1946.* Rpt., Freeport, N.Y.: Books for Libraries P., 1970. First pub. in 1947.

763 CARLISLE, Carol Jones. *Shakespeare from the Greenroom: Actors' Criticisms of Four Major Tragedies.* Chapel Hill: U. of North Carolina P., 1969.*

764 DOWNER, Alan S. "Mr. Dangle's Defense: Acting and Stage History." *EIE 1946* (1947):159–90.

765 EVANS, Gareth Lloyd, ed. *Shakespeare in the Limelight: An Anthology of Theatre Criticism.* Glasgow and London: Blackie, 1968.

766 FINDLATER, Richard. *The Player Kings.* New York: Stein & Day, 1971. About famous actors from Garrick and Kemble to the present day.

767 HACKETT, James Henry. *Notes and Comments upon Certain Plays and Actors of Shakespeare.* New York: Carleton, 1863. Rpt., New York: Blom, 1968, with the title *Notes, Criticisms, and Correspondence upon Shakespeare's Plays and Actors.*

768 JACOBS, Henry E., and Claudia D. JOHNSON, comps. *An Annotated Bibliography of Shakespearean Burlesques, Parodies, and Travesties.* New York and London: Garland, 1976.

769 JOSEPH, Bertram L. *The Tragic Actor.* London: Routledge & K. Paul, 1959.

770 MERCHANT, W. Moelwyn. "Classical Costume in Shakesperian Productions." *ShS* 10 (1957):71–76.

771 ODELL, George C. D. *Shakespeare from Betterton to Irving.* 2 vols. New York: Scribner's, 1920. Rpt., New York: Blom, 1963; Dover, 1966.*

772 PRICE, Joseph G., ed. *The Triple Bond: Plays, Mainly Shakespearean, in Performance.* University Park and London: Pennsylvania State U.P., 1975.

773 SALGĀDO, Gāmini. *Eyewitnesses of Shakespeare: First Hand Accounts of Performances 1597–1890.* New York: Barnes & Noble, 1975.

774 SHATTUCK, Charles H. *The Shakespeare Promptbooks: A Descriptive Catalogue.* Urbana: U. of Illinois P., 1965.

775 SHATTUCK, Charles H. "The Shakespeare Promptbooks: First Supplement." *TN* 24 (1969):5–17.

776 SPEAIGHT, Robert. *Shakespeare on the Stage: An Illustrated History of Shakespearian Performance.* London: Collins; Boston and Toronto: Little, Brown, 1973.

777 SPRAGUE, Arthur Colby. *The Doubling of Parts in Shakespeare's Plays.* London: Society for Theatre Research, 1966.

778 SPRAGUE, Arthur Colby. *Shakespeare and the Actors: The Stage Business in His Plays (1660–1905).* Cambridge, Mass.: Harvard U.P., 1944. Rpt., New York: Russell & Russell, 1963.*

779 SPRAGUE, Arthur Colby. *Shakespeare's Histories: Plays for the Stage.* London: Society for Theatre Research, 1964.

780 SPRAGUE, Arthur Colby. *Shakespearian Players and Performances.* Cambridge, Mass.: Harvard U.P., 1953; London: Black, 1954. Rpt., Westport, Conn.: Greenwood.*

781 THALER, Alwin. *Shakspere to Sheridan: A Book about the Theatre of Yesterday and Today.* Cambridge, Mass.: Harvard U.P., 1922. Rpt., New York: Blom.

782 WINTER, William. *Shakespeare on the Stage.* 3 series. New York: Moffat, Yard, 1911, 1915, and 1916. Rpt., New York: Blom.

The Restoration and Eighteenth Century (1660–1776)

See also **636, 974, 976, 998, 1000, 1074,** and **4033.**

783 APPLETON, William W. *Charles Macklin: An Actor's Life.* Cambridge, Mass.: Harvard U.P., 1960.

784 AVERY, Emmett L., Charles Beecher HOGAN, A. H. SCOUTEN, George Winchester STONE, Jr., and William VAN LENNEP. *The London Stage 1660– 1800: A Calendar of Plays, Entertainments, and Afterpieces.* 11 vols. Carbondale: Southern Illinois U.P., 1960–68.*

785 AVERY, Emmett L., et al. [as above]. *The London Stage, 1660–1800: A Critical Introduction.* 5 vols. Carbondale: Southern Illinois U.P.; London: Feffer & Simons, 1968.*

786 BLACK, James. "An Augustan Stage-History: Nahum Tate's *King Lear.*" *Restoration & 18th-Century Theatre Research* 6.1 (1967):36–54.

787 BRANAM, George C. *Eighteenth-Century Adaptations of Shakespearean Tragedy.* Berkeley and Los Angeles: U. of California P., 1956.

788 BYRNE, Muriel St. Clare. "The Stage Costuming of *Macbeth* in the Eighteenth Century." *Studies in English Theatre History in Memory of Gabrielle Enthoven.* London: Society for Theatre Research, 1952.

789 *Cornmarket Acting Versions of Shakespeare's Plays from the Restoration to the Death of David Garrick.* Seventy-Eight Rare Texts from the Birmingham Shakespeare Library Reprinted. 86 vols. London: Cornmarket, 1969.

790 DONOHUE, Joseph W., Jr. *"Macbeth* in the Eighteenth Century." *Theatre Quarterly* 1.3 (1971):20–25.

791 EVANS, G. Blakemore. *Shakespearean Prompt-Books of the Seventeenth Century.* 4 vols. Charlottesville: Bibliographical Society of the U. of Virginia, 1960–66.

792 HARRIS, Arthur John. "Garrick, Colman, and *King Lear:* A Reconsideration." *SQ* 22 (1971):57–66.

793 HIGHFILL, Philip H., Jr., Kalman A. BURNIM, and Edward A. LANGHANS. *A Biographical Dictionary of Actors, Actresses, Musicians, Dancers, Managers, and Other Stage Personnel in London, 1660–1800.* 12 vols. proposed. Carbondale: Southern Illinois U.P., 1973–.

794 HOGAN, Charles Beecher. *Shakespeare in the Theatre: A Record of Performances in London, 1701–1800.* 2 vols. Oxford: Clarendon, 1952–57.

795 ITZIN, Catherine. *"Macbeth* in the Restoration." *Theatre Quarterly* 1.3 (1971): 14–20.

796 LEECH, Clifford. "Shakespeare, Cibber, and the Tudor Myth." In **1171.**

797 MERCHANT, W. Moelwyn. "Shakespeare 'Made Fit.' " *Restoration Theatre.* Eds. John Russell BROWN and Bernard HARRIS. Stratford-upon-Avon Studies 6. London: Arnold, 1965.

798 MONACO, Marion. *Shakespeare on the French Stage in the Eighteenth Century.* Paris: Didier, 1974.

799 SCOUTEN, A. H. "The Increase in Popularity of Shakespeare's Plays in the Eighteenth Century: A *Caveat* for Interpretors of Stage History." *SQ* 7 (1956): 189–202.

800 SPENCER, Christopher. " 'Count Paris's Wife': *Romeo and Juliet* on the Early Restoration Stage." *TSLL* 7 (1966):309–16.

801 SPENCER, Christopher, ed. *Five Restoration Adaptations of Shakespeare*. Urbana: U. of Illinois P., 1965.

802 SPENCER, Hazelton. *Shakespeare Improved: The Restoration Versions in Quarto and on the Stage*. Cambridge, Mass.: Harvard U.P., 1927. Rpt., New York: Ungar, 1963.

803 STONE, George Winchester, Jr. "Bloody, Cold, and Complex Richard: David Garrick's Interpretation." *On Stage and Off.* Ed. John W. EHRSTINE, et al. Seattle: Washington State U.P., 1968.

804 STONE, George Winchester, Jr. "A Century of *Cymbeline;* or Garrick's Magic Touch." *PQ* 54 (1975):310–22.

805 STONE, George Winchester, Jr. "Garrick and *Othello.*" *PQ* 45 (1966):304–20.

806 STONE, George Winchester, Jr. "Garrick's Handling of *Macbeth.*" *SP* 38 (1941): 609–28.

807 STONE, George Winchester, Jr. "Garrick's Presentation of *Antony and Cleopatra.*" *RES* 13 (1937):20–38.

808 STONE, George Winchester, Jr. "Garrick's Production of *King Lear:* A Study in the Temper of the Eighteenth-Century Mind." *SP* 45 (1948):89–103.

809 STONE, George Winchester, Jr. "The God of His Idolatry: Garrick's Theory of Acting and Dramatic Composition with Especial Reference to Shakespeare." In **1154.**

810 STONE, George Winchester, Jr. "*A Midsummer Night's Dream* in the Hands of Garrick and Colman." *PMLA* 54 (1939):467–82.

811 SUMMERS, Montague, ed. *Shakespeare Adaptations: The Tempest, The Mock Tempest, and King Lear.* London: Cape, 1922. Rpt., New York: Blom, 1966.

812 WOOD, Frederick T. "*The Merchant of Venice* in the Eighteenth Century." *ES* 15 (1933):209–18.

Romantic and Victorian (1776–1903)

See also **927** and **1009.**

813 ALLEN, Shirley S. *Samuel Phelps and Sadler's Wells Theatre.* Middletown, Conn.: Wesleyan U.P., 1971.

814 BAKER, Herschel. *John Philip Kemble: The Actor in His Theatre.* Cambridge, Mass.: Harvard U.P., 1942.

815 BARKER, Kathleen M. D. "Macready's Early Productions of *King Richard II.*" *SQ* 23 (1972):95–100.

816 CARLISLE, Carol Jones. "The Nineteenth-Century Actors *versus* the Closet Critics of Shakespeare." *SP* 51 (1954):599–615.

817 CHILD, Harold. *The Shakespearian Productions of John Philip Kemble.* London: for the Shakespeare Association by Oxford U.P., 1935.

818 CRAIG, E. Gordon. *Henry Irving.* London and New York: Longmans, Green, 1930. Rpt., New York: Blom, 1969.

819 DONOHUE, Joseph W., Jr. *Dramatic Character in the English Romantic Age.* Princeton: Princeton U.P., 1970.*

820 DONOHUE, Joseph W., Jr. "Kemble and Mrs. Siddons in *Macbeth:* The Romantic Approach to Tragic Character." *TN* 22 (1967–68):65–86.

821 DOWNER, Alan S. *The Eminent Tragedian, William Charles Macready.* Cambridge, Mass.: Harvard U.P., 1966.*

822 HILLEBRAND, Harold Newcomb. *Edmund Kean.* New York: Columbia U.P., 1933.

823 IRVING, Laurence. *Henry Irving: The Actor and His World.* London: Faber & Faber, 1951; New York: Macmillan, 1952.

824 MANVELL, Roger. *Ellen Terry.* London: Heinemann; New York: Putnam's, 1968.

825 MANVELL, Roger. *Sarah Siddons: Portrait of an Actress.* London: Heinemann, 1970; New York: Putnam's, 1971.

826 NILAN, Mary M. "Shakespeare Illustrated: Charles Kean's 1857 Production of *The Tempest.*" *SQ* 26 (1975):196–204.

827 NILAN, Mary M. "*The Tempest* at the Turn of the Century: Cross-Currents in Production." *ShS* 25 (1972):113–23.

828 ROSTRON, David. "Contemporary Political Comment in Four of J. P. Kemble's Shakespearean Productions." *ThR* 12 (1972):113–19.

829 SHATTUCK, Charles H. *The Hamlet of Edwin Booth.* Urbana: U. of Illinois P., 1969.

830 SHATTUCK, Charles H. *Shakespeare on the American Stage from the Hallams to Edwin Booth.* Washington: Folger Shakespeare Library, 1976.*

831 SHATTUCK, Charles H., ed. *Bulwer and Macready: A Chronicle of the Early Victorian Theatre.* Urbana: U. of Illinois P., 1958.

832 SHATTUCK, Charles H., ed. *John Philip Kemble Promptbooks.* 11 vols. Charlottesville: U.P. of Virginia, 1974–75.

833 SHATTUCK, Charles H., ed. *Mr. Macready Produces "As You Like It"; A Prompt-Book Study.* Urbana, Ill.: Beta Phi Mu, 1962.

834 SPRAGUE, Arthur Colby. "Shakespeare and Melodrama." *E&S,* n.s. 18 (1965): 1–12.

835 TREWIN, J. C. "*Macbeth* in the Nineteenth Century." *Theatre Quarterly* 1 (1971):26–35.

836 TREWIN, J. C. *Mr. Macready: A Nineteenth-Century Tragedian and His Theatre.* London: Harrap, 1955.

837 VAN DIJK, Maarten. "John Philip Kemble as King John: Two Scenes." *TN* 29 (1975):22–32.

838 WADSWORTH, Frank W. "Hamlet and Iago: Nineteenth-Century Breeches Parts." *SQ* 17 (1966):129–39.

839 WILLIAMSON, Jane. *Charles Kemble, Man of the Theatre.* Lincoln: U. of Nebraska P., 1964.

The Twentieth-Century Stage

See also **1863, 2866, 2929, 3348–51, 3813, 3969,** and **4238.**

840 AGATE, James. *Brief Chronicles: A Survey of the Plays of Shakespeare and the Elizabethans in Actual Performance.* London: Cape, 1943. Rpt., New York: Blom, 1971. Covers the years 1923–42.

841 ARMSTRONG, William A. "The Art of Shakespearean Production in the Twentieth Century." *E&S,* n.s. 15 (1962):74–87.

842 BARISH, Jonas A. "The New Theater and the Old: Reversions and Rejuvenations." In **1164.**

843 BROWN, Ivor. *Shakespeare Memorial Theatre, 1948–1950.* New York: Theatre Arts Books, 1951. *1951–1953,* 1953; *1954–1956,* 1956; *1957–1959,* 1959.

844 BROWN, John Russell. "English Criticism of Shakespeare Performances Today." *SJH* (1967):163–74.

845 BROWNE, E. Martin. "English Hamlets of the Twentieth Century." *ShS* 9 (1956):16–23.

846 BYRNE, Muriel St. Clare. "Fifty Years of Shakespearian Production: 1898–1948." *ShS* 2 (1949):1–20.

847 COHN, Ruby. *Modern Shakespeare Offshoots.* Princeton: Princeton U.P., 1976. On modern adaptations.*

848 CROSSE, Gordon. *Shakespearean Playgoing, 1890–1952.* London: Mowbray, 1953.

849 DAVID, Richard. "Actors and Scholars: A View of Shakespeare in the Modern Theatre." *ShS* 12 (1959):76–87.

850 DAVID, Richard. "Shakespeare's Comedies and the Modern Stage." *ShS* 4 (1951):129–38. A review of the 1949–50 season.

851 DAY, M. C., and J. C. TREWIN. *The Shakespeare Memorial Theatre.* London and Toronto: Dent, 1932.

852 DOWNER, Alan S. "For Jesus' Sake Forbear: Shakespeare *vs.* the Modern Theater." *SQ* 13 (1962):219–30.

853 DOWNER, Alan S. "Shakespeare in the Contemporary American Theater." *SJ* 93 (1957):154–69.

854 ELLIS, Ruth. *The Shakespeare Memorial Theatre.* London: Winchester, 1948.

855 EVANS, Gareth Lloyd. "*Macbeth* in the Twentieth Century." *Theatre Quarterly* 1.3 (1971):36–53.

856 EVANS, Gareth Lloyd. "Shakespeare, the Twentieth Century, and 'Behaviourism.' " *ShS* 20 (1967):133–42.

857 FARJEON, Herbert. *The Shakespearean Scene: Dramatic Criticisms.* London and New York: Hutchinson, 1949. Covers the years 1913–44.

858 GLICK, Claris. "William Poel: His Theories and Influence." *SQ* 15.1 (1964): 15–25.

859 KEMP, T. C. "Acting Shakespeare: Modern Tendencies in Playing and Production." *ShS* 7 (1954):121–27.

860 KEMP, T. C., and J. C. TREWIN. *The Stratford Festival: A History of the Shakespeare Memorial Theatre.* Birmingham: Cornish, 1953.

861 KOZINTSEV, Grigori. *Shakespeare: Time and Conscience.* Trans. Joyce VINING. New York: Hill & Wang, 1966.

862 LINTON, Calvin D. "Some Recent Trends in Shakespearean Staging." *ELH* 7 (1940):300–24.

863 LONEY, Glen, and Patricia MACKAY. *The Shakespeare Complex: A Guide to Summer Festivals and Year-Round Repertory in North America.* New York: Drama Book Specialists, 1975.

864 MOORE, Edward M. "William Poel." *SQ* 23 (1972):21–36.

865 NOWAK, Helen, trans. *Stanislavsky Produces "Othello."* London: Bles, 1948.

866 PEARSON, Hesketh. *Beerbohm Tree: His Life and Laughter.* London: Methuen; New York: Harper, 1956.

867 POEL, William. *Shakespeare in the Theatre.* London and Toronto: Sidgwick & Jackson, 1913. Rpt., New York: Blom, 1968.*

868 PURDOM, C. B. *Harley Granville-Barker: Man of the Theatre, Dramatist, and Scholar.* London: Rockliff, 1955. Rpt., Westport, Conn.: Greenwood.

869 RABY, Peter, ed. *The Stratford Scene 1958–1968.* Toronto and Vancouver: Clarke, Irwin, 1968.

870 SANDERS, Norman. "The Popularity of Shakespeare: An Examination of the Royal Shakespeare Theatre's Repertory." *ShS* 16 (1963):18–29.

871 *Shakespeare-Jahrbuch* (Heidelberg). Contains annual reviews of current productions in West Germany and in Switzerland, including film. *SJ* (Weimar) annually reviews productions in East Germany.*

872 *Shakespeare Quarterly.* Contains annual reviews of current productions in Britain and North America.*

873 *Shakespeare Survey.* Contains annual reviews of current productions throughout the British-speaking world.*

874 SPEAIGHT, Robert. *William Poel and the Elizabethan Revival.* London: for the Society for Theatre Research by Heinemann; Cambridge: Cambridge U.P., 1954.*

875 SPRAGUE, Arthur Colby. "Shakespeare and William Poel." *UTQ* 17 (1947): 29–37.

876 SPRAGUE, Arthur Colby, and J. C. TREWIN. *Shakespeare's Plays Today: Some Customs and Conventions of the Stage.* London: Sidgwick & Jackson; Columbia: U. of South Carolina P., 1970.*

877 TREE, Herbert Beerbohm. *Thoughts and After-Thoughts.* London and New York: Cassell, 1913.

878 TREWIN, J. C. *Shakespeare on the English Stage, 1900–1964: A Survey of Productions.* London: Barrie & Rockliff, 1964.*

879 TROUSDALE, Marion. "The Question of Harley Granville-Barker and Shakespeare on Stage." *RenD,* n.s. 4 (1971):3–36.

880 TYNAN, Kenneth. *Curtains.* New York: Atheneum, 1961.

881 WILLIAMS, E. Harcourt. *Old Vic Saga.* London: Winchester, 1949.

882 WOOD, Roger, Mary CLARKE, and others. *Shakespeare at the Old Vic.* 5 vols. London: A. & C. Black, 1954–58.

Shakespeare on Film

See also **861, 912,** and **4029.**

883 BALL, Robert Hamilton. *Shakespeare on Silent Film.* London: Allen & Unwin; New York: Theatre Arts, 1968.

884 CHAPLIN, William. "Our Darker Purpose: Peter Brook's *King Lear.*" *Arion,* n.s. 1 (1973):168–87.

885 ECKERT, Charles W., ed. *Focus on Shakespearean Films.* Englewood Cliffs, N.J.: Prentice-Hall, 1972. A collection of essays.

886 FUEGI, John. "Explorations in No Man's Land: Shakespeare's Poetry as Theatrical Film." *SQ* 23 (1972):37–49.

887 GEDULD, Harry M. *Filmguide to "Henry V."* Bloomington: Indiana U.P., 1973.*

888 GRIFFIN, Alice S. "Shakespeare through the Camera's Eye." In 4 parts. *SQ* 4 (1953):331–36; 6 (1955):63–66; 7 (1956):235–40; and 17 (1966):383–87.

889 HAPGOOD, Robert. "Shakespeare and the Included Spectator." In **1164.**

890 JORGENS, Jack L. *Shakespeare on Film.* Bloomington: Indiana U.P., 1977.*

891 KERMODE, Frank. "Shakespeare in the Movies." *New York Review of Books* 18.8 (4 May 1972):18–21.

892 KITCHIN, Laurence. "Shakespeare on the Screen." *ShS* 18 (1965):70–74.

893 KOZINTSEV, Grigori. "*Hamlet* and *King Lear:* Stage and Film." In **1151.**

894 LIPPMANN, Max, ed. *Shakespeare im Film.* Deutsches Institut für Filmkunde. Wiesbaden: Saaten-Verlag, 1964.

895 *Literature/Film Quarterly* 1.4 (1973). Entire issue devoted to Shakespeare on Film, with articles on film versions of *Macbeth, Hamlet, Othello,* and *Romeo and Juliet.* See also 4.2 (1976).*

896 MCLEAN, Andrew M. "Teaching Shakespeare on Film: A Checklist." *Teaching Shakespeare: Ideas for the Classroom* 1.1 (1976):6–8. See **1114.**

897 MANVELL, Roger. *Shakespeare and the Film.* London: Dent; New York: Praeger, 1971.*

898 MANVELL, Roger, ed. *Journal of the Society of Film and Television Arts* 37 (Autumn, 1969). Special issue on Shakespeare and film.

899 MARDER, Louis, ed. *ShN* 23.5 (1973):42–50. Issue primarily devoted to film, including a bibliography. See also *ShN* 25.6 (1975):53.

900 MORRIS, Peter. "Shakespeare on Film." *Films in Review* 24 (1973):132–63.

901 REEVES, Geoffrey. "Finding Shakespeare on Film." From an interview with Peter BROOK. *TDR* 11.1 (T33; 1966):117–21.

902 TAYLOR, John Russell. "Shakespeare in Film, Radio, and Television." In **56.**

903 THORP, Margaret Farrand. "Shakespeare and the Movies." *SQ* 9 (1958):357–66.

On Producing Shakespeare Today

The following items offer guidelines for today's Shakespearean producer, based on a knowledge of the Elizabethan stage and of the history of Shakespearean production. They also stress the importance of viewing Shakespeare as a writer for the theater.

See also **649, 772, 1289, 1296,** and **2829.**

904 BROWN, John Russell. *Free Shakespeare.* London: Heinemann, 1974.

905 BROWN, John Russell. *Shakespeare's Plays in Performance.* London: Arnold, 1966; Harmondsworth: Penguin, 1969.*

906 BROWN, John Russell. "The Study and Practice of Shakespeare Production." *ShS* 18 (1965):58–69. A response to **909.**

907 BROWN, John Russell, ed. *Shakespeare in Performance: An Introduction Through Six Major Plays.* New York: Harcourt Brace Jovanovich, 1976.

908 DE BANKE, Cécile. *Shakespearean Stage Production: Then and Now: A Manual for the Scholar-Player.* New York: McGraw-Hill, 1953; London: Hutchinson, 1954.

909 HARBAGE, Alfred. *Theatre for Shakespeare.* Toronto: U. of Toronto P., 1955.*

910 HOSLEY, Richard. "Shakespearian Stage Curtains: Then and Now." *CE* 25 (1964):488–92.

911 JOSEPH, Bertram L. *Acting Shakespeare.* 2nd ed., London: Routledge & K. Paul; New York: Theatre Arts, 1960.*

912 KELLY, F. M. *Shakespearian Costume for Stage and Screen.* 2nd ed., rev. Alan MANSFIELD. London: A. & C. Black, 1970.

913 KERNODLE, George R. "The Open Stage: Elizabethan or Existentialist?" *ShS* 12 (1959):1–7.

914 KNIGHT, G. Wilson. *Shakespeare's Dramatic Challenge.* New York: Barnes & Noble, 1976. On the challenge of performing Shakespeare's tragic heroes.

915 KNIGHT, G. Wilson. *Shakespearian Production, with Especial Reference to the Tragedies.* Evanston, Ill.: Northwestern U.P., 1964; London: Routledge & K. Paul, 1968. Orig. pub. as *Principles of Shakespearian Production.* London: Faber & Faber, 1936.*

916 LEECH, Clifford. "The 'Capability' of Shakespeare." *SQ* 11 (1960):123–36.

917 MCMULLAN, Frank. *The Theatre Student: Directing Shakespeare in the Contemporary Theatre.* New York: Richards Rosen, 1974.

918 MARSHALL, Norman. *The Producer and the Play.* 2nd ed., London: Macdonald, 1962. 3rd ed., London: Davis-Poynter, 1975.

919 PAYNE, Ben Iden. *A Life in a Wooden O: Memoirs of the Theatre.* New Haven and London: Yale U.P., 1977.

920 PURDOM, C. B. *Producing Shakespeare.* London: Pitman, 1950.

921 WATKINS, Ronald. *On Producing Shakespeare.* London: Joseph, 1950.

922 WATKINS, Ronald, and Jeremy LEMMON. *In Shakespeare's Playhouse.* Vol. 1: *The Poet's Method.* Vol. 2: *Macbeth.* Vol. 3: *Hamlet.* Vol. 4: *A Midsummer Night's Dream.* Newton Abbot: David & Charles; Totowa, N.J.: Rowman & Littlefield, 1974.

923 WEBSTER, Margaret. *Shakespeare without Tears.* New York: Whittlesley House (McGraw-Hill), 1942. Rev. ed., Cleveland: World, 1955; New York: Capricorn (Putnam's), 1975.*

The History of Shakespeare Criticism; His Reputation and Influence

General Surveys

See also **172, 763, 802, 1163, 1559, 1883, 2426, 2626, 3566, 4187,** and **4610.**

924 ANDREWS, W. T., ed. *Critics on Shakespeare.* London: Allen & Unwin, 1973.

925 BROWN, Ivor, and George FEARON. *This Shakespeare Industry: Amazing Monument.* New York and London: Harper, 1939.

926 CROW, Charles R. "Chiding the Plays: Then Till Now." *ShS* 18 (1965):1–10.

927 DUNN, Esther Cloudman. *Shakespeare in America.* New York: Macmillan, 1939. Rpt., New York: Blom.

928 EASTMAN, Arthur M. *A Short History of Shakespearean Criticism.* New York: Random House; Ann Arbor: Michigan U.P., 1968. Rpt., New York: Norton, 1975.

929 EASTMAN, Arthur M., and G. B. HARRISON, eds. *Shakespeare's Critics from Jonson to Auden: A Medley of Judgments.* Ann Arbor: U. of Michigan P., 1964.

930 EVANS, G. Blakemore, ed. *Shakespeare: Aspects of Influence.* Cambridge, Mass., and London: Harvard U.P., 1976. A collection of essays concerning Shakespeare's influence on the dramatists of his time, and on Johnson, Keats, Shelley, Dickens, Melville, etc.*

931 FALK, Robert. "Shakespeare in America: A Survey to 1900." *ShS* 18 (1965): 102–18.

932 GARDNER, Helen. *The Business of Criticism.* Oxford: Clarendon, 1959, chaps. 2 and 3.*

933 HALLIDAY, F. E. *The Cult of Shakespeare.* London: Duckworth, 1957.

934 HALLIDAY, F. E. *Shakespeare and His Critics.* Rev. ed., London: Duckworth, 1958; New York: Schocken, 1958, 1963.*

935 JACOBS, Henry E., and Claudia D. JOHNSON, comps. *An Annotated Bibliography of Shakespearean Burlesques, Parodies, and Travesties.* See **768.**

936 JOHNSON, Charles F. *Shakespeare and His Critics.* Boston: Houghton Mifflin, 1909. Rpt., New York: AMS.

937 KERMODE, Frank, ed. *Four Centuries of Shakespearian Criticism.* New York: Avon, 1965.

938 LEVIN, Harry. "The Primacy of Shakespeare." *SQ* 26 (1975):99–112. Rpt. in **1233.**

939 MARDER, Louis. *His Exits and His Entrances: The Story of Shakespeare's Reputation.* Philadelphia and New York: Lippincott; London: Murray, 1963.

940 PILLAI, V. K. Ayappan. *Shakespeare Criticism: From the Beginnings to 1765.* London and Glasgow: Blackie, 1932.

941 RALLI, Augustus. *A History of Shakespearian Criticism.* 2 vols. London: Oxford U.P., 1932.*

942 SCHUELLER, Herbert M., ed. *The Persistence of Shakespeare Idolatry: Essays in Honor of Robert W. Babcock.* Detroit: Wayne State U.P., 1964.

943 SHAABER, M. A. "Shakespeare Criticism: Dryden to Bradley." In **55.**

944 SIEGEL, Paul N., ed. *His Infinite Variety: Major Shakespearean Criticism since Johnson.* Philadelphia: Lippincott, 1964. Rpt., Freeport, N.Y.: Books for Libraries P., 1972.

945 SISSON, Charles J. "The Mythical Sorrows of Shakespeare." *PBA* 20 (1935 for 1934):45–70.

946 SMITH, D. Nichol, ed. *Shakespeare Criticism: A Selection.* London: Oxford U.P., 1916. Rpt., 1949, 1954.

947 SPENCER, T. J. B. "The Course of Shakespeare Criticism." In **1170.**

948 SPENCER, T. J. B. "The Tyranny of Shakespeare." *PBA* 45 (1960 for 1959): 153–71.

949 VICKERS, Brian, ed. *Shakespeare: The Critical Heritage. Vol. 1, 1623–1692. Vol. 2, 1693–1733. Vol. 3, 1733–1752. Vol. 4, 1753–1765.* London and Boston: Routledge & K. Paul, 1974–.*

950 WAGNER, Bernard M., ed. *The Appreciation of Shakespeare: A Collection of Criticism—Philosophic, Literary, and Esthetic—by Great Writers and Scholar-Critics of the Eighteenth, Nineteenth, and Twentieth Centuries.* Washington, D.C.: Georgetown U.P., 1949.

951 WELLS, Stanley. "Shakespearian Burlesque." *SQ* 16 (1965):49–61.

952 WESTFALL, Alfred Van Rensselaer. *American Shakespearean Criticism, 1607–1865.* New York: H. W. Wilson, 1939. Rpt., New York: Blom.

The Late Sixteenth and Early Seventeenth Centuries

See also **2612** and **2930.**

953 BENTLEY, Gerald Eades. *Shakespeare and Jonson: Their Reputations in the Seventeenth Century Compared.* 2 vols. Chicago: U. of Chicago P., 1945. Issued as 2 vols. in one, 1965.*

954 CHARNEY, Maurice. "Webster vs. Middleton, or the Shakespearean Yardstick in Jacobean Tragedy." In **1143.**

955 FREEHAFER, John. "Leonard Digges, Ben Jonson, and the Beginning of Shakespeare Idolatry." *SQ* 21 (1970):63–75.

956 FROST, David L. *The School of Shakespeare: The Influence of Shakespeare on English Drama 1600–42.* Cambridge: Cambridge U.P., 1968.*

957 FROST, David L. "Shakespeare in the Seventeenth Century." *SQ* 16 (1965): 81–89.

958 GARROD, H. W. "Milton's Lines on Shakespeare." *E&S* 12 (1926):7–23.

959 MCGINN, Donald Joseph. *Shakespeare's Influence on the Drama of His Age, Studied in "Hamlet."* New Brunswick: Rutgers U.P., 1938. Rpt., New York: Octagon.

960 MUNRO, John, ed. *The Shakspere Allusion Book: A Collection of Allusions to Shakspere from 1591 to 1700.* 2 vols. Orig. compiled by C. M. INGLEBY and others. London: Chatto & Windus; New York: Duffield, 1909. Reissued by E. K. CHAMBERS. London: Oxford U.P., 1932. Rpt., Freeport, N.Y.: Books for Libraries P.*

961 MURAOKA, Isamu. "Shakespeare and George Herbert." *ShStud* 11 (1975 for 1972–73):37–59.

962 PRICE, Hereward T. "Shakespeare as a Critic." *PQ* 20 (1941):390–99.

963 RICHMOND, Hugh M. "Donne's Master: The Young Shakespeare." *Criticism* 15 (1973):126–44.

964 SCHANZER, Ernest. "Heywood's *Ages* and Shakespeare." *RES,* n.s. 11 (1960): 18–28.

965 SPINGARN, J. E., ed. *Critical Essays of the Seventeenth Century.* 3 vols. Vol. 1: 1605–1650. Oxford: Clarendon, 1908. Rpt., Bloomington: Indiana U.P., 1957.

966 TOLMAN, Albert H. "The Early History of Shakespeare's Reputation." In **1267.**

The Restoration and Eighteenth Century

See also **402–03, 787, 811–12,** and **2756.**

967 ALEXANDER, Nigel. "Thomas Rymer and *Othello.*" *ShS* 21 (1968):67–77.

968 BABCOCK, Robert Witbeck. *The Genesis of Shakespeare Idolatry, 1766–1799.* Chapel Hill: U. of North Carolina P., 1931. Rpt., New York: Russell & Russell, 1964.

969 BABCOCK, Robert Witbeck. "William Richardson's Criticism of Shakespeare." *JEGP* 28 (1929):117–36.

970 BEAM, Marjorie. " 'The Reach and Wit of the Inventor': Swift's *Tale of a Tub* and *Hamlet.*" *UTQ* 46 (1976):1–13.

971 BELL, Mary. "Walter Whiter's Notes on Shakespeare." *ShS* 20 (1967):83–94.

972 BUTT, John. *Pope's Taste in Shakespeare.* London: for the Shakespeare Association by Oxford U.P., 1936.

973 CARVER, P. L. "The Influence of Maurice Morgann." *RES* 6 (1930):320–22.

974 DEELMAN, Christian. *The Great Shakespeare Jubilee.* London: Joseph; New York: Viking, 1964.

975 EIDSON, John Olin. "Dryden's Criticism of Shakespeare." *SP* 33 (1936):273–80.

976 ENGLAND, Martha Winburn. *Garrick's Jubilee.* Columbus: Ohio State U.P., 1964.

977 FETROW, Fred M. "Disclaimers Reclaimed: A Consideration of Johnson's Praise of Shakespeare." *Essays in Literature* 2 (1975):24–31.

978 FINEMAN, Daniel A., ed. *Maurice Morgann: Shakespearian Criticism.* Oxford: Clarendon, 1972.*

979 GRIFFITH, Philip Mahone. "Joseph Warton's Criticism of Shakespeare." *TSE* 14 (1965):17–27.

980 HOBSBAUM, Philip. "*King Lear* in the Eighteenth Century." *MLR* 68 (1973): 494–506.

981 HOOKER, Edward N., ed. *The Critical Works of John Dennis.* 2 vols. Baltimore: The Johns Hopkins P.; London: Oxford U.P., 1939–43. Includes *The Grounds of Criticism in Poetry* (vol. 1) and *Essay on the Genius and Writings of Shakespeare* (vol. 2).*

982 HUDSON, William Henry, ed. *Dramatic Essays by John Dryden.* London and Toronto: Dent; New York: Dutton, 1912.

983 KER, W. P., ed. *Essays of John Dryden.* 2 vols. Oxford: Clarendon, 1900.

984 KILBY, Clyde S. "Horace Walpole on Shakespeare." *SP* 38 (1941):480–93.

985 KIRSCH, Arthur C., ed. *Literary Criticism of John Dryden.* Lincoln: U. of Nebraska P., 1966.*

986 LOVETT, David. *Shakespeare's Characters in Eighteenth-Century Criticism.* Baltimore: The Johns Hopkins P., 1935.

987 MONK, Samuel Holt. "Dryden and the Beginnings of Shakespeare Criticism in the Augustan Age." In **942.**

988 NEUMANN, Joshua H. "Shakespearean Criticism in the *Tatler* and the *Spectator.*" *PMLA* 39 (1924):612–23.

989 RALEIGH, Walter. *Johnson on Shakespeare.* London: Oxford U.P., 1908. Rev. ed., 1925.*

990 RAYSOR, Thomas M. "The Study of Shakespeare's Characters in the Eighteenth Century." *MLN* 42 (1927):495–500.

991 ROBINSON, Herbert Spencer. *English Shakesperian Criticism in the Eighteenth Century.* New York: H. W. Wilson, 1932. Rpt., New York: Gordian, 1968.

992 SEN, Sailendra Kumar. "A Neglected Critic of Shakespeare: Walter Whiter." *SQ* 13 (1962):173–85.

993 SHERBO, Arthur, ed. *Johnson on Shakespeare.* Vols. 7 and 8 of *The Yale Edition of the Works of Samuel Johnson.* New Haven and London: Yale U.P., 1968.*

994 SHERBO, Arthur, ed. *Samuel Johnson: Notes to Shakespeare.* Augustan Reprint Society, 59–60, 65–66, 71. Los Angeles: William Andrews Clark Library, 1956–58.

995 SMITH, D. Nichol, ed. *Dryden's Essay of Dramatic Poesy.* London and Glasgow: Blackie, 1900.

996 SMITH, D. Nichol, ed. *Eighteenth-Century Essays on Shakespeare.* Glasgow: Maclehose, 1903. Rpt., New York: Russell & Russell, 1962. 2nd ed., Oxford: Clarendon, 1963.

997 SMITH, D. Nichol. *Shakespeare in the Eighteenth Century.* Oxford: Clarendon, 1928.

998 STOCHHOLM, Johanne M. *Garrick's Folly: The Stratford Jubilee of 1769 at Stratford and Drury Lane.* London: Methuen; New York: Barnes & Noble, 1964.

999 STOCK, R. D. *Samuel Johnson and Neoclassical Theory: The Intellectual Context of the "Preface to Shakespeare."* Lincoln: U. of Nebraska P., 1973.

1000 STONE, George Winchester, Jr. "David Garrick's Significance in the History of Shakespearean Criticism." *PMLA* 65 (1950):183–97.

1001 STONE, George Winchester, Jr. "Shakespeare in the Periodicals, 1700–1740." *SQ* 2 (1951):221–31; 3 (1952):313–28.

1002 TAVE, Stuart M. "Corbyn Morris: Falstaff, Humor, and Comic Theory in the Eighteenth Century." *MP* 50 (1952):102–15.

1003 WAIN, John, ed. *Johnson as Critic.* London and Boston: Routledge & K. Paul, 1973.

1004 WALLERSTEIN, Ruth. "Dryden and the Analysis of Shakespeare's Techniques." *RES* 19 (1943):165–85.

1005 WHATELY, Thomas. *Remarks on Some of the Characters of Shakespeare.* 1st ed., 1765; 3rd ed., 1839. Ed. Richard WHATELY. Rpt., New York: AMS; Augustus M. Kelly, 1970.

1006 WHITER, Walter. *A Specimen of a Commentary on Shakespeare.* 1st ed., 1794. Rpt., New York: AMS; Garland, 1970. 2nd rev. ed., London: Methuen, 1967.

1007 WIMSATT, William K., Jr., ed. *Samuel Johnson on Shakespeare.* New York: Hill & Wang, 1960. Rpt., Harmondsworth: Pelican, 1969.

1008 ZIMANSKY, Curt A., ed. *The Critical Works of Thomas Rymer.* New Haven: Yale U.P.; London: Oxford U.P., 1956.*

The Nineteenth Century

See also **816, 2624,** and **4418.**

1009 ADES, John I. "Charles Lamb, Shakespeare, and Early Nineteenth-Century Theater." *PMLA* 85 (1970):514–26.

1010 ARCHER, William, and Robert LOWE, eds. *Hazlitt on Theatre.* New York: Hill & Wang [1957]. Selections from *A View of the English Stage* and *Criticisms and Dramatic Essays.*

1011 BADAWI, M. M. *Coleridge: Critic of Shakespeare.* Cambridge: Cambridge U.P., 1973.*

1012 BARNET, Sylvan. "Coleridge on Shakespeare's Villains." *SQ* 7 (1956):9–20.

1013 COLDWELL, Joan. "The Playgoer as Critic: Charles Lamb on Shakespeare's Characters." *SQ* 26 (1975):184–95.

1014 FOAKES, R. A., ed. *Coleridge on Shakespeare: The Text of the Lectures of 1811–12.* Charlottesville: U.P. of Virginia for the Folger Library; London: Routledge & K. Paul, 1971.*

1015 HARDY, Barbara. " 'I Have a Smack of Hamlet': Coleridge and Shakespeare's Characters." *EIC* 8 (1958):238–55.

1016 HAWKES, Terence, ed. *Coleridge's Writings on Shakespeare: A Selection of the Essays, Notes, and Lectures.* New York: Capricorn (Putnam's), 1959; Harmondsworth: Penguin, 1969.

1017 HAZLITT, William. *Characters of Shakespear's Plays.* Orig. ed., London: C. H. Reynell for R. Hunter, 1817. London: Oxford U.P., 1966.

1018 HOUTCHENS, Lawrence Huston, and Carolyn Washburn HOUTCHENS, eds. *Leigh Hunt's Dramatic Criticism, 1808–1831.* New York: Columbia U.P., 1949.*

1019 HOWE, P. P., ed. *The Complete Works of William Hazlitt.* 21 vols. London and Toronto: Dent, 1933. Vol. 4: *Characters of Shakespear's Plays;* Vol. 5: *Lectures on the English Poets* and *A View of the English Stage;* Vol. 6: *Lectures on the English Comic Writers* and *Lectures on the Dramatic Literature of the Age of Elizabeth;* and Vol. 18: *Art and Dramatic Criticism.* *

1020 JACKSON, J. R. de J. "Coleridge on Shakespeare's Preparation." *REL* 7.1 (1966):53–62.

1021 JACKSON, J. R. de J. "Free Will in Coleridge's Shakespeare." *UTQ* 38 (1968): 34–50.

1022 KINNAIRD, John. "Hazlitt and the 'Design' of Shakespearean Tragedy: A 'Character' Critic Revisited." *SQ* 28 (1977):22–39.

1023 RAYSOR, Thomas M., ed. *Samuel Taylor Coleridge: Shakespearean Criticism.* 2 vols. 2nd ed., London: Dent; New York: Dutton, 1960.*

1024 RIBNER, Irving. "Lear's Madness in the Nineteenth Century." *ShAB* 22 (1947): 117–29.

1025 SANDERLIN, George. "The Repute of Shakespeare's Sonnets in the Early Nineteenth Century." *MLN* 54 (1939):462–66.

1026 SHAFFER, Elinor S. "Iago's Malignity Motivated: Coleridge's Unpublished 'Opus Magnum.' " *SQ* 19 (1968):195–203.

1027 SPENCER, T. J. B. "Shakespeare and the Noble Woman." *SJH* (1966):49–62. Concerns the Victorian ideal of womanhood and its debt to Shakespeare.

1028 SPURGEON, Caroline F. E. *Keats's Shakespeare.* 2nd ed., London: Oxford U.P., 1929. Rpt., Oxford: Clarendon, 1966; Folcroft, Pa.: Folcroft, 1975.

1029 STAVISKY, Aron Y. *Shakespeare and the Victorians: Roots of Modern Criticism.* Norman: U. of Oklahoma P., 1969.

1030 VELZ, John W. "Joseph Crosby and the Shakespeare Scholarship of the Nineteenth Century." *SQ* 27 (1976):316–28.

1031 WASSERMAN, Earl R. "Shakespeare and the English Romantic Movement." In **942.**

The Twentieth Century

See also **617, 669, 1568, 1627, 1634, 1669, 1747, 1785, 1810, 1837, 1905, 1937, 1962, 2043, 2121, 2616, 2619, 2896, 3092, 3260, 3268, 3691, 4562, and 4585.**

1032 BABCOCK, Robert Witbeck. "Historical Criticism of Shakespeare." *MLQ* 13 (1952):6–20.

1033 BRADBROOK, M. C. "Fifty Years of the Criticism of Shakespeare's Style: A Retrospect." *ShS* 7 (1954):1–11.

1034 BRADBY, Anne, ed. *Shakespeare Criticism, 1919–35*. London: Oxford U.P., 1936. Rpt., 1962 under the name of Anne RIDLER.

1035 BROCKBANK, J. Philip. "Shakespeare and the Fashion of These Times." *ShS* 16 (1963):30–41. Concerns critical trends in the understanding of certain dramatic conventions.

1036 BROWN, John Russell. "Mr. Beckett's Shakespeare." *CritQ* 5 (1963):310–26.

1037 BROWN, John Russell. "Mr. Pinter's Shakespeare." *CritQ* 5 (1963):251–65.

1038 BROWN, John Russell. "The Theatrical Element of Shakespeare Criticism." In **1164.**

1039 CAMPBELL, Lily B. "Concerning Bradley's *Shakespearean Tragedy*." *HLQ* 13 (1949):1–18.

1040 CAMPBELL, Oscar James. "Shakespeare and the 'New' Critics." In **1154.**

1041 CLARK, Richard C. "Review Article: Shakespeare's 'Contemporary Relevance' —From Klein to Kott to Knight." *RNL* 3.2 (1972):185– 97.

1042 COLLINS, P. A. W. "Shaw on Shakespeare." *SQ* 8 (1957):1–13.

1043 COOKE, Katharine. *A. C. Bradley and His Influence in Twentieth-Century Shakespeare Criticism*. Oxford: Clarendon, 1972.*

1044 CRAIG, Hardin. "Trend of Shakespeare Scholarship." *ShS* 2 (1949):107–14.

1045 HAPGOOD, Robert. "Shakespeare and the Ritualists." *ShS* 15 (1962):111–24. Concerns myth criticism.

1046 HARBAGE, Alfred. "Shakespeare and the Myth of Perfection." *SQ* 15.2 (1964): 1–10. Also in **1153.** Rpt. in **172.** Concerns the myth of Shakespeare's omniscience and its effect on current criticism.*

1047 HASTINGS, William T. "The New Critics of Shakespeare." *SQ* 1 (1950):165–76.

1048 HUNTER, G. K. "A. C. Bradley's *Shakespearean Tragedy*." *E&S*, n.s. 21 (1968): 101–17.*

1049 KETTLE, Arnold. "Some Tendencies in Shakespearian Criticism." *SJW* 102 (1966):23–36.

1050 KNIGHTS, L. C. "On Historical Scholarship and the Interpretation of Shakespeare." *SR* 63 (1955):223–40.* For a reply by John LAWLOR, see *SR* 64 (1956):186–206.

1051 KNIGHTS, L. C. "Shakespeare and Shakespeareans." In **1228.**

1052 LEVIN, Richard. "Refuting Shakespeare's Endings." *MP* 72 (1975):337–49. A reply to recent critical tendencies to render Shakespeare's endings ironic and to see a central theme in most of his work.

1053 LUTZ, Jerry. *Pitchman's Melody: Shaw about "Shakespear."* Lewisburg, Pa.: Bucknell U.P., 1974.

1054 MAJOR, John M. "Santayana on Shakespeare." *SQ* 10 (1959):469–79.

1055 MORTIMER, Anthony. "Wilson Knight and Shakespearean Interpretation." *Studi e Ricerche di Letteratura Inglese e Americana.* Vol. I, pp. 47–73. Milan: Varese, 1967.

1056 MUIR, Kenneth. "Fifty Years of Shakespearian Criticism: 1900–1950." *ShS* 4 (1951):1–25.

1057 MUIR, Kenneth. "Shaw and Shakespeare." *Festschrift: Rudolf Stamm*. Eds. Eduard KOLB and Jörg HASLER. Bern and Munich: Francke, 1969.

1058 MURRAY, Patrick. *The Shakespearian Scene: Some Twentieth-Century Perspectives*. London: Longmans, Green, 1969.

1059 ORNSTEIN, Robert. "Historical Criticism and the Interpretation of Shakespeare." *SQ* 10 (1959):1–9. Rpt. in **1163**.

1060 RIBNER, Irving. "Shakespeare Criticism 1900–1964." In **1121**.

1061 RIDLER, Anne, ed. *Shakespeare Criticism, 1935–60*. London: Oxford U.P., 1963.

1062 ROBERTSON, J. M. *Croce as Shakespearean Critic*. London: Routledge, 1922.

1063 ROBERTSON, J. M. *The State of Shakespeare Study: A Critical Conspectus*. London: Routledge, 1931.

1064 SMITH, J. Percy. "Superman versus Man: Bernard Shaw on Shakespeare." In **1145** (1963 for 1962).

1065 TAYLOR, Michael. "A. C. Bradley and Shakespearean Tragedy." *MLR* 68 (1973):734–40.

1066 WATSON, Curtis Brown. "T. S. Eliot and the Interpretation of Shakespearean Tragedy in Our Time." *EA* 17 (1964):502–21.

1067 WEISINGER, Herbert. "The Study of Shakespearian Tragedy since Bradley." *SQ* 6 (1955):387–96.

1068 WELLEK, René. "A. C. Bradley, Shakespeare, and the Infinite." *PQ* 54 (1975): 85–103.

1069 WELLS, Stanley. "Shakespeare Criticism since Bradley." In **55**.

1070 WEST, E. J. "G[eorge] B[ernard] S[haw] on Shakespearean Production." *SP* 45 (1948):216–35.

1071 WILSON, Edwin, ed. *Shaw on Shakespeare: An Anthology*. New York: Dutton, 1961. Rpt., Harmondsworth: Penguin, 1969.*

Shakespeare on the Continent

For bibliographical information on Shakespeare's reputation and influence in other countries, see Gordon Ross Smith, *A Classified Shakespeare Bibliography*, XIII, 3.

1072 BESTERMAN, Theodore. *Shakespeare and Voltaire*. New York: Pierpont Morgan Library, 1965.

1073 BESTERMAN, Theodore, ed. *Voltaire on Shakespeare*. Vol. 54 of *Studies on Voltaire and the Eighteenth Century*. Geneva: Institut et Musée Voltaire, 1967.*

1074 BRENNECKE, Ernest, in collaboration with Henry BRENNECKE. *Shakespeare in Germany, 1590–1700, with Translations of Five Early Plays*. Chicago: U. of Chicago P., 1964.

1075 COLLISON-MORLEY, Lacy. *Shakespeare in Italy*. Stratford-upon-Avon: Shakespeare Head, 1916. Rpt., New York: Blom, 1967.

1076 FLUCHÈRE, Henri. "Shakespeare in France: 1900–1948." *ShS* 2 (1949):115–25.

1077 FRANCE, Anna Kay. "Iago and Othello in Boris Pasternak's Translation." *SQ* 28 (1977):73–84.

1078 HAINES, C. M. *Shakespeare in France: Criticism, Voltaire to Victor Hugo.* London: Oxford U.P., 1925. Rpt., New York: AMS, 1975.

1079 HAVENS, George R. *Voltaire and the English Critics of Shakespeare.* New York: American Society of the French Legion of Honor, 1944.

1080 JUSSERAND, J. J. *Shakespeare in France under the Ancien Régime.* London: T. Fisher Unwin; New York: Putnam's, 1899. Rpt., New York: American Scholar, 1966.

1081 LAWRENCE, W. W., ed. *Goethe on the Theater: Selections from the Conversations with Eckermann.* Trans. John OXENFORD. New York: Dramatic Museum of Columbia U., 1919.*

1082 LAWRENSON, T. E. "Voltaire and Shakespeare: Ordeal by Translation." In **1134.**

1083 LEWINTER, Oswald, ed. *Shakespeare in Europe.* Cleveland and New York: World, 1963; Harmondsworth: Penguin, 1970.

1084 LOUNSBURY, Thomas R. *Shakespeare and Voltaire.* New York: Scribner's, 1902.

1085 PASCAL, R., ed. *Shakespeare in Germany, 1740–1815.* Cambridge: Cambridge U.P., 1937. Rpt., New York: Octagon, 1971.

1086 PEYRE, Henri. "Shakespeare and Modern French Criticism." In **942.**

1087 SCHLEGEL, Augustus William. *A Course of Lectures on Dramatic Art and Literature.* Trans. John BLACK. Rev. ed., A. J. W. MORRISON. London: H. G. Bohn, 1846. Rpt., New York: AMS.*

1088 WEIGAND, Hermann J. "Shakespeare in German Criticism." In **942.**

Teaching Shakespeare

For a more comprehensive bibliography on the teaching of Shakespeare, consult **1105.**

1089 BERSTEIN, Abraham. "The Shakespearean Play." *Teaching English in the High School.* New York: Random House, 1961.

1090 BOWDEN, William R. "Teaching Structure in Shakespeare: *1 Henry IV, Twelfth Night, Hamlet.*" *CE* 23 (1962):525–31.

1091 DUKE, Charles R. "Shakespearean Drama." *Creative Approaches to the Teaching of English.* Ed. R. Baird SHUMAN. Ithaca, Ill.: Peacock, 1974.

1092 DUNCAN, Charles F., Jr. "A Blackboard Model of Shakespearean Irony." *CE* 34 (1973):791–95.

1093 DUNNING, Stephen, and Alan B. HOWES. *"Macbeth."* *Literature for Adolescents: Teaching Poems, Stories, Novels, and Plays.* Glenview, Ill.: Scott, Foresman, 1975.

1094 EAVES, Morris. "The Real Thing: A Plan for Producing Shakespeare in the Classroom." *CE* 31 (1970):463–72.

1095 ENRIGHT, D. J. *Shakespeare and the Students.* See **1204.**

1096 EVANS, Bertrand. *Teaching Shakespeare in the High School.* New York: Macmillan, 1966.

1097 FISHER, Mildred Ogg. "Shakespeare: Why Ignore the Comedies and the Histories?" *EJ* 60 (1971):587–90.

1098 GRIFFIN, Alice S., ed. *Rebels and Lovers: Shakespeare's Young Heroes and Heroines. A New Approach to Acting and Reading.* New York: New York U.P., 1976. An edition of four plays with an introductory essay.

1099 HELLENGA, Robert R. "*Hamlet* in the Classroom." *CE* 35 (1973):32–39.

1100 JACKSON, Elizabeth. "The Kittredge Way." *CE* 4 (1943):483–87.

1101 KNAPP, Peggy Ann. " 'Stay, Illusion,' or How to Teach *Hamlet.* " *CE* 36 (1974): 75–85.

1102 KNIGHTS, L. C. "The Teaching of Shakespeare." In **1145** (1969 for 1965–67).*

1103 LOVEALL, James. "Shakespeare Is for Adults." *EJ* 36 (1947):363–66.

1104 MACK, Maynard. "Teaching Drama: *Julius Caesar.* " *Essays on the Teaching of English.* Eds. Edward J. GORDON and Edward S. NOYES. New York: Appleton-Century-Crofts, 1960.*

1105 MCLEAN, Andrew M. "Bibliography on Teaching Shakespeare." *ShN* 25 (1975):13–15. See also other pages of the April 1975 issue of *ShN* for abstracts of articles on teaching Shakespeare.*

1106 MARDER, Louis. "Teaching Shakespeare." *ShN* 4 (1954):2, 14, and 22.

1107 MILLS, Gordon. *Hamlet's Castle: The Study of Literature as a Social Experience.* Austin: U. of Texas P., 1976.

1108 MIZENER, Arthur, ed. *Teaching Shakespeare: A Guide to the Teaching of "Macbeth," "Julius Caesar," "The Merchant of Venice," "Hamlet," "Romeo and Juliet," "A Midsummer Night's Dream," "Othello," "As You Like It," "Twelfth Night," "Richard II," "Henry IV, Part One," and "The Tempest."* New York: New American Library, 1969.*

1109 MURPHY, Geraldine. "Advanced Play Reading: Shakespeare." *The Study of Literature in High School.* Waltham, Mass.: Blaisdell, 1968. Chiefly on *Julius Caesar.*

1110 ORNSTEIN, Robert. *Shakespeare in the Classroom.* Urbana, Ill.: Educational Illustrators, 1960.*

1111 ORNSTEIN, Robert. "Teaching *Hamlet.* " *CE* 25 (1964):502–08.*

1112 *Shakespeare Quarterly* 25 (1974):151–271. Spring issue devoted to discussions on the teaching of Shakespeare.*

1113 TAYLOR, Richard V., ed. *Shakespeare for Secondary Schools.* London: Macmillan, 1961.

1114 *Teaching Shakespeare: Ideas for the Classroom* 1.1 (1976):1–8. First issue of a journal devoted entirely to the teaching of Shakespeare, published by Scott, Foresman Co.

1115 WALSH, William. "Shakespeare in the Classroom: An Approach." *Journal of Education* (London), 84 (1952):16–18.

General Criticism Relating to Shakespeare's Works as a Whole

Collections of Essays by Several Authors

See also **55, 604, 607, 929,** and **944.**

1116 ALEXANDER, Peter, ed. *Studies in Shakespeare: British Academy Lectures.* London: Oxford U.P., 1964.* See also **1152.**

1117 ALLEN, Don Cameron, ed. *Studies in Honor of T. W. Baldwin.* Urbana: U. of Illinois P., 1958.

1118 BAIM, Joseph, Ann L. HAYES, and Robert J. GANGEWERE, eds. *In Honor of Austin Wright.* Pittsburgh: Carnegie-Mellon, 1972.

1119 BENNETT, Josephine Waters, Oscar James CARGILL, and Vernon HALL, Jr., eds. *Studies in English Renaissance Drama in Memory of Karl Julius Holzknecht.* New York: New York U.P., 1959.*

1120 BLISTEIN, Elmer M., ed. *The Drama of the Renaissance: Essays for Leicester Bradner.* Providence: Brown U.P., 1970.*

1121 BLOOM, Edward A., ed. *Shakespeare 1564–1964: A Collection of Modern Essays by Various Hands.* Providence: Brown U.P., 1964.*

1122 BRADBY, Anne, ed. *Shakespeare Criticism, 1919–35.* See **1034.**

1123 BROWER, Reuben A., and Richard POIRIER, eds. *In Defense of Reading: A Reader's Approach to Literary Criticism.* New York: Dutton, 1962. Contains, among other matters, three essays on Shakespeare.*

1124 *Bulletin de la Faculté des Lettres de Strasbourg,* 63.8 (1965). Issue devoted to "Hommage à Shakespeare."

1125 CALDERWOOD, James L., and Harold E. TOLIVER, eds. *Essays in Shakespearean Criticism.* Englewood Cliffs, N.J.: Prentice-Hall, 1970.*

1126 *Carnegie Series in English.* Vols. 1, 4, 8, and 10. Pittsburgh: Carnegie Institute of Technology, 1953–.

1127 CHAPMAN, Gerald W., ed. *Essays on Shakespeare.* Princeton: Princeton U.P., 1965.*

1128 CORDER, Jim W., ed. *Shakespeare 1964.* Fort Worth: Texas Christian U.P., 1965.

1129 CRAIG, Hardin, ed. *Essays in Dramatic Literature: The Parrott Presentation Volume.* Princeton: Princeton U.P., 1935. Rpt., New York: Russell & Russell.

1130 CRANE, Milton, ed. *Shakespeare's Art: Seven Essays.* Chicago: U. of Chicago P., 1973.

1131 DAVIS, Herbert, and Helen GARDNER, eds. *Elizabethan and Jacobean Studies Presented to Frank Percy Wilson.* Oxford: Clarendon, 1959.*

1132 DEAN, Leonard F., ed. *Shakespeare: Modern Essays in Criticism.* Rev. ed., New York: Oxford U.P., 1967.*

1133 DOBRÉE, Bonamy, ed. *Shakespeare: The Writer and His Work.* London: Longmans, 1964.

1134 DUTHIE, George Ian, ed. *Papers Mainly Shakespearian.* Edinburgh and London: Oliver & Boyd, 1964.

1135 *Études Anglaises* 17 (1964). Issue devoted to Shakespeare, 1564–1964.

1136 FABER, M. D., ed. *The Design Within.* See **1401.**

1137 FISCHER, Walther, and Karl P. WENTERSDORF, eds. *Shakespeare-Studien: Festschrift für Heinrich Mutschmann.* Marburg: Elwert, 1951.

1138 GARRETT, John, ed. *More Talking of Shakespeare.* London: Longmans, Green; New York: Theatre Arts Books, 1959.*

1139 GARRETT, John, ed. *Talking of Shakespeare.* London: Hodder & Stoughton in association with Max Reinhardt; New York: Theatre Arts Books, 1954.*

1140 GITTINGS, Robert, ed. *The Living Shakespeare.* London: Heinemann, 1960. Rpt., New York: Barnes & Noble, 1967.

1141 GOLLANCZ, Israel, ed. *A Book of Homage to Shakespeare.* Oxford: Clarendon, 1916.

1142 HARRISON, Thomas P., et al., eds. *Studies in Honor of DeWitt T. Starnes.* Austin: U. of Texas P., 1967.

1143 HENNING, Standish, Robert KIMBROUGH, and Richard KNOWLES, eds. *English Renaissance Drama: Essays in Honor of Madeleine Doran and Mark Eccles.* Carbondale and Edwardsville: Southern Illinois U.P.; London and Amsterdam: Feffer & Simons, 1976. Most of the essays are on Shakespeare.

1144 HOSLEY, Richard, ed. *Essays on Shakespeare and Elizabethan Drama in Honor of Hardin Craig.* Columbia: U. of Missouri P., 1962.*

1145 JACKSON, B. A. W., ed. *Stratford Papers on Shakespeare.* Toronto: Gage, 1961 (for the 1960 session of the Shakespeare Seminar). Also 1962 (for 1961); 1963 (for 1962); 1964 (for 1963); 1965 (for 1964); 1969 (for 1965–67); and 1972 (for 1968–69). Last two volumes published by the McMaster U. Library Press and in Ireland by the Irish U.P., Shannon.*

1146 JEFFERSON, D. W., ed. *The Morality of Art: Essays Presented to G. Wilson Knight by His Colleagues and Friends.* London: Routledge & K. Paul; New York: Barnes & Noble, 1969.*

1147 KERNAN, Alvin B., ed. *Modern Shakespearean Criticism: Essays on Style, Dramaturgy, and the Major Plays.* New York: Harcourt, Brace, & World, 1970.*

1148 KETTLE, Arnold, ed. *Shakespeare in a Changing World: Essays on His Times and His Plays.* London: Lawrence & Wishart; New York: International, 1964. Generally Marxist interpretation.*

1149 KIRBY, Thomas Austin, and William John OLIVE, eds. *Essays in Honor of Esmond Linworth Marilla.* Baton Rouge: Louisiana State U.P., 1970.

1150 LAWRENCE, Natalie Grimes, and J. A. REYNOLDS, eds. *Sweet Smoke of Rhetoric: A Collection of Renaissance Essays.* Coral Gables, Fla.: U. of Miami P., 1964.

1151 LEECH, Clifford, and J. M. R. MARGESON, eds. *Shakespeare 1971: Proceedings of the World Shakespeare Congress, Vancouver, August 1971.* Toronto: U. of Toronto P., 1972.*

1152 MACKAIL, J. W., ed. *Aspects of Shakespeare: Being British Academy Lectures.* Oxford: Clarendon, 1933.* See also **1116.**

1153 MCMANAWAY, James G., ed. *Shakespeare 400: Essays by American Scholars on the Anniversary of the Poet's Birth.* New York: Holt, Rinehart, & Winston, 1964. Identical in contents with *SQ* 15.2 (1964).*

1154 MCMANAWAY, James G., Giles E. DAWSON, and Edwin E. WILLOUGHBY, eds. *Joseph Quincy Adams Memorial Studies.* Washington, D.C.: Folger Shakespeare Library, 1948.*

1155 MCNEIR, Waldo F., ed. *Studies in English Renaissance Literature [Dedicated to John Earle Uhler].* Baton Rouge: Louisiana State U.P., 1962.

1156 MCNEIR, Waldo F., and Thelma N. GREENFIELD, eds. *Pacific Coast Studies in Shakespeare.* Eugene: U. of Oregon P., 1966.*

1157 MATTHEWS, Arthur D., and Clark M. EMERY, eds. *Studies in Shakespeare.* Coral Gables, Fla.: U. of Miami P., 1953. Rpt., New York: AMS.

1158 MATTHEWS, Brander, and Ashley H. THORNDIKE, eds. *Shakespearian Studies.* New York: Columbia U.P., 1916.

1159 MINER, Earl, ed. *English Criticism in Japan.* Tokyo: U. of Tokyo P., 1972.

1160 PAOLUCCI, Anne, ed. *Shakespeare Encomium.* New York: City College, 1964.

1161 PROUTY, Charles Tyler, ed. *Shakespeare: Of an Age and for All Time.* Hamden, Conn.: Shoe String, 1954.

1162 PROUTY, Charles Tyler, ed. *Studies in Honor of A. H. R. Fairchild.* Columbia: U. of Missouri, 1946.

1163 RABKIN, Norman, ed. *Approaches to Shakespeare.* New York: McGraw-Hill, 1964.*

1164 RABKIN, Norman, ed. *Reinterpretations of Elizabethan Drama.* Selected Papers from the English Institute. New York: Columbia U.P., 1969.*

1165 RIDLER, Anne, ed. *Shakespeare Criticism, 1935–60.* See **1061.**

1166 SAMARIN, Roman Mikhailovich, and Alexander NIKOLYUKIN, eds. *Shakespeare in the Soviet Union: A Collection of Articles.* Trans. Avril PYMAN. Moscow: Progress, 1966.

1167 SMITH, Gordon Ross, ed. *Essays on Shakespeare.* University Park: Pennsylvania State U.P., 1965.*

1168 SPENCER, T. J. B., ed. *Shakespeare: A Celebration, 1564–1964.* See **56.**

1169 STAFFORD, Tony J., ed. *Shakespeare in the Southwest: Some New Directions.* El Paso: Texas Western P., 1969.

1170 SUTHERLAND, James, and Joel HURSTFIELD, eds. *Shakespeare's World.* London: Arnold; New York: St. Martin's, 1964.

1171 THALER, Alwin, and Norman SANDERS, eds. *Shakespearean Essays.* Knoxville: U. of Tennessee P., 1964.

1172 WEST, E. J., ed. *Elizabethan Studies and Other Essays in Honor of George F. Reynolds.* Boulder: U. of Colorado, 1945.

1173 Wisconsin, University of. *Shakespeare Studies by Members of the Department of English of the University of Wisconsin.* Madison: U. of Wisconsin, 1916.

1174 WOODS, Charles B., and Curt A. ZIMANSKY, eds. *Studies in English Drama Presented to Baldwin Maxwell.* State U. of Iowa, 1962. Identical in contents with *PQ* 41.1 (1962).

1175 WRIGHT, Louis B., ed. *Shakespeare Celebrated: Anniversary Lectures Delivered at the Folger Library.* Ithaca: Cornell U.P., 1966.

General Studies and Collections of Essays by a Single Author

See also **45, 50, 188–95, 465, 475, 555, 923, 1277, 1279, 1286, 1289, 1292, 1352, 1423, 1466, 1489, 1495, 1516, 1522, 1524,** and **1601.**

1176 ALEXANDER, Peter. *Shakespeare.* London: Oxford U.P., 1964.

1177 ARTHOS, John. *The Art of Shakespeare.* London: Bowes & Bowes; New York: Barnes & Noble, 1964. Rpt., Norwood, Pa.: Norwood, 1974.

1178 AUCHINCLOSS, Louis. *Motiveless Malignity.* Boston: Houghton Mifflin, 1969.

1179 AUDEN, W. H. *"The Dyer's Hand" and Other Essays.* New York: Random House, 1948.*

1180 BAKER, George Pierce. *The Development of Shakespeare as a Dramatist.* New York: Macmillan, 1907. Rpt., New York: AMS.

1181 BILTON, Peter. *Commentary and Control in Shakespeare's Plays.* New York: Humanities P.; Oslo: Universitetsforlaget, 1974.

1182 BRADBROOK, M. C. *The Living Monument: Shakespeare and the Theatre of His Time.* London and New York: Cambridge U.P., 1976.

1183 BRADBROOK, M. C. *Shakespeare the Craftsman.* London: Chatto & Windus; New York: Barnes & Noble, 1969.

1184 BRADLEY, A. C. *A Miscellany.* London: Macmillan, 1929.

1185 BRADLEY, A. C. *Oxford Lectures on Poetry.* London: Macmillan, 1909. Rpt., 1959. New York: St. Martin's, 1959.*

1186 BROOKE, C. F. Tucker. *Essays on Shakespeare and Other Elizabethans.* New Haven: Yale U.P., 1948.

1187 BURKHARDT, Sigurd. *Shakespearean Meanings.* Princeton: Princeton U.P., 1968.*

1188 BURKE, Kenneth. *Language as Symbolic Action: Essays on Life, Literature, and Method.* Berkeley and Los Angeles: U. of California P., 1966.*

1189 CALDERWOOD, James L. *Shakespearean Metadrama: The Argument of the Play in "Titus Andronicus," "Love's Labour's Lost," "Romeo and Juliet," "A Midsummer Night's Dream," and "Richard II."* Minneapolis: U. of Minnesota P., 1971.*

1190 CHAMBERS, E. K. *Shakespeare: A Survey.* London: Sidgwick & Jackson, 1925. Rpt., New York: Hill & Wang, n.d.

1191 CHAMBERS, E. K. *Shakespearean Gleanings.* London: Oxford U.P., 1944.

1192 CLEMEN, Wolfgang. *Das Drama Shakespeares.* Göttingen: Vandenhoeck & Ruprecht, 1969.

1193 CLEMEN, Wolfgang. *Shakespeare's Dramatic Art: Collected Essays.* London: Methuen; New York: Barnes & Noble, 1972. Contains some of the same essays as in **1192.**

1194 COLIE, Rosalie L. *Shakespeare's Living Art.* Princeton: Princeton U.P., 1974.*

1195 CRAIG, Hardin. *An Interpretation of Shakespeare.* New York: Dryden, 1948.

1196 CROCE, Benedetto. *Ariosto, Shakespeare, and Corneille.* Trans. Douglas AINS-LIE. New York: Holt; London: Allen & Unwin, 1920. Rpt., New York: Russell & Russell, 1966.

1197 CUNNINGHAM, J. V. *Tradition and Poetic Structure.* Denver: Swallow, 1960.*

1198 DAVIS, Edward. *Essays on English Drama.* Cape Town: Simondium, 1965.

1199 DOWDEN, Edward. *Shakspere: A Critical Study of His Mind and Art.* London: Routledge & K. Paul, 1875. 3rd ed., 1905.

1200 DUTHIE, George Ian. *Shakespeare.* London: Hutchinson's University Library, 1951.

1201 EAGLETON, Terence. *Shakespeare and Society: Critical Studies in Shakespearean Drama.* London: Chatto & Windus; New York: Schocken, 1967.*

1202 EDWARDS, Philip. *Shakespeare and the Confines of Art.* London: Methuen; New York: Barnes & Noble, 1968.*

1203 ELLIS-FERMOR, Una. *Shakespeare the Dramatist and Other Papers.* Ed. Kenneth MUIR. London: Methuen; New York: Barnes & Noble, 1961.

1204 ENRIGHT, D. J. *Shakespeare and the Students.* London: Chatto & Windus; New York: Schocken, 1970.

1205 EVANS, Gareth Lloyd. *Shakespeare.* Vol. 1: 1564–1592. Edinburgh: Oliver & Boyd, 1969–.

1206 FARRELL, Kirby. *Shakespeare's Creation: The Language of Magic and Play.* See **1357.**

1207 FERGUSSON, Francis. *The Human Image in Dramatic Literature.* Garden City, N.Y.: Doubleday, 1957. Rpt., Gloucester, Mass.: P. Smith, 1969.*

1208 FERGUSSON, Francis. *Shakespeare: The Pattern in His Carpet.* New York: Delacorte, 1970.

1209 FLATTER, Richard. *Triumph der Gnade: Shakespeare-Essays.* Vienna: Kurt Desch, 1956.

1210 FLUCHÈRE, Henri. *Shakespeare and the Elizabethans.* Trans. Guy HAMILTON. New York: Hill & Wang, 1956.

1211 FLY, Richard D. *Shakespeare's Mediated World.* Amherst: U. of Massachusetts P., 1976. A study of go-betweens as either ineffectual or as inadvertent distorters of the unions they intend to effect, in *Romeo and Juliet, Measure for Measure, Troilus and Cressida, King Lear,* and *Timon of Athens.* *

1212 GARBER, Marjorie B. *Dream in Shakespeare: From Metaphor to Metamorphosis.* See **1358.**

1213 GILBERT, Allan H. *The Principles and Practice of Criticism: "Othello," "The Merry Wives," "Hamlet."* Detroit: Wayne State U.P., 1959.

1214 GODDARD, Harold C. *The Meaning of Shakespeare.* Orig. 1 vol.; 2 vols. in paperback. Chicago: U. of Chicago P., 1951.

1215 GODSHALK, William Leigh. *Patterning in Shakespearean Drama.* The Hague, Paris: Mouton, 1973.

1216 GOLDMAN, Michael. *Shakespeare and the Energies of Drama.* Princeton: Princeton U.P., 1972.*

1217 GRANVILLE-BARKER, Harley. *More Prefaces to Shakespeare.* Ed. Edward M. MOORE. Princeton: Princeton U.P., 1974.

1218 GRANVILLE-BARKER, Harley. *Prefaces to Shakespeare.* 2 vols.; later, 4 vols. in paperback. Princeton: Princeton U.P., 1946–47; London: Batsford, 1958.*

1219 HARBAGE, Alfred. *A Kind of Power: The Shakespeare-Dickens Analogy.* Philadelphia: American Philosophical Society, 1975.

1220 HARBAGE, Alfred. *Shakespeare Without Words and Other Essays.* Cambridge, Mass.: Harvard U.P., 1972.

1221 HOWARTH, Herbert. *The Tiger's Heart: Eight Essays on Shakespeare.* London: Chatto & Windus; New York: Oxford U.P., 1970.

1222 HUNTER, Edwin R. *Shakspere and Common Sense.* Boston: Christopher, 1954.

1223 KERMODE, Frank. *Shakespeare, Spenser, Donne: Renaissance Essays.* London: Routledge & K. Paul; New York: Viking, 1971.

1224 KERNAN, Alvin B. "The Plays and the Playwrights." In **602.**

1225 KNIGHT, G. Wilson. *The Olive and the Sword: A Study of England's Shakespeare.* London: Oxford U.P., 1944.

1226 KNIGHT, G. Wilson. *The Shakespearian Tempest.* London: Oxford U.P., 1932. 3rd ed., London: Methuen, 1953. A survey of all the works.

1227 KNIGHT, G. Wilson. *The Sovereign Flower: On Shakespeare as the Poet of Royalism Together with Related Essays and Indexes to Earlier Volumes.* London: Methuen; New York: Macmillan, 1958.

1228 KNIGHTS, L. C. *Explorations: Essays in Criticism, Mainly on the Literature of the Seventeenth Century.* London: Chatto & Windus, 1946.*

1229 KNIGHTS, L. C. *Further Explorations.* London: Chatto & Windus; Stanford: Stanford U.P., 1965.* See also *Explorations 3.* Pittsburgh: U. of Pittsburgh P., 1977.

1230 KNIGHTS, L. C. *Some Shakespearean Themes.* London: Chatto & Windus, 1959.*

1231 KOTT, Jan. *Shakespeare Our Contemporary.* Trans. Boleslaw TABORSKI. New York: Norton; Garden City, N.Y.: Doubleday, 1964. For a critical rejoinder, see Patrick CRUTTWELL, "Shakespeare Is Not Our Contemporary." *YR* 59 (1969): 33–49.

1232 LEAVIS, F. R. *The Common Pursuit.* London: Chatto & Windus, 1952. Essays collected from *Scrutiny,* of which a few (though not most) are on Shakespeare.*

1233 LEVIN, Harry. *Shakespeare and the Revolution of the Times: Perspectives and Commentaries.* New York: Oxford U.P., 1976.

1234 LUDOWYK, E. F. C. *Understanding Shakespeare.* Cambridge: Cambridge U.P., 1962.

1235 MACKAIL, J. W. *The Approach to Shakespeare.* Oxford: Clarendon, 1930.

1236 MATTHEWS, Honor. *Character and Symbol in Shakespeare's Plays: A Study of Certain Christian and Pre-Christian Elements in Their Structure and Imagery.* Cambridge: Cambridge U.P., 1962.

1237 MOULTON, Richard G. *Shakespeare as a Dramatic Artist.* 3rd ed., Oxford: Clarendon, 1906. Rpt., New York: Dover, 1966; Gloucester, Mass.: P. Smith.

1238 MUIR, Kenneth. *Shakespeare the Professional, and Related Studies.* London: Heinemann, 1973.

1239 MURRAY, Patrick. *The Shakespearian Scene: Some Twentieth-Century Perspectives.* London: Longmans, Green; New York: Barnes & Noble, 1969.

1240 MURRY, John Middleton. *Shakespeare.* London: Cape; New York: Harcourt, Brace, 1936.

1241 OPPEL, Horst. *Shakespeare: Studien zum Werk und zur Welt des Dichters.* Heidelberg: Winter, 1963.

1242 QUILLER-COUCH, Arthur. *Shakespeare's Workmanship.* London: T. Fisher Unwin, 1918; New York: Macmillan; Cambridge: Cambridge U.P., 1931.

1243 RABKIN, Norman. *Shakespeare and the Common Understanding.* New York: The Free Press; London: Collier-Macmillan, 1967.*

1244 RIDLEY, M. R. *Shakespeare's Plays: A Commentary.* London: Dent, 1937.

1245 ROSSITER, A. P. *Angel with Horns and Other Shakespeare Lectures.* Ed. Graham STOREY. London: Longmans, Green, 1961.*

1246 SANDERS, Wilbur. *The Dramatist and the Received Idea: Studies in the Plays of Marlowe and Shakespeare.* Cambridge: Cambridge U.P., 1968.*

1247 SEWELL, Arthur. *Character and Society in Shakespeare.* Oxford: Clarendon, 1951.*

1248 SHACKFORD, Martha Hale. *Shakespeare, Sophocles: Dramatic Themes and Modes.* New York: Bookman, 1960.

1249 SIEGEL, Paul N. *Shakespeare in His Time and Ours.* Notre Dame: U. of Notre Dame P., 1968.

1250 SIMPSON, Percy. *Studies in Elizabethan Drama.* Oxford: Clarendon, 1955.

1251 SKULSKY, Harold. *Spirits Finely Touched: The Testing of Value and Integrity in Four Shakespearean Plays.* Athens: U. of Georgia P., 1976. A study of *Hamlet, Measure for Measure, King Lear,* and *Othello.*

1252 SMITH, Marion Bodwell. *Dualities in Shakespeare.* Toronto: U. of Toronto P., 1966.

1253 SOELLNER, Rolf. *Shakespeare's Patterns of Self-Knowledge.* See **1443.**

1254 SQUIRE, John. *Shakespeare as a Dramatist.* Orig. pub., 1935. Rpt., New York: Haskell House, 1971.

1255 STAMM, Rudolf. *The Shaping Powers at Work: Fifteen Essays on Poetic Transmutation.* Heidelberg: Winter, 1967.

1256 STAUFFER, Donald A. *Shakespeare's World of Images: The Development of His Moral Ideas.* New York: Norton, 1949. Rpt., Bloomington: Indiana U.P., 1966.*

1257 STEWART, J. I. M. *Character and Motive in Shakespeare.* See **1391.***

1258 STOLL, Elmer Edgar. *From Shakespeare to Joyce.* Garden City, N.Y.: Doubleday, 1944. Rpt., New York: Ungar.

1259 STOLL, Elmer Edgar. *Poets and Playwrights: Shakespeare, Jonson, Spenser, Milton.* Minneapolis: U. of Minnesota P., 1930. Rpt., New York: Russell & Russell, 1965.

1260 STOLL, Elmer Edgar. *Shakespeare and Other Masters.* Cambridge, Mass.: Harvard U.P.; London: Oxford U.P., 1940. Rpt., New York: Russell & Russell.

1261 STOLL, Elmer Edgar. *Shakespeare Studies: Historical and Comparative in Method.* New York: Macmillan, 1927.

1262 SWINBURNE, Algernon Charles. *A Study of Shakespeare.* London: Chatto & Windus, 1880. Rpt., New York: AMS, 1965.

1263 SWINBURNE, Algernon Charles. *Three Plays of Shakespeare.* New York and London: Harper, 1909. A study of *King Lear, Othello,* and *Richard II.*

1264 THALER, Alwin. *Shakespeare and Our World.* Knoxville: U. of Tennessee P., 1966.

1265 THOMPSON, Karl F. *Modesty and Cunning: Shakespeare's Use of Literary Tradition.* Ann Arbor: U. of Michigan P., 1971.

1266 TILLYARD, E. M. W. *Essays, Literary and Educational.* London: Chatto & Windus; New York: Barnes & Noble, 1962.

1267 TOLMAN, Albert H. *Falstaff and Other Shakespearean Topics.* New York: Macmillan, 1925.

1268 TRAVERSI, Derek. *An Approach to Shakespeare.* 2nd ed., Garden City, N.Y.: Doubleday, 1956; Glasgow: Sands, 1957. Orig. pub. as *Approach to Shakespeare.* London: Sands, 1938.*

1269 URE, Peter. *Elizabethan and Jacobean Drama: Critical Essays.* Ed. J. C. MAXWELL. Liverpool: Liverpool U.P.; New York: Barnes & Noble, 1974.

1270 VAN DOREN, Mark. *Shakespeare.* New York: Holt, 1939; London: Allen & Unwin, 1941. Rpt., Garden City, N.Y.: Doubleday Anchor, 1953.*

1271 WAIN, John. *The Living World of Shakespeare: A Playgoer's Guide.* London: Macmillan; New York: St. Martin's, 1964.

1272 WILSON, F. P. *Shakespearian and Other Studies.* Ed. Helen GARDNER. Oxford: Clarendon, 1969.

Shakespeare's Dramaturgy

See also **153, 499, 719, 722, 725, 747, 1182, 1515, 1588, 1601, 1633,** and **1723.**

1273 ADAMS, Robert M. "Trompe-L'Oeil in Shakespeare and Keats." *SR* 63 (1955): 238–55.

1274 ALDUS, Paul J. "Analogical Probability in Shakespeare's Plays." *SQ* 6 (1955): 397–414. On analysis of dramatic construction through analogy or parallelism between scenes and characters, in terms of the Aristotelian concept of probability.

1275 ARNOLD, Morris LeRoy. *The Soliloquies of Shakespeare: A Study in Technic.* New York: Columbia U.P., 1911.

1276 BECKERMAN, Bernard. "Shakespeare and the Life of the Scene." In **1143.** Deals with one aspect of the structure of a scene in Shakespeare: "the shape of its energy."

1277 BERRY, Francis. *The Shakespearean Inset: Word and Picture.* London: Routledge & K. Paul, 1965. A study of episodes in which the imagined spectacle is at odds with the actual spectacle.*

1278 BERRY, Francis. "Shakespeare's Stage Geometry." *SJH* (1974):160–71. On symbolic meaning of stage movement, such as rise and fall.

1279 BETHELL, S. L. *Shakespeare and the Popular Dramatic Tradition.* London and New York: King & Staples; Durham, N.C.: Duke U.P., 1944. Rpt., New York: Octagon. On conventions versus naturalism, anachronism and treatment of time, use of direct address and soliloquy, etc.*

1280 BILTON, Peter. "Shakespeare Criticism and the 'Choric Character.'" *ES* 50 (1969):254–60.

1281 BLACK, Matthew W. "Repeated Situations in Shakespeare's Plays." In **1144.**

1282 BOAS, Frederick S. "The Play within the Play." In **619.**

1283 BOWDEN, William R. "The Bed Trick, 1603–1642: Its Mechanics, Ethics, and Effects." *ShakS* 5 (1970 for 1969):112–23.

1284 BOWERS, Fredson. "Shakespeare's Art: The Point of View." *Literary Views: Critical and Historical Essays.* Ed. Carroll CAMDEN. Chicago: U. of Chicago P., 1964.

1285 BOWERS, Fredson. "Shakespeare's Dramatic Vagueness." *VQR* 39 (1963):475–84.

1286 BRADBROOK, M. C. *Elizabethan Stage Conditions: A Study of Their Place in the Interpretation of Shakespeare's Plays.* London: Cambridge U.P., 1932.

1287 BRADBROOK, M. C. "Shakespeare and the Use of Disguise in Elizabethan Drama." *EIC* 2 (1952):159–68.

1288 BROWN, Arthur. "The Play within a Play: An Elizabethan Dramatic Device." *E&S,* n.s. 13 (1960):36–48.

1289 BROWN, John Russell. *Shakespeare's Dramatic Style: "Romeo and Juliet," "As You Like It," "Julius Caesar," "Twelfth Night," "Macbeth."* London: Heinemann, 1970; New York: Barnes & Noble, 1971.

1290 CLEMEN, Wolfgang. *Schein und Sein bei Shakespeare.* Munich: Bayerische Akademie der Wissenschaften, 1959.

1291 CLEMEN, Wolfgang. *Shakespeare's Soliloquies.* Cambridge: Cambridge U.P., 1964. Rpt. in **1193.***

1292 COGHILL, Nevill. *Shakespeare's Professional Skills.* Cambridge: Cambridge U.P., 1964. On Shakespeare's craftsmanship in shaping a story into a play.*

1293 CONNOLLY, Thomas F. "Shakespeare and the Double Man." *SQ* 1 (1950): 30–35. A study of alter egos, such as Cassius to Brutus and Iago to Othello.

1294 CRAIG, Hardin. "Shakespeare's Development as a Dramatist in the Light of His Experience." *SP* 39 (1942):226–38.

1295 CRANE, R. S. "Toward a More Adequate Criticism of Poetic Structure." *The Languages of Criticism and the Structure of Poetry.* Toronto: U. of Toronto P., 1953.*

1296 DESSEN, Alan C. *Elizabethan Drama and the Viewer's Eye.* Chapel Hill: U. of North Carolina P., 1977. Contains discussions of theatrical techniques in Shakespeare, including the use of visual analogies.

1297 DORAN, Madeleine. "Shakespeare as an Experimental Dramatist: The Word Is 'Boldly.'" In **1175.**

1298 FIEDLER, Leslie A. "The Defense of the Illusion and the Creation of Myth: Device and Symbol in the Plays of Shakespeare." *EIE 1948* (1949):74–94.

1299 GREYERZ, Georg von. *The Reported Scenes in Shakespeare's Plays.* Bern: Pochon-Jent, 1965.

1300 HABICHT, Werner. "'With an Auspicious and a Dropping Eye': Antithetische Mimik in Shakespeares Dramen." *Anglia* 87 (1969):147–66.

1301 HAPGOOD, Robert. "Shakespeare's Delayed Reactions." *EIC* 13 (1963):9–16.

1302 HAWKINS, Harriett. *Likenesses of Truth in Elizabethan and Restoration Drama.* Oxford: Clarendon, 1972. On devices of theatrical illusion.

1303 HOLLOWAY, John. "Dramatic Irony in Shakespeare." *The Charted Mirror: Literary and Critical Essays.* London: Routledge & K. Paul, 1960; New York: Horizon, 1962.

1304 HUNTER, G. K. "Were There Act-Pauses on Shakespeare's Stage?" In **1143.**

1305 ISER, Wolfgang. "Das Spiel im Spiel: Formen dramatischer Illusion bei Shakespeare." *Archiv für das Studium der neueren Sprachen und Literaturen* 198 (1961–62):209–26.

1306 JONES, Emrys. *Scenic Form in Shakespeare.* Oxford: Clarendon, 1971.

1307 JUMP, John. "Shakespeare's Ghosts." *CritQ* 12 (1970):339–51. On ghosts' theatrical function and the "objectivity" of their dramatic existence.

1308 KERNAN, Alvin B. "This Goodly Frame, the Stage: The Interior Theater of Imagination in English Renaissance Drama." *SQ* 25 (1974):1–5.

1309 KREIDER, Paul V. *Repetition in Shakespeare's Plays.* Princeton: Princeton U.P., 1941. Rpt., New York: Octagon, 1975.

1310 LAWLOR, John. "Continuity and Innovation in Shakespeare's Dramatic Career." *REL* 5.2 (1964):11–23.

1311 LAWRENCE, W. J. *Speeding up Shakespeare: Studies of the Bygone Theatre and Drama.* London: Argonaut, 1937. Rpt., New York: Blom.

1312 LEECH, Clifford. "Ephesus, Troy, Athens: Shakespeare's Use of Locality." In **1145** (1964 for 1963).

1313 LEECH, Clifford. "The Function of Locality in the Plays of Shakespeare and His Contemporaries." In **607,** vol. 1 (1969 for 1968).

1314 LEECH, Clifford. "Shakespeare's Prologues and Epilogues." In **1117.**

1315 LEECH, Clifford. "Shakespeare's Use of a Five-Act Structure." *NS,* n.s. 6 (1957): 249–63.

1316 LEVIN, Harry. "The Shakespearean Overplot." *RenD* 8 (1965):63–71. Rpt. in **1233.**

1317 LEVIN, Richard. *The Multiple Plot in English Renaissance Drama.* Chicago and London: U. of Chicago P., 1971.*

1318 MCCLOSKEY, John C. "The Plot Device of False Report." *ShAB* 21 (1926): 147–58.

1319 MACK, Maynard. "Engagement and Detachment in Shakespeare's Plays." In **1144.**

1320 MEHL, Dieter. *The Elizabethan Dumb Show: The History of a Dramatic Convention*. London: Methuen, 1965; Cambridge, Mass.: Harvard U.P., 1966. First pub. in German, 1964.

1321 MOORMAN, F. W. "Shakespeare's Ghosts." *MLR* 1 (1906):192–201.

1322 NASSAR, Eugene Paul. "Shakespeare's Games with His Audience." *The Rape of Cinderella: Essays in Literary Continuity*. Bloomington and London: Indiana U.P., 1970.

1323 NELSON, Robert J. *Play within a Play: The Dramatist's Conception of His Art: Shakespeare to Anouilh*. New Haven: Yale U.P., 1958.

1324 OPPEL, Horst. "Kontrast und Kontrapunkt im Shakespeare-Drama." *SJ* 97 (1961):153–82. Rpt. in **1241.**

1325 PARKER, Robert B. "Dramaturgy in Shakespeare and Brecht." *UTQ* 32 (1963): 229–46.

1326 PARSONS, Philip. "Shakespeare and the Mask." *ShS* 16 (1963):121–31.

1327 PEARN, B. R. "Dumb-Show in Elizabethan Drama." *RES* 11 (1935):385–405.

1328 PRESSON, Robert K. "Some Traditional Instances of Setting in Shakespeare's Plays." *MLR* 61 (1966):12–22.

1329 PRICE, Hereward T. *Construction in Shakespeare*. Ann Arbor: U. of Michigan P., 1951.*

1330 PRICE, Hereward T. "Mirror-Scenes in Shakespeare." In **1154.**

1331 RIGHTER, Anne. *Shakespeare and the Idea of the Play*. London: Chatto & Windus; New York: Barnes & Noble, 1962. Rpt., Harmondsworth and Baltimore: Penguin, 1967. On the device of the play within the play and other images of playacting.*

1332 ROSE, Mark. *Shakespearean Design*. Cambridge, Mass.: Harvard U.P., 1972.

1333 SALTER, F. M. "Shakespeare's Use of Silence." *PTRSC,* 3rd ser. 45.2 (1951): 59–81.

1334 SCHANZER, Ernest. "Plot-Echoes in Shakespeare's Plays." *SJH* (1969):103–21.

1335 SCRIMGEOUR, Gary J. "The Messenger as a Dramatic Device in Shakespeare." *SQ* 19 (1968):41–54.

1336 SEDGEWICK, G. G. *Of Irony, Especially in Drama*. 2nd ed., Toronto: U. of Toronto P., 1948. 1st edition, 1935.

1337 SEN GUPTA, S. C. *The Whirligig of Time: The Problem of Duration in Shakespeare's Plays*. Bombay: Orient Longmans, 1961.

1338 SEWELL, Arthur. "Place and Time in Shakespeare's Plays." *SP* 42 (1945): 205–24.

1339 SHARPE, Robert Boies. *Irony in the Drama: An Essay on Impersonation, Shock, and Catharsis*. Chapel Hill: U. of North Carolina P., 1959. Rpt., Westport, Conn.: Greenwood, 1975.

1340 SIEMON, James Edward. "Disguise in Marston and Shakespeare." *HLQ* 38 (1975):105–23.

1341 SMITH, Irwin. "Dramatic Time versus Clock Time in Shakespeare." *SQ* 20 (1969):65–69.

1342 SNUGGS, Henry L. *Shakespeare and Five Acts: Studies in a Dramatic Convention*. New York: Vantage, 1960.

1343 SPRAGUE, Arthur Colby. *Shakespeare and the Audience: A Study in the Technique of Exposition.* Cambridge, Mass.: Harvard U.P., 1935. Rpt., New York: Russell & Russell, 1966.

1344 STAMM, Rudolf. *Shakespeare's Word-Scenery, with Some Remarks on Stage-History and the Interpretation of His Plays.* Zurich: Polygraphischer, 1954.

1345 STYAN, J. L. *Drama, Stage, and Audience.* London: Cambridge U.P., 1975.

1346 SZENCZI, Miklós. "The Nature of Shakespeare's Realism." *SJW* 102 (1966): 37–59.

1347 THALER, Alwin. "Delayed Exposition in Shakespeare." *SQ* 1 (1950):140–45.

1348 THALER, Alwin. *Shakespeare's Silences.* Cambridge, Mass.: Harvard U.P.; London: Oxford U.P., 1929. Contains various essays on Shakespeare's epilogues and other technical aspects.

1349 VISWANATHAN, S. "A Shakespearian Device: The Scene within the Scene." *Anglia* 90 (1972):456–69.

1350 WALKER, Albert L. "Convention in Shakespeare's Description of Emotion." *PQ* 17 (1938):26–66.

1351 WILLIAMS, Clyde V. "A Glass of Wine, A 'Dram of Eale': Claudius, Cassio, and Shakespeare's Dramatic Art." In **1149.** On the importance of drinking references and scenes to plot, characterization, and thematic continuity.

Shakespeare's Conception of Poetry and the Imagination

See also **316, 475, 1236, 1331, 1447, 1576, 2357, 3189, 3577,** and **3581.**

1352 ARMSTRONG, Edward A. *Shakespeare's Imagination: A Study of the Psychology of Association and Inspiration.* London: Drummond, 1946. Rev. ed., Lincoln: U. of Nebraska P.; Gloucester, Mass.: P. Smith, 1963.*

1353 ARTHOS, John. *Shakespeare's Use of Dream and Vision.* Totowa, N.J.: Rowman & Littlefield, announced for 1977.

1354 BRADBROOK, M. C. *Shakespeare and Elizabethan Poetry.* See **1580.**

1355 BRADBROOK, M. C. "Shakespeare's Primitive Art." *PBA* 51 (1966 for 1965): 214–34. Concerns Shakespeare's imagination and his indebtedness to the popular drama of his time.

1356 DAICHES, David. "Shakespeare's Poetry." In **1140.**

1357 FARRELL, Kirby. *Shakespeare's Creation: The Language of Magic and Play.* Amherst: U. of Massachusetts P., 1975. About Shakespeare's conception of creation, and about the conflict between vision and the more rational uses of the imagination.*

1358 GARBER, Marjorie B. *Dream in Shakespeare: From Metaphor to Metamorphosis.* New Haven and London: Yale U.P., 1974.*

1359 HALLIDAY, F. E. *The Poetry of Shakespeare's Plays.* See **464.**

1360 HAWKINS, Harriett. *Poetic Freedom and Poetic Truth: Chaucer, Shakespeare, Marlowe, Milton.* Oxford: Clarendon, 1976. About the poet's freedom to challenge social and critical orthodoxies.

1361 HOY, Cyrus. "Shakespeare and the Revenge of Art." *Rice U. Studies* 60.2 (1974): 71–94. Concerning the "revenge" which the poet takes on the world for being the way it is—cruel, unjust, subject to time, etc.

1362 MANDEL, Jerome. "Dream and Imagination in Shakespeare." *SQ* 24 (1973): 61–68.

1363 PETTET, E. C. "Shakespeare's Conception of Poetry." *E&S,* n.s. 3 (1950):29–46. About Shakespeare's ideas concerning inspiration, spontaneity, poetic fury, feigning, and the like.*

1364 PRICE, Hereward T. "Shakespeare as a Critic." *PQ* 20 (1941):390–99.

1365 RYLANDS, George. "Shakespeare's Poetic Energy." *PBA* 37 (1952 for 1951): 99–119.

Studies in Characterization

For discussions of Shakespeare's comic and tragic character types, see **1694–1711** and **1982–2004**. See also **458, 572, 584, 634, 973, 986, 990, 1013, 1015, 1017, 1022, 1211, 1236, 1247, 1293, 1350, 1455, 1583, 1924, 2213, 2326,** and **3129.** See also sections on "Character Studies" under various individual plays, including *Coriolanus, Hamlet, Julius Caesar, King Lear, Macbeth, Measure for Measure, The Merchant of Venice, Othello, Romeo and Juliet, The Tempest, Troilus and Cressida, Twelfth Night,* and *The Winter's Tale.*

1366 ANDERSON, Ruth L. *Elizabethan Psychology and Shakespeare's Plays.* New York: Russell & Russell, 1966. See also Louise C. Turner FOREST, "A Caveat for Critics Against Invoking Elizabethan Psychology." *PMLA* 61 (1946):651–72.

1367 BLACK, Michael. "Character in Shakespeare." *CR* 17 (1974):110–19.

1368 CRANFILL, Thomas M. "Flesh's Thousand Natural Shocks in Shakespeare." *TSLL* 17 (1975):27–60. Concerns aging and frailty.

1369 CRANFILL, Thomas M. "Shakespeare's Old Heroes." *TSLL* 15 (1973):215–30.

1370 ELLIS, Roger. "The Fool in Shakespeare: A Study in Alienation." *CritQ* 10 (1968):245–68.

1371 EVANS, Gareth Lloyd. "Shakespeare's Fools: The Shadow and the Substance of Drama." In **1722.**

1372 FARNHAM, Willard. *The Shakespearean Grotesque: Its Genesis and Transformations.* Oxford: Clarendon, 1971. With particular focus on Falstaff, Hamlet, Thersites, Iago, and Caliban as grotesques.

1373 FRICKER, Robert. *Kontrast und Polarität in den Charakterbildern Shakespeares.* Bern: Francke, 1951.

1374 GOLDSMITH, Robert Hillis. *Wise Fools in Shakespeare.* East Lansing: Michigan State U.P., 1955.

1375 HOTSON, Leslie. *Shakespeare's Motley.* London: Hart-Davis, 1952. Rpt., New York: Haskell House, 1971.

1376 JOSEPHS, Lois. "Shakespeare and a Coleridgean Synthesis: Cleopatra, Leontes, and Falstaff." *SQ* 18 (1967):17–21.

1377 KIRSCHBAUM, Leo. *Character and Characterization in Shakespeare.* Detroit: Wayne State U.P., 1962.*

1378 KNIGHTS, L. C. "The Question of Character in Shakespeare." In **1138.***

1379 LANGBAUM, Robert. "Character Versus Action in Shakespeare." *SQ* 8 (1957): 57–69.

1380 LEWIS, Wyndham. *The Lion and the Fox: The Role of the Hero in the Plays of Shakespeare.* New York and London: Harper, 1927; Grant Richards, 1927; London: Methuen, 1951.

1381 MCNEAL, Thomas H. "Shakespeare's Cruel Queens." *HLQ* 22 (1958):41–50.

1382 MATHESON, Belle Seddon. *The Invented Personages in Shakespeare's Plays.* Philadelphia: U. of Pennsylvania, 1932.

1383 MILES, L. Wardlaw. "Shakespeare's Old Men." *ELH* 7 (1940):286–99.

1384 NUTTALL, A. D. "The Argument about Shakespeare's Characters." *CritQ* 7 (1965):107–19.

1385 ORNSTEIN, Robert. "Character and Reality in Shakespeare." In **1121.**

1386 PALMER, John. *Political and Comic Characters of Shakespeare.* London: Macmillan; New York: St. Martin's, 1962.* Two series of essays, originally published separately; see **1481** and **1708.**

1387 SCHELL, J. Stewart. "Shakspere's Gulls." *ShAB* 15 (1940):23–33. On Slender, Sir Andrew Aguecheek, Osric, Roderigo, Cloten, etc.

1388 SCHÜCKING, Levin L. *Character Problems in Shakespeare's Plays.* London: Harrap; New York: Holt, 1922. Rpt., New York: P. Smith, 1948. Orig. pub. in German, 1919.*

1389 SCOTT, W. I. D. *Shakespeare's Melancholics.* London: Mills & Boon, 1962. On Jaques, Hamlet, Antonio in *The Merchant of Venice,* Don John, Orsino, Timon, Leontes, etc.

1390 SPENCER, Theodore. "The Elizabethan Malcontent." In **1154.**

1391 STEWART, J. I. M. *Character and Motive in Shakespeare.* London and New York: Longmans, Green, 1949. Rpt., New York: Barnes & Noble, 1959.*

1392 STEWART, J. I. M. "Shakespeare's Men and Their Morals." In **1138.**

1393 STOCKTON, Eric W. "The Adulthood of Shakespeare's Heroines." In **1171.**

1394 STOLL, Elmer Edgar. *Shakespeare's Young Lovers.* See **1527.**

1395 URE, Peter. "Character and Role from Richard III to Hamlet." In **1269.**

1396 WELSFORD, Enid. *The Fool: His Social and Literary History.* London: Faber & Faber, 1935. Rpt., Gloucester, Mass.: P. Smith, 1966.*

1397 WHITEHOUSE, J. Howard. *The Boys of Shakespeare.* Birmingham: Cornish, 1953. On Arthur in *King John,* young Edward V in *Richard III,* etc.

1398 WILLEFORD, William. *The Fool and His Scepter: A Study in Clowns and Jesters and Their Audience.* Evanston, Ill.: Northwestern U.P.; London: Arnold, 1969. Includes a chapter each on *Hamlet* and *King Lear.*

Psychological Criticism

For psychologically-oriented analyses of separate plays and poems, see under the various individual works.

1399 ARONSON, Alex. *Psyche & Symbol in Shakespeare.* Bloomington and London: Indiana U.P., 1972.

1400 EDGAR, Irving I. *Shakespeare, Medicine, and Psychiatry: An Historical Study in Criticism and Interpretation.* New York: Philosophical Library, 1970.

1401 FABER, M. D., ed. *The Design Within: Psychoanalytic Approaches to Shakespeare.* New York: Science House, 1970.*

1402 FIEDLER, Leslie A. *The Stranger in Shakespeare.* New York: Stein & Day, 1972.

1403 HARDING, D. W. "Women's Fantasy of Manhood: A Shakespearian Theme." *SQ* 20 (1969):245–53.

1404 HOLLAND, Norman N. *Psychoanalysis and Shakespeare.* New York: McGraw-Hill, 1964. Rpt., New York: Octagon.*

1405 HOLLAND, Norman N. *The Shakespearean Imagination.* New York: Macmillan, 1964.*

1406 LUCAS, F. L. *Literature and Psychology.* London: Cassell, 1951; Ann Arbor: U. of Michigan P., 1957. Especially on *Hamlet, Macbeth, Othello,* and *King Lear.**

1407 MUIR, Kenneth. "Some Freudian Interpretations of Shakespeare." *PLPLS-LHS* 7 (1952):43–52.

1408 RAVICH, Robert A. "Shakespeare and Psychiatry." *L&P* 14 (1964):97–105.

Shakespeare's Thought: Religion, Philosophy, Nature and Science, the Supernatural

See also **107, 111, 119, 132, 166, 179, 215, 295, 298–99, 342–43, 1256, 1392, 1518, 1651, 1813, 1826, 1979, 2014, 2026, 2496, 2986, 3258, 3434–41,** and **3600.**

1409 ALLEN, Don Cameron. "Shakspere and the Doctrine of Cosmic Identities." *ShAB* 14 (1939):182–89.

1410 ARTHOS, John. "The Undiscovered Country." *CompD* 10 (1976):16–28.

1411 BARNET, Sylvan. "Some Limitations of a Christian Approach to Shakespeare." *ELH* 22 (1955):81–92. Rpt. in **1163** and **1887.***

1412 BATTENHOUSE, Roy W. *Shakespearean Tragedy: Its Art and Its Christian Premises.* See **1921.**

1413 BRYANT, J. A., Jr. *Hippolyta's View: Some Christian Aspects of Shakespeare's Plays.* Lexington: U. of Kentucky P., 1961.

1414 BUSH, Geoffrey. *Shakespeare and the Natural Condition.* Cambridge, Mass.: Harvard U.P., 1956.*

1415 COURSEN, Herbert R., Jr. *Christian Ritual and the World of Shakespeare's Tragedies.* See **1928.**

1416 CRAIG, Hardin. "A Cutpurse of the Empire: On Shakespeare's Cosmology." *A Tribute to George Coffin Taylor.* Ed. Arnold WILLIAMS. Chapel Hill: U. of North Carolina P., 1952.

1417 CRAIG, Hardin. "Shakespeare and the All-Inclusive Law of Nature." In **1142.**

1418 DAICHES, David. "Guilt and Justice in Shakespeare." *Literary Essays.* Edinburgh and London: Oliver & Boyd, 1956. 2nd impression, Chicago: U. of Chicago P., 1967.

1419 FERGUSSON, Francis. *Trope and Allegory: Themes Common to Dante and Shakespeare.* Athens: U. of Georgia P., 1977.

1420 FITCH, Robert E. *Shakespeare: The Perspective of Value.* Philadelphia: Westminster, 1969.

1421 FRYE, Roland Mushat. *Shakespeare and Christian Doctrine.* Princeton: Princeton U.P., 1963.* For a reply, see Edward M. WILSON, "Shakespeare and Christian Doctrine: Some Qualifications." *ShS* 23 (1970):79–89.

1422 HARBAGE, Alfred. *As They Liked It: A Study of Shakespeare's Moral Artistry.* New York: Macmillan, 1947. Rpt., New York: Harper, 1961; Gloucester, Mass.: P. Smith.*

1423 HARBAGE, Alfred. *Shakespeare and the Rival Traditions.* New York: Macmillan, 1952. Rpt., New York: Barnes & Noble, 1968; Bloomington: Indiana U.P., 1970.*

1424 HOBSON, Alan. *Full Circle: Shakespeare and Moral Development.* London: Chatto & Windus; New York: Barnes & Noble, 1972.

1425 HOROWITZ, David. *Shakespeare: An Existentialist View.* New York: Hill & Wang; London: Tavistock, 1965.

1426 HOWSE, Ernest Marshall. *Spiritual Values in Shakespeare.* Nashville: Abingdon, 1955; Toronto and New York: Abingdon, 1965.

1427 HUBLER, Edward. "Three Shakespearean Myths: Mutability, Plenitude, and Reputation." *EIE 1948* (1949):95–119.

1428 HUHNER, Max. "Shakspere's Conception of the Clergy." *ShAB* 11 (1936): 161–70.

1429 HUNTER, Robert Grams. *Shakespeare and the Mystery of God's Judgments.* Athens: U. of Georgia P., 1976. Focus on *Richard III, Hamlet, Othello, Macbeth,* and *King Lear.**

1430 KNIGHT, G. Wilson. *Shakespeare and Religion: Essays of Forty Years.* London: Routledge & K. Paul; New York: Barnes & Noble, 1967.

1431 KNOWLTON, Edgar C. "Nature and Shakespeare." *PMLA* 51 (1936):719–44.

1432 KUCKHOFF, Armin-Gerd. "Zufall und Notwendigkeit im Drama William Shakespeares." *SJW* 105 (1969):121–39.

1433 LEVIN, Richard. "On Fluellen's Figures, Christ Figures, and James Figures." *PMLA* 89 (1974):302–11. A caveat about allegorized readings of Shakespeare.*

1434 MENDL, R. W. S. *Revelation in Shakespeare: A Study of the Supernatural, Religious, and Spiritual Elements in His Art.* London: Calder, 1964.

1435 MERCHANT, W. Moelwyn. "Shakespeare's Theology." *REL* 5.4 (1964):72–88.

1436 MILWARD, Peter. *Shakespeare's Religious Background.* See **129.**

1437 NAIK, M. K. "Humanitarianism in Shakespeare." *SQ* 19 (1968):139–47.

1438 OHM, Karl. *Shakespeare und das Gewissen: Eine Studie über die Bedeutung des Gewissens bei Personen in Shakespeareas Dramen.* Frankfurt: Athenaion, 1975.

1439 PAOLUCCI, Anne. "Shakespeare and the Genius of the Absurd." *CompD* 7 (1973):231–46.

1440 PARKER, M. D. H. *The Slave of Life: A Study of Shakespeare and the Idea of Justice*. London: Chatto & Windus, 1955. Concerns ideas of damnation and salvation, nature and grace.

1441 RIBNER, Irving. "Shakespeare, Christianity, and the Problem of Belief." *CentR* 8 (1964):99–108.

1442 SEHRT, Ernst Thodor. *Vergebung und Gnade bei Shakespeare*. Stuttgart: Koehler, 1952.

1443 SOELLNER, Rolf. *Shakespeare's Patterns of Self-Knowledge*. Columbus: Ohio State U.P., 1972.*

1444 SPALDING, K. J. *The Philosophy of Shakespeare*. New York: Philosophical Library, 1953.

1445 STEVENSON, Robert. *Shakespeare's Religious Frontier*. The Hague: Nijhoff, 1958.

1446 VYVYAN, John. *The Shakespearean Ethic*. London: Chatto & Windus, 1959. Rpt., New York: Barnes & Noble.

1447 WATKINS, W. B. C. *Shakespeare and Spenser*. Princeton: Princeton U.P., 1950. A comparison in terms of poetic qualities and spiritual values.*

1448 WEST, Robert H. *Shakespeare and the Outer Mystery*. Lexington: U. of Kentucky P., 1968.*

1449 WICHT, Wolfgang. "Christliches in Shakespeares Dramen." *ZAA* 12 (1964): 350–74.

Shakespeare's Thought: Politics, Law, War, Honor

See also **215, 325, 339, 1506, 1793, 1802, 1807, 1832–33, 1872–73, 1959, 2167, 2341–52, 2932–42, 3285,** and **3442–49.**

1450 AKRIGG, G. P. V. "Shakespeare the King-Maker." In **1143.** Studies the importance of the ideal of kingship to Shakespeare's imagination.

1451 ARMSTRONG, William A. "The Elizabethan Conception of the Tyrant." *RES* 22 (1946):161–81.

1452 ARMSTRONG, William A. "The Influence of Seneca and Machiavelli on the Elizabethan Tyrant." *RES* 24 (1948):19–35.

1453 BEVINGTON, David. *Tudor Drama and Politics: A Critical Approach to Topical Meaning*. Cambridge, Mass.: Harvard U.P., 1968.

1454 BLOOM, Allan, with Harry V. JAFFA. *Shakespeare's Politics*. New York and London: Basic Books, 1964.*

1455 BROMLEY, John C. *The Shakespearean Kings*. Boulder: Colorado Associated U.P., 1971. On the history plays and *Julius Caesar, Hamlet, Macbeth,* and *King Lear*.

1456 CHARLTON, H. B. *Shakespeare, Politics and Politicians*. Oxford: Oxford U.P., 1929.

1457 CLARKSON, Paul S., and Clyde T. WARREN. *The Law of Property in Shakespeare and the Elizabethan Drama*. See **232.**

1458 COOPER, Duff. *Sergeant Shakespeare.* London: Hart-Davis, 1949; New York: Viking, 1950. On Shakespeare and the military life.

1459 COUNCIL, Norman. *When Honour's at the Stake: Ideas of Honour in Shakespeare's Plays.* London: Allen & Unwin; New York: Barnes & Noble, 1973.

1460 CROSBY, Ernest H. "Shakespeare and the Working Classes." *Tolstoy on Shakespeare.* Trans. V. TCHERTKOFF, I. F. M. and E. A. Christchurch: The Free Age Press; London: Everett, n.d.*

1461 EDWARDS, Philip. "Person and Office in Shakespeare's Plays." *PBA* 56 (1972 for 1970):93–109.

1462 ELLIS-FERMOR, Una. "Shakespeare's Political Plays." *The Frontiers of Drama.* 2nd ed., London: Methuen, 1946.

1463 EURE, John D. "Shakespeare and the Legal Process: Four Essays." *Virginia Law Review* 61 (1975):390–433.

1464 FABER, M. D. "Freud and Shakespeare's Mobs." *L&P* 15 (1965):238–55.

1465 FARNAM, Henry W. *Shakespeare's Economics.* New Haven: Yale U.P.; London: Oxford U.P., 1931.

1466 FINKELSTEIN, Sidney. *Who Needs Shakespeare?* New York: International, 1973. A survey from a political point of view.

1467 FRIESNER, Donald Neil. "William Shakespeare, Conservative." *SQ* 20 (1969): 165–78.

1468 FUJITA, Minoru. "The Concept of the Royal in Shakespeare." In **1159.**

1469 JORGENSEN, Paul A. "A Formative Shakespearean Legacy: Elizabethan Views of God, Fortune, and War." *PMLA* 90 (1975):222–33.

1470 JORGENSEN, Paul A. *Shakespeare's Military World.* Berkeley and Los Angeles: U. of California P., 1956.*

1471 KEETON, George W. *Shakespeare and His Legal Problems.* London: A. & C. Black, 1930.

1472 KEETON, George W. *Shakespeare's Legal and Political Background.* London: Pitman, 1967.*

1473 KNIGHT, G. Wilson. *This Sceptred Isle: A Study of Shakespeare's Kings.* Oxford: Blackwell, 1940. Rpt. in **1227.**

1474 KNIGHT, W. Nicholas. *Shakespeare's Hidden Life: Shakespeare at the Law, 1585–1595.* New York: Mason & Lipscomb, 1973.

1475 KNIGHTS, L. C. *Poetry, Politics, and the English Tradition.* London: Chatto & Windus, 1954. Rpt. in **1229.***

1476 KNIGHTS, L. C. "Shakespeare's Politics: With Some Reflections on the Nature of Tradition." *PBA* 43 (1958 for 1957):115–32. Rpt. in **1229.***

1477 LYMAN, Stanford M., and Marvin B. SCOTT. *The Drama of Social Reality.* New York: Oxford U.P., 1975. On Shakespeare's political and social views, and on the function of theater in society.

1478 MCCANLES, Michael. "The Dialectic of Right and Power in Eight Plays of Shakespeare, 1595–1604." *Dialectical Criticism and Renaissance Literature.* Berkeley and Los Angeles: U. of California P., 1975. Discusses the second tetralogy of history plays together with *Julius Caesar, Troilus and Cressida, Hamlet,* and *Measure for Measure.*

1479 MARRIOTT, J. A. R. "Shakespeare and Politics." *Cornhill* 63 (1927):678–90.

1480 MUIR, Kenneth. "Shakespeare and Politics." In **1148.**

1481 PALMER, John. *Political Characters of Shakespeare.* London: Macmillan, 1945. Rpt. in **1386.***

1482 PATRIDES, C. A. " 'The Beast with Many Heads': Renaissance Views on the Multitude." *SQ* 16 (1965):241–46.

1483 PHILLIPS, James Emerson, Jr. *The State in Shakespeare's Greek and Roman Plays.* See **2045.***

1484 PHILLIPS, O. Hood. *Shakespeare and the Lawyers.* London: Methuen; New York: Barnes & Noble, 1972.

1485 RABKIN, Norman. "The Polity." In **1243.***

1486 RICHMOND, Hugh M. *Shakespeare's Political Plays.* New York: Random House, 1967.***

1487 SCHNEIDER, Reinhold. "Das Bild der Herrschaft in Shakespeares Drama." *SJ* 93 (1957):9–37.

1488 SIEGEL, Paul N. "Shakespeare and the Neo-Chivalric Cult of Honor." *CentR* 8 (1964):39–70.

1489 SMIRNOV, A. A. *Shakespeare: A Marxist Interpretation.* Trans. Sonia VOLO-CHOVA, et al. New York: Critics Group, 1936.

1490 SPEAIGHT, Robert. *Shakespeare and Politics.* London: distributed by Simpkin Marshall for the Royal Society of Literature, 1941.

1491 SPENCER, T. J. B. "Social Assent and Dissent in Shakespeare's Plays." *RNL* 3.2 (1972):20–38.

1492 STEWART, J. I. M. "Shakespeare's Lofty Scene." *PBA* 57 (1973 for 1971): 181–95.

1493 STIRLING, Brents. *The Populace in Shakespeare.* New York: Columbia U.P.; London: Oxford U.P., 1949. Rpt., New York: AMS.***

1494 TALBERT, Ernest William. *The Problem of Order: Elizabethan Political Commonplaces and an Example of Shakespeare's Art.* Chapel Hill: U. of North Carolina P., 1962.***

1495 THALER, Alwin. *Shakespeare and Democracy.* Knoxville: U. of Tennessee P., 1941.

1496 TISON, John L., Jr. "Shakespeare's *Consolatio* for Exile." *MLQ* 21 (1960): 142–57.

1497 TOLIVER, Harold E. "Shakespeare's Kingship: Institution and Dramatic Form." In **1125.**

1498 TUPPER, Frederick, Jr. "The Shaksperean Mob." *PMLA* 27 (1912):486–523.

1499 WATSON, Curtis Brown. *Shakespeare and the Renaissance Concept of Honor.* Princeton: Princeton U.P., 1960.***

1500 WEIMANN, Robert. "The Soul of the Age: Towards a Historical Approach to Shakespeare." In **1148.**

1501 WEST, Rebecca. *The Court and the Castle: The Interaction of Political and Religious Ideas.* See **2496.**

1502 WHITE, Howard B. *Copp'd Hills Towards Heaven: Shakespeare and the Classical Polity.* The Hague: Nijhoff, 1970.

1503 WOOD, Frederick T. "Shakespeare and the Plebs." *E&S* 18 (1933 for 1932): 53–73.

1504 ZEEVELD, W. Gordon. *The Temper of Shakespeare's Thought.* New Haven and London: Yale U.P., 1974.*

Shakespeare on History and the Nature of Time

See also **1337–38, 1341, 1812, 1861, 1874, 1967, 2731, 2900, 3067, 3724, 3886,** and **3995.**

1505 BORINSKI, Ludwig. "Shakespeare's Conception of History." *BFLS* 63.8 (1965): 835–54.

1506 BULLOUGH, Geoffrey. "The Uses of History." In **1170.**

1507 CLEMEN, Wolfgang. "Past and Future in Shakespeare's Drama." *PBA* 52 (1967 for 1966):231–52. Rpt. in **1193.**

1508 DRIVER, Tom F. *The Sense of History in Greek and Shakespearean Drama.* New York: Columbia U.P., 1960.*

1509 GEYL, Pieter. "Shakespeare as a Historian." *Encounters in History.* Cleveland: Meridian, 1962.

1510 IWASAKI, Soji. *The Sword and the Word: Shakespeare's Tragic Sense of Time.* Tokyo: Shinozaki Shorin, 1973.

1511 LEECH, Clifford. "Shakespeare and the Idea of the Future." *UTQ* 35 (1966): 213–28.

1512 MAGUIN, François. "The Breaking of Time: *Richard II, Hamlet, King Lear, Macbeth* (The Hero's Stand In and Against Time)." *CahiersE* 7 (1975):25–41.

1513 MORTON, A. L. "Shakespeare's Historical Outlook." *SJW* 100–01 (1964–65): 208–26. Also in *ZAA* 12 (1964):229–43.

1514 QUINONES, Ricardo J. *The Renaissance Discovery of Time.* See **334.***

1515 SCHANZER, Ernest. "Shakespeare and the Doctrine of the Unity of Time." *ShS* 28 (1975):57–61. Argues that Shakespeare deliberately contradicts the classical unity as a fatuous tyranny.

1516 SYPHER, Wylie. *The Ethic of Time: Structures of Experience in Shakespeare.* New York: Seabury, 1976. Focuses on the way Shakespeare's characters perceive time.

1517 TOLIVER, Harold E. "Shakespeare and the Abyss of Time." *JEGP* 64 (1965): 234–54.

1518 TURNER, Frederick. *Shakespeare and the Nature of Time: Moral and Philosophical Themes in Some Plays and Poems of William Shakespeare.* Oxford: Clarendon; New York: Oxford U.P., 1971.*

Shakespeare on Women, Love, and Marriage

See also **226, 229, 240, 248, 1589, 1594, 1668, 1682, 1727, 1896,** and **2056–61.**

1519 DUSINBERRE, Juliet. *Shakespeare and the Nature of Women.* London: Macmillan; New York: Barnes & Noble, 1975.*

1520 FERGUSSON, Francis. "Romantic Love in Dante and Shakespeare." *SR* 83 (1975):253–66.

1521 HEILBRUN, Carolyn G. *Toward a Recognition of Androgyny.* New York: Knopf, 1973.*

1522 HERFORD, C. H. *Shakespeare's Treatment of Love and Marriage and Other Essays.* London: T. Fisher Unwin, 1921.

1523 HOY, Cyrus. "Shakespeare, Sidney, and Marlowe: The Metamorphoses of Love." *VQR* 51 (1975):448–58.

1524 LYONS, Charles R. *Shakespeare and the Ambiguity of Love's Triumph.* The Hague and Paris: Mouton, 1971.

1525 MEADER, William G. *Courtship in Shakespeare: Its Relation to the Tradition of Courtly Love.* New York: King's Crown, 1954. Rpt., New York: Octagon.

1526 PEARSON, Lu Emily. *Elizabethan Love Conventions.* Berkeley: U. of California P., 1933.

1527 STOLL, Elmer Edgar. *Shakespeare's Young Lovers.* London: Oxford U.P., 1937. Rpt., New York: AMS.

1528 VYVYAN, John. *Shakespeare and Platonic Beauty.* London: Chatto & Windus; New York: Barnes & Noble, 1961.

Shakespeare's Lore: Natural History, Folklore, Medicine, Sports and Pastimes, Heraldry, the Sea

See also **66, 215, 332,** and **1400.**

1529 COOK, Phyllis. "William Shakspere, Botanist." *ShAB* 15 (1940):149–65.

1530 DENT, Alan. *World of Shakespeare: Animals and Monsters.* Reading: Osprey, 1972; New York: Taplinger, 1973. Other volumes in this series include *Plants* (1971, 1973), *Sports and Pastimes* (1973, 1974), *Technology,* and *Magic and Superstition.**

1531 FALCONER, Alexander Frederick. *Shakespeare and the Sea.* London: Constable, 1964.

1532 HENN, T. R. *The Living Image; Shakespearean Essays.* London: Methuen; New York: Barnes & Noble, 1972. Studies in hunting, angling, archery, the army, etc.*

1533 MADDEN, D. H. *The Diary of Master William Silence: A Study of Shakespeare and of Elizabethan Sport.* London: Longmans, Green, 1897. Rpt., Westport, Conn.: Greenwood, 1969.*

1534 SCHULTZ, John Howard. "A Glossary of Shakespeare's Hawking Language." *UTSE* 18 (1938):194–205.

1535 SCOTT-GILES, C. W. *Shakespeare's Heraldry.* London: Dent, 1950. Rpt., New York: AMS, 1971.

1536 SEAGER, H. W. *Natural History in Shakespeare's Time.* London: Elliot Stock, 1896.

1537 SIMPSON, R. R. *Shakespeare and Medicine.* Edinburgh and London: Livingstone, 1959.

1538 SMITH, Charles G. *Shakespeare's Proverb Lore.* Cambridge, Mass.: Harvard U.P., 1963.

1539 THISELTON DYER, T. F. *Folk-Lore of Shakespeare.* London: Griffith & Farran; New York: Dutton, 1883. Rpt., New York: Dover, 1966.

Shakespeare and the Arts: Music, Dance, Painting, Sculpture, Architecture

See also **215, 1746, 1754, 1765, 2020, 2762, 3718, 4096,** and **4477.**

1540 ALLENTUCK, Marcia. "Sir Thomas Hanmer Instructs Francis Hayman: An Editor's Notes to His Illustrator (1744)." *SQ* 27 (1976):288–315.

1541 AUDEN, W. H. "Music in Shakespeare: Its Dramatic Use in His Plays." *Encounter* 9.6 (1957):31–44. Rpt. in **1179.**

1542 BOUSTED, Alan. *Music to Shakespeare: A Practical Catalogue of Current Incidental Music, Song Settings, and Other Related Music.* London and New York: Oxford U.P., 1964.

1543 BRISSENDEN, Alan. "Shakespeare and Dance." In **1145** (1972 for 1968–69).

1544 CLEMEN, Wolfgang. "Shakespeare und die Musik." *SJH* (1966):30–48.

1545 COWLING, G. H. *Music on the Shakespearian Stage.* Cambridge: Cambridge U.P., 1913.

1546 DEAN, Winton. "Shakespeare in the Opera House." *ShS* 18 (1965):75–93.

1547 DICKINSON, A. E. F. "Shakespeare in Music." *DUJ* 56, n.s. 25 (1964):113–22.

1548 ELSON, Louis C. *Shakespeare in Music: A Collection of the Chief Musical Allusions in the Plays of Shakespeare.* 1st ed., 1900. Rpt., Freeport, N.Y.: Books for Libraries P., 1970.

1549 FAIRCHILD, Arthur H. R. *Shakespeare and the Arts of Design—Architecture, Sculpture, and Painting.* Columbia: U. of Missouri P., 1937.

1550 GREENFIELD, Thelma N. "Nonvocal Music: Added Dimension in Five Shakespeare Plays." In **1156.**

1551 HARTNOLL, Phyllis, ed. *Shakespeare in Music.* London: Macmillan; New York: St Martin's, 1964.

1552 HECKSCHER, William S. "Shakespeare in His Relationship to the Visual Arts: A Study in Paradox." *RORD* 13–14 (1970–71):5–71.

1553 HOFFMAN, D. S. "Some Shakespearian Music, 1660–1900." *ShS* 18 (1965): 94–101.

1554 INGRAM, R. W. "Music as Structural Element in Shakespeare." In **1151.**

1555 INGRAM, R. W. " 'The True Concord of Well-Tuned Sounds': Shakespeare and Music." *RNL* 3.2 (1972):138–62.

1556 LINGS, Martin. *Shakespeare in the Light of Sacred Art.* New York: Humanities P., 1966.

1557 LONG, John H. *Shakespeare's Use of Music: A Study of the Music and Its Performance in the Original Production of Seven Comedies.* Gainesville: U. of Florida P., 1955. *The Final Comedies,* 1961. *The Histories and Tragedies,* 1971.*

1558 MANIFOLD, J. S. *The Music in English Drama: From Shakespeare to Purcell.* London: Rockliff, 1956.

1559 MERCHANT, W. Moelwyn. *Shakespeare and the Artist.* London: Oxford U.P., 1959.*

1560 NAYLOR, Edward W. *Shakespeare and Music.* Rev. ed., London: Dent; New York: Dutton, 1931. Rpt., New York: Da Capo and Blom, 1965. Rpt. of first ed. of 1896, New York: AMS.

1561 NOBLE, Richmond. *Shakespeare's Use of Song, with the Text of the Principal Songs.* London: Oxford U.P., 1923.

1562 SALAMAN, Malcolm, and Charles HOLME, eds. *Shakespeare in Pictorial Art.* London: The Studio, 1916.

1563 SENG, Peter J. *The Vocal Songs in the Plays of Shakespeare: A Critical History.* Cambridge, Mass.: Harvard U.P.; London: Oxford U.P., 1967.*

1564 SORRELL, Walter. "Shakespeare and the Dance." *SQ* 8 (1957):367–84.

1565 STERNFELD, F. W. *Music in Shakespearean Tragedy.* London: Routledge & K. Paul; New York: Dover, 1963.*

1566 STERNFELD, F. W. "Shakespeare and Music." In **55.**

1567 STERNFELD, F. W. "Shakespeare's Use of Popular Song." In **1131.**

1568 STERNFELD, F. W. "Twentieth-Century Studies in Shakespeare's Songs, Sonnets, and Poems: 1. Songs and Music." *ShS* 15 (1962):1–10.

1569 WOERMANN, Karl. *Shakespeare und die Bildenden Künste.* Leipzig: S. Hirzel, 1930.

Studies in the Chronology and Development of Shakespeare's Art

General Studies

See also **442** and **1199.**

1570 BARROLL, J. Leeds. "The Chronology of Shakespeare's Jacobean Plays and the Dating of *Antony and Cleopatra.*" In **1167**.

1571 EVERITT, Ephraim B. *The Young Shakespeare: Studies in Documentary Evidence.* Anglistica, 2. Copenhagen: Rosenkilde & Bagger, 1954.

1572 FEUILLERAT, Albert. *The Composition of Shakespeare's Plays: Authorship, Chronology.* New Haven: Yale U.P., 1953.

1573 GRANVILLE-BARKER, Harley. "From *Henry V* to *Hamlet.*" *PBA* 11 (1926 for 1924–25):283–309.*

1574 LEECH, Clifford. "Shakespeare, Elizabethan and Jacobean." *QQ* 72 (1965):5–25.

1575 MCMANAWAY, James G. "Recent Studies in Shakespeare's Chronology." *ShS* 3 (1950):22–33.

1576 MATCHETT, William H. "Shylock, Iago, and *Sir Thomas More:* With Some Further Discussion of Shakespeare's Imagination." *PMLA* 92 (1977):217–30.

1577 WENTERSDORF, Karl P. "Shakespearean Chronology and the Metrical Tests." In **1137**.

The Early Writings

For genre studies of the early Shakespeare, see "The Early Comedies, c.1589–c.1595," **1712–18**; "The First Historical Tetralogy, *Henry VI–Richard III,*" **1850–62**; and "The Early Tragedies," **2005–10**.

See also **151** and **565**.

1578 ARTHOS, John. *Shakespeare: The Early Writings.* London: Bowes & Bowes; Totowa, N.J.: Rowman & Littlefield, 1972.

1579 BALDWIN, T. W. *William Shakspere's Five-Act Structure.* Urbana: U. of Illinois P., 1947. Concerned primarily with structure in the early plays.

1580 BRADBROOK, M. C. *Shakespeare and Elizabethan Poetry: A Study of His Earlier Work in Relation to the Poetry of the Time.* London: Chatto & Windus, 1951.

1581 BROOKS, Harold F. "Marlowe and Early Shakespeare." See **103**.

1582 BROWN, John Russell, and Bernard HARRIS, gen eds. *Early Shakespeare.* Stratford-upon-Avon Studies 3. London: Arnold, 1961; New York: Schocken, 1966. A collection of essays.*

1583 BURELBACH, Frederick M., Jr. "Character Disintegration in the Early Shakespeare." *ShStud* 6 (1967–68):62–74.

1584 CUTTS, John P. *The Shattered Glass: A Dramatic Pattern in Shakespeare's Early Plays.* Detroit: Wayne State U.P., 1968.

1585 DRAPER, John W. *Stratford to Dogberry: Studies in Shakespeare's Earlier Plays.* Pittsburgh: U. of Pittsburgh P., 1961.

1586 HAMILTON, A. C. *The Early Shakespeare.* San Marino, Calif.: Huntington Library, 1967.*

1587 ISAACS, J. "Shakespeare's Earliest Years in the Theatre." *PBA* 39 (1954 for 1953):119–38.

1588 LEECH, Clifford. "The Two-Part Play: Marlowe and the Early Shakespeare." *SJ* 94 (1958):90–106.

1589 MARCOTTE, Paul J. *Priapus Unbound: Shakespeare's Concept of Love Inferred from Six Early Works.* Ottawa: U. of Ottawa P., 1971.

1590 MINCOFF, Marco. "The Chronology of Shakespeare's Early Works." *ZAA* 12 (1964):173–82. Also in *SJW* 100–01 (1964–65):253–65.

1591 PRICE, Hereward T. "Shakespeare and His Young Contemporaries." *PQ* 41 (1962):37–57. Also in **1174.**

1592 TALBERT, Ernest William. *Elizabethan Drama and Shakespeare's Early Plays.* Chapel Hill: U. of North Carolina P., 1963.*

1593 TURNER, Robert Y. *Shakespeare's Apprenticeship.* Chicago: U. of Chicago P., 1974.*

1594 VYVYAN, John. *Shakespeare and the Rose of Love: A Study of the Early Plays in Relation to the Medieval Philosophy of Love.* London: Chatto & Windus; New York: Barnes & Noble, 1960.

1595 WEISS, Theodore. *The Breath of Clowns and Kings: Shakespeare's Early Comedies and Histories.* London: Chatto & Windus; New York: Atheneum, 1971.*

1596 WILLCOCK, Gladys D. "Language and Poetry in Shakespeare's Early Plays." *PBA* 40 (1955 for 1954):103–17.

1597 WILSON, F. P. *Marlowe and the Early Shakespeare.* See **155.***

The Late Plays

For studies dealing chiefly with Shakespeare's late romances, see below under The Comedies: The Late Romances (**1740–77**). The works listed here deal with Shakespeare's late tragedies and with his late history play, *Henry VIII,* as well as with the romances.

See also **736, 1762, 2872,** and **4115.**

1598 ARMSTRONG, John. *The Paradise Myth.* London: Oxford U.P., 1969. Deals specifically with *Antony and Cleopatra, The Winter's Tale,* and *The Tempest.*

1599 BROWN, John Russell, and Bernard HARRIS, eds. *Later Shakespeare.* Stratford-upon-Avon Studies 8. London: Arnold, 1966; New York: St. Martin's, 1967. A collection of essays.*

1600 DANBY, John F. *Poets on Fortune's Hill: Studies in Sidney, Shakespeare, Beaumont and Fletcher.* London: Faber & Faber, 1952. Rpt., Port Washington, N.Y.: Kennikat, 1966. Rpt. with the title *Elizabethan and Jacobean Poets.* London: Faber & Faber, 1964.*

1601 EGAN, Robert. *Drama within Drama: Shakespeare's Sense of His Art in "King Lear," "The Winter's Tale," and "The Tempest."* New York and London: Columbia U.P., 1975.

1602 FOAKES, R. A. *Shakespeare, The Dark Comedies to the Last Plays: From Satire to Celebration.* London: Routledge & K. Paul; Charlottesville: U.P. of Virginia, 1971.*

1603 GAJDUSEK, R. E. "Death, Incest, and the Triple Bond in the Later Plays of Shakespeare." *AI* 31 (1974):109–58.

1604 JAMES, D. G. "The Failure of the Ballad-Makers." *Scepticism and Poetry.* London: Allen & Unwin, 1937. Argues that Shakespeare failed in his tragedies to come to terms with life as a whole, and so resorted in his late romances to the myth of finding what is lost.*

1605 KNIGHT, G. Wilson. *The Crown of Life: Essays in Interpretation of Shakespeare's Final Plays.* London: Oxford U.P., 1947. 2nd ed., London: Methuen, 1948. Rpt., 1961.*

1606 LEECH, Clifford. "The Structure of the Last Plays." *ShS* 11 (1958):19–30.

1607 MUIR, Kenneth. "Theophanies in the Last Plays." In **1613.**

1608 OPPEL, Horst. *Shakespeares Tragödien und Romanzen: Kontinuität oder Umbruch?* Wiesbaden: Akademie der Wissenschaften und der Literatur in Mainz, in Kommission bei Franz Steiner, 1954.

1609 OPPEL, Horst. *Der Späte Shakespeare.* Hamburg: Ellermann, 1949.

1610 RABKIN, Norman. "The Great Globe Itself." In **1243.***

1611 ROBERTSON, D. A., Jr., ed. "Myth in the Later Plays of Shakespeare." *EIE 1948* (1949):29–119. Four essays by various authors.

1612 STRACHEY, Lytton. "Shakespeare's Final Period." *Books and Characters.* London: Chatto & Windus; New York: Harcourt, Brace, 1922.

1613 TOBIAS, Richard C., and Paul G. ZOLBROD, eds. *Shakespeare's Late Plays: Essays in Honor of Charles Crow.* Athens: Ohio U.P., 1974.*

1614 WEINSTOCK, Horst. "Loyal Service in Shakespeare's Mature Plays." *SN* 43 (1971):446–73.

1615 YATES, Frances A. *Shakespeare's Last Plays: A New Approach.* London: Routledge & K. Paul, 1975.

Studies in Genre

Essays in Definition of Genre

See also **1573** and **1608.**

1616 COLIE, Rosalie L. *The Resources of Kind: Genre-Theory in the Renaissance.* Ed. Barbara K. LEWALSKI. Berkeley: U. of California P., 1973.

1617 DORAN, Madeleine. *Endeavors of Art: A Study of Form in Elizabethan Drama.* Madison: U. of Wisconsin P., 1954.*

1618 FRYE, Northrop. *Anatomy of Criticism.* Princeton: Princeton U.P., 1957. Rpt., New York: Atheneum, 1968.*

1619 HEILMAN, Robert B. *Tragedy and Melodrama: Versions of Experience.* Seattle: U. of Washington P., 1968.

1620 HOY, Cyrus. *The Hyacinth Room: An Investigation into the Nature of Comedy, Tragedy, and Tragicomedy.* New York: Knopf; London: Chatto & Windus, 1964.*

1621 LEECH, Clifford. "Shakespeare's Greeks." In **1145** (1964 for 1963). Concerns the problem of classifying Shakespeare's plays with Greek or Hellenistic setting.

1622 LEECH, Clifford. "Shakespeare's Tragic Fiction."*PBA* 59 (1975 for 1973):159–74. Concerns the interrelationship of tragedy and the history play.

1623 WAITH, Eugene M. *Ideas of Greatness: Heroic Drama in England.* New York: Barnes & Noble; London: Routledge & K. Paul, 1971. Includes discussion of *Henry V, Antony and Cleopatra, Coriolanus, Cymbeline, Hamlet, Henry IV,* etc.*

The Comedies

General Studies; Comic Theory

See also **507, 509, 1520, 1522, 1524–25, 1557, 1719–39, 2759, 3488,** and **4399.**

1624 BERRY, Ralph. "Shakespearean Comedy and Northrop Frye." *EIC* 22 (1972): 33–40.

1625 BRADBROOK, M. C. *The Growth and Structure of Elizabethan Comedy.* London: Chatto & Windus, 1955. Rev. ed., 1973.*

1626 BROWN, Arthur. "Shakespeare's Treatment of Comedy." In **1170.**

1627 BROWN, John Russell. "The Interpretation of Shakespeare's Comedies: 1900–1953." *ShS* 8 (1955):1–13.

1628 BROWN, John Russell. *Shakespeare and His Comedies.* London: Methuen, 1957. 2nd ed., enl., 1962.*

1629 CECIL, David. "Shakespearean Comedy." *The Fine Art of Reading, and Other Literary Studies.* London: Constable; New York: Bobbs-Merrill, 1957. Rpt. in **1731.**

1630 CHAMPION, Larry S. *The Evolution of Shakespeare's Comedy: A Study in Dramatic Perspective.* Cambridge, Mass.: Harvard U.P., 1970.

1631 CHARLTON, H. B. *Shakespearian Comedy.* London: Methuen, 1938. Rpt., London: Methuen; New York: Barnes & Noble, 1966.*

1632 COGHILL, Nevill. "The Basis of Shakespearian Comedy: A Study in Medieval Affinities." *E&S,* n.s. 3 (1950):1–28. Rpt. in **1061.**

1633 COPE, Jackson I. *The Theater and the Dream: From Metaphor to Form in Renaissance Drama.* Baltimore: The Johns Hopkins U.P., 1973.*

1634 CRANE, Milton. "Shakespeare's Comedies and the Critics." *SQ* 15.2 (1964): 67–73. Also in **1153.**

1635 DAVID, Richard. "The Comedies." In **1140.**

1636 DESAI, Chintamani N. *Shakespearean Comedy.* Indore City: published by the author, 1952. Rpt., New York: AMS, 1975.

1637 EVANS, Bertrand. *Shakespeare's Comedies.* Oxford: Clarendon, 1960.*

1638 FARNHAM, Willard. "The Mediaeval Comic Spirit in the English Renaissance." In **1154.**

1639 FELDMAN, Sylvia D. *The Morality-Patterned Comedy of the Renaissance.* The Hague: Mouton, 1970.

1640 FRYE, Northrop. "The Argument of Comedy." *EIE 1948* (1949):58–73. Rpt. in **1125, 1132,** and **1656.***

1641 FRYE, Northrop. "Comic Myth in Shakespeare." *PTRSC,* 3rd. ser. 46.2 (1952): 47–58. Rpt. in **1731.***

1642 FRYE, Northrop. *A Natural Perspective: The Development of Shakespearean Comedy and Romance.* New York and London: Columbia U.P., 1965.*

1643 FRYE, Northrop. "Old and New Comedy." *ShS* 22 (1969):1–5.

1644 FRYE, Northrop. "The Structure and Spirit of Comedy." In **1145** (1965 for 1964).

1645 GESNER, Carol. *Shakespeare and the Greek Romance: A Study of Origins.* Lexington: U. of Kentucky P., 1970.*

1646 GORDON, George. *Shakespearian Comedy and Other Studies.* Ed. E. K. CHAMBERS. London: Oxford U.P., 1944.

1647 HASSEL, R. Chris. "Shakespeare's Comic Epilogues: Invitations to Festive Communion." *SJH* (1970):160–69.

1648 HAWKINS, Sherman H. "The Two Worlds of Shakespearean Comedy." *ShakS* 3 (1968 for 1967):62–80.*

1649 HERRICK, Marvin T. *Comic Theory in the Sixteenth Century.* Urbana: U. of Illinois P., 1950. Concerns comic types such as senex and parasite.

1650 HUBLER, Edward. "The Range of Shakespeare's Comedy." *SQ* 15.2 (1964): 55–66. Also in **1153.**

1651 HUNTER, Robert Grams. *Shakespeare and the Comedy of Forgiveness.* New York and London: Columbia U.P., 1965.*

1652 KANTAK, V. Y. "An Approach to Shakespearian Comedy." *ShS* 22 (1969): 7–14.

1653 KAUL, A. N. *The Action of English Comedy: Studies in the Encounter of Abstraction and Experience from Shakespeare to Shaw.* New Haven and London: Yale U.P., 1970.

1654 LASCELLES, Mary. "Shakespeare's Comic Insight." *PBA* 48 (1963 for 1962): 171–86.

1655 LEIMBERG, Inge. "Shakespeares Komödien und Sidney 'Goldene Welt.' " *SJH* (1969):174–97.

1656 LERNER, Laurence, ed. *Shakespeare's Comedies: An Anthology of Modern Criticism.* Harmondsworth and Baltimore: Penguin, 1967.

1657 LOW, J. T. *Shakespeare's Folio Comedies.* Norwood, Pa.: Norwood, 1974.

1658 MINCOFF, Marco. "Shakespeare's Comedies and the Five-Act Structure." *BFLS* 63.8 (1965):919–34.

1659 MUIR, Kenneth. "Didacticism in Shakespearean Comedy: Renaissance Theory and Practice." *RNL* 3.2 (1972):39–53.

1660 MUIR, Kenneth, ed. *Shakespeare, The Comedies: A Collection of Critical Essays.* Englewood Cliffs, N.J.: Prentice-Hall, 1965.*

1661 MURRAY, Peter B. " 'Much Virtue in If' in Shakespeare's Comedies." *LC* 32 (1966):31–39.

1662 OLSON, Elder. *The Theory of Comedy.* Bloomington: Indiana U.P., 1968.

1663 ORNSTEIN, Robert. "Shakespearian and Jonsonian Comedy." *ShS* 22 (1969): 43–46.

1664 OYAMA, Toshiko. "Form and Rhetoric in Shakespearean Comedy." *ShStud* 11 (1975 for 1972–73):1–27.

1665 PARROTT, Thomas Marc. *Shakespearean Comedy.* New York: Oxford U.P., 1949.

1666 PETTET, E. C. *Shakespeare and the Romance Tradition.* London and New York: Staples, 1949. Rpt., London: Methuen, 1970.*

1667 PHIALAS, Peter G. "Comic Truth in Shakespeare and Jonson." *SAQ* 62 (1963): 78–91.

1668 RICHMOND, Hugh M. *Shakespeare's Sexual Comedy: A Mirror for Lovers.* Indianapolis: Bobbs-Merrill, 1971.

1669 ROBERTS, Jeanne Addison. "American Criticism of Shakespeare's Comedies." *ShakS* 9 (1976):1–10.

1670 ROSSITER, A. P. " 'Comic Relief.' " In **1245.**

1671 SALINGAR, Leo. *Shakespeare and the Traditions of Comedy.* Cambridge: Cambridge U.P., 1974.*

1672 SCHULZ, Volker. *Studien zum Komischen in Shakespeares Komödien.* Darmstadt: Wissenschaftliche Buchgesellschaft, 1971.

1673 SEHRT, Ernst Thodor. *Wandlungen der Shakespeareschen Komödie.* Göttingen: Vandenhoeck & Ruprecht, 1961.

1674 SEN GUPTA, S. C. *Shakespearian Comedy.* London: Oxford U.P., 1950. Rpt., 1967.

1675 SHAABER, M. A. "The Comic View of Life in Shakespeare's Comedies." In **1120.**

1676 *Shakespeare Studies* 8 (1955) and 22 (1969). Largely devoted to the comedies.

1677 SIDER, John Wm. "The Serious Elements of Shakespeare's Comedies." *SQ* 24 (1973):1–11.

1678 SIEGEL, Paul N. "Shakespearean Comedy and the Elizabethan Compromise." In **1249.**

1679 SMITH, J. Percy. "Imaginary Forces and the Ways of Comedy." In **1145** (1972 for 1968–69).

1680 SMITH, James. *Shakespearian and Other Essays.* Cambridge: Cambridge U.P., 1974. Focuses on the comedies.

1681 SPRAGUE, Arthur Colby. "The Moments of Seriousness in Shakespearian Comedy." *SJH* (1965):240–47.

1682 STEVENSON, David Lloyd. *The Love-Game Comedy.* New York: Columbia U.P., 1946. Rpt., New York: AMS, 1966. Chiefly on *Love's Labour's Lost, As You Like It, The Taming of the Shrew, Much Ado About Nothing,* and *Troilus and Cressida.*

1683 STYAN, J. L. *The Dark Comedy: The Development of Modern Comic Tragedy.* Cambridge: Cambridge U.P., 1962. 2nd ed., 1968.

1684 STYAN, J. L. "The Delicate Balance: Audience Ambivalence in the Comedy of Shakespeare and Chekhov." *Costerus* 2 (1972):159–84.

1685 SWINDEN, Patrick. *An Introduction to Shakespeare's Comedies.* London: Macmillan; New York: Barnes & Noble, 1973.

1686 TILLYARD, E. M. W. *The Nature of Comedy and Shakespeare.* London: Oxford U.P., 1958. Rpt. in **1266.**

1687 VELIE, Alan R. *Shakespeare's Repentance Plays: The Search for an Adequate Form.* Rutherford, N.J.: Fairleigh Dickinson U.P., 1972. Chiefly on *Measure for Measure, Pericles, Cymbeline, The Winter's Tale,* and *The Tempest.*

1688 VYVYAN, John. *Shakespeare and Platonic Beauty.* See **1528.**

1689 WELD, John. *Meaning in Comedy: Studies in Elizabethan Romantic Comedy.* Albany: State U. of New York P., 1975. Deals in part with *The Comedy of Errors, A Midsummer Night's Dream, The Taming of the Shrew,* and *The Merchant of Venice.*

1690 WELLS, Stanley. "Happy Endings in Shakespeare." *SJH* (1966):103–23.

1691 WILSON, Elkin Calhoun. *Shakespeare, Santayana, and the Comic.* University: U. of Alabama P.; London: Allen & Unwin, 1973.

1692 WILSON, F. P. "Shakespeare's Comedies." In **1272.**

1693 WIMSATT, William K., Jr., ed. *English Stage Comedy. EIE 1954* (1955), entire issue. Includes introductory essay by the editor on "The Criticism of Comedy," pp. 3–21.

Comic Character Types

On the Fool as a Shakespearean character type, see **1370–71, 1374–75, 1396, 1398,** and **3129.**

See also **1387, 1989,** and **2253.**

1694 BLISTEIN, Elmer M. "The Object of Scorn: An Aspect of the Comic Antagonist." *WHR* 14 (1960):209–22. Focuses on Parolles and Malvolio.

1695 BOUGHNER, Daniel C. *The Braggart in Renaissance Comedy: A Study in Comparative Drama from Aristophanes to Shakespeare.* Minneapolis: U. of Minnesota P., 1954. Rpt., Westport, Conn.: Greenwood, 1970.

1696 BROOKS, Charles. "Shakespeare's Heroine-Actresses." *SJ* 96 (1960):134–44. On the heroines like Viola and Portia who undertake male disguises.

1697 BROOKS, Charles. "Shakespeare's Romantic Shrews." *SQ* 11 (1960):351–56.

1698 COGHILL, Nevill. "Wags, Clowns, and Jesters." In **1138.**

1699 EVANS, Hugh C. "Comic Constables—Fictional and Historical." *SQ* 20 (1969): 427–33.

1700 FRYE, Northrop. "Characterization in Shakespearian Comedy." *SQ* 4 (1953): 271–77.

1701 HART, John A. "Father-Daughter as Device in Shakespeare's Romantic Comedies." In **1118.**

1702 HERBERT, T. Walter. "The Villain and the Happy End of Shakespeare Comedy." *RenP 1966* (1967):69–74.

1703 HERRICK, Marvin T. *Comic Theory in the Sixteenth Century.* See **1649.**

1704 LEA, Kathleen M. *Italian Popular Comedy: A Study in the Commedia dell' Arte, 1560–1620, with Special Reference to the English Stage.* 2 vols., Oxford: Clarendon, 1934. Rpt., New York: Russell & Russell.*

1705 LEECH, Clifford. "Shakespeare's Comic Dukes." *REL* 5.2 (1964):101–14.

1706 MARES, F. H. "Viola and Other Transvestite Heroines in Shakespeare's Comedies." In **1145** (1969 for 1965–67).

1707 NUTTALL, A. D. "Two Unassimilable Men." In **1722**. On Jaques and Caliban.

1708 PALMER, John. *Comic Characters of Shakespeare.* London: Macmillan, 1946. Rpt. in **1386**.*

1709 PRIESTLEY, J. B. *The English Comic Characters.* London: John Lane, 1925.

1710 ROBERTS, Jeanne Addison. "Laughter and the Law: Shakespeare's Comic Constables." *The Police in Society.* Eds. Emilio C. VIANO and Jeffrey H. REIMAN. Lexington, Mass.: Heath, 1975.

1711 SIEMON, James Edward. "The Canker Within: Some Observations on the Role of the Villain in Three Shakespearean Comedies." *SQ* 23 (1972):435–43.

The Early Comedies, c.1589–c.1595

See also **113, 122, 130, 141, 1578, 1582, 1586, 1589, 1591, 1593–95, 1697,** and **2273.**

1712 BERMAN, Ronald. "Shakespearean Comedy and the Uses of Reason." *SAQ* 63 (1964):1–9. On *Love's Labour's Lost* and *The Taming of the Shrew.*

1713 BONAZZA, Blaze Odell. *Shakespeare's Early Comedies: A Structural Analysis.* The Hague: Mouton, 1966.

1714 CODY, Richard. *The Landscape of the Mind: Pastoralism and Platonic Theory in Tasso's "Aminta" and Shakespeare's Early Comedies.* Oxford: Clarendon, 1969.

1715 HILL, R. F. "Delight and Laughter: Some Aspects of Shakespeare's Early Verbal Comedy." *ShStud* 3 (1964):1–21.

1716 MIOLA, Robert. "Early Shakespearean Comedy: *sub specie ludi.*" *Thoth* 14 (1973–74):23–36.

1717 TILLYARD, E. M. W. *Shakespeare's Early Comedies.* London: Chatto & Windus; New York: Barnes & Noble, 1965.*

1718 TRAVERSI, Derek. *William Shakespeare: The Early Comedies.* London: Longmans, Green, 1960. Rev. ed., 1964.*

Romantic Or Festive Comedies, c.1592–c.1602

The plays most often discussed in this group are *A Midsummer Night's Dream, The Merchant of Venice, Much Ado About Nothing, As You Like It, Twelfth Night,* and *The Merry Wives of Windsor.* The earlier comedies are sometimes included: *The Comedy of Errors, The Two Gentlemen of Verona, Love's Labour's Lost,* and *The Taming of the Shrew.* When other plays are included as well, they are indicated below.

See also **1624–93.**

1719 BARBER, C. L. *Shakespeare's Festive Comedy: A Study of Dramatic Form and Its Relation to Social Custom.* Princeton: Princeton U.P., 1959. Rpt., Cleveland and New York: Meridian (World), 1963. Includes *Henry IV.* *

1720 BAXTER, John S. "Present Mirth: Shakespeare's Romantic Comedies." *QQ* 72 (1965):52–77.

1721 BERRY, Ralph. *Shakespeare's Comedies: Explorations in Form.* Princeton: Princeton U.P., 1972.*

1722 BRADBURY, Malcolm, and D. J. PALMER, eds. *Shakespearian Comedy.* Stratford-upon-Avon Studies 14. London: Arnold; New York: Crane, Russak, 1972. Includes *Measure for Measure.* *

1723 HASLER, Jörg. *Shakespeare's Theatrical Notation: The Comedies.* Bern: Francke, 1974.

1724 HASSEL, R. Chris. "Saint Paul and Shakespeare's Romantic Comedies." *Thought* 46 (1971):371–88.

1725 HUNTER, G. K. *William Shakespeare: The Late Comedies.* London: Longmans, Green, 1962.*

1726 KERMODE, Frank. "The Mature Comedies." In **1582**. Rpt. in **1223**. Includes *Cymbeline.* *

1727 LEGGATT, Alexander. *Shakespeare's Comedy of Love.* London: Methuen; New York: Barnes & Noble, 1974.*

1728 MARTZ, William J. *Shakespeare's Universe of Comedy.* London: Methuen, 1970; New York: D. Lewis, 1971.

1729 PHIALAS, Peter G. *Shakespeare's Romantic Comedies: The Development of Their Form and Meaning.* Chapel Hill: U. of North Carolina P., 1966.

1730 THOMPSON, Karl F. "Shakespeare's Romantic Comedies." *PMLA* 67 (1952): 1079–93.

1731 WEIL, Herbert, Jr., ed. *Discussions of Shakespeare's Romantic Comedy.* Boston: Heath, 1966. A collection of essays.

1732 WELD, John. *Meaning in Comedy: Studies in Elizabethan Romantic Comedy.* See **1689.**

1733 WILSON, J. Dover. *Shakespeare's Happy Comedies.* London: Faber & Faber; Evanston, Ill.: Northwestern U.P., 1962.

Pastoral Plays

This genre overlaps considerably with both romantic comedy and late romance. See also **326, 2224, 2241,** and **3075.**

1734 CODY, Richard. *The Landscape of the Mind.* See **1714.**

1735 CONN, Naomi. "The Promise of Arcadia: Nature and the Natural Man in Shakespeare's Comedies." In **1160.**

1736 EMPSON, William. *Some Versions of Pastoral.* See **2659.**

1737 GREENLAW, Edwin. "Shakespeare's Pastorals." *SP* 13 (1916):122–54. Includes *As You Like It, The Winter's Tale,* and *Cymbeline.*

1738 MCFARLAND, Thomas. *Shakespeare's Pastoral Comedy.* Chapel Hill: U. of North Carolina P., 1972. Includes *Love's Labour's Lost, A Midsummer Night's Dream, As You Like It, The Winter's Tale,* and *The Tempest.* *

1739 YOUNG, David. *The Heart's Forest: A Study of Shakespeare's Pastoral Plays.* New Haven and London: Yale U.P., 1972. Includes *As You Like It, King Lear, The Winter's Tale,* and *The Tempest.* *

The Late Romances, c.1607–c.1612

Studies of *Pericles, Cymbeline, The Winter's Tale,* and *The Tempest.*

See also **150, 316, 490, 736, 1598–1615, 1642, 1687, 2106,** and **4115.**

1740 BERRY, Francis. "Word and Picture in the Final Plays." In **1599.**

1741 BLAND, D. S. "The Heroine and the Sea: An Aspect of Shakespeare's Last Plays." *EIC* 3 (1953):39–44.

1742 BROWN, John Russell. "Laughter in the Last Plays." In **1599.**

1743 CHILDRESS, D. T. "Are Shakespeare's Late Plays Really Romances?" In **1613.**

1744 CUTTS, John P. *Rich and Strange: A Study of Shakespeare's Last Plays.* Pullman: Washington State U.P., 1968.

1745 DANBY, John F. " Sidney and the Late-Shakespearian Romance." In **1600.**

1746 DUNN, Catherine M. "The Function of Music in Shakespeare's Romances." *SQ* 20 (1969):391–405.

1747 EDWARDS, Philip. "Shakespeare's Romances: 1900–1957." *ShS* 11 (1958):1–18.

1748 FELPERIN, Howard. *Shakespearean Romance.* Princeton: Princeton U.P., 1972.*

1749 FRYE, Northrop. *The Secular Scripture: A Study of the Structure of Romance.* Cambridge, Mass.: Harvard U.P., 1976.*

1750 GESNER, Carol. *Shakespeare and the Greek Romance: A Study of Origins.* See **1645.***

1751 GRENE, David. *Reality and the Heroic Pattern: Last Plays of Ibsen, Shakespeare, and Sophocles.* Chicago: U. of Chicago P., 1967.

1752 HARTWIG, Joan. *Shakespeare's Tragicomic Vision.* Baton Rouge: Louisiana State U.P., 1972.

1753 HOENIGER, F. David. "Shakespeare's Romances since 1958: A Retrospect." *ShS* 29 (1976):1–10.

1754 INGRAM, R. W. "Musical Pauses and the Vision Scenes in Shakespeare's Last Plays." In **1156.**

1755 JACQUOT, Jean. "The Last Plays and the Masque." In **1151.**

1756 KERMODE, Frank. *William Shakespeare: The Final Plays.* London: Longmans, Green, 1963. Rpt. in **1223.***

1757 KNIGHT, G. Wilson. *The Crown of Life.* See **1605.***

1758 LEAVIS, F. R. "The Criticism of Shakespeare's Late Plays: A Caveat." *Scrutiny* 10 (1942):339–45. Rpt. in **1232.**

1759 MARSH, D. R. C. *The Recurring Miracle: A Study of "Cymbeline" and the Last Plays.* Pietermaritzburg: U. of Natal P., 1962; Lincoln: U. of Nebraska P., 1969.

1760 MELCHIORI, Barbara. " 'Still Harping on My Daughter.' " *EM* 11 (1960): 59–74. Concerns incest in the late plays.

1761 MOWAT, Barbara A. *The Dramaturgy of Shakespeare's Romances.* Athens: U. of Georgia P., 1976.

1762 MUIR, Kenneth. *Last Periods of Shakespeare, Racine, Ibsen.* Liverpool: U. of Liverpool P.; Detroit: Wayne State U.P., 1961.

1763 NELSON, Thomas Allen. *Shakespeare's Comic Theory: A Study of Art and Artifice in the Last Plays.* The Hague and Paris: Mouton, 1972; New York: Humanities P., 1973.

1764 NICOLL, Allardyce. "Shakespeare and the Court Masque." *SJ* 94 (1958):51–62.

1765 NOSWORTHY, J. M. "Music and Its Function in the Romances of Shakespeare." *ShS* 11 (1958):60–69.

1766 PALMER, D. J., ed. *Shakespeare's Later Comedies: An Anthology of Modern Criticism.* Harmondsworth: Penguin, 1971.

1767 PETERSON, Douglas L. *Time, Tide, and Tempest: A Study of Shakespeare's Romances.* San Marino, Calif.: Huntington Library, 1973.*

1768 RABKIN, Norman. "The Holy Sinner and the Confidence Man: Illusion in Shakespeare's Romances." *Four Essays on Romance.* Ed. Herschel BAKER. Cambridge, Mass.: Harvard U.P., 1971.

1769 SALINGAR, Leo. "Time and Art in Shakespeare's Romances." *RenD* 9 (1966): 3–35. Rpt., rev., in **1671.**

1770 SEMON, Kenneth J. "Fantasy and Wonder in Shakespeare's Last Plays." *SQ* 25 (1974):89–102.

1771 *Shakespeare Survey* 11 (1958) and 29 (1976). Issues largely devoted to the last plays.*

1772 SMITH, Hallett. *Shakespeare's Romances.* San Marino, Calif.: Huntington Library, 1972.

1773 SPENCER, Theodore. "Appearance and Reality in Shakespeare's Last Plays." *MP* 39 (1942):265–74.

1774 TILLYARD, E. M. W. *Shakespeare's Last Plays.* London: Chatto & Windus; Toronto: Clarke, Irwin, 1938. Rpt., New York: Barnes & Noble, 1964.*

1775 TRAVERSI, Derek. *Shakespeare: The Last Phase.* London: Hollis & Carter; New York: Harcourt, Brace, 1954. Rpt., Stanford: Stanford U.P., 1955.*

1776 WELLS, Stanley. "Shakespeare and Romance." In **1599.** Rpt. in **1766.**

1777 WINCOR, Richard. "Shakespeare's Festival Plays." *SQ* 1 (1950):219–40.

Problem Plays and Satire

The works discussed as "problem plays" usually include *All's Well That Ends Well, Measure for Measure,* and *Troilus and Cressida. Hamlet* is included somewhat less often. Exceptions to this pattern are noted individually below. Discussions of "satire" in Shakespeare range widely through such plays as *As You Like It, Twelfth Night, Timon of Athens, Troilus and Cressida, The Merry Wives of Windsor, Love's Labour's Lost, Hamlet, Coriolanus, Measure for Measure,* and *All's Well.*

See also **1683, 4210,** and **4362.**

1778 BEVINGTON, David. "Shakespeare vs. Jonson on Satire." In **1151.** Includes discussions of *As You Like It* and *All's Well.*

1779 BIRNEY, Alice Lotvin. *Satiric Catharsis in Shakespeare: A Theory of Dramatic Structure.* Berkeley and Los Angeles: U. of California P., 1973. Includes discussions of *Richard III, Henry IV, As You Like It, Troilus and Cressida,* and *Timon.*

1780 BOAS, Frederick S. "The Problem Plays." *Shakspere and His Predecessors.* New York: Scribner's, 1896. Rpt., New York: Haskell House, 1968; Greenwich, Conn.: Greenwood. Includes *Hamlet.*

1781 CAMPBELL, Oscar James. *Shakespeare's Satire.* London and New York: Oxford U.P., 1943. Rpt., New York: Gordian.

1782 CHARLTON, H. B. "The Dark Comedies." *BJRL* 21 (1937):78–128. On *Measure for Measure, All's Well,* and *Troilus and Cressida.*

1783 FOAKES, R. A. *Shakespeare, The Dark Comedies to the Last Plays: From Satire to Celebration.* See **1602.***

1784 HAWKES, Terence. *Shakespeare and the Reason: A Study of the Tragedies and the Problem Plays.* See **2016.***

1785 JAMIESON, Michael. "The Problem Plays, 1920–1970: A Retrospect." *ShS* 25 (1972):1–10.

1786 JENSEN, Ejner J. "Spying Scenes and the Problem Plays: A Shakespearean Strategy." *TSE* 20 (1972):23–40.

1787 KERNAN, Alvin B. *The Cankered Muse: Satire of the English Renaissance.* New Haven: Yale U.P., 1959. Includes discussion of *As You Like It, Troilus and Cressida,* and *Timon.***

1788 KIRSCHHEIM, Astrid. *Tragik und Komic in Shakespeares "Troilus and Cressida," "Measure for Measure," und "All's Well That Ends Well."* Frankfurt: Athenäum, 1971.

1789 LAWRENCE, W. W. *Shakespeare's Problem Comedies.* New York: Macmillan, 1931. 2nd ed., New York: Ungar, 1960. Includes *Cymbeline.***

1790 ORNSTEIN, Robert, ed. *Discussions of Shakespeare's Problem Comedies.* Boston: Heath, 1961. A collection of essays.

1791 ROSSITER, A. P. "The Problem Plays." In **1245.**

1792 SCHANZER, Ernest. *The Problem Plays of Shakespeare: A Study of "Julius Caesar," "Measure for Measure," and "Antony and Cleopatra."* London: Routledge & K. Paul; New York: Schocken, 1963.***

1793 SHALVI, Alice. *The Relationship of Renaissance Concepts of Honour to Shakespeare's Problem Plays.* Salzburg: Institut für Englische Sprache und Literatur, 1972. Includes *Hamlet.*

1794 *Shakespeare Survey* 25 (1972). Largely devoted to the problem plays.*

1795 TILLYARD, E. M. W. *Shakespeare's Problem Plays.* Toronto: U. of Toronto P., 1949; London: Chatto & Windus, 1950. Includes *Hamlet.* *

1796 TOOLE, William B. *Shakespeare's Problem Plays: Studies in Form and Meaning.* The Hague: Mouton; New York: Humanities P., 1966.

1797 URE, Peter. *William Shakespeare: The Problem Plays.* London: Longmans, Green, 1961. Includes *Timon.*

The Histories

General Studies

See also **85, 88, 90–91, 1450–1506, 1508–09, 1513, 1557, 1580, 1582, 1586, 1592, 1597, and 3881.**

1798 ARMSTRONG, William A. *Shakespeare's Histories: An Anthology of Modern Criticism.* Harmondsworth and Baltimore: Penguin, 1972.

1799 BENBOW, R. Mark. "The Providential Theory of Historical Causation in Holinshed's Chronicles: 1577 and 1587." *TSLL* 1 (1959):264–76.

1800 BETHELL, S. L. "The Comic Element in Shakespeare's Histories." *Anglia* 71 (1952):82–101.

1801 BRUNNER, Karl. "Middle-Class Attitudes in Shakespeare's Histories." *ShS* 6 (1953):36–38.

1802 CAMPBELL, Lily B. *Shakespeare's "Histories": Mirrors of Elizabethan Policy.* San Marino, Calif.: Huntington Library, 1947.*

1803 CHAPMAN, Raymond. "The Wheel of Fortune in Shakespeare's Historical Plays." *RES,* n.s. 1 (1950):1–7.

1804 CRAIG, Hardin. "Shakespeare and the History Play." In **1154.**

1805 FLEISCHER, Martha Hester. *The Iconography of the English History Play.* Salzburg: Institut für Englische Sprache und Literatur, 1974.

1806 FORKER, Charles R. "Shakespeare's Chronicle Plays as Historical-Pastoral." *ShakS* 1 (1965):85–104.

1807 FREEMAN, Leslie. "Shakespeare's Kings and Machiavelli's Prince." In **1160.**

1808 HUMPHREYS, A. R. "Shakespeare and the Tudor Perception of History." In **1145** (1965 for 1964). Rpt. in **1175.**

1809 HUMPHREYS, A. R. "Shakespeare's Histories and 'the Emotion of Multitude.'" *PBA* 54 (1970 for 1968):265–87.

1810 JENKINS, Harold. "Shakespeare's History Plays: 1900–1951." *ShS* 6 (1953): 1–15.

1811 JUMP, John. "Shakespeare and History." *CritQ* 17 (1975):223–44.

1812 KASTAN, David Scott. "The Shape of Time: Form and Value in the Shakespearean History Play." *CompD* 7 (1973–74):259–77.*

1813 KELLY, Henry Ansgar. *Divine Providence in the England of Shakespeare's Histories.* Cambridge, Mass.: Harvard U.P., 1970.*

1814 KINGSFORD, Charles Lethbridge. "Fifteenth-Century History in Shakespeare's
Plays." *Prejudice and Promise in Fifteenth-Century England.* Oxford: Clarendon,
1925, pp. 1–21.

1815 KITTO, H. D. F. "A Classical Scholar Looks at Shakespeare." In **1138.** On
Shakespeare's historical tragedies, and *Hamlet.*

1816 KLEINSTÜCK, Johannes. "The Problem of Order in Shakespeare's Histories."
Neophil 38 (1954):268–77.

1817 KNIGHTS, L. C. *William Shakespeare: The Histories.* London: Longmans,
Green, 1962.

1818 LAW, Robert Adger. "Links between Shakespeare's History Plays." *SP* 50
(1953):168–87.

1819 LEECH, Clifford. *William Shakespeare: The Chronicles.* London: Longmans,
Green, 1962.

1820 LINDENBERGER, Herbert. *Historical Drama: The Relation of Literature and
Reality.* Chicago and London: U. of Chicago P., 1975.

1821 MACLEAN, Hugh. "Time and Horsemanship in Shakespeare's Histories." *UTQ*
35 (1966):229–45.

1822 MANHEIM, Michael. *The Weak King Dilemma in the Shakespearean History
Play.* Syracuse: Syracuse U.P., 1973.

1823 MARRIOTT, J. A. R. *English History in Shakespeare.* London: Chapman & Hall;
New York: Dutton, 1918.

1824 MEHUS, Donald V. *Shakespeare's English History Plays: Genealogical Table.*
Charlottesville: U.P. of Virginia for the Folger Library, 1975.

1825 MORRIS, Helen. "The Histories." In **1140.**

1826 MROZ, Sister Mary Bonaventure. *Divine Vengeance: A Study in the Philosophical
Backgrounds of the Revenge Motif as It Appears in Shakespeare's Chronicle History
Plays.* Washington, D.C.: Catholic U. of America P., 1941.

1827 MUIR, Kenneth. "Image and Symbol in Shakespeare's Histories." *BJRL* 50
(1967):103–23. Rpt. in **1238.**

1828 MUIR, Kenneth. "Source Problems in the Histories." *SJ* 96 (1960):47–63.

1829 ORNSTEIN, Robert. *A Kingdom for a Stage: The Achievement of Shakespeare's
History Plays.* Cambridge, Mass.: Harvard U.P., 1972.*

1830 PEARCE, Josephine A. "Constituent Elements in Shakespeare's History Plays."
In **1157.**

1831 PIERCE, Robert B. *Shakespeare's History Plays: The Family and the State.*
Columbus: Ohio State U.P., 1971.

1832 PRIOR, Moody E. *The Drama of Power: Studies in Shakespeare's History Plays.*
Evanston, Ill.: Northwestern U. P., 1973.

1833 REESE, M. M. *The Cease of Majesty: A Study of Shakespeare's History Plays.*
London: Arnold; New York: St. Martin's, 1961.*

1834 RIBNER, Irving. *The English History Play in the Age of Shakespeare.* Princeton: Princeton U.P., 1957. Rev. ed., enl., New York: Barnes & Noble; London: Baylis, 1965. London: Methuen, 1965.*

1835 ROSSITER, A. P. "Ambivalence: The Dialectic of the Histories." In **1139.** Rpt. in **1245.***

1836 SACCIO, Peter. *Shakespeare's English Kings: History, Chronicle, and Drama.* New York: Oxford U.P., 1977.

1837 SANDERS, Norman. "American Criticism of Shakespeare's History Plays." *ShakS* 9 (1976):11–23.

1838 SEN GUPTA, S. C. *Shakespeare's Historical Plays.* London: Oxford U.P., 1964.

1839 *Shakespeare Survey* 6 (1953). Largely devoted to the histories.

1840 SNYDER, Karl E. "Kings and Kingship in Four of Shakespeare's History Plays." In **1128.**

1841 SPRAGUE, Arthur Colby. *Shakespeare's Histories: Plays for the Stage.* See **779.**

1842 TILLYARD, E. M. W. "Shakespeare's Historical Cycle: Organism or Compilation?" *SP* 51 (1954):34–39. Rpt. in **1266.**

1843 TILLYARD, E. M. W. *Shakespeare's History Plays.* London: Chatto & Windus, 1944; New York: Macmillan, 1946. Rpt., New York: Barnes & Noble, 1964.*

1844 UTTERBACK, Raymond V., ed. *SLitI* 5.1 (1972). Entire issue devoted to Shakespeare's history plays.

1845 WAITH, Eugene M., ed. *Shakespeare, The Histories: A Collection of Critical Essays.* Englewood Cliffs, N.J.: Prentice-Hall, 1965.

1846 WEDGEWOOD, C. V. "Shakespeare between Two Civil Wars." In **1175.** Examines Shakespeare between the civil wars of the fifteenth and seventeenth centuries.

1847 WILSON, F. P. "The English History Play." In **1272.**

1848 WINNY, James. *The Player King: A Theme of Shakespeare's Histories.* London: Chatto & Windus; New York: Barnes & Noble, 1968.

1849 ZEEVELD, W. Gordon. "The Influence of Hall on Shakespeare's English Historical Plays." *ELH* 3 (1936):317–53.

The First Historical Tetralogy, Henry VI—Richard III

For critical studies focusing on *Henry VI* with incidental reference to *Richard III,* see "The Henry VI Plays," **2821–40.**

See also **1581–82, 1586, 1588, 1590, 1592–93,** and **1595.**

1850 ALEXANDER, Peter. *Shakespeare's "Henry VI" and "Richard III."* Cambridge: Cambridge U.P., 1929. Rpt., New York: Octagon.

1851 BERRY, Edward I. *Patterns of Decay: Shakespeare's Early Histories.* Charlottesville: U.P. of Virginia, 1975.

1852 BURKHART, Robert E. "Obedience and Rebellion in Shakespeare's Early History Plays." *ES* 55 (1974):108–17.

1853 CLEMEN, Wolfgang. "Anticipation and Foreboding in Shakespeare's Early Histories." *ShS* 6 (1953):25–35.*

1854 FRENCH, A. L. "The Mills of God and Shakespeare's Early History Plays." *ES* 55 (1974):313–24.

1855 LEECH, Clifford. "The Two-Part Play: Marlowe and the Early Shakespeare." *SJ* 94 (1958):90–106.

1856 MCNEAL, Thomas H. "Margaret of Anjou: Romantic Princess and Troubled Queen." *SQ* 9 (1958):1–10.

1857 QUINN, Michael. "Providence in Shakespeare's Yorkist Plays." *SQ* 10 (1959): 45–52.*

1858 RICHARDSON, Arleigh D., III. "The Early Historical Plays." In **1161.**

1859 ROWSE, A. L. *Bosworth Field.* Garden City, N.Y.: Doubleday, 1966.

1860 SCHLÖSSER, Anselm. "Shakespeares Erste Tetralogie." *SJW* 102 (1966):168–208.

1861 STŘÍBRNÝ, Zdeněk. "The Idea and Image of Time in Shakespeare's Early Histories." *SJW* 110 (1974):129–38.

1862 TURNER, Robert Y. "Characterization in Shakespeare's Early History Plays." *ELH* 31 (1964):241–58.

The Second Historical Tetralogy, Richard II—Henry V

See also **474, 2769, 2803–04, 2818,** and **3867.**

1863 DAVID, Richard. "Shakespeare's History Plays: Epic or Drama?" *ShS* 6 (1953): 129–39. A review of productions at Stratford-upon-Avon in 1951.

1864 DEAN, Leonard F. "*Richard II* to *Henry V:* A Closer View." In **1142.** Rpt. in **1132.**

1865 DORIUS, R. J., ed. *Discussions of Shakespeare's Histories: "Richard II" to "Henry V."* Boston: Heath, 1964. An anthology of essays.

1866 HAPGOOD, Robert. "Shakespeare's Thematic Modes of Speech: *Richard II* to *Henry V.*" *ShS* 20 (1967):41–49.

1867 KELLY, Robert L. "Shakespeare's Scroops and the 'Spirit of Cain.'" *SQ* 20 (1969):71–80.

1868 KERNAN, Alvin B. "The Henriad: Shakespeare's Major History Plays." *YR* 59 (1969):3–32. Rpt. in **1147.***

1869 LA GUARDIA, Eric. "Ceremony and History: The Problem of Symbol from *Richard II* to *Henry V.*" In **1156.**

1870 LAW, Robert Adger. "The Composition of Shakespeare's Lancastrian Tetralogy." *TSLL* 3 (1961):321–27.

1871 MICHEL, Laurence, and Cecil C. SERONSY. "Shakespeare's History Plays and Daniel: An Assessment." *SP* 52 (1955):549–77.

1872 PARKER, Robert B. "The Prince and the King: Shakespeare's Machiavellian Cycle." *Revue des Langues Vivantes* 38 (1972):241–53.

1873 RIBNER, Irving. "The Political Problem in Shakespeare's Lancastrian Tetralogy." *SP* 49 (1952):171–84.

1874 STŘÍBRNÝ, Zdeněk. "The Idea and Image of Time in Shakespeare's Second Historical Tetralogy." *SJW* 111 (1975):51–66.

1875 TOLIVER, Harold E. "Falstaff, the Prince, and the History Play." *SQ* 16 (1965): 63–80.

1876 TRAVERSI, Derek. *Shakespeare from "Richard II" to "Henry V."* London: Hollis & Carter; Palo Alto: Stanford U.P., 1957.*

1877 WEBBER, Joan. "The Renewal of the King's Symbolic Role: From *Richard II* to *Henry V."* *TSLL* 4 (1963):530–38.*

The Tragedies

Principles of Tragedy

See also **3094.**

1878 BRERETON, Geoffrey. *Principles of Tragedy: A Rational Examination of the Tragic Concept in Life and Literature.* Coral Gables, Fla.: U. of Miami P., 1968.

1879 CALARCO, N. Joseph. *Tragic Being: Apollo and Dionysus in Western Drama.* Minneapolis: U. of Minnesota P.; London: Oxford U.P., 1969.

1880 JASPERS, Karl. *Tragedy Is Not Enough.* Trans. Harald A. T. REICHE, Harry T. MOORE, and Karl W. DEUTSCH. Boston: Beacon, 1952.

1881 KERMODE, Frank. "World without End or Beginning." *The Sense of an Ending: Studies in the Theory of Fiction.* Oxford and New York: Oxford U.P., 1967.*

1882 KOELB, Clayton. "The Problem of 'Tragedy' as a Genre." *Genre* 8 (1975): 248–66.

1883 KOELB, Clayton. " 'Tragedy' as an Evaluative Term." *CLS* 11 (1974):69–82.

1884 KROOK, Dorothea. *Elements of Tragedy.* New Haven and London: Yale U.P., 1969.

1885 MICHEL, Laurence. "The Possibility of a Christian Tragedy." *Thought* 31 (1956):403–28. Rpt. in **1887.**

1886 MICHEL, Laurence. "Yardsticks for Tragedy." *EIC* 5 (1955):81–88.

1887 MICHEL, Laurence, and Richard B. SEWALL, eds. *Tragedy: Modern Essays in Criticism.* Englewood Cliffs, N.J.: Prentice-Hall, 1963.

1888 MYERS, Henry Alonzo. *Tragedy: A View of Life.* Ithaca: Cornell U.P., 1956.

1889 OLSON, Elder. *Tragedy and the Theory of Drama.* Detroit: Wayne State U.P., 1961.

1890 PRIOR, Moody E. *The Language of Tragedy.* See **482.**

1891 WEISINGER, Herbert. *Tragedy and the Paradox of the Fortunate Fall.* East Lansing: Michigan State College P., 1953.

Elizabethan and Jacobean Tragedy

See also **7, 1985,** and **3322.**

1892 BOWERS, Fredson. *Elizabethan Revenge Tragedy, 1587–1642.* Princeton: Princeton U.P., 1940. Paperback ed., 1966. Rpt., Gloucester, Mass.: P. Smith, 1959.*

1893 BRADBROOK, M. C. *Themes and Conventions of Elizabethan Tragedy.* 2nd ed., Cambridge: Cambridge U.P., 1952.

1894 BRODWIN, Leonora Leet. *Elizabethan Love Tragedy, 1587–1625.* New York: New York U.P.; London: U. of London P., 1971.

1895 DORAN, Madeleine. *Endeavors of Art.* See **1617.**

1896 FORKER, Charles R. "The Love-Death Nexus in English Renaissance Tragedy." *ShakS* 8 (1975):211–30.

1897 GARDNER, Helen. "Milton's 'Satan' and the Theme of Damnation in Elizabethan Tragedy." *E&S,* n.s. 1 (1948):46–66.

1898 HARBAGE, Alfred. "Intrigue in Elizabethan Tragedy." In **1144.**

1899 HARDISON, O. B., Jr. "Three Types of Renaissance Catharsis." *RenD,* n.s. 2 (1969):3–22.

1900 HERNDL, George C. *The High Design: English Renaissance Tragedy and the Natural Law.* Lexington: U.P. of Kentucky, 1970.

1901 HOY, Cyrus. "Jacobean Tragedy and the Mannerist Style." *ShS* 26 (1973):49–67.

1902 JENKINS, Harold. "The Tragedy of Revenge in Shakespeare and Webster." *ShS* 14 (1961):45–55.

1903 LEECH, Clifford. "The Incredible in Jacobean Tragedy." *Rice U. Studies* 60.2 (1974):109–22.

1904 LEECH, Clifford. *Shakespeare's Tragedies and Other Studies in Seventeenth-Century Drama.* London: Chatto & Windus; New York: Oxford U.P., 1950.

1905 LEECH, Clifford. "Studies in Shakespearian and Other Jacobean Tragedy, 1918–1972: A Retrospect." *ShS* 26 (1973):1–9.

1906 LUCAS, F. L. *Seneca and Elizabethan Tragedy.* Cambridge: Cambridge U.P., 1922. Rpt., New York: Haskell House, 1966.

1907 MCDONALD, Charles Osborne. *The Rhetoric of Tragedy: Form in Stuart Drama.* See **476.**

1908 MARGESON, J. M. R. *The Origins of English Tragedy.* Oxford: Clarendon, 1967.*

1909 MINCOFF, Marco. "Shakespeare, Fletcher, and Baroque Tragedy." *ShS* 20 (1967):1–15.

1910 OLIVER, H. J. "Literary Allusions in Jacobean Drama." *Rice U. Studies* 60.2 (1974):131–40.

1911 ORNSTEIN, Robert. *The Moral Vision of Jacobean Tragedy.* Madison: U. of Wisconsin P., 1960. Rpt., New York: Greenwood, 1975.*

1912 SCHÜCKING, Levin L. "The Baroque Character of the Elizabethan Tragic Hero." *PBA* 24 (1939 for 1938):85–111.

1913 *Shakespeare Survey* 20 (1967). Largely devoted to Shakespearean and other tragedy.

1914 SPENCER, Theodore. *Death and Elizabethan Tragedy: A Study of Convention and Opinion in the Elizabethan Drama.* Cambridge, Mass.: Harvard U.P.; London: Oxford U.P., 1936.

1915 STROUP, Thomas B. "The Testing Pattern in Elizabethan Tragedy." *SEL* 3 (1963):175–90.

1916 STROZIER, Robert M. "Politics, Stoicism, and the Development of Elizabethan Tragedy." *Costerus* 8 (1973):193–218.

1917 TOMLINSON, T. B. *A Study of Elizabethan and Jacobean Tragedy.* Cambridge: Cambridge U.P., 1964.

1918 WHITAKER, Virgil K. "Shakespeare the Elizabethan." *Rice U. Studies* 60.2 (1974):141–51.

General Studies in Shakespearean Tragedy

See also **457, 475, 521, 577, 769, 915, 1066–67, 1413, 1429, 1510, 1557, 1565, 1622, 1902, 1904–05, 1909, 1911, 1918, 1983, 1988, 1995, 1999, 2004, 2011–31, 3159, 3359, 3698,** and **4623.**

1919 BARROLL, J. Leeds. "Structure in Shakespearean Tragedy." *ShakS* 7 (1974): 345–78.

1920 BARROLL, J. Leeds. "The Structure of a Shakespearean Tragedy." *ShakS* 8 (1975):1–27.

1921 BATTENHOUSE, Roy W. *Shakespearean Tragedy: Its Art and Its Christian Premises.* Bloomington: Indiana U.P., 1969.

1922 BLACK, Matthew W. "Aristotle's Mythos and the Tragedies of Shakespeare." *SJH* (1968):43–55.

1923 BOWERS, Fredson. "Death in Victory: Shakespeare's Tragic Reconciliations." In **1142.***

1924 BROWER, Reuben A. *Hero and Saint: Shakespeare and the Graeco-Roman Heroic Tradition.* New York and Oxford: Oxford U.P., 1971.*

1925 CADY, Frank W. "Motivation of the Inciting Force in Shakespeare's Tragedies." In **1172.**

1926 CHAMPION, Larry S. *Shakespeare's Tragic Perspective: The Development of His Dramatic Technique.* Athens: U. of Georgia P., 1976.

1927 CHARLTON, H. B. *Shakespearian Tragedy.* Cambridge: Cambridge U.P., 1948.*

1928 COURSEN, Herbert R., Jr. *Christian Ritual and the World of Shakespeare's Tragedies.* Lewisburg, Pa.: Bucknell U.P.; London: Associated U.P., 1976.

1929 CUNNINGHAM, J. V. *Woe or Wonder: The Emotional Effect of Shakespearean Tragedy.* Denver: U. of Denver P., 1951. Rpt. in **1197.***

1930 DANBY, John F. "The Tragedies." In **1140.**

1931 DANSON, Lawrence. *Tragic Alphabet: Shakespeare's Drama of Language.* New Haven and London: Yale U.P., 1974.

1932 DAVIDSON, Clifford. "Organic Unity and Shakespearian Tragedy." *JAAC* 30 (1971):171–76. Concerns critical misapplication of Coleridge's terminology.

1933 ELIOT, T. S. "Shakespeare and the Stoicism of Seneca." *Selected Essays of T. S. Eliot.* New York: Harcourt, Brace; London: Faber & Faber, 1932.*

1934 EVANS, Gareth Lloyd. "Shakespeare, Seneca, and the Kingdom of Violence." *Roman Drama.* Eds. T. A. DOREY and Donald R. DUDLEY. London: Routledge & K. Paul, 1965.

1935 FLY, Richard D. " 'So Workmanly the Blood and Tears Are Drawn': Tragic Vision and Formal Beauty in Shakespearean Drama." *Essays in Literature* 2 (1975):131–48.

1936 FORTIN, René E. "Shakespearean Tragedy and the Problem of Transcendence." *ShakS* 7 (1974):307–25.

1937 FRENCH, A. L. *Shakespeare and the Critics.* Cambridge and New York: Cambridge U.P., 1972. On *Hamlet, Othello, King Lear,* and *Antony and Cleopatra.**

1938 FRYE, Northrop. *Fools of Time: Studies in Shakespearean Tragedy.* Toronto: U. of Toronto P., 1967.

1939 FRYE, Roland Mushat. "Theological and Non-Theological Structures in Tragedies." *ShakS* 4 (1969 for 1968):132–48.

1940 GRACE, William J. "The Cosmic Sense in Shakespearean Tragedy." *SR* 50 (1942):433–45.

1941 HANFORD, James Holly. "Suicide in the Plays of Shakespeare." *PMLA* 27 (1912):380–97.

1942 HARBAGE, Alfred, ed. *Shakespeare, The Tragedies: A Collection of Critical Essays.* Englewood Cliffs, N.J.: Prentice-Hall, 1964.

1943 HARRISON, G. B. *Shakespeare's Tragedies.* London: Routledge & K. Paul; New York: Oxford U.P., 1951.

1944 HEILMAN, Robert B. *Shakespearian Tragedy and the Drama of Disaster.* Vancouver: U. of British Columbia, 1960.

1945 HEILMAN, Robert B. "To Know Himself: An Aspect of Tragic Structure." *REL* 5.2 (1964):36–57.

1946 HENN, T. R. "Towards a Shakespearian Synthesis." *The Harvest of Tragedy.* London: Methuen, 1956; New York: Barnes & Noble, 1966.

1947 HONIGMANN, E. A. J. *Shakespeare: Seven Tragedies; The Dramatist's Manipulation of Response.* New York: Barnes & Noble, 1976. On *Julius Caesar, Hamlet, Othello, King Lear, Macbeth, Antony and Cleopatra,* and *Coriolanus.*

1948 HONIGMANN, E. A. J. *Shakespearean Tragedy and the Mixed Response.* Newcastle: U. of Newcastle Upon Tyne, 1971.

1949 JENKINS, Harold. *The Catastrophe in Shakespearean Tragedy.* Edinburgh: Edinburgh U.P., 1969.

1950 KITTO, H. D. F. "Why Blame Aristotle?" In **1151.** A comparison of Sophocles' *Trachiniae* and *Ajax* with *Coriolanus.*

1951 KNIGHT, G. Wilson. *The Wheel of Fire: Interpretation of Shakespeare's Tragedy.* 4th rev. ed., London: Methuen, 1949; Cleveland: Meridian, 1957; New York: Barnes & Noble, 1965.*

1952 KNIGHTS, L. C. "Shakespeare's Tragedies and the Question of Moral Judgment." *Shenandoah* 19.3 (1968):29–45. Rpt. in *Explorations 3;* see **1229.**

1953 LAWLOR, John. *The Tragic Sense in Shakespeare.* London: Chatto & Windus, 1960.

1954 LEECH, Clifford, ed. *Shakespeare: The Tragedies. A Collection of Critical Essays.* Chicago: U. of Chicago P., 1965.

1955 LERNER, Laurence, ed. *Shakespeare's Tragedies: An Anthology of Modern Criticism.* Baltimore: Penguin, 1963; Harmondsworth: Penguin, 1964.

1956 LONG, Michael. *The Unnatural Scene: A Study in Shakespearean Tragedy.* London: Methuen; New York: Barnes & Noble, 1976. A study of ways in which Shakespeare's tragedies develop the idea of a conflict between nature and the social structure.

1957 MCFARLAND, Thomas. *Tragic Meanings in Shakespeare.* New York: Random House, 1966. Focuses on *Hamlet, Othello, Antony and Cleopatra,* and *King Lear.*

1958 MACK, Maynard. "The Jacobean Shakespeare: Some Observations on the Construction of the Tragedies." *Jacobean Theatre.* Eds. John Russell BROWN and Bernard HARRIS. Stratford-upon-Avon Studies 1. London: Arnold, 1960; New York: Capricorn, 1967. Rpt. in **1125.***

1959 MACK, Maynard, Jr. *Killing the King: Three Studies in Shakespeare's Tragic Structure.* New Haven and London: Yale U.P., 1973. On *Hamlet, Macbeth,* and *Richard II.*

1960 MICHEL, Laurence. "Shakespearean Tragedy: Critique of Humanism from the Inside." *Massachusetts Review* 2 (1961):633–50.

1961 MINCOFF, Marco. "The Structural Pattern of Shakespeare's Tragedies." *ShS* 3 (1950):58–65.

1962 MUIR, Kenneth. "American Criticism of Shakespeare's Tragedies." *ShakS* 9 (1976):25–30.

1963 MUIR, Kenneth. "Shakespeare and the Tragic Pattern." *PBA* 44 (1959 for 1958): 145–62.

1964 MUIR, Kenneth. *Shakespeare's Tragic Sequence.* London: Hutchinson, 1972.

1965 NEVO, Ruth. *Tragic Form in Shakespeare.* Princeton: Princeton U.P., 1972.

1966 NOWOTTNY, Winifred M. T. "Shakespeare's Tragedies." In **1170.**

1967 RAYSOR, Thomas M. "Intervals of Time and Their Effect upon Dramatic Values in Shakespeare's Tragedies." *JEGP* 37 (1938):21–47.

1968 RIBNER, Irving. *Patterns in Shakespearian Tragedy.* London: Methuen; New York: Barnes & Noble, 1960.

1969 ROSEN, William. *Shakespeare and the Craft of Tragedy.* Cambridge, Mass.: Harvard U.P., 1960.*

1970 ROSSITER, A. P. "Shakespearian Tragedy." In **1245.**

1971 SEN GUPTA, S. C. *Aspects of Shakespearian Tragedy.* Calcutta and London: Oxford U.P., 1972.

1972 SEWALL, Richard B. "Ahab's Quenchless Feud: The Tragic Vision in Shakespeare and Melville." *CompD* 1 (1967):207–18.

1973 *Shakespeare Studies* 26 (1973). Issue chiefly devoted to Shakespeare's Jacobean tragedies.

1974 SIEGEL, Paul N. *Shakespearean Tragedy and the Elizabethan Compromise.* New York: New York U.P., 1957.

1975 SOMERVILLE, H. *Madness in Shakespearian Tragedy.* London: Richards, 1929.

1976 SPEAIGHT, Robert. *Nature in Shakespearian Tragedy.* London: Hollis & Carter, 1955; New York: Collier, 1962.*

1977 SPENCER, Theodore. *Shakespeare and the Nature of Man.* See **339.***

1978 STIRLING, Brents. *Unity in Shakespearian Tragedy: The Interplay of Theme and Character.* New York: Columbia U.P., 1956.*

1979 WEST, Robert H. "Morality and Its Ground in Shakespeare's Tragedies." *RenP 1964* (1965):43–48. Rpt. in **1448.**

1980 WHITAKER, Virgil K. *The Mirror up to Nature: The Technique of Shakespeare's Tragedies.* San Marino, Calif.: Huntington Library, 1965.*

1981 WILSON, Harold S. *On the Design of Shakespearian Tragedy.* Toronto: U. of Toronto P., 1957.*

Shakespeare's Tragic Characters

For studies of villains in Shakespeare's comedies, see **1702** and **1711.**

See also **914, 1022, 1381, 1387, 1512, 1912, 1978,** and **2035.**

1982 ANDERSON, Ruth L. "Excessive Goodness a Tragic Fault." *ShAB* 19 (1944): 85–96.

1983 BARROLL, J. Leeds. *Artificial Persons: The Formation of Character in the Tragedies of Shakespeare.* Columbia: U. of South Carolina P., 1974.*

1984 BLACK, Matthew W. "*Hamartia* in Shakespeare." *LC* 30 (1964):100–16.

1985 BOYER, Clarence Valentine. *The Villain as Hero in Elizabethan Tragedy.* London: Routledge; New York: Dutton, 1914. Rpt., New York: Russell & Russell. Includes a chapter each on *Macbeth* and *Richard III.*

1986 BROCK, J. H. E. *Iago and Some Shakespearean Villains.* Cambridge, Eng.: Heffer, 1937.

1987 BROWN, Huntington. "Enter the Shakespearean Tragic Hero." *EIC* 3 (1953): 285–302.

1988 CAMPBELL, Lily B. *Shakespeare's Tragic Heroes: Slaves of Passion.* Cambridge: Cambridge U.P., 1930. Rpt., New York: Barnes & Noble, 1952; Gloucester, Mass.: P. Smith.*

1989 COE, Charles Norton. *Shakespeare's Villains.* New York: Bookman, 1957. Rev. as *Demi-Devils: The Character of Shakespeare's Villains.* New York: Bookman, 1963.

1990 EDDY, Darlene Mathis. "Nature's Livery, Fortune's Star: Some Considerations of the Shakespearean Tragic Hero." *BSUF* 16.3 (1975):26–48.

1991 HEILMAN, Robert B. "Manliness in the Tragedies: Dramatic Variations." In **1121.**

1992 HOLLAND, Norman N. "Shakespearean Tragedy and the Three Ways of Psychoanalytic Criticism." *HudR* 15 (1962):217–27. Rpt. in **1404.**

1993 MINCOFF, Marco. "Shakespeare and *Hamartia.*" *ES* 45 (1964):130–36.

1994 MURAKAMI, Toshio. "Cleopatra and Volumnia." *ShStud* 9 (1970–71):28–55.

1995 PROSER, Matthew N. *The Heroic Image in Five Shakespearean Tragedies.* Princeton: Princeton U.P., 1965. On *Julius Caesar, Macbeth, Othello, Coriolanus,* and *Antony and Cleopatra.* *

1996 SCHWARTZ, Elias. "The Idea of the Person and Shakespearian Tragedy." *SQ* 16 (1965):39–47.

1997 SPENCER, Theodore. "The Isolation of the Shakespearean Hero." *SR* 52 (1944): 313–31.

1998 SPEVACK, Marvin. "Hero and Villain in Shakespeare: On Dualism and Tragedy." *TSL* 12 (1967):1–11.

1999 SPIVACK, Bernard. *Shakespeare and the Allegory of Evil: The History of a Metaphor in Relation to His Major Villains.* New York: Columbia U.P., 1958. Discusses *Richard III, Othello, King Lear, Much Ado About Nothing,* and *Titus Andronicus.* *

2000 STRATHMANN, Ernest A. "The Devil Can Cite Scripture." *SQ* 15.2 (1964): 19–23. On the seemingly good advice offered by such evil characters as Iago in *Othello,* Goneril and Regan in *King Lear,* and the weird sisters in *Macbeth.*

2001 URE, Peter. "Character and Role from Richard III to Hamlet." In **2418.**

2002 URE, Peter. *Shakespeare and the Inward Self of the Tragic Hero.* Durham: U. of Durham P., 1961. Rpt. in **1269.**

2003 WEIDHORN, Manfred. "The Relation of Title and Name to Identity in Shakespearean Tragedy." *SEL* 9 (1969):303–19.

2004 WILDS, Lillian. *Shakespeare's Character-Dramatists: A Study of a Character Type in Shakespearean Tragedy Through "Hamlet."* Salzburg: Institut für Englische Sprache und Literatur, 1975. On the dramatic type known as "the character as dramatist."

The Early Tragedies

Studies of the early tragedies generally include *Titus Andronicus, Romeo and Juliet, Richard II,* and *Richard III.* Exceptions are noted below.

See also **1582, 1586, 1593,** and **4001.**

2005 BROOKE, Nicholas. *Shakespeare's Early Tragedies.* London: Methuen, 1968. Includes *Julius Caesar* and *Hamlet.* *

2006 DYSON, H. V. D. "The Emergence of Shakespeare's Tragedy." *PBA* 36 (1951 for 1950):69–93.

2007 HAPGOOD, Robert. "Shakespeare's Maimed Rites: The Early Tragedies." *CentR* 9 (1965):494–508. Includes *Julius Caesar.*

2008 HILL, R. F. "Shakespeare's Early Tragic Mode." *SQ* 9 (1958):455–69.

2009 HUNTER, G. K. "Shakespeare's Earliest Tragedies: *Titus Andronicus* and *Romeo and Juliet.*" *ShS* 27 (1974):1–9.

2010 *Shakespeare Survey* 27 (1974). Devoted in part to the early tragedies.

The "Major" or "Great" Tragedies

Except as otherwise noted, the following studies focus on *Hamlet, Othello, King Lear,* and *Macbeth.*

See also **763, 1065, 1429, 1927–29, 1937–38, 1947, 1953–55, 1969,** and **1976–81.**

2011 BRADLEY, A. C. *Shakespearean Tragedy: Lectures on "Hamlet," "Othello," "King Lear," and "Macbeth."* London: Macmillan, 1904. 2nd ed., 1905. Rpt., London: Macmillan; New York: St. Martin's, 1967.*

2012 CAMPBELL, Lily B. *Shakespeare's Tragic Heroes: Slaves of Passion.* See **1988.**

2013 COX, Roger L. *Between Earth and Heaven: Shakespeare, Dostoevsky, and the Meaning of Christian Tragedy.* New York: Holt, Rinehart, & Winston, 1969. On *Hamlet, King Lear,* and *Macbeth.*

2014 CREETH, Edmund. *Mankynde in Shakespeare.* Athens: U. of Georgia P., 1976. A study of *Macbeth, Othello,* and *King Lear* as avatars of English theological dramas.

2015 FAIRCHILD, Arthur H. R. *Shakespeare and the Tragic Theme.* Columbia: U. of Missouri P., 1944.

2016 HAWKES, Terence. *Shakespeare and the Reason: A Study of the Tragedies and the Problem Plays.* London: Routledge & K. Paul, 1964.*

2017 HEILMAN, Robert B. " 'Twere Best Not Know Myself: *Othello, Lear, Macbeth.* " *SQ* 15.2 (1964):89–98. Also in **1153.**

2018 HOLLOWAY, John. *The Story of the Night: Studies in Shakespeare's Major Tragedies.* London: Routledge & K. Paul; Lincoln: U. of Nebraska P., 1961. Includes *Antony and Cleopatra* and *Coriolanus.* *

2019 HUNTER, Robert Grams. *Shakespeare and the Mystery of God's Judgments.* See **1429.** Includes *Richard III.*

2020 INGRAM, R. W. "*Hamlet, Othello,* and *King Lear:* Music and Tragedy." *SJ* 100 (1964):159–72.

2021 KETTLE, Arnold. "From *Hamlet* to *King Lear.* " In **1148.**

2022 KIRSCH, James. *Shakespeare's Royal Self.* New York: Putnam's, 1966. On *Hamlet, King Lear,* and *Macbeth.*

2023 LENGELER, Rainer. *Tragische Wirklichkeit als groteske Verfremdung bei Shakespeare.* Cologne: Böhlau, 1964.

2024 LUCAS, F. L. *Literature and Psychology.* See **1406.***

2025 MCELROY, Bernard. *Shakespeare's Mature Tragedies.* Princeton: Princeton U.P., 1973.*

2026 MORRIS, Ivor. *Shakespeare's God: The Role of Religion in the Tragedies.* London: Allen & Unwin; New York: St. Martin's, 1972.

2027 MUIR, Kenneth. *William Shakespeare: The Great Tragedies.* London: Longmans, Green, 1961.

2028 MYRICK, Kenneth O. "The Theme of Damnation in Shakespearean Tragedy." *SP* 38 (1941):221–45. In *Hamlet, Macbeth,* and *Othello.*

2029 QUINN, Edward James Ruoff, and Joseph GRENNEN, comps. *The Major Shakespearean Tragedies: A Critical Bibliography.* New York: Free Press; London: Collier-Macmillan, 1973.

2030 SISSON, Charles J. *Shakespeare's Tragic Justice.* Scarborough, Ont.: Gage, 1961; London: Methuen, 1962.

2031 STOLL, Elmer Edgar. *Art and Artifice in Shakespeare.* Cambridge: Cambridge U.P., 1933. Rpt., London: Methuen, 1963.

The Final Tragedies

These studies of the "final" tragedies generally focus on *Timon of Athens, Coriolanus,* and *Antony and Cleopatra,* sometimes also including *King Lear* and *Macbeth.*

See also **1599–1602, 1604, 1608,** and **1613.**

2032 FARNHAM, Willard. *Shakespeare's Tragic Frontier: The World of His Final Tragedies.* Berkeley and Los Angeles: U. of California P., 1950. Rpt., New York: Harper & Row, 1973.*

2033 FOAKES, R. A. "Shakespeare's Later Tragedies." In **1121.**

2034 HEILMAN, Robert B. " 'From Mine Own Knowledge': A Theme in the Late Tragedies." *CentR* 8 (1964):17–38.

2035 HUNTER, G. K. "The Last Tragic Heroes." In **1599.**

The Roman Plays

Except as otherwise noted, the following studies focus on *Titus Andronicus, Julius Caesar, Coriolanus,* and *Antony and Cleopatra.* Under the somewhat broader generic category of "classical tragedies" are also to be found *Timon of Athens* and *Troilus and Cressida.*

See also **28, 86, 94, 96–97, 121, 133, 1456, 1462, 1478, 1481, 1493, 1495, 1498,** and **2032–35.**

2036 BARROLL, J. Leeds. "Shakespeare and Roman History." *MLR* 53 (1958):327–43.

2037 BROWER, Reuben A. *Hero and Saint: Shakespeare and the Graeco-Roman Heroic Tradition.* See **1924.***

2038 CANTOR, Paul A. *Shakespeare's Rome: Republic and Empire.* Ithaca and London: Cornell U.P., 1976. On *Antony and Cleopatra* and *Coriolanus.*

2039 CHARNEY, Maurice. *Shakespeare's Roman Plays: The Function of Imagery in the Drama.* Cambridge, Mass.: Harvard U.P., 1961.*

2040 CHARNEY, Maurice, ed. *Discussions of Shakespeare's Roman Plays.* Boston: Heath, 1964. An anthology of essays.

2041 KNIGHT, G. Wilson. *The Imperial Theme: Further Interpretations of Shakespeare's Tragedies Including the Roman Plays.* London: Oxford U.P., 1931. 3rd ed., London: Methuen, 1951. Includes *Macbeth.*

2042 MACCALLUM, M. W. *Shakespeare's Roman Plays and Their Background.* London: Macmillan, 1910. Reissued, London: Macmillan; New York: St. Martin's, 1967. Rpt., New York: Russell & Russell, 1964.

2043 MAXWELL, J. C. "Shakespeare's Roman Plays: 1900–1956." *ShS* 10 (1957):1–11.

2044 PAYNE, Michael. *Irony in Shakespeare's Roman Plays.* Salzburg: Institut für Englische Sprache und Literatur, 1974.

2045 PHILLIPS, James Emerson, Jr. *The State in Shakespeare's Greek and Roman Plays.* New York: Columbia U.P., 1940. Rpt., New York: Octagon, 1972.*

2046 PLATT, Michael. *Rome and Romans According to Shakespeare.* Salzburg: Institut für Englische Sprache und Literatur, 1976. Includes *The Rape of Lucrece.*

2047 *Shakespeare Survey* 10 (1957). Chiefly devoted to the Roman plays.

2048 SIMMONS, J. L. *Shakespeare's Pagan World: The Roman Tragedies.* Charlottesville: U.P. of Virginia, 1973.

2049 SISSON, Charles J. "The Roman Plays." In **1140.**

2050 SPENCER, T. J. B. "Shakespeare and the Elizabethan Romans." *ShS* 10 (1957): 27–38. Rpt. in **2040.**

2051 SPENCER, T. J. B. *William Shakespeare: The Roman Plays.* London: Longmans, Green, 1963. 2nd ed., 1973.

2052 STAMPFER, Judah. *The Tragic Engagement: A Study of Shakespeare's Classical Tragedies.* New York: Funk & Wagnalls, 1968.

2053 THOMSON, J. A. K. *Shakespeare and the Classics.* See **149.**

2054 TRAVERSI, Derek. *Shakespeare: The Roman Plays.* London: Hollis & Carter; Stanford: Stanford U.P., 1963.

2055 WALKER, Roy. "The Northern Star: An Essay on the Roman Plays." *SQ* 2 (1951):287–93.

The Love Tragedies

This grouping overlaps substantially with others already presented under Tragedy.

See also **1527, 1896, 2181, 2197,** and **4005.**

2056 BRODWIN, Leonora Leet. *Elizabethan Love Tragedy, 1587–1625.* See **1894.**

2057 DICKEY, Franklin M. *Not Wisely But Too Well: Shakespeare's Love Tragedies.* San Marino, Calif.: Huntington Library, 1957. On *Romeo and Juliet, Troilus and Cressida, Antony and Cleopatra,* and the Sonnets.*

2058 MARSH, D. R. C. *Passion Lends Them Power: A Study of Shakespeare's Love Tragedies.* Manchester: U. of Manchester P.; New York: Barnes & Noble, 1976. Focuses on *Romeo and Juliet, Othello,* and *Antony and Cleopatra.*

2059 MASON, H. A. *Shakespeare's Tragedies of Love: An Examination of the Possibility of Common Readings of "Romeo and Juliet," "Othello," "King Lear," and "Antony and Cleopatra."* London: Chatto & Windus; New York: Barnes & Noble, 1970.

2060 RABKIN, Norman. "Eros and Death." In **1243.**

2061 SELTZER, Daniel. " 'Their Tragic Scene': *The Phoenix and Turtle* and Shakespeare's Love Tragedies." *SQ* 12 (1961):91–101.

Part II
Individual Works

All's Well That Ends Well

See also **1177, 1202, 1227, 1245, 1258, 1283, 1370, 1374, 1396, 1628, 1631, 1637, 1651, 1694, 1780–86, 1788–91,** and **1793–97.**

2062 ADAMS, John F. "*All's Well That Ends Well:* The Paradox of Procreation." *SQ* 12 (1961):261–70.

2063 ARTHOS, John. "The Comedy of Generation." *EIC* 5 (1955):97–117.

2064 BENNETT, Josephine Waters. "New Techniques of Comedy in *All's Well That Ends Well.*" *SQ* 18 (1967):337–62.

2065 BERGERON, David M. "The Mythical Structure of *All's Well That Ends Well.*" *TSLL* 14 (1973):559–68.

2066 BERGERON, David M. "The Structure of Healing in *All's Well That Ends Well.*" *SAB* 37.4 (1972):25–34.

2067 BERTHOFF, Warner. " 'Our Means Will Make Us Means': Character as Virtue in *Hamlet* and *All's Well.*" *NLH* 5 (1974):319–51.

2068 BRADBROOK, M. C. "Virtue Is the True Nobility: A Study of the Structure of *All's Well That Ends Well.*" *RES,* n.s. 1 (1950):289–301. Rpt. in **1660.***

2069 CALDERWOOD, James L. "The Mingled Yarn of *All's Well.*" *JEGP* 62 (1963): 61–76.

2070 CALDERWOOD, James L. "Styles of Knowing in *All's Well.*" *MLQ* 25 (1964): 272–94.

2071 CARTER, Albert Howard. "In Defense of Bertram." *SQ* 7 (1956):21–31.

2072 COGHILL, Nevill. "*All's Well* Revalued." *Studies in English Language and Literature in Honour of Margaret Schlauch.* Ed. Mieczyslaw BRAHMER et al. Warsaw: PWN-Polish Scientific Publ., 1966.

2073 DENNIS, Carl. "*All's Well That Ends Well* and the Meaning of *Agape.*" *PQ* 50 (1971):75–84.

2074 DONALDSON, Ian. "*All's Well That Ends Well:* Shakespeare's Play of Endings." *EIC* 27 (1977):34–55.

2075 GODSHALK, William Leigh. "*All's Well That Ends Well* and the Morality Play." *SQ* 25 (1974):61–70.

2076 HALIO, Jay L. "*All's Well That Ends Well.*" *SQ* 15.1 (1964):33–43.

2077 HAPGOOD, Robert. "The Life of Shame: Parolles and *All's Well.*" *EIC* 15 (1965):269–78.

2078 HETHMON, Robert H. "The Case for *All's Well:* What Is Wrong with the King?" *Drama Critique* 7 (1964):26–31.

2079 HILL, W. Speed. "Marriage as Destiny: An Essay on *All's Well That Ends Well.*" *ELR* 5 (1975):344–59.

2080 HUNTER, G. K., ed. *All's Well That Ends Well.* In the Arden Shakespeare. See **350.***

2081 HUSTON, J. Dennis. " 'Some Stain of Soldier': The Functions of Parolles in *All's Well That Ends Well.*" *SQ* 21 (1970):431–38.

2082 KING, Walter N. "Shakespeare's 'Mingled Yarn.' " *MLQ* 21 (1960):33–44.

2083 KRAPP, George Philip. "Parolles." In **1158.**

2084 LA GUARDIA, Eric. "Chastity, Regeneration, and World Order in *All's Well That Ends Well.*" *Myth and Symbol: Critical Approaches and Applications by Northrop Frye, L. C. Knights, and Others.* Ed. Bernice SLOTE. Lincoln: U. of Nebraska P., 1963.

2085 LA GUARDIA, Eric. *Nature Redeemed: The Imitation of Order in Three Renaissance Poems.* The Hague: Mouton, 1966, pp. 148–68.

2086 LAYMAN, B. J. "Shakespeare's Helena, Boccaccio's Giletta, and the Riddles of 'Skill' and 'Honesty.' " *EM* 23 (1972):39–53.

2087 LEECH, Clifford. "The Theme of Ambition in *All's Well That Ends Well.*" *ELH* 21 (1954):17–29. Rpt. in **1790.***

2088 LEGGATT, Alexander. "*All's Well That Ends Well:* The Testing of Romance." *MLQ* 32 (1971):21–41.*

2089 LEGOUIS, Émile. "La Comtesse de Roussillon." *English* 1 (1937):399–404.

2090 LOVE, John M. " 'Though Many of the Rich Are Damn'd': Dark Comedy and Social Class in *All's Well That Ends Well.*" *TSLL* 18 (1977):517–27.

2091 MAGEE, William H. "Helena, a Female Hamlet." *EM* 22 (1971):31–46.

2092 NAGARAJAN, S. "The Structure of *All's Well That Ends Well.*" *EIC* 10 (1960): 24–31.

2093 PEARCE, Frances M. "Analogical Probability and the Clown in *All's Well That Ends Well.*" *SJW* 108 (1972):129–44.

2094 PEARCE, Frances M. "In Quest of Unity: A Study of Failure and Redemption in *All's Well That Ends Well.*" *SQ* 25 (1974):71–88.

2095 PRICE, Joseph G. *The Unfortunate Comedy: A Study of "All's Well That Ends Well" and Its Critics.* Toronto: U. of Toronto P., 1968.*

2096 RANALD, Margaret Loftus. "The Betrothals of *All's Well That Ends Well.*" *HLQ* 26 (1963):179–92.

2097 ROTHMAN, Jules. "A Vindication of Parolles." *SQ* 23 (1972):183–96.

2098 SCHOFF, Francis G. "Claudio, Bertram, and a Note on Interpretation." *SQ* 10 (1959):11–23.

2099 SHAPIRO, Michael. " 'The Web of Our Life': Human Frailty and Mutual Redemption in *All's Well That Ends Well.*" *JEGP* 71 (1972):514–26.*

2100 SILVERMAN, J. M. "Two Types of Comedy in *All's Well That Ends Well.*" *SQ* 24 (1973):25–34.

2101 SISSON, Charles J. "Shakespeare's Helena and Dr. William Harvey, with a Case-History from Harvey's Practice." *E&S,* n.s. 13 (1960):1–20.

2102 SMALLWOOD, R. L. "The Design of *All's Well That Ends Well.*" *ShS* 25 (1972):45–61.

2103 STENSGAARD, Richard K. "*All's Well That Ends Well* and the Galenico-Paracelsian Controversy." *RenQ* 25 (1972):173–88.

2104 TURNER, Robert Y. "Dramatic Conventions in *All's Well That Ends Well.*" *PMLA* 75 (1960):497–502.

2105 WARREN, Roger. "Why Does It End Well? Helena, Bertram, and the Sonnets." *ShS* 22 (1969):79–92.

2106 WHEELER, Richard P. "The King and the Physician's Daughter: *All's Well That Ends Well* and the Late Romances." *CompD* 8 (1974–75):311–27.

2107 WHEELER, Richard P. "Marriage and Manhood in *All's Well That Ends Well.*" *BuR* 21.1 (1973):103–24.

2108 WILSON, Harold S. "Dramatic Emphasis in *All's Well That Ends Well.*" *HLQ* 13 (1950):217–40. Rpt. in **1790.***

Antony and Cleopatra

General Studies

See also **86, 96, 149, 339, 356, 457, 475, 541, 685, 807, 1035, 1177, 1194, 1196, 1201, 1204, 1218, 1279, 1306, 1477, 1532, 1598–1600, 1792, 1924, 1927, 1937, 1947, 1957–58, 1965, 1969, 1976, 1981, 1995, 2018, 2032–61,** and **2346.**

2109 ADELMAN, Janet. *The Common Liar: An Essay on "Antony and Cleopatra."* New Haven and London: Yale U.P., 1973.*

2110 BARNET, Sylvan. "Recognition and Reversal in *Antony and Cleopatra.*" *SQ* 8 (1957):331–34.

2111 BARROLL, J. Leeds. "Scarrus and the Scarred Soldier." *HLQ* 22 (1958):31–39. Studies a textual problem.

2112 BECKERMAN, Bernard. "Past the Size of Dreaming." In **2166.** On the way in which the play overflows the customary bounds of the drama, both theatrically and imaginatively.

2113 BELL, Arthur H. "Time and Convention in *Antony and Cleopatra.*" *SQ* 24 (1973):253–64.

2114 BLISSETT, William. "Dramatic Irony in *Antony and Cleopatra.*" *SQ* 18 (1967): 151–66.

2115 BONJOUR, Adrien. "From Shakespeare's Venus to Cleopatra's Cupids." *ShS* 15 (1962):73–80.

2116 BRADLEY, A. C. "Shakespeare's *Antony and Cleopatra.*" In **1185.***

2117 BROWN, John Russell, ed. *Shakespeare, "Antony and Cleopatra": A Casebook.* London: Macmillan, 1968.

2118 BURKE, Kenneth. "Shakespearean Persuasion: *Antony and Cleopatra.*" In **1188.***

2119 CAPUTI, Anthony. "Shakespeare's *Antony and Cleopatra:* Tragedy without Terror." *SQ* 16 (1965):183–91.

2120 CECIL, David. *"Antony and Cleopatra."* Glasgow: Jackson, 1943. Rpt. in *Poets and Story-Tellers.* London: Constable; New York: Macmillan, 1949. Rpt., New York: Barnes & Noble, 1961.

2121 COUCHMAN, Gordon W. *"Antony and Cleopatra* and the Subjective Convention." *PMLA* 76 (1961):420–25. Concerns Shaw's criticism of the play.

2122 DAICHES, David. "Imagery and Meaning in *Antony and Cleopatra.*" *ES* 43 (1962):343–58. Rpt. in *More Literary Essays.* Edinburgh: Oliver & Boyd, 1968.

2123 DANBY, John F. *"Antony and Cleopatra:* A Shakespearian Adjustment." In **1600.**

2124 DANBY, John F. "The Shakespearean Dialectic: An Aspect of *Antony and Cleopatra."* *Scrutiny* 16 (1949):196–213.

2125 DORAN, Madeleine. " 'High Events as These': The Language of Hyperbole in *Antony and Cleopatra."* *QQ* 72 (1965):26–51.

2126 DORIUS, R. J. "Shakespeare's Dramatic Modes and *Antony and Cleopatra."* In *Literatur als Kritik des Lebens,* ed. Rudolf HAAS, et al. See **4273.**

2127 FISCH, Harold. *"Antony and Cleopatra:* The Limits of Mythology." *ShS* 23 (1970):59–67.

2128 FITCH, Robert E. "No Greater Crack?" *SQ* 19 (1968):3–17.

2129 FOAKES, R. A. "Vision and Reality in *Antony and Cleopatra."* *DUJ* 56, n.s. 25 (1964):66–76.

2130 GOLDBERG, S. L. "The Tragedy of the Imagination: A Reading of *Antony and Cleopatra."* *CR* 4 (1961):41–64.

2131 GRIFFITHS, G. S. *"Antony and Cleopatra."* *E&S* 31 (1946 for 1945):34–67.

2132 GÜNTHER, Peter. "Shakespeares *Antony and Cleopatra:* Wandel und Gestaltung eines Stoffes." *SJH* (1968):94–108.

2133 HALLETT, Charles A. "Change, Fortune, and Time: Aspects of the Sublunar World in *Antony and Cleopatra."* *JEGP* 75 (1976):75–89.

2134 HAPGOOD, Robert. "Hearing Shakespeare: Sound and Meaning in *Antony and Cleopatra."* *ShS* 24 (1971):1–12.

2135 HEFFNER, Ray L., Jr. "The Messengers in Shakespeare's *Antony and Cleopatra."* *ELH* 43 (1976):154–62.

2136 HOMAN, Sidney R. "Divided Response and the Imagination in *Antony and Cleopatra."* *PQ* 49 (1970):460–68.

2137 JENKIN, Bernard. *"Antony and Cleopatra:* Some Suggestions on the Monument Scenes." *RES* 21 (1945):1–14.

2138 JORGENSEN, Paul A. "Antony and the Protesting Soldiers: A Renaissance Tradition for the Structure of *Antony and Cleopatra.*" In **1167.**

2139 KAULA, David. "The Time Sense of *Antony and Cleopatra."* *SQ* 15.3 (1964): 211–23. Rpt. in **1125.***

2140 KNIGHTS, L. C. "On the Tragedy of *Antony and Cleopatra."* *Scrutiny* 16 (1949):318–23. A reply to **2124.**

2141 KROOK, Dorothea. "Tragic and Heroic in Shakespeare's *Antony and Cleopatra.*" *Studies in the Drama.* Ed. Arieh SACHS. Jerusalem: Magnes P. of Hebrew U., 1967. Rpt. in **1884.**

2142 LEAVIS, F. R. "*Antony and Cleopatra* and *All for Love:* A Critical Exercise." *Scrutiny* 5 (1936):158–69.

2143 LEE, Robin. *Shakespeare, "Antony and Cleopatra."* London: Arnold, 1971.

2144 LLOYD, Michael. "The Roman Tongue." *SQ* 10 (1959):461–68.

2145 LYONS, Charles R. "The Serpent, the Sun, and 'Nilus Slime': A Focal Point for the Ambiguity of Shakespeare's *Antony and Cleopatra.*" *Rivista di Letterature Moderne e Comparate* (Florence), 21 (1968):13–34.

2146 MACK, Maynard. "*Antony and Cleopatra:* The Stillness and the Dance." In **1130.***

2147 MACMULLAN, Katherine Vance. "Death Imagery in *Antony and Cleopatra.*" *SQ* 14 (1963):399–410.

2148 MARKELS, Julian. *The Pillar of the World: "Antony and Cleopatra" in Shakespeare's Development.* Columbus: Ohio State U.P., 1968.

2149 MILLS, Laurens J. *The Tragedies of Shakespeare's "Antony and Cleopatra."* Bloomington: Indiana U.P., 1964.

2150 MOORE, John Rees. "The Enemies of Love: The Example of Antony and Cleopatra." *KR* 31 (1969):646–74.

2151 MORGAN, Margery M. "Your Crown's Awry: *Antony and Cleopatra* in the Comic Tradition." *Komos* 1 (1968):128–39.

2152 MORRIS, Helen. "Shakespeare and Dürer's Apocalypse." *ShakS* 4 (1969 for 1968):252–62. Concerns a possible source.

2153 MUIR, Kenneth. "The Imagery of *Antony and Cleopatra.*" *Kwartalnik Neofilologiczny* 8 (1961):249–64. Rpt., rev., in **1238.**

2154 NANDY, Dipak. "The Realism of *Antony and Cleopatra.*" In **1148.**

2155 NELSON, C. E. "*Antony and Cleopatra* and the Triumph of Rome." *UR* 32 (1966):199–203.

2156 NORMAN, Arthur M. Z. "Daniel's *The Tragedie of Cleopatra* and *Antony and Cleopatra.*" *SQ* 9 (1958):11–18.

2157 OAKESHOTT, Walter. "Shakespeare and Plutarch." In **1139.**

2158 ORNSTEIN, Robert. "The Ethic of the Imagination: Love and Art in *Antony and Cleopatra.*" In **1599.***

2159 PAYNE, Michael. "Erotic Irony and Polarity in *Antony and Cleopatra.*" *SQ* 24 (1973):265–79.

2160 PEARSON, Norman Holmes. "*Antony and Cleopatra.*" In **1161.**

2161 PERRET, Marion. "Shakespeare's Use of Messengers in *Antony and Cleopatra.*" *Drama Survey* 5 (1966):67–72.

2162 RACKIN, Phyllis. "Shakespeare's Boy Cleopatra, the Decorum of Nature, and the Golden World of Poetry." *PMLA* 87 (1972):201–12.***

2163 RIDLEY, M. R., ed. *Antony and Cleopatra.* In the Arden Shakespeare. See **350.**

2164 RIEMER, A. P. *A Reading of Shakespeare's "Antony and Cleopatra."* Sydney: Sydney U.P., 1968.

2165 ROERECKE, Edith M. "Baroque Aspects of *Antony and Cleopatra.*" In **1167.**

2166 ROSE, Mark, ed. *Twentieth Century Interpretations of "Antony and Cleopatra."* Englewood Cliffs, N.J.: Prentice-Hall, 1977.

2167 ROSE, Paul Lawrence. "The Politics of *Antony and Cleopatra.*" *SQ* 20 (1969): 379–89.

2168 ROTHSCHILD, Herbert B., Jr. "The Oblique Encounter: Shakespeare's Confrontation of Plutarch with Special Reference to *Antony and Cleopatra.*" *ELR* 6 (1976):404–29.

2169 SCHWARTZ, Elias. "The Shackling of Accidents: *Antony and Cleopatra.*" *CE* 23 (1962):550–58.

2170 SEATON, Ethel. "*Antony and Cleopatra* and the *Book of Revelation.*" *RES* 22 (1946):219–24.

2171 SHAPIRO, Stephen A. "The Varying Shore of the World: Ambivalence in *Antony and Cleopatra.*" *MLQ* 27 (1966):18–32.

2172 SIEMON, James Edward. " 'The Strong Necessity of Time': Dilemma in *Antony and Cleopatra.*" *ES* 54 (1973):316–25.

2173 SIMMONS, J. L. "*Antony and Cleopatra* and *Coriolanus,* Shakespeare's Heroic Tragedies: A Jacobean Adjustment." *ShS* 26 (1973):95–101. Rpt., rev., in **2048.**

2174 SIMMONS, J. L. "The Comic Pattern and Vision in *Antony and Cleopatra.*" *ELH* 36 (1969):493–510. Rpt., rev., in **2048.**

2175 SMITH, J. Oates. "The Alchemy of *Antony and Cleopatra.*" *BuR* 12.1 (1964): 37–50.

2176 SMITH, Sheila M. " 'This Great Solemnity': A Study of the Presentation of Death in *Antony and Cleopatra.*" *ES* 45 (1964):163–76.

2177 SPENCER, Benjamin T. "*Antony and Cleopatra* and the Paradoxical Metaphor." *SQ* 9 (1958):373–78.

2178 STROUP, Thomas B. "The Structure of *Antony and Cleopatra.*" *SQ* 15.2 (1964): 289–98. Also in **1153.**

2179 THOMAS, Mary Olive. "The Opening Scenes of *Antony and Cleopatra.*" *SAQ* 71 (1972):565–72.

2180 THOMAS, Mary Olive. "The Repetitions in Antony's Death Scene." *SQ* 9 (1958):153–57.

2181 TRACI, Philip J. *The Love Play of "Antony and Cleopatra."* The Hague and Paris: Mouton, 1970.

2182 WADDINGTON, Raymond B. "*Antony and Cleopatra:* 'What Venus Did with Mars.' " *ShakS* 2 (1967 for 1966):210–27.

2183 WEITZ, Morris. "Literature without Philosophy: *Antony and Cleopatra.*" *ShS* 28 (1975):29–36.

2184 WHATLEY, Janet. "L'Orient désert: *Bérénice* and *Antony and Cleopatra.*" *UTQ* 44 (1975):96–114.

2185 WILLIAMSON, Marilyn L. "Fortune in *Antony and Cleopatra.*" *JEGP* 67 (1968):423–29.

2186 WILLIAMSON, Marilyn L. *Infinite Variety: Antony and Cleopatra in Renaissance Drama and Earlier Tradition.* Mystic: Lawrence Verry, 1974.

2187 WILLIAMSON, Marilyn L. "Patterns of Development in *Antony and Cleopatra.*" *TSL* 14 (1969):129–39.

2188 WILLIAMSON, Marilyn L. "The Political Context in *Antony and Cleopatra.*" *SQ* 21 (1970):241–51.

2189 WIMSATT, William K., Jr. "Poetry and Morals: A Relation Reargued." *Thought* 23 (1948):281–99. Rpt. in *The Verbal Icon.* Lexington: U. of Kentucky P., 1954; New York: Noonday, 1958.

Character Studies

See also **1376, 1391, 1978, 1983, 1988,** and **1994–95.**

2190 BARROLL, J. Leeds. "Antony and Pleasure." *JEGP* 57 (1958):708–20.

2191 BARROLL, J. Leeds. "The Characterization of Octavius." *ShakS* 6 (1972 for 1970):231–88.

2192 BARROLL, J. Leeds. "Shakespeare and the Art of Character: A Study of Antony." *ShakS* 5 (1970 for 1969):159–235.

2193 BOWLING, Lawrence Edward. "Antony's Internal Disunity." *SEL* 4 (1964): 239–46.

2194 CUNNINGHAM, Dolora G. "The Characterization of Shakespeare's Cleopatra." *SQ* 6 (1955):9–17.

2195 DONNO, Elizabeth Story. "Cleopatra Again." *SQ* 7 (1956):227–33.

2196 ERSKINE-HILL, Howard. "Antony and Octavius: The Theme of Temperance in Shakespeare's *Antony and Cleopatra.*" *RMS* 14 (1970):26–47.

2197 HAMILTON, Donna B. "*Antony and Cleopatra* and the Tradition of Noble Lovers." *SQ* 24 (1973):245–51.

2198 HUME, Robert D. "Individuation and Development of Character Through Language in *Antony and Cleopatra.*" *SQ* 24 (1973):280–300.

2199 HUNTER, Robert Grams. "Cleopatra and the 'Oestre Junonicque.' " *ShakS* 5 (1970 for 1969):236–39. Deals with allusive comparisons among Cleopatra, Juno, Isis, and Io.

2200 KIRSCHBAUM, Leo. "Shakspere's Cleopatra." *ShAB* 19 (1944):161–71.

2201 LLOYD, Michael. "Antony and the Game of Chance." *JEGP* 61 (1962):548–54.

2202 LLOYD, Michael. "Cleopatra as Isis." *ShS* 12 (1959):88–94.

2203 MCGINN, Donald Joseph. "Cleopatra's Immolation Scene." *Essays in Literary History Presented to J. Milton French.* Eds. Rudolf KIRK and C. F. MAIN. New York: Russell & Russell, 1965.

2204 RINEHART, Keith. "Shakespeare's Cleopatra and England's Elizabeth." *SQ* 23 (1972):81–86. See also Helen MORRIS, "Queen Elizabeth I 'Shadowed' in Cleopatra." *HLQ* 32 (1969):271–78.

2205 SHAW, J. "Cleopatra and Seleucus." *REL* 7.4 (1966):79–86.

2206 STEIN, Arnold. "The Image of Antony: Lyric and Tragic Imagination." *KR* 21 (1959):586–606. Rpt. in **1125.***

2207 STEMPEL, Daniel. "The Transmigration of the Crocodile." *SQ* 7 (1956):59–72. A study of critical attitudes toward Cleopatra and of images associated with her.

2208 STIRLING, Brents. "Cleopatra's Scene with Seleucus: Plutarch, Daniel, and Shakespeare." *SQ* 15.2 (1964):299–311. Also in **1153**.

2209 STOLL, Elmer Edgar. "Cleopatra." *MLR* 23 (1928):145–63.

2210 STULL, Joseph S. "Cleopatra's Magnanimity: The Dismissal of the Messenger." *SQ* 7 (1956):73–78.

2211 THOMAS, Mary Olive. "Cleopatra and the 'Mortal Wretch.' " *SJ* 99 (1963): 174–83. About Cleopatra's death.

2212 WAITH, Eugene M. "Manhood and Valor in Two Shakespearean Tragedies." *ELH* 17 (1950):262–73. Examines *Antony and Cleopatra* and *Macbeth.*

2213 WAITH, Eugene M. *The Herculean Hero in Marlowe, Chapman, Shakespeare, and Dryden.* New York: Columbia U.P.; London: Chatto & Windus, 1962. Includes discussions of *Antony and Cleopatra* and *Coriolanus.* *

2214 WILSON, Elkin Calhoun. "Shakespeare's Enobarbus." In **1154**.

As You Like It

See also **326, 514, 555, 833, 1221, 1289, 1317, 1370, 1374, 1389, 1396, 1518, 1628, 1631, 1637, 1651, 1682, 1707–09, 1719–39, 1778–79, 1781–82, 1787,** and **2538.**

2215 BABB, Lawrence. *The Elizabethan Malady.* See **306**.

2216 BAIRD, Ruth Cates. "*As You Like It* and Its Source." *Essays in Honor of Walter Clyde Curry.* Nashville: Vanderbilt U.P., 1954.

2217 BARNET, Sylvan. " 'Strange Events': Improbability in *As You Like It.*" *ShakS* 4 (1969 for 1968):119–31.

2218 BARTON, Anne. "*As You Like It* and *Twelfth Night:* Shakespeare's Sense of an Ending." In **1722.**

2219 BENNETT, Josephine Waters. "Jaques' Seven Ages." *ShAB* 18 (1943):168–74.

2220 BENNETT, Robert B. "The Reform of a Malcontent: Jaques and the Meaning of *As You Like It.*" *ShakS* 9 (1976):183–204.

2221 BRADFORD, Alan Taylor. "Jaques' Distortion of the Seven-Ages Paradigm." *SQ* 27 (1976):171–76.

2222 CAMPBELL, Oscar James. "Jaques." *Huntington Lib. Bull.* 8 (1935):71–102.

2223 CHEW, Samuel C. " 'This Strange Eventful History.' " In **1154.**

2224 CIRILLO, Albert R. "*As You Like It:* Pastoralism Gone Awry." *ELH* 38 (1971): 19–39.

2225 COLE, Howard C. "The Moral Vision of *As You Like it.*" *CollL* 3 (1976):17–32.

2226 DORAN, Madeleine. " 'Yet Am I Inland Bred.' " *SQ* 15.2 (1964):99–114. Also in **1153**.

2227 FABER, M. D. "On Jaques: Psychoanalytic Remarks." *UR* 36 (1969–70):89–96, 179–82.

2228 FINK, Z. S. "Jaques and the Malcontent Traveler." *PQ* 14 (1935):237–52.

2229 FORTIN, René E. " 'Tongues in Trees': Symbolic Patterns in *As You Like It.*" *TSLL* 14 (1973):569–82.

2230 GARDNER, Helen. "*As You Like It.*" In **1138.** Rpt. in **1656, 1660,** and **1731.***

2231 HALIO, Jay L. " 'No Clock in the Forest': Time in *As You Like It.*" *SEL* 2 (1962):197–207.

2232 HALIO, Jay L., ed. *Twentieth Century Interpretations of "As You Like It."* Englewood Cliffs, N.J.: Prentice-Hall, 1968. An anthology of essays.

2233 HANKINS, John E. "The Penalty of Adam—*As You Like It,* II. i. 5." In **1171.**

2234 HOWARTH, Herbert. "Shakespeare in 1599: The Event and the Art." *LC* 30 (1964):88–99.

2235 JAMIESON, Michael. *Shakespeare: "As You Like It."* London: Arnold, 1965.

2236 JENKINS, Harold. "*As You Like It.*" *ShS* 8 (1955):40–51. Rpt. in **1132.***

2237 KELLY, Thomas. "Shakespeare's Romantic Heroes: Orlando Reconsidered." *SQ* 24 (1973):12–24.

2238 KNOWLES, Richard. "Myth and Type in *As You Like It.*" *ELH* 33 (1966):1–22.

2239 KREIDER, Paul V. "Genial Literary Satire in the Forest of Arden." *ShAB* 10 (1935):212–31.

2240 KUHN, Maura Slattery. "Much Virtue in *If.*" *SQ* 28 (1977):40–50.

2241 LASCELLES, Mary. "Shakespeare's Pastoral Comedy." In **1138.**

2242 LATHAM, Agnes, ed. *As You Like It.* In the Arden Shakespeare. See **350.**

2243 MCINTOSH, Angus. "*As You Like It:* A Grammatical Clue to Character." *REL* 4.2 (1963):68–81.

2244 MINCOFF, Marco. "What Shakespeare Did to *Rosalynde.*" *SJ* 96 (1960):78–89.

2245 MORRIS, Harry. "*As You Like It:* Et in Arcadia Ego." *SQ* 26 (1975):269–75.

2246 PALMER, D. J. "Art and Nature in *As You Like It.*" *PQ* 49 (1970):30–40.

2247 PALMER, D. J. "*As You Like It* and the Idea of Play." *CritQ* 13 (1971):234–45.

2248 PIERCE, Robert B. "The Moral Languages of *Rosalynde* and *As You Like It.*" *SP* 68 (1971):167–76.

2249 SCHUTTE, William M. "The Worlds of *As You Like It.*" *Wisconsin Studies in Literature* 1 (1964):1–10.

2250 SHAW, John. "Fortune and Nature in *As You Like It.*" *SQ* 6 (1955):45–50.

2251 SMITH, James. "*As You Like It.*" *Scrutiny* 9 (1940):9–32.

2252 STAEBLER, Warren. "Shakespeare's Play of Atonement." *ShAB* 24 (1949): 91–105.

2253 STOLL, Elmer Edgar. "Shakspere, Marston, and the Malcontent Type." *MP* 3 (1906):281–303.

2254 TAYLOR, Michael. "*As You Like It:* The Penalty of Adam." *CritQ* 15 (1973): 76–80.

2255 UHLIG, Claus. " 'The Sobbing Deer': *As You Like It,* II. i. 21–66 and the Historical Context." *RenD,* n.s. 3 (1970):79–109.

2256 VAN DEN BERG, Kent Talbot. "Theatrical Fiction and the Reality of Love in *As You Like It.*" *PMLA* 90 (1975):885–93.

2257 WILLIAMSON, Marilyn L. "The Masque of Hymen in *As You Like It.*" *CompD* 2 (1968–69):248–58.

2258 WILSON, Rawdon. "The Way to Arden: Attitudes toward Time in *As You Like It.*" *SQ* 26 (1975):16–24.

2259 WOLK, Anthony. "The Extra Jaques in *As You Like It.*" *SQ* 23 (1972):101–05.

The Comedy of Errors

See also **1226, 1578, 1582, 1586, 1589, 1594–95, 1631–32, 1637, 1640, 1666, 1668, 1671, 1685, 1689, 1697, 1704, 1713–14, 1717–18, 1721,** and **1727.**

2260 ARTHOS, John. "Shakespeare's Transformations of Plautus." *CompD* 1 (1967–68):239–53. Rpt., rev., in **1578.**

2261 BABULA, William. "If I Dream Not: Unity in *The Comedy of Errors.*" *South Atl. Bull.* 38.4 (1973):26–33.

2262 BALDWIN, T. W. *On the Compositional Genetics of "The Comedy of Errors."* Urbana: U. of Illinois P., 1965.

2263 BALDWIN, T. W. "Three Homilies in *The Comedy of Errors.*" In **1144.**

2264 BALDWIN, T. W. *William Shakespeare Adapts a Hanging.* Princeton: Princeton U.P., 1931.

2265 BARBER, C. L. "Shakespearian Comedy in *The Comedy of Errors.*" *CE* 25 (1964):493–97.

2266 BROOKS, Harold F. "Themes and Structure in *The Comedy of Errors.*" In **1582.** Rpt. in **1660.***

2267 CLUBB, Louise George. "Italian Comedy and *The Comedy of Errors.*" *CL* 19 (1967):240–51.

2268 ELLIOTT, G. R. "Weirdness in *The Comedy of Errors.*" *UTQ* 9 (1939):95–106. Rpt. in **1656.**

2269 FERGUSSON, Francis. "Two Comedies: *The Comedy of Errors* and *Much Ado About Nothing.*" *SR* 62 (1954):24–37. Rpt. In *The Human Image in Dramatic Literature.* Garden City, N.Y.: Doubleday, 1957; Gloucester, Mass.: P. Smith, 1969. Rpt. also in **1656** and **1731.***

2270 FOAKES, R. A., ed. *The Comedy of Errors.* In the Arden Shakespeare. See **350.**

2271 GILL, Erma M. "A Comparison of the Characters in *The Comedy of Errors* with Those in the *Menaechmi.*" *UTSE* 5 (1925):79–95.

2272 GILL, Erma M. "The Plot-Structure of *The Comedy of Errors* in Relation to Its Source." *UTSE* 10 (1930):13–65.

2273 GRIVELET, Michel. "Shakespeare, Molière, and the Comedy of Ambiguity." *ShS* 22 (1969):15–26.

2274 HENZE, Richard. "*The Comedy of Errors:* A Freely Binding Chain." *SQ* 22 (1971):35–41.

2275 HOSLEY, Richard. "The Formal Influence of Plautus and Terence." See **122.**

2276 PARKS, George B. "Shakespeare's Map for *The Comedy of Errors.*" *JEGP* 39 (1940):93–97.

2277 PETRONELLA, Vincent F. "Structure and Theme through Separation and Union in Shakespeare's *The Comedy of Errors.*" *MLR* 69 (1974):481–88.

2278 ROSADOR, Kurt Tetzeli von. " 'Intricate Impeach': Die Einheit der *Comedy of Errors.*" *SJH* (1975):137–53.

2279 SĀLGADO, Gāmini. " 'Time's Deformed Hand': Sequence, Consequence, and Inconsequence in *The Comedy of Errors.*" *ShS* 25 (1972):81–91.

2280 SANDERSON, James L. "Patience in *The Comedy of Errors.*" *TSLL* 16 (1975): 603–18.

2281 SCHLÖSSER, Anselm. "Das Motiv der Entfremdung in der *Komödie der Irrungen.*" *SJW* 100–01 (1964–65):57–71.

2282 SEGAL, Erich. *Roman Laughter: The Comedy of Plautus.* Cambridge, Mass.: Harvard U.P., 1968.

2283 THOMAS, Sidney. "The Date of *The Comedy of Errors.*" *SQ* 7 (1956):377–84.

2284 WILLIAMS, Gwyn. "*The Comedy of Errors* Rescued from Tragedy." *REL* 5.4 (1964):63–71.

Coriolanus

General Studies

See also **86, 96, 121, 133, 149, 348, 362, 1201, 1203, 1216, 1218, 1230–31, 1559, 1781, 1783, 1924, 1947, 1950, 1969, 1981, 2018,** and **2032–55.**

2285 BERRY, Ralph. "The Metamorphoses of *Coriolanus.*" *SQ* 26 (1975):172–83.

2286 BRADLEY, A. C. *"Coriolanus."PBA* 5 (1913 for 1911–12):457–73. Rpt. in **1116** and **1184.***

2287 BRITTIN, Norman A. "Coriolanus, Alceste, and Dramatic Genres." *PMLA* 71 (1956):799–807.

2288 BROCKBANK, J. Philip, ed. *Coriolanus.* In the Arden Shakespeare. See **350.**

2289 BRUNKHORST, Martin. *Shakespeares "Coriolanus" in deutscher Bearbeitung.* Berlin and New York: de Gruyter, 1973. On German adaptations.

2290 BYRNE, Muriel St. Clare. "Classical *Coriolanus.*" *National Review* 96 (1931): 426–30.

2291 CARR, W. I. " 'Gracious Silence'—A Selective Reading of *Coriolanus.*" *ES* 46 (1965):221–34.

2292 CHAPPELL, Fred. "Shakespeare's *Coriolanus* and Plutarch's *Life of Cato.*" *RenP 1962* (1963):9–16.

2293 CRAIG, Hardin. "*Coriolanus:* Interpretation." In **1156.**

2294 CROWLEY, Richard C. "*Coriolanus* and the Epic Genre." In **1613.**

2295 ENRIGHT, D. J. *"Coriolanus:* Tragedy or Debate?" *EIC* 4 (1954):1–19. Rpt., rev., in *The Apothecary's Shop.* London: Secker & Warburg, 1957. Rpt. also in **2040.***

2296 FRYE, Dean. "Commentary in Shakespeare: The Case of *Coriolanus."* *ShakS* 1 (1965):105–17.

2297 FRYE, Northrop. "The Tragedies of Nature and Fortune." In **1145** (1962 for 1961).

2298 GASSENMEIER, Michael. "Odi et amo: Das Dilemma von Shakespeares *Coriolan."* *Anglia* 93 (1975):70–110.

2299 HALIO, Jay L. *"Coriolanus:* Shakespeare's 'Drama of Reconciliation.' " *ShakS* 6 (1972 for 1970):289–303.

2300 HEUER, Hermann. "From Plutarch to Shakespeare: A Study of *Coriolanus."* *ShS* 10 (1957):50–59.

2301 HILL, R. F. *"Coriolanus:* Violentest Contrariety." *E&S,* n.s. 17 (1964):12–23.

2302 HOFLING, Charles K. "An Interpretation of Shakespeare's *Coriolanus."* *AI* 14 (1957):407–35.

2303 HONIG, Edwin. *"Sejanus* and *Coriolanus:* A Study in Alienation." *MLQ* 12 (1951):407–21.

2304 HUFFMAN, Clifford Chalmers. *"Coriolanus" in Context.* Lewisburg, Pa.: Bucknell U.P., 1971.

2305 KIRSCHBAUM, Leo. "Shakespeare's Stage Blood and Its Critical Significance." *PMLA* 64 (1949):517–29. Focuses on *Julius Caesar* and *Coriolanus.*

2306 KITTO, H. D. F. *Poiesis: Structure and Thought.* Berkeley and Los Angeles: U. of California P., 1966, chap. vii.

2307 LEES, F. N. *"Coriolanus,* Aristotle, and Bacon." *RES,* n.s. 1 (1950):114–25.

2308 LITTLEWOOD, J. C. F. *"Coriolanus."* *CQ* 2 (1967):339–57; 3 (1967–68):28–50.

2309 MCCANLES, Michael. "The Dialectic of Transcendence in Shakespeare's *Coriolanus."* *PMLA* 82 (1967):44–53.

2310 MESZAROS, Patricia K. " 'There Is a World Elsewhere': Tragedy and History in *Coriolanus."* *SEL* 16 (1976):273–85.

2311 MURRY, John Middleton. *"Coriolanus." Discoveries.* London: Collins, 1924. Rpt. in *John Clare and Other Studies.* London and New York: Nevill, 1950.

2312 NEUMEYER, Peter F. "Ingratitude Is Monstrous: An Approach to *Coriolanus."* *CE* 26 (1964):192–98.

2313 NEUMEYER, Peter F. "Not Local Habitation Nor a Name: *Coriolanus."* *UR* 32 (1966):195–98.

2314 PHILLIPS, James Emerson, Jr., ed. *Twentieth Century Interpretations of "Coriolanus."* Englewood Cliffs, N.J.: Prentice-Hall, 1970. A collection of essays.

2315 RIBNER, Irving. "The Tragedy of *Coriolanus."* *ES* 34 (1953):1–9. Rpt., rev., in **1968.**

2316 ROSSITER, A. P. *"Coriolanus."* In **1245.**

2317 SCHLÖSSER, Anselm. "Reflections upon Shakespeare's *Coriolanus."* *PP* 6 (1963):11–20.

2318 SEN, Sailendra Kumar. "What Happens in *Coriolanus."* *SQ* 9 (1958):331–45.

2319 SHANKER, Sidney. "Some Clues for *Coriolanus.*" *ShAB* 24 (1949):209–13.

2320 SIMMONS, J. L. "*Antony and Cleopatra* and *Coriolanus,* Shakespeare's Heroic Tragedies: A Jacobean Adjustment." *ShS* 26 (1973):95–101.

2321 TENNENHOUSE, Leonard. "*Coriolanus:* History and the Crisis of Semantic Order." *CompD* 10 (1976–77):328–46.

2322 TRAVERSI, Derek. "*Coriolanus.*" *Scrutiny* 6 (1937):43–58.

2323 WICKHAM, Glynne. "*Coriolanus:* Shakespeare's Tragedy in Rehearsal and Performance." In **1599.** Rpt. in **624.**

2324 ZOLBROD, Paul G. "Coriolanus and Alceste: A Study in Misanthropy." *SQ* 23 (1972):51–62.

Character Studies

See also **1380, 1403, 1481, 1994–95,** and **2357.**

2325 BARRON, David B. "*Coriolanus*: Portrait of the Artist as Infant." *AI* 19 (1962): 171–93.

2326 BOWDEN, William R. "The 'Unco Guid' and Shakespeare's Coriolanus." *SQ* 13 (1962):41–48. Concerns virtuous but unattractive characters who are often unrewarded in this life.

2327 BROWNING, I. R. "Coriolanus—Boy of Tears." *EIC* 5 (1955):18–31.*

2328 BRYAN, Margaret B. "Volumnia—Roman Matron or Elizabethan Huswife." *RenP 1972* (1973):43–58.

2329 COLMAN, E. A. M. "The End of Coriolanus." *ELH* 34 (1967):1–20.

2330 JORGENSEN, Paul A. "Shakespeare's Coriolanus: Elizabethan Soldier." *PMLA* 64 (1949):221–35.

2331 MARIENSTRAS, R. "La dégradation des vertus héroïques dans *Othello* et dans *Coriolan.*" *EA* 17 (1964):372–89.

2332 MURRY, John Middleton. "A Neglected Heroine of Shakespeare." *Countries of the Mind.* 1st series. London: Collins; New York: Dutton, 1922. Rev. and enl., London: Oxford U.P., 1931. Rpt., Freeport, N.Y.: Books for Libraries P., 1968. About Virgilia.

2333 OLIVER, H. J. "Coriolanus as Tragic Hero." *SQ* 10 (1959):53–60.

2334 POISSON, Rodney. "Coriolanus as Aristotle's Magnanimous Man." In **1156.**

2335 PUTNEY, Rufus. "Coriolanus and His Mother." *PsyQ* 31 (1962):364–81.

2336 ROUDA, F. H. "*Coriolanus*—A Tragedy of Youth." *SQ* 12 (1961):103–06. Argues that Coriolanus' youth explains his rashness.

2337 SMITH, Gordon Ross. "Authoritarian Patterns in Shakespeare's *Coriolanus.*" *L&P* 9 (1959):45–51.

2338 STOCKHOLDER, Katherine. "The Other Coriolanus." *PMLA* 85 (1970):228–36. A study of Coriolanus as both awesome and ridiculous.

2339 WAITH, Eugene M. *The Herculean Hero in Marlowe, Chapman, Shakespeare, and Dryden.* See **2213.**

2340 WILSON, Emmett, Jr. "Coriolanus: The Anxious Bridegroom." *AI* 25 (1968): 224–41.

Political Studies

See also **1456, 1470, 1482–83, 1486, 1493, 1498,** and **1503.**

2341 BAUMGARTEN, Eduard. "Gemeinschaft und Gewissen in Shakespeares *Coriolan.*" *NS* 43 (1935):363–84, 413–25.

2342 BURKE, Kenneth. "*Coriolanus*—and the Delights of Faction." *HudR* 19 (1966): 185–202. Rpt. in **1125** and **1188.***

2343 DAVIDSON, Clifford. "*Coriolanus:* A Study in Political Dislocation." *ShakS* 4 (1969 for 1968):263–74.

2344 GURR, Andrew. "*Coriolanus* and the Body Politic." *ShS* 28 (1975):63–69.

2345 KNIGHTS, L. C. "Shakespeare and Political Wisdom: A Note on the Personalism of *Julius Caesar* and *Coriolanus.*" *SR* 61 (1953):43–55.***

2346 MACLURE, Millar. "Shakespeare and the Lonely Dragon." *UTQ* 24 (1955): 109–20. Concerns the Earl of Essex.

2347 MITCHELL, Charles. "*Coriolanus:* Power as Honor." *ShakS* 1 (1965):199–226.

2348 MUIR, Kenneth. "The Background of *Coriolanus.*" *SQ* 10 (1959):137–45. Argues that Shakespeare was writing in a literary rather than political tradition.

2349 PETTET, E. C. "*Coriolanus* and the Midlands Insurrection of 1607." *ShS* 3 (1950):34–42.

2350 RABKIN, Norman. "*Coriolanus:* The Tragedy of Politics." *SQ* 17 (1966):195–212.***

2351 WICHT, Wolfgang. "Mensch und Gesellschaft in *Coriolanus.*" *SJW* 102 (1966): 245–97.

2352 ZEEVELD, W. Gordon. "*Coriolanus* and Jacobean Politics." *MLR* 57 (1962): 321–34.

Language and Imagery

See also **457, 538, 554,** and **2039.**

2353 BERRY, Ralph. "Sexual Imagery in *Coriolanus.*" *SEL* 13 (1973):301–16.***

2354 CALDERWOOD, James L. "*Coriolanus:* Wordless Meanings and Meaningless Words." *SEL* 6 (1966):211–24. Rpt. in **1125.***

2355 DANSON, Lawrence. "Metonymy and *Coriolanus.*" *PQ* 52 (1973):30–42. Rpt., rev., in **1931.***

2356 DEAN, Leonard F. "Voice and Deed in *Coriolanus.*" *UKCR* 21 (1955):177–84.

2357 GORDON, D. J. "Name and Fame: Shakespeare's *Coriolanus.*" In **1134.** Rpt. in *The Renaissance Imagination.* Collected and edited by Stephen ORGEL. Berkeley and Los Angeles: U. of California P., 1975.

2358 GRANVILLE-BARKER, Harley. "Verse and Speech in *Coriolanus.*" *RES* 23 (1947):1–15.

2359 HALE, David G. "*Coriolanus:* The Death of a Political Metaphor." *SQ* 22 (1971):197–202.

2360 HALE, David G. "Intestine Sedition: The Fable of the Belly." *CLS* 5 (1968): 377–88.

2361 MAXWELL, J. C. "Animal Imagery in *Coriolanus.*" *MLR* 42 (1947):417–21.

2362 SICHERMAN, Carol M. "*Coriolanus:* The Failure of Words." *ELH* 39 (1972): 189–207.

2363 TANSELLE, G. Thomas, and Florence W. DUNBAR. "Legal Language in *Coriolanus.*" *SQ* 13 (1962):231–38.

Cymbeline

See also **804, 1218, 1242, 1255–56, 1604, 1637, 1642, 1651, 1666, 1687, 1737,** and **1740–77.**

2364 BROCKBANK, J. Philip. "History and Histrionics in *Cymbeline.*" *ShS* 11 (1958):42–49.

2365 CAMDEN, Carroll. "The Elizabethan Imogen." *RIP* 38.1 (1951):1–17.

2366 COLLEY, John Scott. "Disguise and New Guise in *Cymbeline.*" *ShS* 7 (1974): 233–52.

2367 FOAKES, R. A. "Character and Dramatic Technique in *Cymbeline* and *The Winter's Tale.*" *Studies in the Arts: Proceedings of the St. Peter's College Literary Society.* Oxford: Blackwell, 1968.

2368 GESNER, Carol. "*Cymbeline* and the Greek Romance: A Study in Genre." In **1155.** Rpt., rev., in **1645.**

2369 HARRIS, Bernard. " 'What's Past Is Prologue': *Cymbeline* and *Henry VIII.*" In **1599.***

2370 HILL, Geoffrey. " 'The True Conduct of Human Judgment': Some Observations on *Cymbeline.*" In **1146.**

2371 HOENIGER, F. David. "Irony and Romance in *Cymbeline.*" *SEL* 2 (1962): 219–28.

2372 HOFLING, Charles K. "Notes on Shakespeare's *Cymbeline.*" *ShakS* 1 (1965): 118–36.

2373 JONES, Emrys. "Stuart Cymbeline." *EIC* 11 (1961):84–99. Rpt. in **1766.***

2374 KIRSCH, Arthur C. "*Cymbeline* and Coterie Dramaturgy." *ELH* 34 (1967): 285–306. Rpt. in **1766.***

2375 LAWRENCE, W. W. "The Wager in *Cymbeline.*" In **1789.**

2376 MARSH, D. R. C. *The Recurring Miracle: A Study of "Cymbeline" and the Last Plays.* See **1759.**

2377 MAXWELL, J. C., ed. *Cymbeline.* In the New Cambridge Shakespeare. See **363.**

2378 MOFFET, Robin. *"Cymbeline* and the Nativity." *SQ* 13 (1962):207–18.

2379 MOWAT, Barbara A. *"Cymbeline:* Crude Dramaturgy and Aesthetic Distance." *RenP 1966* (1967):39–47. Rpt., rev., in **1761.**

2380 NOSWORTHY, J. M. "The Integrity of Shakespeare: Illustrated from *Cymbeline." ShS* 8 (1955):52–56.

2381 NOSWORTHY, J. M. "The Sources of the Wager Plot in *Cymbeline." N&Q* 197 (1952):93–96.

2382 NOSWORTHY, J. M., ed. *Cymbeline.* In the Arden Shakespeare. See **350.**

2383 POWLICK, Leonard. *"Cymbeline* and the Comedy of Anticlimax." In **1613.**

2384 RIBNER, Irving. "Shakespeare and Legendary History: *Lear* and *Cymbeline." SQ* 7 (1956):47–52.

2385 RICHMOND, Hugh M. "Shakespeare's Roman Trilogy: The Climax in *Cymbeline." SLitI* 5.1 (1972):129–39.

2386 SCHORK, R. J. "Allusion, Theme, and Characterization in *Cymbeline." SP* 69 (1972):210–16.

2387 SHAHEEN, Naseeb. "The Use of Scripture in *Cymbeline." ShakS* 4 (1969 for 1968):294–315.

2388 SIEMON, James Edward. "Noble Virtue in *Cymbeline." ShS* 29 (1976):51–62.

2389 SMITH, Warren D. "Cloten with Caius Lucius." *SP* 49 (1952):185–94.

2390 STEPHENSON, A. A. "The Significance of *Cymbeline." Scrutiny* 10 (1942): 329–38.

2391 SWANDER, Homer D. *"Cymbeline* and the 'Blameless Hero.' " *ELH* 31 (1964): 259–70.

2392 SWANDER, Homer D. *"Cymbeline:* Religious Idea and Dramatic Design." In **1156.**

2393 THORNE, William Barry. *"Cymbeline:* 'Lopp'd Branches' and the Concept of Regeneration." *SQ* 20 (1969):143–59.

2394 THRALL, William Flint. *"Cymbeline,* Boccaccio, and the Wager Story in England." *SP* 28 (1931):639–51.

2395 TINKLER, F. C. *"Cymbeline." Scrutiny* 7 (1938):5–20.

2396 WARREN, Roger. "Theatrical Virtuosity and Poetic Complexity in *Cymbeline." ShS* 29 (1976):41–50.

2397 WILSON, Harold S. *"Philaster* and *Cymbeline." EIE 1951* (1952):146–67.

Hamlet

Textual Commentary and Sources

See also **382, 389,** and **2461.**

2398 BLIGH, John. "The Women in the Hamlet Story." *DR* 53 (1973):275–85. A source study.

2399 BOWERS, Fredson. "The Printing of *Hamlet* Q2." *SB* 7 (1955):41–50.

2400 BOWERS, Fredson. "The Textual Relation of Q2 to Q1 *Hamlet* (I)." *SB* 8 (1956):39–66.

2401 BROWN, John Russell. "The Compositors of *Hamlet* Q2 and *The Merchant of Venice.*" *SB* 7 (1955):17–40.

2402 DUTHIE, George Ian. *The "Bad" Quarto of "Hamlet": A Critical Study.* Cambridge: Cambridge U.P., 1941. Rpt., Norwood, Pa.: Norwood, 1975.

2403 FREEMAN, James A. "Hamlet, Hecuba, and Plutarch." *ShakS* 7 (1974):197–201.

2404 GOLLANCZ, Israel. *The Sources of "Hamlet," with an Essay on the Legend.* London: Oxford U.P., 1926. Rpt., London: Cass, 1967; New York: Octagon.

2405 JENKINS, Harold. "Playhouse Interpolations in the Folio Text of *Hamlet.*" *SB* 13 (1960):31–47.

2406 JENKINS, Harold. "The Relation between the Second Quarto and the Folio Text of *Hamlet.*" *SB* 7 (1955):69–83.

2407 JOSEPH, Bertram L. "*The Spanish Tragedy* and *Hamlet:* Two Exercises in English Seneca." *Classical Drama and Its Influence: Essays Presented to H. D. F. Kitto.* Ed. M. J. ANDERSON. London: Methuen; New York: Barnes & Noble, 1965.

2408 KAULA, David. "*Hamlet* and the *Sparing Discoverie.*" *ShS* 24 (1971):71–77. A source study.

2409 LAW, Robert Adger. "Belleforest, Shakespeare, and Kyd." In **1154.**

2410 LEWIS, Charlton M. *The Genesis of "Hamlet."* Port Washington, N.Y.: Kennikat, 1967. Orig. pub. in 1907 by H. Holt.

2411 MCCOMBIE, Frank. "*Hamlet* and the *Moriae Encomium.*" *ShS* 27 (1974):59–69.

2412 STABLER, A. P. "Elective Monarchy in the Sources of *Hamlet.*" *SP* 62 (1965):654–61.

2413 TAYLOR, Marion A. *A New Look at the Old Sources of "Hamlet."* The Hague: Mouton, 1968.

2414 WALKER, Alice. "Collateral Substantive Texts (with Special Reference to *Hamlet*)." *SB* 7 (1955):51–67.

2415 WALKER, Alice. "The Textual Problem of *Hamlet:* A Reconsideration." *RES,* n.s. 2 (1951):328–38.

2416 WILSON, J. Dover. *The Manuscript of Shakespeare's "Hamlet" and the Problem of Its Transmission.* 2 vols. Cambridge: Cambridge U.P., 1934. Rpt. in 1963 with foreword by G. I. DUTHIE.

Collections of Essays

2417 BEVINGTON, David, ed. *Twentieth Century Interpretations of "Hamlet."* Englewood Cliffs, N.J.: Prentice-Hall, 1968.

2418 BROWN, John Russell, and Bernard HARRIS, eds. *Hamlet.* Stratford-upon-Avon Studies 5. London: Arnold, 1963; New York: St. Martin's; Schocken, 1966.

2419 HOLZBERGER, William G., and Peter B. WALDOCK, eds. *Perspectives on "Hamlet."* Lewisburg, Pa.: Bucknell U.P.; London: Associated U.P., 1975. Nine essays by various hands presented at Bucknell and Susquehanna Universities in April, 1973.

2420 HOY, Cyrus, ed. *Hamlet.* New York: Norton, 1963. An edition with introduction and selections from sources and criticism.

2421 JUMP, John, ed. *Shakespeare, "Hamlet": A Casebook.* London: Macmillan, 1968.

2422 LEAVENWORTH, Russell E., ed. *Interpreting "Hamlet": Materials for Analysis.* San Francisco: Chandler, 1960.

2423 LEVENSON, J. C., ed. *Discussions of "Hamlet."* Boston: Heath, 1960.

2424 SACKS, Claire, and Edgar WHAN, eds. *"Hamlet": Enter Critic.* New York: Appleton-Century-Crofts, 1960.

2425 *Shakespeare Survey* 9 (1956). Issue largely devoted to *Hamlet.*

2426 WILLIAMSON, Claude C. H., ed. *Readings on the Character of Hamlet, 1661–1947.* London: Allen & Unwin, 1950.

General Studies

See also **134, 339, 453, 1183, 1201–02, 1213, 1216, 1218, 1221, 1231, 1245, 1260, 1448, 1477, 1508, 1781, 1793, 1795, 1815, 1878, 1880, 1892, 1899, 1911, 1923–24, 1927–28, 1937, 1947, 1951, 1953, 1957–59, 1969, 1976, 1978, 1980–81, 2001, 2004–05, 2011–30, and 3581.**

2427 ABEL, Lionel. "Hamlet Q.E.D." *Metatheatre: A New View of Dramatic Form.* New York: Hill & Wang, 1963.

2428 ALDUS, Paul J. *Mousetrap: Structure and Meaning in "Hamlet."* Toronto: U. of Toronto P., 1977.

2429 ALEXANDER, Nigel. *Poison, Play, and Duel: A Study in "Hamlet."* London: Routledge & K. Paul; Lincoln: U. of Nebraska P., 1971.

2430 ALEXANDER, Peter. *Hamlet: Father and Son.* Oxford: Clarendon, 1955.*

2431 BABCOCK, Weston. *Hamlet: A Tragedy of Errors.* W. Lafayette, Ind.: Purdue U.P., 1961.

2432 BERRY, Ralph. " 'To Say One': An Essay on *Hamlet.*" *ShS* 28 (1975):107–15.

2433 BOKLUND, Gunnar. "Judgment in *Hamlet.*" In **1127.**

2434 BOOTH, Stephen. "On the Value of *Hamlet.*" In **1164.***

2435 BOYER, Eric R. "Hamlet and Absurd Freedom: *The Myth of Sisyphus* as Commentary on Shakespeare's Creation." *BSUF* 16.3 (1975):54–66.

2436 BRADDY, Haldeen. *Hamlet's Wounded Name.* El Paso: Texas Western P., 1964. 2nd ed., enl., Amsterdam: Rodopi, 1974.

2437 BRADLEY, A. C. *Shakespearean Tragedy.* See **2011.***

2438 BRENNECKE, Detlef. "Shakespeares *Hamlet:* Tragödie der Vernunft." *SJH* (1974):201–16.

2439 BROWN, Keith. "Hamlet's Place on the Map." *ShakS* 4 (1969 for 1968):160–82. A study of geographical and cosmological factors.

2440 CALHOUN, Jean S. "*Hamlet* and the Circumference of Action." *Renaissance News* 15 (1962):281–98. A study of how characters shape and are shaped by the action.

2441 CANNON, Charles K. " 'As in a Theater': *Hamlet* in the Light of Calvin's Doctrine of Predestination." *SEL* 11 (1971):203–22.

2442 CUNNINGHAM, J. V. "Plots and Errors: *Hamlet* and *King Lear.*" In **1197.***

2443 DORAN, Madeleine. "That Undiscovered Country: A Problem Concerning the Use of the Supernatural in *Hamlet* and *Macbeth.*" *PQ* 20 (1941):413–27.

2444 DRAPER, John W. *The "Hamlet" of Shakespeare's Audience.* Durham, N.C.: Duke U.P., 1938. Rpt., New York: Octagon.

2445 ELIOT, T. S. "Hamlet and His Problems." *Selected Essays, 1917–1932.* London: Faber & Faber; New York: Harcourt, Brace, 1932. Printed earlier in *The Sacred Wood.* London: Methuen, 1920. Rpt. in *Elizabethan Essays.* London: Faber & Faber, 1934.*

2446 ELLIOTT, G. R. *Scourge and Minister: A Study of "Hamlet" As Tragedy of Revengefulness and Justice.* Durham, N.C.: Duke U.P., 1951. Rpt., New York: AMS.

2447 EMPSON, William. "*Hamlet* When New." *SR* 61 (1953):15–42, 185–205. Concerns the problems Shakespeare must have perceived in writing the play.

2448 FELPERIN, Howard. " 'O'erdoing Termagent: An Approach to Shakespearean Mimesis." *YR* 63 (1974):372–91.

2449 FERGUSSON, Francis. "*Hamlet, Prince of Denmark:* The Analogy of Action." *The Idea of a Theater: A Study of Ten Plays.* Princeton: Princeton U.P., 1949; Garden City, N.Y.: Doubleday, 1953.*

2450 FOAKES, R. A. "*Hamlet* and the Court of Elsinore." *ShS* 9 (1956):35–43. On the contrasting elements of formality and corruption at court.

2451 FORTIN, René E. "*Hamlet* and the Mythic Hypothesis." *TSL* 18 (1973):49–61. Argues that archetypal studies of Hamlet as a full-fledged mythic hero too often ignore the ironies surrounding the mythic actions he attempts.

2452 FREIMAN, Gwenne. "*Hamlet* as Theatre and as a Play." *AI* 29 (1972):377–83.

2453 FRIEDMAN, Alan Warren. "Hamlet the Unready." *MLQ* 37 (1976):15–34. About the role of providence.

2454 GODSHALK, William Leigh. "Hamlet's Dream of Innocence." *ShakS* 9 (1976): 221–32.

2455 GREBANIER, Bernard. *The Heart of Hamlet.* New York: Crowell, 1960. Rpt., 1967.

2456 HOGREFE, Pearl. "Artistic Unity in *Hamlet.*" *SP* 46 (1949):184–95.

2457 HOLMES, Martin. *The Guns of Elsinore.* London: Chatto & Windus; New York: Barnes & Noble, 1964.

2458 HONIGMANN, E. A. J. "The Politics in *Hamlet* and 'The World of the Play.' " In **2418.**

2459 HUGHES, Geoffrey. "The Tragedy of a Revenger's Loss of Conscience: A Study of *Hamlet.*" *ES* 57 (1976):395–409.

2460 JAMES, D. G. *The Dream of Learning: An Essay on "The Advancement of Learning," "Hamlet," and "King Lear."* Oxford: Clarendon, 1951.*

2461 JENKINS, Harold. "Fortinbras and Laertes and the Composition of *Hamlet.*" *Rice U. Studies* 60.2 (1974):95–108.

2462 JORGENSEN, Paul A. "Elizabethan Ideas of War in *Hamlet.*" *ClioW* 3 (1974): 111–28.

2463 JORGENSEN, Paul A. "*Hamlet* and the Restless Renaissance." In **1171.**

2464 JOSEPH, Bertram L. *Conscience and the King: A Study of "Hamlet."* London: Chatto & Windus, 1953.*

2465 KNIGHTS, L. C. *An Approach to "Hamlet."* London: Chatto & Windus, 1960; Stanford: Stanford U.P., 1961.*

2466 LEVIN, Harry. *The Question of "Hamlet."* New York: Oxford U.P., 1959.*

2467 LEWIS, C. S. "Hamlet: The Prince or the Poem?" *PBA* 28 (1943 for 1942): 139–54. Rpt. in *They Asked for a Paper.* London: Bles, 1962. Rpt. also in **1955.***

2468 MACK, Maynard. "The World of *Hamlet.*" *YR* 41 (1952):502–23. Rpt. in **1132, 1942,** and **2417.***

2469 MADARIAGA, Salvador de. *On Hamlet.* London: Hollis & Carter, 1948. 2nd ed., London: Cass, 1964.

2470 MAGUIN, Jean-Marie. "Of Ghosts and Spirits Walking by Night: A Joint Examination of the Ghost Scenes in Robert Garnier's *Cornélie,* Thomas Kyd's *Cornelia,* and Shakespeare's *Hamlet* in the Light of Reformation Thinking as Presented in Lavater's Book." *CahiersE* 1 (1972):25–40.

2471 MARSH, D. R. C. *Shakespeare's "Hamlet."* Sydney: Sydney U.P., 1970.

2472 MIRIAM JOSEPH, Sister. "*Hamlet,* A Christian Tragedy." *SP* 59 (1962):119–40.

2473 MORRIS, Harry. "Hamlet as a *memento mori* Poem." *PMLA* 85 (1970):1035–40.

2474 MUIR, Kenneth. *Shakespeare: "Hamlet."* London: Arnold, 1963.

2475 OLSON, Elder. "*Hamlet* and the Hermeneutics of Drama." *MP* 61 (1964): 225–37.*

2476 PIRIE, David. "*Hamlet* without the Prince." *CritQ* 14 (1972):293–314.

2477 PRIOR, Moody E. "The Thought of *Hamlet* and the Modern Temper." *ELH* 15 (1948):261–85.

2478 PROSSER, Eleanor. *Hamlet and Revenge.* Stanford: Stanford U.P.; London: Oxford U.P., 1967. 2nd ed., 1971.

2479 ROBERTSON, J. M. *The Problem of "Hamlet."* London: Allen & Unwin, 1919.

2480 ROSE, Mark. "*Hamlet* and the Shape of Revenge." *ELR* 1 (1971):132–43.*

2481 SAGAR, Keith. *"Hamlet."* Oxford: Blackwell, 1969.

2482 SANTAYANA, George. *"Hamlet." Essays in Literary Criticism of George Santayana.* Ed. Irving SINGER. New York: Scribner's, 1956.

2483 SCHELL, Edgar T. "Who Said That—Hamlet or *Hamlet?*" *SQ* 24 (1973):135–46. Argues that Hamlet is the voice of a genuine perspective on the play itself.

2484 SCHÜCKING, Levin L. *The Meaning of "Hamlet."* Trans. Graham RAWSON. London: Oxford U.P., 1937. Rpt., New York: Barnes & Noble, 1966.

2485 SIMS, James H. "Some Biblical Light on Shakespeare's *Hamlet.*" *Costerus* 6 (1972):155–61.

2486 SJÖGREN, Gunnar. "The Danish Background in *Hamlet.*" *ShakS* 4 (1969 for 1968):221–30.

2487 SKULSKY, Harold. "Revenge, Honor, and Conscience in *Hamlet.*" *PMLA* 85 (1970):78–87. Rpt., rev., in **1251.***

2488 STOLL, Elmer Edgar. *"Hamlet": An Historical and Comparative Study.* Minneapolis: U. of Minnesota P., 1919. Rpt., New York: Gordian, 1968; Folcroft, Pa.: Folcroft, 1969.

2489 STROUP, Thomas B. *"Doctor Faustus* and *Hamlet:* Contrasting Kinds of Christian Tragedy." *CompD* 5 (1971–72):243–53.

2490 SWART, J. "I Know Not 'Seems': A Study of *Hamlet.*" *REL* 2.4 (1961):60–76.

2491 TRENCH, Wilbraham Fitzjohn. *Shakespeare's "Hamlet": A New Commentary.* London: Smith, Elder, 1913.

2492 WALDOCK, A. J. A. *"Hamlet": A Study in Critical Method.* Cambridge: Cambridge U.P., 1931.

2493 WALKER, Roy. *The Time Is Out of Joint: A Study of "Hamlet."* London: Dakers, 1948.

2494 WARHAFT, Sidney. "The Mystery of *Hamlet.*" *ELH* 30 (1963):193–208.

2495 WEBBER, Joan. *"Hamlet* and the Freeing of the Mind." In **1143.**

2496 WEST, Rebecca. *The Court and the Castle: A Study of the Interactions of Political and Religious Ideas in Imaginative Literature.* New Haven: Yale U.P., 1957; London: Macmillan, 1958, chap. 1.

2497 WEST, Robert H. "King Hamlet's Ambiguous Ghost." *PMLA* 70 (1955):1107–17.

2498 WILSON, J. Dover. *What Happens in "Hamlet."* Cambridge: Cambridge U.P., 1935. 3rd ed., 1951.*

2499 ZITNER, Sheldon P. "Hamlet, Duellist." *UTQ* 39 (1969):1–18. A study of weapons and the duelling code in the play.

Character Studies

See also **1372, 1388–89, 1404, 1406–07, 1988, 2001, 2004, 2426, 2430, 2448,** and **3774.**

2500 ANTHONISEN, Niels L. "The Ghost in *Hamlet.*" *AI* 22 (1965):232–49.

2501 BENNETT, Josephine Waters. "Characterization in Polonius' Advice to Laertes." *SQ* 4 (1953):3–9.

2502 BERTHOFF, Warner. " 'Our Means Will Make Us Means': Character as Virtue in *Hamlet* and *All's Well.*" *NLH* 5 (1974):319–51.

2503 BONJOUR, Adrien. "The Question of Hamlet's Grief." *ES* 43 (1962):336–43.

2504 BROWN, Keith. "Polonius and Fortinbras (and Hamlet?)" *ES* 55 (1974):218–38.

2505   BURGE, Barbara. "*Hamlet:* The Search for Identity." *REL* 5.2 (1964):58–71.

2506   CAMDEN, Carroll. "On Ophelia's Madness." *SQ* 15.2 (1964):247–55. Also in **1153.**

2507   CAMPBELL, Lily B. "Polonius: The Tyrant's Ears." In **1154.**

2508   COOPERMAN, Stanley. "Shakespeare's Anti-Hero: Hamlet and the Underground Man." *ShakS* 1 (1965):37–63.

2509   COX, Roger L. "Hamlet's Hamartía: Aristotle or St. Paul?" *YR* 55 (1966): 347–64. Rpt., rev., in **2013.**

2510   CRAIG, Hardin. "Hamlet as a Man of Action." *HLQ* 27 (1964):229–37.

2511   CRUTTWELL, Patrick. "The Morality of Hamlet—'Sweet Prince' or 'Arrant Knave'?" In **2418.**

2512   EISSLER, K. R. *Discourse on Hamlet and "Hamlet": A Psychoanalytic Inquiry.* New York: International U.P., 1971.*

2513   EISSLER, K. R. "Fortinbras and Hamlet." *AI* 25 (1968):199–223.

2514   FABER, M. D. "Ophelia's Doubtful Death." *L&P* 16 (1966):103–08.

2515   FLATTER, Richard. *Hamlet's Father.* London: Heinemann; New Haven: Yale U.P., 1949.

2516   FOAKES, R. A. "The Art of Cruelty: Hamlet and Vindici." *ShS* 26 (1973):21–31.

2517   GEDO, John E. "Caviare to the General." *AI* 29 (1972):293–317. A commentary on **2512.**

2518   GOTTSCHALK, Paul A. "Hamlet and the Scanning of Revenge." *SQ* 24 (1973): 155–70.

2519   GREENE, Thomas. "The Postures of Hamlet." *SQ* 11 (1960):357–66.

2520   HALIO, Jay L. "Hamlet's Alternatives." *TSLL* 8 (1966):169–88.

2521   HANKINS, John E. *The Character of Hamlet and Other Essays.* Chapel Hill: U. of North Carolina P., 1941.

2522   HARDISON, O. B., Jr. "The Dramatic Triad in *Hamlet.*" *SP* 57 (1960):144–64. A study of the arrangement of three characters, one being the center of interest and contrasted with the other two.*

2523   HARTWIG, Joan. "Parodic Polonius." *TSLL* 13 (1971):215–25.

2524   HEILBRUN, Carolyn G. "The Character of Hamlet's Mother." *SQ* 8 (1957): 201–06.

2525   HELLER, Lora, and Abraham HELLER. "Hamlet's Parents: The Dynamic Formulation of a Tragedy." *AI* 17 (1960):413–21.

2526   HUNTER, G. K. "The Heroism of Hamlet." In **2418.***

2527   HUNTER, G. K. "Isocrates' Precepts and Polonius' Character." *SQ* 8 (1957): 501–06.

2528   HUTTON, Virgil. "Hamlet's Fear of Death." *UR* 37 (1970):11–19.

2529   JENKINS, Harold. "Hamlet and Ophelia." *PBA* 49 (1964 for 1963):135–51.

2530   JOHNSON, S. F. "The Regeneration of Hamlet." *SQ* 3 (1952):187–207.

2531   JONES, Ernest. *Hamlet and Oedipus.* Rev. ed., London: Gollancz; New York: Norton, 1949. Rpt., Garden City, N.Y.: Doubleday Anchor, 1954.*

2532   JORGENSEN, Paul A. "Hamlet's Therapy." *HLQ* 27 (1964):239–58.

2533 KIRSCHBAUM, Leo. "Hamlet and Ophelia." *PQ* 35 (1956):376–93.

2534 KNIGHTS, L. C. "Prince Hamlet." *Scrutiny* 9 (1940):149–60. Rpt. in **1228.***

2535 KOTT, Jan. "Hamlet and Orestes." Trans. Boleslaw TABORSKI. *PMLA* 82 (1967):303–13.

2536 LAWRENCE, W. W. "Ophelia's Heritage." *MLR* 42 (1947):409–16.

2537 LEVITSKY, Ruth M. "Rightly to Be Great." *ShakS* 1 (1965):142–67.

2538 LYONS, Bridget Gellert. "Melancholy and Hamlet." *Voices of Melancholy: Studies in Literary Treatments of Melancholy in Renaissance England.* London: Routledge & K. Paul, 1971; New York: Norton, 1975.

2539 MCLAUCHLAN, Juliet. "The Prince of Denmark and Claudius's Court." *ShS* 27 (1974):43–57.

2540 MAJOR, John M. "The 'Letters Seal'd' in *Hamlet* and the Character of Claudius." *JEGP* 57 (1958):512–21.

2541 MAXWELL, Baldwin. "Hamlet's Mother." *SQ* 15.2 (1964):235–46. Also in **1153.**

2542 MENDEL, Sydney. "The Revolt against the Father: The Adolescent Hero in *Hamlet* and *The Wild Duck.*" *EIC* 14 (1964):171–78.

2543 MURRAY, Gilbert. "Hamlet and Orestes: A Study in Traditional Types." *PBA* 6 (1913–14):389–412. Rpt. in *The Classical Tradition in Poetry.* Cambridge, Mass.: Harvard U.P., 1927.

2544 ORTEGO, Philip D. "Hamlet: The Stamp of One Defect." In **1169.**

2545 PARTEE, Morriss Henry. "Claudius and the Political Background of *Hamlet.*" *EM* 21 (1970):35–53.

2546 PIPER, W. B. "Of Hamlet's Transformation." *SHR* 2 (1968):324–42.

2547 POLLIN, Burton R. "Hamlet, a Successful Suicide." *ShakS* 1 (1965):240–60.

2548 PROSER, Matthew N. "Hamlet and the Name of Action." In **1167.**

2549 PUTZEL, Rosamond. "Queen Gertrude's Crime." *RenP 1961* (1962):37–46.

2550 REED, Robert R., Jr. "Hamlet, the Pseudo-Procrastinator." *SQ* 9 (1958):177–86.

2551 REID, Stephen A. "Hamlet's Melancholia." *AI* 31 (1974):378–400.

2552 RUBIN, Samuel S. "Hamlet: A Psychoanalytic Reinterpretation." *PsyR* 57 (1970–71):660–70.

2553 SKULSKY, Harold. " 'I Know My Course': Hamlet's Confidence." *PMLA* 89 (1974):477–86. Rpt., rev., in **1251.***

2554 SMIDT, Kristian. "Politicians, Courtiers, Soldiers, and Scholars: Type Characters in *Hamlet.*" *ES* 57 (1976):337–47.

2555 SPAETH, J. Duncan. "Horatio's Hamlet." *ShAB* 24 (1949):37–47.

2556 SPENCER, T. J. B. "The Decline of Hamlet." In **2418.**

2557 STIRLING, Brents. "Theme and Character in *Hamlet.*" *MLQ* 13 (1952):323–32. Rpt., rev., in **1978.**

2558 STOCKHOLDER, Katherine. "*Hamlet:* Between Night and Day." *L&P* 21 (1971):7–20. On the oedipal confrontations in the play.

2559 TAYLOR, Michael. "The Conflict in Hamlet." *SQ* 22 (1971):147–61.

2560 TAYLOR, Myron. "Tragic Justice and the House of Polonius." *SEL* 8 (1968): 273–81. Argues that Polonius is justly punished, since he is a practiced machiavellian and not simply an old bore.

2561 WEISBERG, Richard. "Hamlet and Ressentiment." *AI* 29 (1972):318–37.

2562 WORMHOUDT, Arthur. *Hamlet's Mouse Trap: A Psychoanalytical Study of the Drama.* New York: AMS, 1970. Orig. pub. by the Philosophical Library in 1956.

Studies in Dramatic Structure

See also **1959, 2428,** and **2522.**

2563 BARRY, Jackson G. "Shakespeare's 'Deceptive Cadence': A Study in the Structure of *Hamlet.*" *SQ* 24 (1973):117–27.

2564 BOWERS, Fredson. "Dramatic Structure and Criticism: Plot in *Hamlet.*" *SQ* 15.2 (1964):207–18. Also in **1153.***

2565 BOWERS, Fredson. "Hamlet as Minister and Scourge." *PMLA* 70 (1955):740–49.*

2566 BROWN, Keith. " 'Form and Cause Conjoin'd': *Hamlet* and Shakespeare's Workshop." *ShS* 26 (1973):11–20.

2567 COX, Lee Sheridan. *Figurative Design in "Hamlet": The Significance of the Dumb Show.* Columbus: Ohio State U.P., 1973.

2568 HAPGOOD, Robert. "*Hamlet* Nearly Absurd: The Dramaturgy of Delay." *TDR* 9.4 (1965):132–45.

2569 KITTO, H. D. F. *Form and Meaning in Drama: A Study of Six Greek Plays and of "Hamlet."* London: Methuen, 1956. 2nd ed., 1964.

2570 NOSWORTHY, J. M. "The Structural Experiment in *Hamlet.*" *RES* 22 (1946): 282–88.

2571 VAN LAAN, Thomas F. "Ironic Reversal in *Hamlet.*" *SEL* 6 (1966):247–62.

2572 WALTON, J. K. "The Structure of *Hamlet.*" In **2418.**

Particular Scenes or Passages

See also **2567.**

2573 ANDREWS, Michael C. "The Double-Death of Claudius in *Hamlet.*" *RenP 1970* (1971):21–27.

2574 BATTENHOUSE, Roy W. "Hamlet's Apostrophe on Man: Clue to the Tragedy." *PMLA* 66 (1951):1073–1113. For a reply, see Adrien BONJOUR, "*Hamlet* and the Phantom Clue." *ES* 35 (1954):253–59.

2575 BATTENHOUSE, Roy W. "The Significance of Hamlet's Advice to the Players." In **1120.**

2576 BOWERS, Fredson. "The Death of Hamlet: A Study in Plot and Character." In **1119.**

2577 BOWERS, Fredson. "Hamlet's Fifth Soliloquy, 3.2.406–17." In **1144.**

2578 BOWERS, Fredson. "The Moment of Final Suspense in Hamlet: 'We Defy Augury.' " In **1121.***

2579 BOWLIN, Karla, Norman A. BRITTIN, and Revin P. ARRINGTON. "Shakespeare's Dramaturgy: *Hamlet,* Act IV." *BSUF* 16.3 (1975):49–53.

2580 CLAYTON, Thomas. "The Quibbling Polonii and the Pious Bonds: The Rhetoric of *Hamlet* I. iii." *ShakS* 2 (1967 for 1966):59–94.

2481 COURSEN, Herbert R., Jr. "The Rarer Action: Hamlet's Mousetrap." *Literary Monographs.* Eds. Eric ROTHSTEIN and Richard N. RINGLER. Vol. 2. Madison: U. of Wisconsin P., 1969, pp. 59–97.***

2582 DELUCA, Diana Macintyre. "The Movements of the Ghost in *Hamlet.*" *SQ* 24 (1973):147–54.

2583 DETMOLD, George. "Hamlet's 'All But Blunted Purpose.' " *ShAB* 24 (1949): 23–36.

2584 ELIOT, T. S. "Poetry and Drama." *On Poetry and Poets.* London: Faber & Faber; Cambridge, Mass.: Harvard U.P., 1951; New York: Farrar, Straus, & Cudahy, 1957. Partly concerns the first scene in *Hamlet.*

2585 FRENCH, A. L. "Hamlet and the Sealed Commission." *ES* 48 (1966):28–30. Rpt. in **1937.**

2586 GREEN, Andrew J. "The Cunning of the Scene." *SQ* 4 (1953):395–404. On Hamlet's "mousetrap," his advice to the players, and the Pyrrhus speech.

2587 HAMILL, Paul. "Death's Lively Image: The Emblematic Significance of the Closet Scene in *Hamlet.*" *TSLL* 16 (1974):249–62.

2588 HAVELY, Cicely. "The Play-Scene in *Hamlet.*" *EIC* 23 (1973):217–35.

2589 JENKINS, Harold. "Hamlet and the Fishmonger." *SJH* (1975):109–20.

2590 JOHNSTON, Arthur. "The Player's Speech in *Hamlet.*" *SQ* 13 (1962):21–30.

2591 LAWRENCE, W. W. "Hamlet's Sea-Voyage." *PMLA* 59 (1944):45–70.

2592 LE COMTE, Edward. *Poet's Riddles: Essays in Seventeenth-Century Explication.* Port Washington, N.Y.: Kennikat, 1975. Includes an essay on the ending of *Hamlet* as a farewell to Essex.

2593 LEECH, Clifford. "The Hesitation of Pyrrhus." In **1146.**

2594 MIRIAM JOSEPH, Sister. "Discerning the Ghost in *Hamlet.*" *PMLA* 76 (1961): 493–502.

2595 MORGAN, Roberta. "Some Stoic Lines in *Hamlet* and the Problem of Interpretation." *PQ* 20 (1941):549–58.

2596 NEWELL, Alex. "The Dramatic Context and Meaning of Hamlet's 'To Be or Not to Be' Soliloquy." *PMLA* 80 (1965):38–50.

2597 OLSSON, Yngve B. "In Search of Yorick's Skull; Notes on the Background of *Hamlet.*" *ShakS* 4 (1969 for 1968):183–220.

2598 PHIALAS, Peter G. "Hamlet and the Grave-Maker." *JEGP* 63 (1964):226–34.

2599 REEDY, Gerard. " 'Alexander Died': *Hamlet,* V. i. 216–40." *SQ* 24 (1973): 128–34.

2600 REID, B. L. "The Last Act and the Action of *Hamlet.*" *YR* 54 (1964):59–80.

2601 RENO, Raymond H. "Hamlet's Quintessence of Dust." *SQ* 12 (1961):107–13.

2602 REPLOGLE, Carol. "Not Parody, Not Burlesque: The Play Within the Play in *Hamlet.*" *MP* 67 (1969):150–59.

2603 RINGLER, William A., Jr. "Hamlet's Defense of the Players." In **1144.**

2604 ROBSON, W. W. "Did the King See the Dumb-Show?" *CQ* 6 (1975):303–26.

2605 SCHLÖSSER, Anselm. "Über Hamlets Schauspieltheorie und deren Verwirklichung im *Hamlet.*" *SJW* 111 (1975):24–34.

2606 SCHRICKX, Willem. "The Background and Context of Hamlet's Second Soliloquy." *MLR* 68 (1973):241–55.

2607 SHEPARD, Warren V. "Hoisting the Enginer with His Own Petar." *SQ* 7 (1956):281–85.

2608 STEVENS, Martin. "Hamlet and the Pirates: A Critical Reconsideration." *SQ* 26 (1975):276–84.

Critical and Stage History

See also **721, 730, 763, 829, 838, 845, 847, 890, 893, 895, 922, 959,** and **2029.**

2609 ALEXANDER, Nigel. "Critical Disagreement About Oedipus and Hamlet." *ShS* 20 (1967):33–40.

2610 BRASHEAR, William R. "Nietsche and Spengler on Hamlet: An Elaboration and Synthesis." *CompD* 5 (1971):106–16.

2611 BUELL, William Ackerman. *The Hamlets of the Theatre.* New York: Astor-Honor, 1968.

2612 CONKLIN, Paul L. *A History of "Hamlet" Criticism: 1601–1821.* London: Oxford U.P.; New York: King's Crown, 1947; London: Routledge & K. Paul; New York: Humanities P., 1957.

2613 FRENCH, A. L. "*Hamlet* and the Moralists." *Oxford Review* 6 (1967):41–74. Rpt. in **1937.**

2614 GARDNER, Helen. "The Historical Approach." In **932.** Rpt. in **1942.***

2615 GLICK, Claris. "*Hamlet* in the English Theater—Acting Texts from Betterton (1676) to Olivier (1963)." *SQ* 20 (1969):17–35.

2616 GOTTSCHALK, Paul A. *The Meanings of "Hamlet": Modes of Literary Interpretation since Bradley.* Albuquerque: U. of New Mexico P., 1972.

2617 HUNTER, G. K. "*Hamlet* Criticism." *CritQ* 1 (1959):27–32.

2618 JENKINS, Harold. "*Hamlet* Then Till Now." *ShS* 18 (1965):34–45.

2619 LEECH, Clifford. "Studies in *Hamlet,* 1901–1955." *ShS* 9 (1956):1–15.

2620 MANDER, Raymond, and Joe MITCHENSON, comps. "*Hamlet*" *Through the Ages: A Pictorial Record from 1709.* London: Rockliff, 1952. Rev. ed., Freeport, N.Y.: Books for Libraries P., 1955.

2621 RAVEN, Anton Adolph. *A "Hamlet" Bibliography and Reference Guide, 1877–1935.* Chicago: U. of Chicago P., 1936. Rpt., New York: Russell & Russell.

2622 ROWE, Eleanor. "Pushkin, Lermontov, and *Hamlet.*" *TSLL* 17 (1975):337–47.

2623 RUSSELL, D. A. "Hamlet Costumes from Garrick to Gielgud." *ShS* 9 (1956):54–58.

2624 SANDERS, Norman. "Metamorphoses of the Prince: Some Critical and Theatrical Interpretations of *Hamlet* 1864–1964." In **1171.**

2625 TODD, D. K. C. *I Am Not Prince Hamlet: Shakespeare, Criticism, Schools of English.* London: U. of London P.; New York: Barnes & Noble, 1974.

2626 WEITZ, Morris. *"Hamlet" and the Philosophy of Literary Criticism.* Chicago: U. of Chicago P., 1964.

Language and Imagery

See also **457, 474–75, 538–39, 541, 554,** and **572.**

2627 ALTICK, Richard D. "*Hamlet* and the Odor of Mortality." *SQ* 5 (1954):167–76.

2628 CHARNEY, Maurice. *Style in "Hamlet."* Princeton: Princeton U.P., 1969.*

2629 DESSEN, Alan C. "Hamlet's Poisoned Sword: A Study in Dramatic Imagery." *ShakS* 5 (1970 for 1969):53–69.*

2630 DOEBLER, John. "The Play Within the Play: *The Muscipula Diaboli* in *Hamlet.*" *SQ* 23 (1972):161–69. Rpt. in **555.***

2631 DORAN, Madeleine. "The Language of *Hamlet.*" *HLQ* 27 (1964):259–78.

2632 ELLISON, Paul. "Reason to the Dane." *BUSE* 1 (1955):20–37. On the use of dialectic in *Hamlet.*

2633 FALK, Doris V. "Proverbs and the Polonius Destiny." *SQ* 18 (1967):23–36.

2634 FISCH, Harold. *Hamlet and the Word: The Covenant Pattern in Shakespeare.* New York: Ungar, 1971.

2635 FOAKES, R. A. "Character and Speech in *Hamlet.*" In **2418.**

2636 FORKER, Charles R. "Shakespeare's Theatrical Symbolism and Its Function in *Hamlet.*" *SQ* 14 (1963):215–29. Rpt. in **1125.***

2637 FOSTER, Richard. "Hamlet and the Word." *UTQ* 30 (1961):229–45.

2638 GELLERT, Bridget. "The Iconography of Melancholy in the Graveyard Scene in *Hamlet.*" *SP* 67 (1970):57–66.

2639 MCDONALD, Charles Osborne. "The Rhetoric of *Hamlet.*" In **476.**

2640 MUIR, Kenneth. "Imagery and Symbolism in *Hamlet.*" *EA* 17 (1964):352–63. Rpt. in **1238.**

2641 PATERSON, John. "The Word in *Hamlet.*" *SQ* 2 (1951):47–55.

2642 SANFORD, Wendy Coppedge. *Theater as Metaphor in "Hamlet."* Cambridge, Mass.: Harvard U.P., 1967.

2643 SENG, Peter J. "Ophelia's Songs in *Hamlet.*" *DUJ* 56, n.s. 25 (1964):77–85.

2644 SPEVACK, Marvin. "Hamlet and Imagery: The Mind's Eye." *NS,* n.s. 25 (1966): 203–12.

2645 STAFFORD, Tony J. "Hamlet's House of Death." *PLL* 10 (1974):15–20. On images of building structures.

2646 WILLIAMS, George Walton. "Sleep in *Hamlet.*" *RenP 1964* (1965):17–20.

Henry IV

Henry IV, Parts I and II

See also **514, 779, 1187, 1216, 1317, 1459, 1481, 1486, 1585, 1719, 1779, 1800, 1802, 1816, 1829, 1833, 1843, 1863–77, 2738–72, 3853, 3867, 3895,** and **3901.**

2647 BARBER, C. L. "From Ritual to Comedy: An Examination of *Henry IV.*" *EIE 1954* (1955):22–51. Rpt. in **1719.**

2648 BARBER, Charles. "Prince Hal, Henry V, and the Tudor Monarchy." In **1146.**

2649 BARISH, Jonas A. "The Turning Away of Prince Hal." *ShakS* 1 (1965):9–17.*

2650 BECK, Richard J. *Shakespeare: "Henry IV."* London: Arnold, 1965.

2651 BERMAN, Ronald. "The Nature of Guilt in the Henry IV Plays." *ShakS* 1 (1965):18–28.

2652. BLACK, James. "Counterfeits of Soldiership in *Henry IV.*" *SQ* 24 (1973):372–82.

2653 BRADBROOK, M. C. "King Henry IV." In **1145** (1969 for 1965–67).

2654 BRYANT, J. A., Jr. "Prince Hal and the Ephesians." *SR* 67 (1959):204–19. Rpt. in **1413.**

2655 CAIN, H. Edward. "Further Light on the Relation of *1* and *2 Henry IV.*" *SQ* 3 (1952):21–38.

2656 COUNCIL, Norman. "Prince Hal: Mirror of Success." *ShakS* 7 (1974):125–46.

2657 DICKINSON, Hugh. "The Reformation of Prince Hal." *SQ* 12 (1961):33–46.

2658 DORAN, Madeleine. "Imagery in *Richard II* and *Henry IV.*" *MLR* 37 (1942): 113–22. Rpt. in **2702.**

2659 EMPSON, William. *Some Versions of Pastoral.* London: Chatto & Windus, 1935, chaps. 2 and 3.

2660 EVANS, Gareth Lloyd. "The Comical-Tragical-Historical Method: *Henry IV.*" In **1582.**

2661 FISH, Charles. "Henry IV: Shakespeare and Holinshed." *SP* 61 (1964):205–18.

2662 GOSS, Alan Gerald. "The Justification of Prince Hal." *TSLL* 10 (1968):27–35.

2663 HAWKINS, Sherman H. "Virtue and Kingship in Shakespeare's *Henry IV.*" *ELR* 5 (1975):313–43.

2664 HOYLE, James. "Some Emblems in Shakespeare's Henry IV Plays." *ELH* 38 (1971):512–27.

2665 HUMPHREYS, A. R. "Shakespeare's Political Justice in *Richard II* and *Henry IV.*" In **1145** (1965 for 1964).

2666 HUNTER, G. K. "*Henry IV* and the Elizabethan Two-Part Play." *RES,* n.s. 5 (1954):236–48.

2667 HUNTER, G. K. "Shakespeare's Politics and the Rejection of Falstaff." *CritQ* 1 (1959):229–36.*

2668 HUNTER, G. K., ed. *Shakespeare, "Henry IV Parts I and II": A Casebook.* London: Macmillan, 1970.

2669 JENKINS, Harold. *The Structural Problem in Shakespeare's "Henry the Fourth."* London: Methuen, 1956. Rpt., slightly abridged, in **1865**. Rpt. also in **1798, 2668,** and **2737.***

2670 JORGENSEN, Paul A. " 'Redeeming Time' in Shakespeare's *Henry IV."* TSL 5 (1960):101–09. Rpt. in **538**.

2671 KNIGHTS, L. C. "Notes on Comedy." *Scrutiny* 1 (1933):356–67. Rpt. in *Determinations.* Ed. F. R. LEAVIS. London: Chatto & Windus, 1934. Rpt. also in **2702.***

2672 KRIS, Ernst. "Prince Hal's Conflict." *PsyQ* 17 (1948):487–506. Rpt. in **1163.***

2673 LAW, Robert Adger. "Structural Unity in the Two Parts of *Henry the Fourth."* SP 24 (1927):223–42.

2674 MCLUHAN, Herbert Marshall. *"Henry IV,* A Mirror for Magistrates." *UTQ* 17 (1948):152–60.

2675 MCNAMARA, Anne Marie. *"Henry IV:* The King as Protagonist." *SQ* 10 (1959):423–31.

2676 PALMER, D. J. "Casting Off the Old Man: History and St. Paul in *Henry IV."* CritQ 12 (1970):267–83. Concerns biblical echoes.

2677 SCHLÖSSER, Anselm. "Legende, Wunschbild und Wirklichkeit in *Heinrich IV."* ZAA 12 (1964):121–41.

2678 SHAABER, M. A. "The Unity of *Henry IV."* In **1154**. Rpt. in **2702.***

2679 WILSON, J. Dover. "The Political Background of Shakespeare's *Richard II* and *Henry IV."* SJ 75 (1939):36–51.

Henry IV, Part I

See also **2738, 2747, 2752, 2769, 2772,** and **2952.**

2680 BERKELEY, David, and Donald EIDSON. "The Theme of *Henry IV, Part I."* SQ 19 (1968):25–31.

2681 BOWERS, Fredson. "Hal and Francis in *King Henry IV,* Part I." *RenP 1965* (1966):15–20.

2682 BOWERS, Fredson. "Theme and Structure in *King Henry IV,* Part I." In **1120.***

2683 BROOKS, Cleanth, and Robert B. HEILMAN. "Shakespeare, *Henry IV, Part I."* Understanding Drama. New York: Holt, 1945. An edition with introduction and notes.

2684 CALDERWOOD, James L. *"1 Henry IV:* Art's Gilded Lie." *ELR* 3 (1973): 131–44.

2685 CALLAHAN, E. F. "Lyric Origins of the Unity of *1 Henry IV."* Costerus 3 (1972):9–22.

2686 CLARK, Axel. "The Battle of Shrewsbury." *CR* 15 (1972):29–45.

2687 CONNOR, Seymour V. "The Role of Douglas in *Henry IV,* Part One." *UTSE* 27 (1948):215–21.

2688 DESSEN, Alan C. "The Intemperate Knight and the Politic Prince: Late Morality Structure in *1 Henry IV."* ShakS 7 (1974):147–71.

2689 DORIUS, R. J., ed. *Twentieth Century Interpretations of "Henry IV Part I."* Englewood Cliffs, N.J.: Prentice-Hall, 1970. A collection of essays.

2690 FACKLER, Herbert V. "Shakespeare's 'Irregular and Wild' Glendower: The Dramatic Use of Source Materials." *Discourse* 13 (1970):306–14.

2691 GOTTSCHALK, Paul A. "Hal and the 'Play Extempore' in *1 Henry IV.*" *TSLL* 15 (1974):605–14.

2692 HARTMANN, Herbert. "Prince Hal's 'Shew of Zeale.' " *PMLA* 46 (1931): 720–23.

2693 HUMPHREYS, A. R., ed. *The First Part of King Henry IV.* In the Arden Shakespeare. See **350.**

2694 LA BRANCHE, Anthony. " 'If Thou Wert Sensible of Courtesy': Private and Public Virtue in *Henry IV, Part One.*" *SQ* 17 (1966):371–82.

2695 MCGUIRE, Richard L. "The Play-within-the-play in *1 Henry IV.*" *SQ* 18 (1967):47–52.

2696 MCNEIR, Waldo F. "Structure and Theme in the First Tavern Scene (II. iv) of *1 Henry IV.*" In **1156.** Rpt. in **1167.**

2697 MIDDLEMAN, Louis I. "*Henry IV, Part I:* The Two Faces of Revolt." In **1118.**

2698 MITCHELL, Charles. "The Education of the True Prince." *TSL* 12 (1967): 13–21.

2699 RENO, Raymond H. "Hotspur: The Integration of Character and Theme." *RenP 1962* (1963):17–25.

2700 RUBENSTEIN, E. "*1 Henry IV:* The Metaphor of Liability." *SEL* 10 (1970): 287–95.

2701 SALTER, F. M. "The Play within the Play of *First Henry IV.*" *PTRSC,* 3rd ser. 40.2 (1946):209–23.

2702 SANDERSON, James L., ed. *William Shakespeare: "Henry the Fourth, Part I."* A Norton Critical Edition. New York: Norton, 1962. Rev. ed., 1969; rpt., 1972. A collection of essays, with text.

2703 SCOUFOS, Alice Lyle. "Gads Hill and the Structure of Comic Satire." *ShakS* 5 (1970 for 1969):25–52.

2704 SHAW, John. "The Staging of Parody and Parallels in *1 Henry IV.*" *ShS* 20 (1967):61–73.

2705 SHUCHTER, J. D. "Prince Hal and Francis: The Imitation of an Action." *ShakS* 3 (1968 for 1967):129–37.

2706 SPRAGUE, Arthur Colby. "Gadshill Revisited." *SQ* 4 (1953):125–37. Rpt. in **2702.**

2707 STONE, William B. "Literature and Class Ideology: *Henry IV, Part One.*" *CE* 33 (1972):891–900. For a reply, see Richard M. EASTMAN, "Political Values in *Henry IV, Part One:* A Demonstration of Liberal Humanism." *CE* 33 (1972): 901–07.

2708 THOMAS, Mary Olive. "The Elevation of Hal in *1 Henry IV.*" *SLitI* 5.1 (1972): 73–89.

2709 TRAVERSI, Derek. "*Henry IV, Part I.*" *Scrutiny* 15 (1947):24–35. Rpt. in **1876.**

2710 WALDOCK, A. J. A. "The Men in Buckram." *RES* 23 (1947):16–23.

2711 WALKER, Alice. "The Folio Text of *1 Henry IV.*" *SB* 6 (1954):45–59.

2712 ZEEVELD, W. Gordon. " 'Food for Powder'—'Food for Worms.' " *SQ* 3 (1952):249–53.

2713 ZITNER, Sheldon P. "Anon, Anon: or, a Mirror for a Magistrate." *SQ* 19 (1968):63–70.

Henry IV, Part II

See also **389** and **2738–72.**

2714 BLANPIED, John W. " 'Unfathered Heirs and Loathly Births of Nature': Bringing History to Crisis in *2 Henry IV.*" *ELR* 5 (1975):212–31.*

2715 BOUGHNER, Daniel C. "Pistol and the Roaring Boys." *ShAB* 11 (1936):226–37.

2716 HART, Alfred. "Was the Second Part of *Henry the Fourth* Censored?" In **119.**

2717 HOLLINDALE, Peter. *A Critical Commentary on Shakespeare's "King Henry IV Part 2."* London: Macmillan; New York: Fernhill House, 1971.

2718 HOTSON, Leslie. "Ancient Pistol." *YR* 38 (1948):51–66. Rpt. in **4538.**

2719 HUMPHREYS, A. R., ed. *The Second Part of King Henry IV.* In the Arden Shakespeare. See **350.**

2720 JORGENSEN, Paul A. "The 'Dastardly Treachery' of Prince John of Lancaster." *PMLA* 76 (1961):488–92.*

2721 KNIGHTS, L. C. "Time's Subjects: The Sonnets and *King Henry IV, Part II.*" In **1230.**

2722 KNOWLES, Richard. "Unquiet and the Double Plot of *2 Henry IV.*" *ShakS* 2 (1967 for 1966):133–40.

2723 LEECH, Clifford. "The Unity of *2 Henry IV.*" *ShS* 6 (1953):16–24. Rpt. in **1165, 1865,** and **2737.**

2724 MCMANAWAY, James G. "The Cancel in the Quarto of *2 Henry IV.*" In **1162.**

2725 MANLEY, Frank. "The Unity of Betrayal in *II Henry IV.*" *SLitI* 5.1 (1972): 91–110.

2726 PETTIGREW, John. "The Mood of *Henry IV, Part 2.*" In **1145** (1969 for 1965–67).

2727 SCHÄFER, Jürgen. " 'When They Marry, They Get Wenches.' " *SQ* 22 (1971): 203–11. On the importance of male heirs in the royal line.

2728 SCHELL, Edgar T. "Prince Hal's Second 'Reformation.' " *SQ* 21 (1970):11–16.

2729 SHAABER, M. A. "The Folio Text of *2 Henry IV.*" *SQ* 6 (1955):135–44.

2730 SMITH, John Hazel. "The Cancel in the Quarto of *2 Henry IV* Revisited." *SQ* 15.3 (1964):173–78.

2731 SPENCER, Benjamin T. "*2 Henry IV* and the Theme of Time." *UTQ* 13 (1944): 394–99.

2732 TRAVERSI, Derek. *"Henry IV, Part II."* Scrutiny 15 (1948):117–27. Rpt. in **1876.**

2733 WAGGONER, George R. "An Elizabethan Attitude toward Peace and War." *PQ* 33 (1954):20–33.

2734 WALKER, Alice. "Quarto 'Copy' and the 1623 Folio: *2 Henry IV.*" *RES,* n.s. 2 (1951):217–25.

2735 WALTER, J. H. " 'With Sir John in It.' " *MLR* 41 (1946):237–45.

2736 WILLIAMS, George Walton. "The Text of *2 Henry IV:* Facts and Problems." *ShakS* 9 (1976):173–82.

2737 YOUNG, David, ed. *Twentieth Century Interpretations of "Henry IV, Part Two."* Englewood Cliffs, N.J.: Prentice-Hall, 1968.

Falstaff

Included here are discussions of Falstaff's role in *Henry V* and *The Merry Wives of Windsor* as well as in the *Henry IV* plays.

See also **513, 1002, 1261, 1372, 1376, 1380, 1396, 1638, 1709, 2667, 2688, 2696, 2735, 2787, 2799, 3554, 3562, 3566,** and **3569.**

2738 AUDEN, W. H. "The Prince's Dog." In **1179.** Rpt. in **2668.** Orig. pub. as "The Fallen City: Some Reflections on Shakespeare's *Henry IV*" in *Encounter* 13.5 (Nov. 1959):21–31.*

2739 BATTENHOUSE, Roy. "Falstaff as Parodist and Perhaps Holy Fool." *PMLA* 90 (1975):32–52.

2740 BOUGHNER, Daniel C. "Traditional Elements in Falstaff." *JEGP* 43 (1944): 417–28.

2741 BOUGHNER, Daniel C. "Vice, Braggart, and Falstaff." *Anglia* 72 (1954):35–61.

2742 BRADLEY, A. C. "The Rejection of Falstaff." In **1185.** Rpt. in **1865, 2668,** and **2702.***

2743 BRYANT, J. A., Jr. "Shakespeare's Falstaff and the Mantle of Dick Tarleton." *SP* 51 (1954):149–62.

2744 CHARLTON, H. B. "Falstaff." *BJRL* 19 (1935):46–89. Rpt. in **1631.***

2745 DEAN, Leonard F. "Three Notes on Comic Morality: Celia, Bobadill, and Falstaff." *SEL* 16 (1976):263–71.

2746 EMPSON, William. "Falstaff and Mr. Dover Wilson." *KR* 15 (1953):213–62. Rpt. in **2668.*** A reply to **2772.**

2747 FABER, M. D. "Falstaff Behind the Arras." *AI* 27 (1970):197–225.

2748 FIEHLER, Rudolph. *The Strange History of Sir John Oldcastle.* New York: American P., 1965.

2749 HAPGOOD, Robert. "Falstaff's Vocation." *SQ* 16 (1965):91–98.

2750 HEMINGWAY, Samuel B. "On Behalf of That Falstaff." *SQ* 3 (1952):307–11.

2751 JEMBER, Gregory K. "Glory, Jest, and Riddle: The Three Deaths of Falstaff." *Thoth* 12.3 (1972):30–38.

2752 JORGENSEN, Paul A. "Valor's Better Parts: Backgrounds and Meanings of Shakespeare's Most Difficult Proverb." *ShakS* 9 (1976):141–58. On Falstaff's "The better part of valor is discretion" (V, iv).

2753 KAISER, Walter. "Shakespeare's Falstaff." *Praisers of Folly: Erasmus, Rabelais, Shakespeare.* Cambridge, Mass.: Harvard U.P., 1963.

2754 LANDT, D. B. "The Ancestry of Sir John Falstaff." *SQ* 17 (1966):69–76.

2755 LANGBAUM, Robert. "Character versus Action in Shakespeare." *The Poetry of Experience.* New York: Random House; London: Chatto & Windus, 1957. New York: Norton, 1957, 1963. Rpt. in **1865.***

2756 MORGANN, Maurice. *An Essay on the Dramatic Character of Sir John Falstaff.* London: T. Davies, 1777. Ed. William Arthur GILL. London: Frowde, 1912. Rpt. in **946, 996, 2668,** and **2689.***

2757 NAHM, Milton C. "Falstaff, Incongruity and the Comic; An Essay in Aesthetic Criticism." *Personalist* 49 (1968):289–321.

2758 NEWMAN, Franklin B. "The Rejection of Falstaff and the Rigorous Charity of the King." *ShakS* 2 (1967 for 1966):153–61.

2759 PRIOR, Moody E. "Comic Theory and the Rejection of Falstaff." *ShakS* 9 (1976):159–71.

2760 ROTHSCHILD, Herbert B., Jr. "Falstaff and the Picaresque Tradition." *MLR* 68 (1973):14–21.

2761 SCOUFOS, Alice Lyle. "The 'Martyrdom' of Falstaff." *ShakS* 2 (1967 for 1966): 174–91.

2762 SENG, Peter J. "Songs, Time, and the Rejection of Falstaff." *ShS* 15 (1962): 31–40.

2763 SHIRLEY, John W. "Falstaff, an Elizabethan Glutton." *PQ* 17 (1938):271–87.

2764 SIEGEL, Paul N. "Falstaff and His Social Milieu." *SJW* 110 (1974):139–45.

2765 SIMS, Ruth E. "The Green Old Age of Falstaff." *Bulletin of the History of Medicine* 13 (1943):144–57.

2766 SPIVACK, Bernard. "Falstaff and The Psychomachia." *SQ* 8 (1957):449–59.

2767 STEWART, Douglas J. "Falstaff the Centaur." *SQ* 28 (1977):5–21.

2768 STEWART, J. I. M. "The Birth and Death of Falstaff." In **1391.***

2769 TOLIVER, Harold E. "Falstaff, the Prince, and the History Play." *SQ* 16 (1965): 63–80.*

2770 WILLIAMS, Philip. "The Birth and Death of Falstaff Reconsidered." *SQ* 8 (1957):359–65. Rpt. in **1125.** A comment on **2768** above.

2771 WILSON, Elkin Calhoun. "Falstaff—Clown and Man." In **1119.**

2772 WILSON, J. Dover. *The Fortunes of Falstaff.* Cambridge: Cambridge U.P., 1943.*

Henry V

See also **514, 538, 779, 1216, 1234, 1236, 1259, 1317, 1458, 1469–70, 1473, 1481, 1486, 1573, 1800–02, 1807, 1813, 1817, 1822, 1829, 1833–36, 1843, 1863–77, 2648, 2715, 2718, 2735, 3907,** and **4538.**

2773 AKRIGG, G. P. V. "*Henry V:* The Epic Hero as Dramatic Protagonist." In **1145** (1969 for 1965–67).

2774 BATTENHOUSE, Roy W. "*Henry V* as Heroic Comedy." In **1144.**

2775 BATTENHOUSE, Roy W. "The Relation of Henry V to Tamburlaine." *ShS* 27 (1974):71–79.

2776 BERMAN, Ronald. "Shakespeare's Alexander: Henry V." *CE* 23 (1962):532–39.

2777 BERMAN, Ronald, ed. *Twentieth Century Interpretations of "Henry V."* Englewood Cliffs, N.J.: Prentice-Hall, 1968. A collection of essays.

2778 BOKLUND, Gunnar. "Henry V—A Hero for Our Time?" *Denver Quarterly* 10.2 (1975):83–92.

2779 BRADDY, Haldeen. "Shakespeare's *Henry V* and the French Nobility." *TSLL* 3 (1961):189–96.

2780 BURNS, Landon C., Jr. "Three Views of King Henry V." *Drama Survey* 1 (1962):278–300.

2781 CAIRNCROSS, Andrew S. "Quarto Copy for Folio *Henry V.*" *SB* 8 (1956): 67–93.

2782 COOK, Dorothy. "*Henry V:* Maturing of Man and Majesty." *SLitI* 5.1 (1972): 111–28.

2783 COURSEN, Herbert R., Jr. "Henry V and the Nature of Kingship." *Discourse* 13 (1970):279–305.

2784 DRAPER, John W. "The Humor of Corporal Nym." *ShAB* 13 (1938):131–38. Rpt. in **1585.**

2785 DUTHIE, George Ian. "The Quarto of Shakespeare's *Henry V.*" In **1134.**

2786 EGAN, Robert. "A Muse of Fire: *Henry V* in the Light of *Tamburlaine.*" *MLQ* 29 (1968):15–28.

2787 FLEISSNER, Robert F. "Falstaff's Green Sickness Unto Death." *SQ* 12 (1961): 47–55.

2788 GEDULD, Harry M. *Filmguide to "Henry V."* See **887.**

2789 GILBERT, Allan H. "Patriotism and Satire in *Henry V.*" In **1157.**

2790 GOULD, Gerald. "A New Reading of *Henry V.*" *English Review* 29 (1919): 42–55. Rpt. as "Irony and Satire in *Henry V,*" in **2806.** Examines the motives of the churchmen, in strategically urging the French war as a way of preventing passage of an expropriation bill.

2791 HOBDAY, C. H. "Imagery and Irony in *Henry V.*" *ShS* 21 (1968):107–13.

2792 HUTCHISON, Harold F. *Henry V: A Biography.* London: Eyre & Spottiswoode; New York: Day, 1967.

2793 JORGENSEN, Paul A. "Accidental Judgments, Casual Slaughters, and Purposes Mistook: Critical Reactions to Shakspere's *Henry the Fifth.*" *ShAB* 22 (1947): 51–61.

2794 JORGENSEN, Paul A. "The Courtship Scene in *Henry V.*" *MLQ* 11 (1950): 180–88.

2795 LEVER, J. W. "Shakespeare's French Fruits." *ShS* 6 (1953):79–90. Finds a source for *Henry V* in a work by Thomas Elyot.

2796 MCCLOSKEY, John C. "The Mirror of All Christian Kings." *ShAB* 19 (1944): 36–40.

2797 MAGUIN, Jean-Marie. "Shakespeare's Structural Craft and Dramatic Technique in *Henry V.*" *CahiersE* 7 (1975):51–67.

2798 MAXWELL, J. C. "Simple or Complex?: Some Problems in the Interpretation of Shakespeare." *DUJ* 46, n.s. 15 (1954):112–15.

2799 MENDILOW, A. A. "Falstaff's Death of a Sweat." *SQ* 9 (1958):479–83.

2800 MERCHANT, W. Moelwyn. "The Status and Person of Majesty." *SJ* 90 (1954): 285–89. About the language of majesty.

2801 MERRIX, Robert P. "The Alexandrian Allusion in Shakespeare's *Henry V.*" *ELR* 2 (1972):321–33.

2802 MITCHELL, Charles. "Henry V: The Essential King." In **1171.**

2803 PETRONELLA, Vincent F. "Shakespeare's *Henry V* and the Second Tetralogy: Meditation as Drama." *Costerus* 4 (1972):169–82.

2804 PHIALAS, Peter G. "Shakespeare's Henry V and the Second Tetralogy." *SP* 62 (1965):155–75.

2805 PRICE, George R. "Henry V and Germanicus." *SQ* 12 (1961):57–60.

2806 QUINN, Michael, ed. *Shakespeare, "Henry V": A Casebook.* London: Macmillan, 1969.

2807 SAHEL, Pierre. "Henry V, Roi Idéal?" *EA* 28 (1975):1–14.

2808 SCHLÖSSER, Anselm. "Der Widerstreit von Patriotismus und Humanismus in *Heinrich V.*" *ZAA* 12 (1964):244–56.

2809 SMITH, Gordon Ross. "Shakespeare's *Henry V:* Another Part of the Critical Forest." *JHI* 37 (1976):3–26.

2810 SMITH, Warren D. "The *Henry V* Choruses in the First Folio." *JEGP* 53 (1954):38–57.

2811 STŘÍBRNÝ, Zdeněk. "*Henry V* and History." In **1148.**

2812 TRAVERSI, Derek. "*Henry the Fifth.*" *Scrutiny* 9 (1941):352–74. Rpt. in **1876.**

2813 TUCKER, E. F. J. "Legal Fiction and Human Reality: Hal's Role in *Henry V.*" *ETJ* 26 (1974):308–14.

2814 WALKER, Alice. "Some Editorial Principles (with Special Reference to Henry V)." *SB* 8 (1956):95–111.

2815 WALTER, J. H., ed. *King Henry the Fifth.* In the Arden Shakespeare. See **350.**

2816 WENTERSDORF, Karl P. "The Conspiracy of Silence in *Henry V.*" *SQ* 27 (1976):264–87. Concerns the silence of the play regarding the Mortimers' dynastic claim to the English throne.

2817 WILLIAMS, Charles. "*Henry V.*" In **1034.**

2818 WILLIAMSON, Marilyn L. "The Courtship of Katherine and the Second Tetralogy." *Criticism* 17 (1975):326–34.

2819 WILLIAMSON, Marilyn L. "The Episode with Williams in *Henry V.*" *SEL* 9 (1969):275–82.

2820 ZIMBARDO, Rose A. "The Formalism of *Henry V.*" In **1160.**

Henry VI

The Henry VI Plays

For critical studies embracing all four plays in Shakespeare's first historical tetralogy, see **1850–62.**

See also **155, 643, 779, 1236, 1330, 1470, 1472, 1486, 1493, 1578, 1581–82, 1586, 1592, 1802, 1813, 1822, 1826–27, 1829, 1831–36, 1843,** and **1848–49.**

2821 ALEXANDER, Peter. *Shakespeare's "Henry VI" and "Richard III."* See **1850.**

2822 BERMAN, Ronald. "Fathers and Sons in the Henry VI Plays." *SQ* 13 (1962): 487–97.*

2823 BILLINGS, Wayne L. "Ironic Lapses: Plotting in *Henry VI.*" *SLitI* 5.1 (1972): 27–49.

2824 BORN, Hanspeter. "The Date of *2, 3 Henry VI.*" *SQ* 25 (1974):323–34.

2825 BROCKBANK, J. Philip. "The Frame of Disorder: *Henry VI.*" In **1582.** Rpt. in **1125, 1798,** and **1845.***

2826 DORAN, Madeleine. *"Henry VI," Parts II and III: Their Relation to the "Contention" and the "True Tragedy."* Iowa City: U. of Iowa P., 1928.

2827 FRENCH, A. L. "*Henry VI* and the Ghost of Richard II." *ES* (Anglo-American Supplement) 50 (1969):xxxvii–xliii.

2828 HASLER, Jörg. "Gestische Leitmotive in Shakespeares *Henry VI.*" *SJH* (1975): 163–73.

2829 JACKSON, Barry. "On Producing *Henry VI.*" *ShS* 6 (1953):49–52.

2830 KAY, Carol McGinnis. "Traps, Slaughter, and Chaos: A Study of Shakespeare's *Henry VI* Plays." *SLitI* 5.1 (1972):1–26.

2831 KELLY, Faye L. "Oaths in Shakespeare's *Henry VI* Plays." *SQ* 24 (1973): 357–71.

2832 LAW, Robert Adger. "The Chronicles and the Three Parts of *Henry VI.*" *UTSE* 33 (1954):13–32.

2833 LEECH, Clifford. "The Two-Part Play: Marlowe and the Early Shakespeare." See **1855.**

2834 MÜLLER, Heiner. "Die Gestaltung des Volkes in Shakespeares Historiendramen, untersucht am Beispiel *Heinrichs VI.*" *SJW* 106 (1970):127–75.

2835 PRATT, Samuel M. "Shakespeare and Humphrey, Duke of Gloucester: A Study in Myth." *SQ* 16 (1965):201–16.

2836 RICKS, Don M. *Shakespeare's Emergent Form: A Study of the Structures of the "Henry VI" Plays.* Logan: Utah State U.P., 1968.

2837 RIGGS, David. *Shakespeare's Heroical Histories: "Henry VI" and Its Literary Tradition.* Cambridge, Mass.: Harvard U.P., 1971.*

2838 TURNER, Robert Y. "Shakespeare and the Public Confrontation Scene in Early History Plays." *MP* 62 (1964):1–12. Rpt. in modified form in **1593.** (Focuses on the *Henry VI* plays rather than on *Richard III.*)

2839 WATKINS, Ronald. "The Only Shake-Scene." *PQ* 54 (1975):47–67. On the authorship of the Henry VI plays.

2840 WILLIAMS, Gwyn. "Suffolk and Margaret: A Study of Some Sections of Shakespeare's *Henry VI.*" *SQ* 25 (1974):310–22.

Henry VI, Part I

See also **2835** and **2840**.

2841 BEVINGTON, David. "The Domineering Female in *1 Henry VI.*" *ShakS* 2 (1967 for 1966):51–58.

2842 BLANPIED, John W. " 'Art and Baleful Sorcery': The Counterconsciousness of *Henry VI, Part I.*" *SEL* 15 (1975):213–27.

2843 BOAS, Frederick S. "Joan of Arc in Shakespeare, Schiller, and Shaw." *SQ* 2 (1951):35–45.

2844 BURKHARDT, Sigurd. " 'I Am But Shadow of Myself': Ceremony and Design in *1 Henry VI.*" *MLQ* 28 (1967):139–58. Rpt. in **1187.***

2845 CAIRNCROSS, Andrew S., ed. *The First Part of King Henry VI.* In the Arden Shakespeare. See **350.**

2846 FRENCH, A. L. "Joan of Arc and *Henry VI.*" *ES* 49 (1968):425–29.

2847 GAW, Allison. *The Origin and Development of "1 Henry VI" in Relation to Shakespeare, Marlowe, Peele, and Greene.* Los Angeles: U. of Southern California P., 1926. Rpt., New York: AMS.

2848 GREER, Clayton Alvis. "The Place of *1 Henry VI* in the York-Lancaster Tetralogy." *PMLA* 53 (1938):687–701.

2849 KIRSCHBAUM, Leo. "The Authorship of *1 Henry VI.*" *PMLA* 67 (1952): 809–22.

2850 LAMBIN, G. "Here Lyeth Iohn Talbot." *EA* 24 (1971):361–76.

2851 MINCOFF, Marco. "The Composition of *Henry VI, Part I.*" *SQ* 16 (1965): 279–87.

2852 RIDDELL, James A. "Talbot and the Countess of Auvergne." *SQ* 28 (1977): 51–57.

Henry VI, Part II

See also **2824, 2826, 2835,** and **2840.**

2853 CAIRNCROSS, Andrew S., ed. *The Second Part of King Henry VI.* In the Arden Shakespeare. See **350.**

2854 CALDERWOOD, James L. "Shakespeare's Evolving Imagery: *2 Henry VI.*" *ES* 48 (1967):481–93.

2855 CARR, Virginia M. "Animal Imagery in *2 Henry VI.*" *ES* 53 (1972):408–12.

2856 MCMANAWAY, James G. "*The Contention* and *2 Henry VI.*" *Studies in English Language and Literature.* Ed. Siegfried KORNINGER. Wiener Beiträge zur Englishen Philologie 65. Stuttgart: Braumüller, 1957, pp. 143–54.

2857 PROUTY, Charles Tyler. *"The Contention" and Shakespeare's "2 Henry VI": A Comparative Study.* New Haven: Yale U.P., 1954.

2858 TURNER, Robert Y. "Significant Doubling of Roles in *Henry VI, Part Two.*" *LC* 30 (1964):77–84.

Henry VI, Part III

See also **2824** and **2826.**

2859 CAIRNCROSS, Andrew S., ed. *The Third Part of King Henry VI.* In the Arden Shakespeare. See **350.**

2860 KERNAN, Alvin B. "A Comparison of the Imagery in *3 Henry VI* and *The True Tragedie of Richard Duke of York.*" *SP* 51 (1954):431–42.

2861 MINCOFF, Marco. "*Henry VI, Part III* and *The True Tragedy.*" *ES* 42 (1961): 273–88.

Henry VIII

See also **779, 1221, 1559, 1606, 1829, 1833–34, 1836, 1843, 4679,** and **4684.**

2862 ALEXANDER, Peter. "Conjectural History, or Shakespeare's *Henry VIII.*" *E&S* 16 (1931 for 1930):85–120.

2863 BERMAN, Ronald. "*King Henry the Eighth:* History and Romance." *ES* 48 (1967):112–21.

2864 BERTRAM, Paul. "*Henry VIII:* The Conscience of the King." In **1123.**

2865 BLISS, Lee. "The Wheel of Fortune and the Maiden Phoenix of Shakespeare's *King Henry the Eighth.*" *ELH* 42 (1975):1–25.

2866 BYRNE, Muriel St. Clare. "A Stratford Production: *Henry VIII.*" *ShS* 3 (1950): 120–29.

2867 CUTTS, John P. "Shakespeare's Song and Masque Hand in *Henry VIII.*" *SJ* 99 (1963):184–95.

2868 FELPERIN, Howard. "Shakespeare's *Henry VIII:* History as Myth." *SEL* 6 (1966):225–46. Rpt., rev., in **1748.***

2869 FOAKES, R. A. "On the First Folio Text of *Henry VIII.*" *SB* 11 (1958):55–60.

2870 FOAKES, R. A., ed. *King Henry VIII.* In the Arden Shakespeare. See **350.**

2871 HARRIS, Bernard. " 'What's Past is Prologue': *Cymbeline* and *Henry VIII.*" In **1599.***

2872 HOWARTH, Herbert. "An Old Man Looking at Life: *Henry VIII* and the Late Plays." In **1145** (1962 for 1961).

2873 KERMODE, Frank. "What Is Shakespeare's *Henry VIII* About?" *DUJ* 40, n.s. 9 (1948):48–55. Rpt. in **1798** and **1845.***

2874 KNIGHT, G. Wilson. *"Henry VIII* and the Poetry of Conversion." In **1605.***

2875 MAXWELL, J. C., ed. *King Henry the Eighth.* In the New Cambridge Shakespeare. See **363.**

2876 MINCOFF, Marco. *"Henry VIII* and Fletcher." *SQ* 12 (1961):239–60.

2877 NICOLSON, Marjorie. "The Authorship of *Henry the Eighth." PMLA* 37 (1922):484–502.

2878 PARKER, A. A. "Henry VIII in Shakespeare and Calderón." *MLR* 43 (1948): 327–52.

2879 PARTRIDGE, A. C. *The Problem of "Henry VIII" Reopened.* Cambridge, Eng.: Bowes & Bowes, 1949. Rpt. in **504.**

2880 RICHMOND, Hugh M. "Shakespeare's *Henry VIII:* Romance Redeemed by History." *ShakS* 4 (1969 for 1968):334–49.*

2881 SCHLÖSSER, Anselm. "Konturen unter der Oberfläche in *Heinrich VIII." ZAA* 12 (1964):257–65.

2882 TILLYARD, E. M. W. "Why Did Shakespeare Write *Henry VIII?" CritQ* 3 (1961):22–27. Rpt. in **1266.**

2883 WAAGE, Frederick O., Jr. *"Henry VIII* and the Crisis of the English History Play." *ShakS* 8 (1975):297–309.

2884 WAITH, Eugene M. *"Henry VIII* and the More Historical Tragedies." *The Pattern of Tragicomedy in Beaumont and Fletcher.* New Haven: Yale U.P.; London: Oxford U.P., 1952.

2885 WASSON, John. "In Defense of *King Henry VIII." RS* 32 (1964):261–76.

2886 WATERS, D. Douglas. "Shakespeare and the 'Mistress-Missa' Tradition in *King Henry VIII." SQ* 24 (1973):459–62.

2887 WILEY, Paul L. "Renaissance Exploitation of Cavendish's *Life of Wolsey." SP* 43 (1946):121–46.

Julius Caesar

General Studies

See also **133, 149, 1183, 1187, 1218, 1234, 1237, 1243, 1289, 1358, 1792, 1811, 1924, 1927, 1941, 1947, 1951, 1978, 1981, 2005,** and **2036–55.**

2888 AUFFRET, Jean. "The Philosophic Background of *Julius Caesar." CahiersE* 5 (1974):66–92.

2889 AYRES, Harry Morgan. "Shakespeare's *Julius Caesar* in the Light of Some Other Versions." *PMLA* 25 (1910):183–227.

2890 BELLRINGER, A. W. *"Julius Caesar:* Room Enough." *CritQ* 12 (1970):31–48. A study of the play as both a tragedy and a play about Roman history.

2891 BONJOUR, Adrien. *The Structure of "Julius Caesar."* Liverpool: Liverpool U.P., 1958.*

2892 BREYER, Bernard R. "A New Look at *Julius Caesar.*" *Essays in Honor of Walter Clyde Curry.* Nashville: Vanderbilt U.P., 1954. Rpt. in **2913.**

2893 CHANG, Joseph S. M. J. "*Julius Caesar* in the Light of Renaissance Historiography." *JEGP* 69 (1970):63–71.

2894 COLES, Blanche. *Shakespeare Studies: "Julius Caesar."* New York: Richard R. Smith, 1940.

2895 CREWE, J. V. "Shakespeare's *Julius Caesar.*" *Theoria* 37 (1971):31–44.

2896 DEAN, Leonard F. "*Julius Caesar* and Modern Criticism." *EJ* 50 (1961):451–56.

2897 DEAN, Leonard F., ed. *Twentieth Century Interpretations of "Julius Caesar."* Englewood Cliffs, N.J.: Prentice-Hall, 1968. A collection of essays.

2898 DORSCH, T. S., ed. *Julius Caesar.* In the Arden Shakespeare. See **350.**

2899 EDINBOROUGH, Arnold. "*Julius Caesar.*" In **1145** (1969 for 1965–67).

2900 FELHEIM, Marvin. "The Problem of Time in *Julius Caesar.*" *HLQ* 13 (1950): 399–405.

2901 FOAKES, R. A. "An Approach to *Julius Caesar.*" *SQ* 5 (1954):259–70.

2902 FORTIN, René E. "*Julius Caesar:* An Experiment in Point of View." *SQ* 19 (1968):341–47.

2903 GERENDAY, Lynn de. "Play, Ritualization, and Ambivalence in *Julius Caesar.*" *L&P* 24 (1974):24–33.

2904 HARTSOCK, Mildred E. "The Complexity of *Julius Caesar.*" *PMLA* 81 (1966): 56–62.

2905 HERBERT, Edward T. "Myth and Archetype in *Julius Caesar.*" *PsyR* 57 (1970): 303–08.

2906 HOMAN, Sidney R. "Dion, Alexander, and Demetrius—Plutarch's Forgotten *Parallel Lives*—as Mirrors for Shakespeare's *Julius Caesar.*" *ShakS* 8 (1975): 195–210.

2907 KAUFMANN, R. J., and Clifford J. RONAN. "Shakespeare's *Julius Caesar:* An Apollonian and Comparative Reading." *CompD* 4 (1970):18–51.

2908 KIRSCHBAUM, Leo. "Shakespeare's Stage-Blood and Its Critical Significance." See **2305.**

2909 MACK, Maynard. "*Julius Caesar.*" In **1147.**

2910 MCNEIR, Waldo F. *Shakespeare's "Julius Caesar": A Tragedy Without a Hero.* Wiesbaden: Akademie der Wissenschaften und der Literatur in Mainz, in Kommission bei Franz Steiner, 1971.

2911 MAGUIN, Jean-Marie. "Play Structure and Dramatic Technique in Shakespeare's *Julius Caesar.*" *CahiersE* 5 (1974):93–106.

2912 MAGUIN, Jean-Marie. "Preface to a Critical Approach to *Julius Caesar:* Renaissance Interests in Caesar; Shakespeare and North's Plutarch." *CahiersE* 4 (1973): 16–49.

2913 MARKELS, Julian, ed. *Shakespeare's "Julius Caesar."* New York: Scribner's, 1961. Contains text and nine previously published essays.

2914 MONSARRAT, Gilles. "Le Stoïcisme dans *Julius Caesar,* ou les Préjugés de la Critique." *EA* 27 (1974):2–6.

2915 MUSGROVE, Sydney. *Julius Caesar*. Sydney: for the Australian English Association, 1941.

2916 PARKER, Barbara L. " 'This Monstrous Apparition': The Role of Perception in *Julius Caesar.*" *BSUF* 16.3 (1975):70–77.

2917 REES, Joan. "*Julius Caesar*—An Earlier Play, and an Interpretation." *MLR* 50 (1955):135–41.

2918 RICE, Julian C. "*Julius Caesar* and the Judgment of the Senses." *SEL* 13 (1973): 238–55.

2919 SCHLÖSSER, Anselm. "Shakespeares *Julius Caesar*—ein Interpretationsversuch." *ZAA* 19 (1971):229–60.

2920 SIMMONS, J. L. "Shakespeare's Julius Caesar: The Roman Actor and the Man." *TSE* 16 (1968):1–28. Rpt., rev., in **2048.**

2921 SMITH, Warren D. "The Duplicate Revelation of Portia's Death." *SQ* 4 (1953): 153–61. On a textual problem in IV, iii. Rpt. in **2913.**

2922 SPAKOWSKI, R. E. "Deification and Myth-Making in the Play *Julius Caesar.*" *UR* 36 (1969):135–40.

2923 STIRLING, Brents. "Brutus and the Death of Portia." *SQ* 10 (1959):211–17. On the textual problem in IV, iii. The author reverses his position in "*Julius Caesar* in Revision." *SQ* 13 (1962):187–205.

2924 TAYLOR, Myron. "Shakespeare's *Julius Caesar* and the Irony of History." *SQ* 24 (1973):301–08.

2925 URE, Peter, ed. *Shakespeare, "Julius Caesar": A Casebook*. London: Macmillan, 1969.

2926 VAWTER, Marvin L. " 'After Their Fashion': Cicero and Brutus in *Julius Caesar.*" *ShakS* 9 (1976):205–19.

2927 VELZ, John W. "Clemency, Will, and Just Cause in *Julius Caesar.*" *ShS* 22 (1969):109–18.

2928 VELZ, John W. "Undular Structure in *Julius Caesar.*" *MLR* 66 (1971):21–30.

2929 WALKER, Roy. "Unto Caesar: A Review of Recent Productions." *ShS* 11 (1958):128–35.

2930 WILSON, J. Dover. "Ben Jonson and *Julius Caesar.*" *ShS* 2 (1949):36–43. On Jonson's criticism of Shakespeare's first real Roman tragedy.

2931 YODER, R. A. "History and the Histories in *Julius Caesar.*" *SQ* 24 (1973): 309–27.

Political Studies

See also **1454–55, 1459, 1478, 1486,** and **1492–93.**

2932 ANSON, John S. "*Julius Caesar:* The Politics of the Hardened Heart." *ShakS* 2 (1967 for 1966):11–33.

2933 HALL, Vernon, Jr. "*Julius Caesar:* A Play without Political Bias." In **1119.**

2934 HENZE, Richard. "Power and Spirit in *Julius Caesar.*" *UR* 36 (1970):307–14.

2935 HUNTER, Mark. "Politics and Character in Shakespeare's *Julius Caesar.*" *Essays by Divers Hands, being the Transactions of the Royal Society of Literature,* n. s. 10 (1931):109–40.

2936 KNIGHTS, L. C. "Personality and Politics in *Julius Caesar.*" In **1229.***

2937 KNIGHTS, L. C. "Shakespeare and Political Wisdom: A Note on the Personalism of *Julius Caesar* and *Coriolanus.*" *SR* 61 (1953):43–55.*

2938 ORNSTEIN, Robert. "Seneca and the Political Drama of *Julius Caesar.*" *JEGP* 57 (1958):51–56.

2939 PAYNE, Michael. "Political Myth and Rhetoric in *Julius Caesar.*" *BuR* 19.2 (1971):85–106.

2940 RIBNER, Irving. "Political Issues in *Julius Caesar.*" *JEGP* 56 (1957):10–22.

2941 SANDERS, Norman. "The Shift of Power in *Julius Caesar.*" *REL* 5.2 (1964): 24–35.

2942 UHLER, John Earle. "*Julius Caesar*—A Morality of Respublica." In **1157.**

Character Studies

See also **1391, 1481, 1955, 1983, 1988,** and **2201.**

2943 BARROLL, J. Leeds. "The Characterization of Octavius." See **2191.**

2944 BOWDEN, William R. "The Mind of Brutus." *SQ* 17 (1966):57–67.

2945 BREWER, D. S. "Brutus' Crime: A Footnote to *Julius Caesar.*" *RES* 3 (1952): 51–54.

2946 BURKE, Kenneth. "Antony in Behalf of the Play." *SoR* 1 (1935):308–19. Rpt. in *The Philosophy of Literary Form.* Baton Rouge: Louisiana State U.P., 1941. Rpt., New York: Vintage, 1957. Rpt. also in **2913.**

2947 FELDMAN, Harold. "Unconscious Envy in Brutus." *AI* 9 (1952):307–35.

2948 GASQUET, Emile. "Le Machiavelisme d'Antoine dans *Julius Caesar.*" *EA* 27 (1974):7–15.

2949 GUNDOLF, Friedrich. *The Mantle of Caesar.* Trans. Jacob Wittmer HARTMANN. New York: Macy-Masius, Vanguard, 1928; London: Cayme [1929], chap. 3.

2950 HOUPPERT, Joseph W. "Fatal Logic in *Julius Caesar.*" *SAB* 39.4 (1974):3–9. On Brutus' errors.

2951 LEVITSKY, Ruth M. "The Elements Were So Mix'd . . . " *PMLA* 88 (1973): 240–45.

2952 LORDI, Robert J. "Brutus and Hotspur." *SQ* 27 (1976):177–85. On *1 Henry IV* as an inspirational "source" for *Julius Caesar.*

2953 PALMER, D. J. "Tragic Error in *Julius Caesar.*" *SQ* 21 (1970):399–409.

2954 PAOLUCCI, Anne. "The Tragic Hero in *Julius Caesar.*" *SQ* 11 (1960):329–33.

2955 PETERSON, Douglas L. " 'Wisdom Consumed in Confidence': An Examination of Shakespeare's Julius Caesar." *SQ* 16 (1965):19–28.

2956 PRIOR, Moody E. "The Search for a Hero in *Julius Caesar.*" *RenD,* n.s. 2 (1969):81–101.*

2957 RACKIN, Phyllis. "The Pride of Shakespeare's Brutus." *LC* 32 (1966):18–30.

2958 SACHAROFF, Mark. "Suicide and Brutus' Philosophy in *Julius Caesar.*" *JHI* 33 (1972):115–22.

2959 SCHANZER, Ernest. "The Tragedy of Shakespeare's Brutus." *ELH* 22 (1955): 1–15. Rpt. in **2040.** Rpt., rev., in **1792.**

2960 SMITH, Gordon Ross. "Brutus, Virtue, and Will." *SQ* 10 (1959):367–79. Rpt. in **2913.**

2961 VAWTER, Marvin L. " 'Division 'tween Our Souls': Shakespeare's Stoic Brutus." *ShakS* 7 (1974):173–95.

2962 VELZ, John W. "Cassius as a 'Great Observer.' " *MLR* 68 (1973):256–59.

2963 VELZ, John W. " 'If I Were Brutus Now . . .': Role-Playing in *Julius Caesar.*" *ShakS* 4 (1969 for 1968):149–59.

2964 WELSH, Alexander. "Brutus Is an Honorable Man." *YR* 64 (1975):496–513.

2965 WILKINSON, Andrew M. "A Psychological Approach to *Julius Caesar.*" *REL* 7.4 (1966):65–78.

2966 YU, Anthony C. "O Hateful Error: Tragic *Hamartia* in Shakespeare's Brutus." *CLAJ* 16 (1973):345–56.

Language and Imagery

See also **457** and **2039.**

2967 ANDERSON, Peter S. "Shakespeare's *Caesar:* The Language of Sacrifice." *CompD* 3 (1969):3–26.

2968 COURSEN, Herbert R., Jr. "The Fall and Decline of *Julius Caesar.*" *TSLL* 4 (1962):241–51. On the imagery that is connected with plotting and assassination.

2969 FRYE, Roland Mushat. "Rhetoric and Poetry in *Julius Caesar.*" *Quarterly Journal of Speech* 37 (1951):41–48.

2970 FUZIER, Jean. "Rhetoric *versus* Rhetoric: A Study of Shakespeare's *Julius Caesar,* Act III, scene 2." *CahiersE* 5 (1974):25–65.

2971 HAPGOOD, Robert. "Speak Hands for Me: Gesture as Language in *Julius Caesar.*" *Drama Survey* 5 (1966):162–70. Rpt. in **1125.***

2972 REYNOLDS, Robert C. "Ironic Epithet in *Julius Caesar.*" *SQ* 24 (1973):329–33.

2973 TOOLE, William B. "The Metaphor of Alchemy in *Julius Caesar.*" *Costerus* 5 (1972):135–51.

2974 VAWTER, Marvin L. "*Julius Caesar:* Rupture in the Bond." *JEGP* 72 (1973): 311–28. On the play of meanings having to do with bonds and bondage, master-servant relations, etc.

2975 VELZ, John W. "Two Emblems in Brutus' Orchard." *RenQ* 25 (1972):307–15.

2976 ZANDVOORT, R. W. "Brutus' Forum Speech in *Julius Caesar.*" *RES* 16 (1940):62–66. Rpt. in *Collected Papers.* Groningen: Wolters, 1954. A rhetorical analysis.

King John

See also **779, 837, 1256, 1486, 1802, 1822, 1828–29, 1833–34, 1836,** and **1843.**

2977 ASH, D. F. "Anglo-French Relations in *King John.*" *EA* 3 (1939):349–58.

2978 BERMAN, Ronald. "Anarchy and Order in *Richard III* and *King John.*" *ShS* 20 (1967):51–59.

2979 BOKLUND, Gunnar. "The Troublesome Ending of *King John.*" *SN* 40 (1968): 175–84.

2980 BONJOUR, Adrien. "Bastinado for the Bastard?" *ES* 45 Supplement (1964): 169–76.

2981 BONJOUR, Adrien. "The Road to Swinstead Abbey: A Study of the Sense and Structure of *King John.*" *ELH* 18 (1951):253–74.*

2982 BURKHARDT, Sigurd. "*King John:* The Ordering of This Present Time." *ELH* 33 (1966):133–53. Rpt. in **1187.***

2983 CALDERWOOD, James L. "Commodity and Honour in *King John.*" *UTQ* 29 (1960):341–56. Rpt. in **1845.***

2984 ELLIOTT, John R., Jr. "Shakespeare and the Double Image of King John." *ShakS* 1 (1965):64–84.*

2985 ELSON, John. "Studies in the King John Plays." In **1154.** See also Yoshiko UÉNO, "An Essay on the King John Plays from History to Romance." *ShStud* 12 (1973–74):1–30.

2986 GREENEWALD, Gerard M. *Shakespeare's Attitude towards the Catholic Church in "King John."* Washington, D.C.: Catholic U. of America P., 1938.

2987 HARRISON, G. B. "Shakespeare's Topical Significances: I. *King John.*" *LTLS,* Nov. 13, 1930, p. 939. Rpt. in **1034.**

2988 HONIGMANN, E. A. J., ed. *King John.* In the Arden Shakespeare. See **350.**

2989 LEWIS, Allan. "Shakespeare and the Morality of Money." *Social Research* 36 (1969):373–88.

2990 MATCHETT, William H. "Richard's Divided Heritage in *King John.*" *EIC* 12 (1962):231–53. Rpt. in **1125** and **1798.***

2991 ORTEGO, Philip D. "Shakespeare and the Doctrine of Monarchy in *King John.*" *CLAJ* 13 (1970):392–401.

2992 PETIT-DUTAILLIS, Charles. *Le Roi Jean et Shakespeare.* 3rd ed., Paris: Gallimard, 1944.

2993 PETTET, E. C. "Hot Irons and Fever: A Note on Some of the Imagery of *King John.*" *EIC* 4 (1954):128–44.

2994 PRICE, Jonathan R. "*King John* and Problematic Art." *SQ* 21 (1970):25–28.

2995 SALTER, F. M. "The Problem of *King John.*" *PTRSC,* 3rd ser. 43.2 (1949): 115–36.

2996 SIBLY, John. "The Anomalous Case of *King John.*" *ELH* 33 (1966):415–21.

2997 SIMMONS, J. L. "Shakespeare's *King John* and Its Source: Coherence, Pattern, and Vision." *TSE* 17 (1969):53–72.

2998 SISSON, Charles J. *"King John:* A History Play for Elizabethans." In **1145** (1961 for 1960).

2999 STEVICK, Robert D. " 'Repentant Ashes': The Matrix of 'Shakespearian' Poetic Language." *SQ* 13 (1962):366–70.

3000 STROUD, Ronald. "The Bastard to the Time in *King John." CompD* 6 (1972): 154–66.

3001 VAN DE WATER, Julia C. "The Bastard in *King John." SQ* 11 (1960):137–46.

3002 WARREN, W. L. *King John.* London: Eyre & Spottiswoode; New York: Norton, 1961. An historical and biographical study.

3003 WEIMANN, Robert. "Vice-Tradition und Renaissance-Gestalt in *King John." SJW* 108 (1972):24–34.

3004 WHITE, Howard B. "Bastards and Usurpers: Shakespeare's *King John." Ancients and Moderns: Essays on the Tradition of Political Philosophy in Honor of Leo Strauss.* Ed. Joseph CROPSEY. New York: Basic Books, 1964.

King Lear

Textual Criticism and Sources

See also **106, 389,** and **2384.**

3005 CAIRNCROSS, Andrew S. "The Quartos and the Folio Text of *King Lear." RES,* n.s. 6 (1955):252–58.

3006 CAUTHEN, Irby B., Jr. "Compositor Determination in the First Folio *King Lear." SB* 5 (1952–53):73–80.

3007 DORAN, Madeleine. *The Text of "King Lear."* Stanford, Calif.: Stanford U.P.; London: Oxford U.P., 1931. Rpt., New York: AMS.

3008 DUTHIE, George Ian. *Elizabethan Shorthand and the First Quarto of "King Lear."* Oxford: Blackwell, 1949.

3009 GREG, W. W. "The Date of *King Lear* and Shakespeare's Use of Earlier Versions of the Story." *Library,* 4th ser. 20 (1940):377–400.

3010 GREG, W. W. *The Variants in the First Quarto of "King Lear": A Bibliographical and Critical Inquiry.* London: Oxford U.P. for the Bibliographical Society, 1940 (for 1939).

3011 HAMILTON, Donna B. "Some Romance Sources for *King Lear: Robert of Sicily* and *Robert the Devil." SP* 71 (1974):173–91.

3012 HENDERSON, W. B. Drayton. "Montaigne's *Apologie of Raymond Sebond,* and *King Lear." ShAB* 14 (1939):209–25 and 15 (1940):40–54.

3013 LASCELLES, Mary. *"King Lear* and Doomsday." *ShS* 26 (1973):69–79. On Shakespeare's probable debt to a Doomsday painting.

3014 LAW, Robert Adger. "Holinshed's Leir Story and Shakespeare's." *SP* 47 (1950): 42–50.

3015 MENDONÇA, Barbara Heliodora Carneiro de. "The Influence of *Gorboduc* on *King Lear.*" *ShS* 13 (1960):41–48.

3016 MUIR, Kenneth. "Samuel Harsnett and *King Lear.*" *RES,* n.s. 2 (1951):11–21.

3017 PERKINSON, Richard H. "Shakespeare's Revision of the Lear Story and the Structure of *King Lear.*" *PQ* 22 (1943):315–29.

3018 PRESSON, Robert K. "Boethius, King Lear, and 'Maystresse Philosophie.' " *JEGP* 64 (1965):406–24.

3019 PYLE, Fitzroy. *"Twelfth Night, King Lear,* and *Arcadia."* *MLR* 43 (1948): 449–55.

3020 SMIDT, Kristian. "The Quarto and the Folio *Lear:* Another Look at the Theories of Textual Derivation." *ES* 45 (1964):149–62.

3021 WILLIAMS, Philip. "The Compositor of the 'Pied Bull' *Lear.*" *SB* 1 (1948–49):59–68.

3022 WILLIAMS, Philip. "Two Problems in the Folio Text of *King Lear.*" *SQ* 4 (1953):451–60.

3023 YOUNG, Alan R. "The Written and Oral Sources of *King Lear* and the Problem of Justice in the Play." *SEL* 15 (1975):309–19.

Collections of Essays

3024 BONHEIM, Helmut, ed. *The "King Lear" Perplex.* San Francisco: Wadsworth, 1960.

3025 COLIE, Rosalie L., and F. T. FLAHIFF, eds. *Some Facets of "King Lear": Essays in Prismatic Criticism.* Toronto: U. of Toronto P., 1974.*

3026 KERMODE, Frank, ed. *Shakespeare, "King Lear": A Casebook.* London: Macmillan, 1969.

3027 *Shakespeare Survey* 13 (1960). Deals mainly with *King Lear.*

General Studies

See also **339, 980, 1187, 1204, 1211, 1216, 1218, 1230–31, 1249, 1263, 1306, 1429, 1448, 1601, 1646, 1739, 1748, 1887, 1889, 1911, 1924, 1927–29, 1937, 1947, 1951, 1957, 1969, 1976, 1978, 1981, 2011–31, and 2625.**

3028 ALLGAIER, Johannes. "Is *King Lear* an Antiauthoritarian Play?" *PMLA* 88 (1973):1033–39.*

3029 ALPERS, Paul J. *"King Lear* and the Theory of the 'Sight Pattern.' " In **1123.***

3030 ANDERSON, Peter S. "The Fragile World of *Lear.*" *CompD* 5 (1971–72): 269–82.

3031 BARNET, Sylvan. "Some Limitations of a Christian Approach to Shakespeare." *ELH* 22 (1955):81–92. Rpt. in **1163** and **1887.***

3032 BERMAN, Ronald. "Sense and Substance in *King Lear.*" *NM* 65 (1964):96–103.

3033 BICKERSTETH, Geoffrey L. "The Golden World of *King Lear.*" *PBA* 32 (1947 for 1946):147–71.

3034 BLISSETT, W. F. "Recognition in *King Lear.*" In **3025.**

3035 BLOCK, Alexander. "Shakespeare's *King Lear.*" In **1166.**

3036 BLOCK, Edward A. "*King Lear:* A Study in Balanced and Shifting Sympathies." *SQ* 10 (1959):499–512.

3037 BRADLEY, A. C. *Shakespearean Tragedy.* See **2011.***

3038 BROOKE, Nicholas. *Shakespeare: "King Lear."* London: Arnold, 1963.

3039 BURKE, Kenneth. "*King Lear:* Its Form and Psychosis." *Shenandoah* 21.1 (1969):3–18.*

3040 CALARCO, N. Joseph. "The Tragic Universe of *King Lear.*" In **1879.**

3041 CAVELL, Stanley. "The Avoidance of Love: A Reading of *King Lear.*" *Must We Mean What We Say? A Book of Essays.* New York: Scribner's, 1969.*

3042 CHAMBERS, R. W. *King Lear.* Glasgow U. Publications 54. Glasgow: Jackson, 1940.

3043 COLIE, Rosalie L. "Reason and Need: *King Lear* and the 'Crisis' of the Aristocracy." In **3025.**

3044 CRAIG, Hardin. "The Ethics of *King Lear.*" *PQ* 4 (1925):97–109.

3045 CUNNINGHAM, J. V. "Plots and Errors: *Hamlet* and *King Lear.*" In **1197.**

3046 DANBY, John F. "*King Lear* and Christian Patience: A Culmination." In **1600.**

3047 DANBY, John F. *Shakespeare's Doctrine of Nature: A Study of "King Lear."* London: Faber & Faber, 1949.*

3048 ELTON, William R. *"King Lear" and the Gods.* San Marino: Huntington Library, 1966.*

3049 EVERETT, Barbara. "The New *King Lear.*" *CritQ* 2 (1960):325–39.*

3050 FLY, Richard D. "Beyond Extremity: A Reading of *King Lear.*" *TSLL* 16 (1974):45–63. Rpt., rev., in **1211.***

3051 FRENCH, Carolyn S. "Shakespeare's 'Folly': *King Lear.*" *SQ* 10 (1959):523–29. Sees the play as about Christian folly.

3052 GARDNER, Helen. *King Lear.* London: Athlone, 1967.

3053 GOLDBERG, S. L. *An Essay on "King Lear."* Cambridge: Cambridge U.P., 1974.*

3054 GOTTSCHALK, Paul A. "The Universe of Madness in *King Lear.*" *BuR* 19.3 (1971):51–68.

3055 GREG, W. W. "Time, Place, and Politics in *King Lear.*" *MLR* 35 (1940):431–46.

3056 HARDISON, O. B., Jr. "Myth and History in *King Lear.*" *SQ* 26 (1975):227–42.*

3057 HARRISON, Thomas P. "*Titus Andronicus* and *King Lear:* A Study in Continuity." In **1171.**

3058 HEILMAN, Robert B. "The Lear World." *EIE 1948* (1949):29–57.

3059 HEILMAN, Robert B. *This Great Stage: Image and Structure in "King Lear."* Baton Rouge: Louisiana State U.P., 1948. 2nd ed., Seattle: U. of Washington P., 1963.*

3060 HOBDAY, C. H. The Social Background of *King Lear.*" *Modern Quarterly Miscellany* 1 (1947):37–56.

3061 HOCKEY, Dorothy C. "The Trial Pattern in *King Lear.*" *SQ* 10 (1959):389–95.

3062 HOENIGER, F. David. "The Artist Exploring the Primitive: *King Lear.*" In **3025.**

3063 HOLE, Sandra. "The Background of Divine Action in *King Lear.*" *SEL* 8 (1968): 217–33.

3064 HOLLY, Marcia. "*King Lear:* The Disguised and Deceived." *SQ* 24 (1973): 171–80.

3065 HUNTER, G. K., ed. *King Lear.* In the New Penguin Shakespeare. See **362.**

3066 HUTCHENS, Eleanor N. "The Transfer of Power in *King Lear* and *The Tempest.*" *REL* 4.2 (1963):82–93.

3067 IWASAKI, Soji. "Time and Truth in *King Lear.*" In **1159.**

3068 JAFFA, Harry V. "The Limits of Politics: *King Lear,* Act I, scene i." In **1454.** *

3069 JAMES, D. G. *The Dream of Learning: An Essay on "The Advancement of Learning," "Hamlet," and "King Lear."* Oxford: Clarendon, 1951.*

3070 JAYNE, Sears. "Charity in *King Lear.*" *SQ* 15.2 (1964):277–88. Also in **1153.**

3071 JENKINS, Raymond. "The Socratic Imperative and *King Lear.*" *RenP 1963* (1964):85–93. On attaining self-knowledge.

3072 KERNODLE, George R. "The Symphonic Form of *King Lear.*" In **1172.**

3073 KOLVE, V. A. "The Modernity of *Lear.*" In **1156.**

3074 LEVINSON, Jill. "What the Silence Said: Still Points in *King Lear.*" In **1151.**

3075 LINDHEIM, Nancy R. "*King Lear* as Pastoral Tragedy." In **3025.**

3076 LOTHIAN, John M. "*King Lear*": *A Tragic Reading of Life.* Toronto: Clarke, Irwin, 1949.

3077 LYONS, Bridget Gellert. "The Subplot as Simplification in *King Lear.*" In **3025.** *

3078 MACK, Maynard. "*King Lear" in Our Time.* Berkeley and Los Angeles: U. of California P., 1965. Paperback edition, 1972.*

3079 MAGUIN, Jean-Marie. "Imagination and Image Types in *King Lear.*" *CahiersE* 9 (1976):9–28.

3080 MARKELS, Julian. "Shakespeare's Confluence of Tragedy and Comedy: *Twelfth Night* and *King Lear.*" *SQ* 15.2 (1964):75–88. Also in **1153.**

3081 MASON, H. A. "Can We Derive Wisdom about Old Age from *King Lear?*" *CQ* 6 (1975):203–13.

3082 MAXWELL, J. C. "The Technique of Invocation in *King Lear.*" *MLR* 45 (1950):142–47.

3083 MILWARD, Peter. "The Religious Dimension of *King Lear.*" *ShStud* 8 (1969–70):48–73. See also Hideo HIRAMATSU, "The Structure and Theme of *King Lear.*" *ShStud* 12 (1973–74):31–45.

3084 MUIR, Edwin. "The Politics of *King Lear.*" *Essays on Literature and Society.* London: Hogarth, 1949. Enl. and rev. ed., Cambridge, Mass.: Harvard U.P., 1965.*

3085 MUIR, Kenneth, ed. *King Lear.* In the Arden Shakespeare. See **350.**

3086 MYRICK, Kenneth O. "Christian Pessimism in *King Lear.*" In **1121.**

3087 OATES, Joyce Carol. " 'Is This the Promised End?': The Tragedy of King Lear." *JAAC* 33 (1974):19–32.*

3088 PROVOST, Foster. "On Justice and the Music in *Richard II* and *King Lear.*" *Annuale Mediaevale* 2 (1961):55–71.

3089 RACKIN, Phyllis. "Delusion and Resolution in *King Lear.*" *SQ* 21 (1970): 29–34.*

3090 RIBNER, Irving. "The Gods Are Just: A Reading of *King Lear.*" *TDR* 2.3 (1958):34–54. Rpt., rev., in **1968.**

3091 RIEMER, A. P. *Darker Purpose: An Approach to Shakespeare's "King Lear."* Sydney: The English Association, 1968.

3092 ROSENBERG, John D. "King Lear and His Comforters." *EIC* 16 (1966):135–46. A critique of the modern critical tendency to stress the "redemption" of King Lear.

3093 ROSIER, James L. "The Lex Aeterna and *King Lear.*" *JEGP* 53 (1954):574–80.

3094 SEWALL, Richard B. *"King Lear." The Vision of Tragedy.* New Haven and London: Yale U.P., 1959.

3095 SHAPIRO, Arnold. " 'Childe Roland,' *Lear,* and the Ability to See." *PLL* 11 (1975):88–94.

3096 SIEGEL, Paul N. "Adversity and the Miracle of Love in *King Lear.*" *SQ* 6 (1955):325–36.

3097 SKULSKY, Harold. *"King Lear* and the Meaning of Chaos." *SQ* 17 (1966):3–17. Rpt., rev., in **1251.***

3098 SNYDER, Susan. *"King Lear* and the Prodigal Son." *SQ* 17 (1966):361–69. Argues that Lear's progress through the play is parallel to that of the prodigal son.

3099 STAMPFER, Judah. "The Catharsis of *King Lear.*" *ShS* 13 (1960):1–10.

3100 STUART, Betty Kantor. "Truth and Tragedy in *King Lear.*" *SQ* 18 (1967): 167–80.

3101 TALBERT, Ernest William. *"King Lear." Critical Approaches to Six Major English Works: "Beowulf" through "Paradise Lost."* Eds. Robert M. LUMIANSKY and Herschel BAKER. Philadelphia: U. of Pennsylvania P., 1968.

3102 TRAVERSI, Derek. *"King Lear." Scrutiny* 19 (1952–53):43–64, 126–42, and 206–30.

3103 VAN LAAN, Thomas F. "Acting as Action in *King Lear.*" In **3025.**

3104 VICKERS, Brian. *"King Lear* and Renaissance Paradoxes." *MLR* 63 (1968): 305–14.

3105 WALLER, G. F. "Time, Providence, and Tragedy in *The Atheist's Tragedy* and *King Lear.*" *EM* 23 (1972):55–74.

3106 WATKINS, W. B. C. "The Two Techniques in *King Lear.*" *RES* 18 (1942):1–26. Rpt. in **1447.**

3107 WEITZ, Morris. "The coinage of Man: *King Lear* and Camus's *L'etranger.*" *MLR* 66 (1971):31–39.

3108 WEST, Robert H. "Sex and Pessimism in *King Lear.*" *SQ* 11 (1960):55–60. Rpt. in **1448.**

3109 WICKHAM, Glynne. "From Tragedy to Tragi-Comedy: *King Lear* as Prologue." *ShS* 26 (1973):33–48. Published also in German in *SJH* (1974):7–33.

Character Studies

See also **1247, 1370, 1374, 1381, 1391, 1396, 1398, 1406, 1988, 1999, 2017, 2022,** and **3485.**

3110 ADAMS, Robert P. "King Lear's Revenges." *MLQ* 21 (1960):223–27.

3111 ANSHUTZ, H. L. "Cordelia and the Fool." *RS* 32 (1964):240–60.

3112 ARNOLD, Judd. "How Do We Judge King Lear?" *Criticism* 14 (1972):207–26.

3113 BACHE, William B. "Lear as Old Man—Father—King." *CLAJ* 19 (1975):1–9.

3114 BALD, R. C. " 'Thou, Nature, Art My Goddess': Edmund and Renaissance Free-Thought." In **1154.**

3115 BAUER, Robert J. "Despite of Mine Own Nature: Edmund and the Orders, Cosmic and Moral." *TSLL* 10 (1968):359–66.

3116 BENNETT, Josephine Waters. "The Storm Within: The Madness of Lear." *SQ* 13 (1962):137–55.

3117 BUCKLEY, George T. "Was Edmund Guilty of Capital Treason?" *SQ* 23 (1972): 87–94.

3118 CAMPBELL, Oscar James. "The Salvation of Lear." *ELH* 15 (1948):93–109.

3119 CHAPLIN, William H. "Form and Psychology in *King Lear.*" *L&P* 19.3–4 (1969):31–45.

3120 DAVIS, Arthur G. *The Royalty of Lear.* Jamaica, N.Y.: St. John's U.P., 1974.

3121 DONNELLY, John. "Incest, Ingratitude, and Insanity: Aspects of the Psychopathology of King Lear." *PsyR* 40 (1953):149–55.

3122 FLAHIFF, F. T. "Edgar: Once and Future King." In **3025.**

3123 GRINSTEIN, Alexander. "King Lear's Impending Death." *AI* 30 (1973):121–41.

3124 ISENBERG, Arnold. "Cordelia Absent." *SQ* 2 (1951):185–94.

3125 JORGENSEN, Paul A. *Lear's Self-Discovery.* Berkeley and Los Angeles: U. of California P., 1967.*

3126 KAHN, Sholom J. "Enter Lear Mad." *SQ* 8 (1957):311–29.

3127 KIRSCHBAUM, Leo. "Albany." *ShS* 13 (1960):20–29.

3128 KIRSCHBAUM, Leo. "Banquo and Edgar: Character or Function?" *EIC* 7 (1957):1–21.

3129 LIPPINCOTT, H. F. "*King Lear* and the Fools of Robert Armin." *SQ* 26 (1975):243–53.

3130 MCCULLEN, Joseph T., Jr. "Edgar: The Wise Bedlam." In **1169.**

3131 MCEWAN, Neil. "The Lost Childhood of Lear's Fool." *EIC* 26 (1976):209–17.

3132 MACLEAN, Hugh. "Disguise in *King Lear:* Kent and Edgar." *SQ* 11 (1960): 49–54.

3133 MCNEIR, Waldo F. "The Role of Edmund in *King Lear.*" *SEL* 8 (1968): 187–216.

3134 MATTHEWS, Richard. "Edmund's Redemption in *King Lear.*" *SQ* 26 (1975): 25–29.

3135 MORRIS, Ivor. "Cordelia and Lear." *SQ* 8 (1957):141–58.

3136 MORTENSON, Peter. "The Role of Albany." *SQ* 16 (1965):217–25.

3137 MUIR, Kenneth. "Madness in *King Lear.*" *ShS* 13 (1960):30–40.

3138 NOJIMA, Hidekatsu. "Exit the Fool." In **1159.**

3139 NOWOTTNY, Winifred M. T. "Lear's Questions." *ShS* 10 (1957):90–97.

3140 ORWELL, George. "Lear, Tolstoy, and the Fool." *Shooting an Elephant and Other Essays.* London: Secker & Warburg; New York: Harcourt, Brace, & World, 1950. Rpt. in **937.***

3141 PARR, Johnston. "Edmund's Nativity in *King Lear.*" *ShAB* 21 (1946):181–85. Rpt. in *Tamburlaine's Malady and Other Essays.* University: U. of Alabama P., 1953.

3142 PAUNCE, Arpad. "Psychopathology of Shakespeare's *King Lear.*" *AI* 9 (1952): 57–78.

3143 REID, Stephen A. "In Defense of Goneril and Regan." *AI* 27 (1970):226–44.

3144 ROSINGER, Lawrence. "Gloucester and Lear: Men Who Act Like Gods." *ELH* 35 (1968):491–504.

3145 SCHOFF, Francis G. "King Lear: Moral Example or Tragic Protagonist?" *SQ* 13 (1962):157–72.

3146 SINFIELD, Alan. "Lear and Laing." *EIC* 26 (1976):1–16. On Laing's concept of "reason in madness."

3147 STETNER, S. C. V., and Oscar B. GOODMAN. "Lear's Darker Purpose." *L&P* 18 (1968):82–90.

3148 STEVENSON, Warren. "Albany as Archetype in *King Lear.*" *MLQ* 26 (1965): 257–63.

3149 STROUP, Thomas B. "Cordelia and the Fool." *SQ* 12 (1961):127–32.

3150 WEIDHORN, Manfred. "Lear's Schoolmasters." *SQ* 13 (1962):305–16. On the education of Lear.

3151 WOOD, Glena D. "The Tragi-Comic Dimensions of Lear's Fool." *Costerus* 5 (1972):197–226.

Particular Scenes or Passages

See also **3068** and **4236.**

3152 BROOKE, Nicholas. "The Ending of *King Lear.*" In **1121.***

3153 BROWN, Stephen J. "Shakespeare's King and Beggar." *YR* 64 (1975):370–95. On III, iv.

3154 DONNER, H. W. " 'Is This the Promised End?': Reflections on the Tragic Ending of *King Lear.*" *ES* 50 (1969):503–10.

3155 DUNN, E. Catherine. "The Storm in *King Lear.*" *SQ* 3 (1952):329–33.

3156 ELLIS, John. "The Gulling of Gloucester: Credibility in the Subplot of *King Lear.*" *SEL* 12 (1972):275–89.

3157 FROST, William. "Shakespeare's Rituals and the Opening of *King Lear.*" *HudR* 10 (1957–58):577–85. Rpt. in **1954.***

3158 FRYE, Dean. "The Context of Lear's Unbuttoning." *ELH* 32 (1965):17–31.

3159 HARRIS, Duncan S. "The End of *Lear* and a Shape for Shakespearean Tragedy." *ShakS* 9 (1976):253–67.

3160 HENNEDY, Hugh L. "*King Lear:* Recognizing the Ending." *SP* 71 (1974): 371–84.

3161 HOBSBAUM, Philip. "Survival Values." *A Theory of Communication.* London: Macmillan, 1970. About the history of *Lear* criticism, focusing on the last scene.*

3162 KERNAN, Alvin B. "Formalism and Realism in Elizabethan Drama: The Miracles in *King Lear.*" *RenD* 9 (1966):59–66.*

3163 KREIDER, Paul V. "Gloucester's Eyes." *ShAB* 8 (1933):121–32.

3164 LEVIN, Harry. "The Heights and the Depths: A Scene from *King Lear.*" In **1138.** Rpt. in **1233.** Focuses on IV, vi.

3165 MCLAUGHLIN, Ann L. "The Journeys in *King Lear.*" *AI* 29 (1972):384–99.

3166 MACLEAN, Norman. "Episode, Scene, Speech, and Word: The Madness of Lear." *Critics and Criticism.* Ed. R. S. CRANE. Chicago: U. of Chicago P., 1952.*

3167 MCNEIR, Waldo F. "The Staging of the Dover Cliff Scene in *King Lear.*" In **1155.**

3168 MARKS, Carol L. " 'Speak What We Feel': The End of *King Lear.*" *ELN* 5 (1968):163–71.

3169 MEHL, Dieter. "King Lear and the 'Poor Naked Wretches.' " *SJH* (1975): 154–62. On III, iv.

3170 NELSON, William. " 'Complement of Leave-Taking' between Lear and the King of France." *RenQ* 27 (1974):193–95.

3171 OPPEL, Horst. *Die Gerichtsszene in "King Lear."* Wiesbaden: Akademie der Wissenschaften und der Literatur in Mainz, in Kommission bei Franz Steiner, 1968.

3172 PECK, Russell A. "Edgar's Pilgrimage: High Comedy in *King Lear.*" *SEL* 7 (1967):219–37.

3173 SHAW, John. "*King Lear:* The Final Lines." *EIC* 16 (1966):261–67.

3174 STEWART, J. I. M. "The Blinding of Gloster." *RES* 21 (1945):264–70.

3175 WALTON, J. K. "Lear's Last Speech." *ShS* 13 (1960):11–19.

3176 WEIMANN, Robert. "Lear und das Bild der 'armen nackten Elenden.' " *SJW* 109 (1973):62–73. On III, iv.

3177 WILLSON, Robert F., Jr. "Lear's Auction." *Costerus* 6 (1972):163–77. On I, i.

Staging and Stage History

See also **718, 731, 746, 763, 786, 792, 808, 847, 884, 893, 1024, 1559, 1937,** and **3167.**

3178 CLEMEN, Wolfgang, and others. *"König Lear:* Der theatralische Vorwurf Shakespeares und seine Verwirkichung auf der Bühne. Das Bochumer Podiumsgespräch vom 20. April 1968." *SJH* (1969):10–80.

3179 JACKSON, Esther Merle. *"King Lear:* The Grammar of Tragedy." *SQ* 17 (1966):25–40. On the problem of recovering the theatrical "language" of Shakespeare's original play.

3180 ROSENBERG, Marvin. *The Masks of "King Lear."* Berkeley and Los Angeles: U. of California P., 1972.*

Language and Imagery

See also **457, 512, 554,** and **3079.**

3181 ANDRESEN, Martha. " 'Ripeness Is All': Sententiae and Commonplaces in *King Lear."* In **3025.**

3182 BARISH, Jonas A., and Marshall WAINGROW. " 'Service' in *King Lear." SQ* 9 (1958):347–55.

3183 CHARNEY, Maurice. " 'We Put Fresh Garments on Him': Nakedness and Clothes in *King Lear."* In **3025.**

3184 COLIE, Rosalie L. "The Energies of Endurance: Biblical Echo in *King Lear."* In **3025.**

3185 DORAN, Madeleine. "Command, Question, and Assertion in *King Lear."* In **1130.**

3186 DRY, Helen. "Words in *King Lear." Thoth* 13.2 (1973):11–17.

3187 EMPSON, William. "Fool in *Lear."* In **530.**

3188 FLY, Richard D. "Revelations of Darkness: The Language of Silence in *King Lear." BuR* 20.3 (1972):73–92. Rpt., rev., in **1211.**

3189 FRASER, Russell A. *Shakespeare's Poetics in Relation to "King Lear."* London: Routledge & K. Paul, 1962.

3190 GREENFIELD, Thelma N. "The Clothing Motif in *King Lear." SQ* 5 (1954): 281–86.

3191 HAWKES, Terence. " 'Love' in *King Lear." RES,* n.s. 10 (1959):178–81. Rpt., rev., in **465.**

3192 KANZER, Mark. "Imagery in *King Lear." AI* 22 (1965):3–13.

3193 KEAST, W. R. "Imagery and Meaning in the Interpretation of *King Lear." MP* 47 (1949):45–64. Rpt. under the title "The 'New Criticism' and *King Lear"* in *Critics and Criticism.* Ed. R. S. CRANE. Chicago: U. of Chicago P., 1952.*

3194 KNIGHTS, L. C. *"King Lear* as Metaphor." In **1229.** Rpt. in *Myth and Symbol.* See **2084.**

3195 LEIDER, Emily W. "Plainness of Style in *King Lear." SQ* 21 (1970):45–53.

3196 MCCLOSKEY, John C. "The Emotive Use of Animal Imagery in *King Lear." SQ* 13 (1962):321–25.

3197 MUSGROVE, Sydney. "The Nomenclature of *King Lear." RES,* n.s. 7 (1956): 294–98.

3198 NOWOTTNY, Winifred M. T. "Some Aspects of the Style of *King Lear.*" *ShS* 13 (1960):49–57.

3199 REIBETANZ, John. "Theatrical Emblems in *King Lear.*" In **3025.**

3200 WILLIAMS, George Walton. "The Poetry of the Storm in *King Lear.*" *SQ* 2 (1951):57–71.

3201 ZITNER, Sheldon P. "*King Lear* and Its Language." In **3025.**

Love's Labour's Lost

See also **514, 1189, 1202, 1218, 1226, 1326, 1578–79, 1586, 1589, 1592, 1595, 1628, 1637, 1668, 1682, 1699, 1704, 1708, 1710, 1712–21, 1727, 1730, 1733, 1738,** and **1781.**

3202 AGNEW, Gates K. "Berowne and the Progress of *Love's Labour's Lost.*" *ShakS* 4 (1969 for 1968):40–72.

3203 ANDERSON, J. J. "The Morality of *Love's Labour's Lost.*" *ShS* 24 (1971):55–62.

3204 BABCOCK, Weston. "Fools, Fowls, and Perttaunt-Like in *Love's Labour's Lost.*" *SQ* 2 (1951):211–19.

3205 BOUGHNER, Daniel C. "Don Armado and the *Commedia dell' Arte.*" *SP* 37 (1940):201–24.

3206 BOUGHNER, Daniel C. "Don Armado as a Gallant." *Revue Anglo-Américaine* 13 (1935):18–28.

3207 BRADBROOK, M. C. *The School of Night: A Study in the Literary Relationships of Sir Walter Ralegh.* Cambridge: Cambridge U.P., 1936.

3208 BRONSON, Bertrand H. "Daisies Pied and Icicles." *MLN* 63 (1948):35–38.

3209 BROWNE, Ray B. "The Satiric Use of 'Popular' Music in *Love's Labour's Lost.*" *Southern Folklore Quarterly* 23 (1959):137–49.

3210 CAMPBELL, Oscar James. "*Love's Labour's Lost* Re-studied." *Studies in Shakespeare, Milton, and Donne* by Members of the English Department of the University of Michigan. New York: Macmillan, 1925.

3211 CARROLL, William C. *The Great Feast of Language in "Love's Labour's Lost."* Princeton: Princeton U.P., 1976.*

3212 COURSEN, Herbert R., Jr. "*Love's Labour's Lost* and the Comic Truth." *PLL* 6 (1970):316–22.

3213 CUNNINGHAM, J. V. " 'With That Facility': False Starts and Revisions in *Love's Labour's Lost.*" In **1127.**

3214 DAVID, Richard, ed. *Love's Labour's Lost.* In the Arden Shakespeare. See **350.**

3215 DRAPER, John W. "Tempo in *Love's Labour's Lost.*" *ES* 29 (1948):129–37.

3216 ELLIS, Herbert A. *Shakespeare's Lusty Punning in "Love's Labour's Lost."* The Hague and Paris: Mouton, 1973.

3217 EVANS, Malcolm. "Mercury Versus Apollo: A Reading of *Love's Labour's Lost.*" *SQ* 26 (1975):113–27.

3218 GODSHALK, William Leigh. "Pattern in *Love's Labour's Lost.*" *RenP 1968* (1969):41–48. Rpt. in **1215.**

3219 GOLDSTIEN, Neal L. "*Love's Labour's Lost* and the Renaissance Vision of Love." *SQ* 25 (1974):335–50.

3220 GREENE, Thomas M. "*Love's Labour's Lost:* The Grace of Society." *SQ* 22 (1971):315–28.

3221 GREENFIELD, Stanley B. "Moth's *L'Envoy* and the Courtiers in *Love's Labour's Lost.*" *RES,* n.s. 5 (1954):167–68.

3222 HARBAGE, Alfred. "*Love's Labour's Lost* and the Early Shakespeare." *PQ* 41 (1962):18–36. Also in **1174.** Rpt. in **1220** and in **1145** (1962 for 1961).*

3223 HASLER, Jörg. "Enumeration in *Love's Labour's Lost.*" *ES* 50 (1969):176–85.

3224 HENINGER, S. K., Jr. "The Pattern of *Love's Labour's Lost.*" *ShakS* 7 (1974): 25–53.*

3225 HOY, Cyrus. "*Love's Labour's Lost* and the Nature of Comedy." *SQ* 13 (1962): 31–40.

3226 HOY, Cyrus. "Navarre and His Bookmen." In **1620.**

3227 HUNT, John Dixon. "Grace, Art, and the Neglect of Time in *Love's Labour's Lost.*" In **1722.**

3228 HUNTER, Robert Grams. "The Function of the Songs at the End of *Love's Labour's Lost.*" *ShakS* 7 (1974):55–64.*

3229 KODAMA, Hisao. "Armado's 'You that way; we this way.' " *ShStud* 8 (1969–70):1–17.

3230 LAWRENCE, Natalie Grimes. "A Study of Taffeta Phrases ... and Honest Kersey Noes." In **1150.**

3231 LEFRANC, Abel. "Les Éléments français de *Peines d'amour perdues* de Shakespeare." *Revue Historique* 178 (1936):411–32.

3232 LEFRANC, Abel. *Sous le Masque de "William Shakespeare."* 2 vols. Paris: Payot, 1918–19.

3233 LENNAM, Trevor. " 'The Ventricle of Memory': Wit and Wisdom in *Love's Labour's Lost.*" *SQ* 24 (1973):54–60.

3234 LEWIS, Anthony J. "Shakespeare's Via Media in *Love's Labour's Lost.*" *TSLL* 16 (1974):241–48.

3235 LORD, Gisela. "Die Figur des Pedanten bei Shakespeare." *SJH* (1969):213–44.

3236 MCLAY, Catherine M. "The Dialogues of Spring and Winter: A Key to the Unity of *Love's Labour's Lost.*" *SQ* 18 (1967):119–27.

3237 MATTHEWS, William. "Language in *Love's Labour's Lost.*" *E&S,* n.s. 17 (1964):1–11.

3238 MEMMO, Paul E., Jr. "The Poetry of the *Stilnovisti* and *Love's Labour's Lost.*" *CL* 18 (1966):1–15.

3239 MONTROSE, Louis A. " 'Sport By Sport O'erthrown': *Love's Labour's Lost* and the Politics of Play." *TSLL* 18 (1977):528–52.

3240 NEVINSON, John L. "A Show of Nine Worthies." *SQ* 14 (1963):103–07.

3241 ROESEN, Bobbyann. "*Love's Labour's Lost.*" *SQ* 4 (1953):411–26. Rpt. in **1125** under the name of Anne BARTON.

3242 SCHLÖSSER, Anselm. "*Love's Labour's Lost:* Shakespeares Jahrmarkt der Eitelkeit." *ZAA* 13 (1965):25–34.

3243 SCHRICKX, Willem. *Shakespeare's Early Contemporaries: The Background of the Harvey-Nashe Polemic and "Love's Labour's Lost."* Antwerp: Nederlandsche Boekhandel, 1956. Rpt., New York: AMS.

3244 SPEVACK, Marvin. "Shakespeare's Early Use of Wordplay: *Love's Labour's Lost." Festschrift für Edgar Mertner.* Eds. Bernhard FABIAN and Ulrich SUERBAUM. Munich: Fink, 1969.

3245 THORNE, William Barry. "*Love's Labour's Lost:* The Lyly Gilded." *HAB* 21.3 (1970):32–37.

3246 WESTLUND, Joseph. "Fancy and Achievement in *Love's Labour's Lost." SQ* 18 (1967):37–46.

3247 WILDERS, John. "The Unresolved Conflicts of *Love's Labour's Lost." EIC* 27 (1977):20–33.

3248 YATES, Frances A. *A Study of "Love's Labour's Lost."* Cambridge: Cambridge U.P., 1936.

Macbeth

General Studies

See also **339, 343, 382, 932, 1177, 1201, 1204, 1218, 1234, 1238, 1246–47, 1256, 1258, 1261, 1268, 1289, 1306, 1413, 1419, 1429, 1448, 1451–52, 1477, 1508, 1518, 1878, 1897, 1911, 1927–28, 1947, 1951, 1953, 1958–59, 1969, 1976, 1978, 1981,** and **2011–32.**

3249 BAUDUIN, Janine. "Les Éléments baroques dans *Macbeth* et leur utilisation." *EA* 24 (1971):1–21.

3250 BERNAD, Miguel A. "The Five Tragedies in *Macbeth." SQ* 13 (1962):49–61.

3251 BIGGINS, Dennis. "Sexuality, Witchcraft, and Violence in *Macbeth." ShakS* 8 (1975):255–77.

3252 BLISSETT, William. "The Secret'st Man of Blood: A Study of Dramatic Irony in *Macbeth." SQ* 10 (1959):397–408.*

3253 BRADBROOK, M. C. "The Sources of *Macbeth." ShS* 4 (1951):35–48.

3254 BRADLEY, A. C. *Shakespearean Tragedy.* See **2011.***

3255 BROWN, John Russell. *Shakespeare: "The Tragedy of Macbeth."* London: Arnold, 1963.

3256 BURRELL, Margaret D. "*Macbeth:* A Study in Paradox." *SJ* 90 (1954):167–90.

3257 COURSEN, Herbert R., Jr. "In Deepest Consequence: *Macbeth." SQ* 18 (1967): 375–88. On the myth of the fall from a state of grace.

3258 CURRY, Walter Clyde. *Shakespeare's Philosophical Patterns.* Baton Rouge: Louisiana State U.P., 1937. 2nd ed., 1959. Rpt., Gloucester, Mass.: P. Smith. Contains essays on *Macbeth* and *The Tempest.* *

3259 DAVIDSON, Clifford. *The Primrose Way: A Study of Shakespeare's "Macbeth."* Conesville, Iowa: J. Westburg, 1970.

3260 DEAN, Leonard F. *"Macbeth* and Modern Criticism." *EJ* 47 (1958):57–67.

3261 DORAN, Madeleine. "That Undiscovered Country: A Problem Concerning the Use of the Supernatural in *Hamlet* and *Macbeth."* *PQ* 20 (1941):413–27.

3262 DUTHIE, George Ian. "Antithesis in *Macbeth."* *ShS* 19 (1966):25–33.

3263 ELLIOTT, G. R. *Dramatic Providence in "Macbeth."* Princeton: Princeton U.P., 1958. Rpt., Westport, Conn.: Greenwood.

3264 FERGUSSON, Francis. *"Macbeth* as the Imitation of an Action." *EIE 1951* (1952):31–43. Rpt. in **1125, 1207,** and **1942.***

3265 FOAKES, R. A. *"Macbeth."* In **1145** (1963 for 1962).

3266 FRYE, Roland Mushat. "Macbeth and the Powers of Darkness." *EUQ* 8 (1952): 164–74.

3267 HALIO, Jay L., ed. *Approaches to "Macbeth."* Belmont, Calif.: Wadsworth, 1966. A collection of essays.

3268 HUNTER, G. K. *"Macbeth* in the Twentieth Century." *ShS* 19 (1966):1–11.

3269 HUNTER, G. K., ed. *Macbeth.* In the New Penguin Shakespeare. See **362.**

3270 IDE, Richard S. "The Theatre of the Mind: An Essay on *Macbeth."* *ELH* 42 (1975):338–61.

3271 JACK, Jane H. *"Macbeth,* King James, and the Bible." *ELH* 22 (1955):173–93.

3272 JORGENSEN, Paul A. *Our Naked Frailties: Sensational Art and Meaning in "Macbeth."* Berkeley and Los Angeles: U. of California P., 1971.***

3273 KISTNER, A. L., and M. K. KISTNER. *"Macbeth:* A Treatise of Conscience." *Thoth* 13.2 (1973):27–43.

3274 KITTREDGE, George Lyman. *Witchcraft in Old and New England.* Cambridge, Mass.: Harvard U.P.; London: Oxford U.P., 1929. Rpt., New York: Russell & Russell, 1956.

3275 KNIGHTS, L. C. *"Macbeth."* In **1230.** Rpt. in **1942.***

3276 KNIGHTS, L. C. "On the Background of Shakespeare's Use of Nature in *Macbeth."* *SR* 64 (1956):207–17.

3277 LEECH, Clifford. "The Dark Side of *Macbeth."* *Literary Half-Yearly* 8 (1967): 27–34.

3278 MCGEE, Arthur R. *"Macbeth* and the Furies." *ShS* 19 (1966):55–67.

3279 MARKELS, Julian. "The Spectacle of Deterioration: *Macbeth* and the 'Manner' of Tragic Imitation." *SQ* 12 (1961):293–303.

3280 MORRIS, Harry. *"Macbeth,* Dante, and the Greatest Evil." *TSL* 12 (1967): 23–38.

3281 MUIR, Kenneth, ed. *Macbeth.* In the Arden Shakespeare. See **350.**

3282 MUIR, Kenneth, and Philip EDWARDS. *Aspects of "Macbeth."* London and New York: Cambridge U.P., 1977.

3283 PACK, Robert. *"Macbeth:* The Anatomy of Loss." *YR* 45 (1956):533–48.

3284 PAOLUCCI, Anne. *"Macbeth* and *Oedipus Rex:* A Study in Paradox." In **1160.**

3285 PAUL, Henry N. *The Royal Play of "Macbeth."* New York: Macmillan, 1950. Rpt., New York: Octagon.

3286 RAUBER, D. F. "Macbeth, Macbeth, Macbeth." *Criticism* 11 (1969):59–67. On the pattern of three's in the play.

3287 REID, B. L. "*Macbeth* and the Play of Absolutes." *SR* 73 (1965):19–46.

3288 RIBNER, Irving. "*Macbeth:* The Pattern of Idea and Action." *SQ* 10 (1959): 147–59. Rpt., rev., in **1968.**

3289 RIBNER, Irving. "Political Doctrine in *Macbeth.*" *SQ* 4 (1953):202–05.

3290 ROGERS, H. L. *"Double Profit" in "Macbeth."* Melbourne: Melbourne U.P.; London and New York: Cambridge U.P., 1964.

3291 ROSSITER, A. P. *"Macbeth."* In **1245.**

3292 *Shakespeare Survey* 19 (1966). Devoted largely to *Macbeth.* *

3293 SMITH, Fred Manning. "The Relation of *Macbeth* to *Richard the Third.*" *PMLA* 60 (1945):1003–20.

3294 SPENDER, Stephen. "Time, Violence, and *Macbeth.*" *Penguin New Writing* 3 (1940–41):115–26.

3295 STIRLING, Brents. "The Unity of *Macbeth.*" *SQ* 4 (1953):385–94. Rpt. in **1978.**

3296 STOLL, Elmer Edgar. "Source and Motive in *Macbeth* and *Othello.*" *RES* 19 (1943):25–32. Rpt. in **1258.**

3297 TOMLINSON, T. B. "Action and Soliloquy in *Macbeth.*" *EIC* 8 (1958):147–55.

3298 URE, Peter. *"Macbeth."* In **1269.**

3299 WAIN, John, ed. *Shakespeare, "Macbeth": A Casebook.* London: Macmillan, 1968.

3300 WALKER, Roy. *The Time Is Free: A Study of "Macbeth."* London: Dakers, 1949.

3301 WALTON, J. K. *"Macbeth."* In **1148.**

Character Studies

See also **1381, 1391, 1403, 1406, 1985, 1988, 1991, 1995, 2017,** and **2022.**

3302 ANDERSON, Ruth L. "The Pattern of Behavior Culminating in *Macbeth.*" *SEL* 3 (1963):151–73.

3303 ARTHOS, John. "The Naive Imagination and the Destruction of Macbeth." *ELH* 14 (1947):114–26.

3304 BARRON, David B. "The Babe that Milks: An Organic Study of *Macbeth.*" *AI* 17 (1960):133–61. Rpt. in **1401.**

3305 BERLIN, Normand. "Ross in *Macbeth.*" *Neophil* 58 (1974):411–24.

3306 BOOTH, Wayne. "Shakespeare's Tragic Villain." In **1955.** Orig. pub. as "Macbeth as Tragic Hero" in *JGE* 6 (1951):17–25.*

3307 CLARKE, C. C. "Darkened Reason in *Macbeth.*" *DUJ* 53, n.s. 22 (1960):11–18.

3308 CORIAT, Isador H. *The Hysteria of Lady Macbeth.* New York: Moffat, Yard, 1912.

3309 CUNNINGHAM, Dolora G. "*Macbeth:* The Tragedy of the Hardened Heart." *SQ* 14 (1963):39–47.

3310 EWBANK, Inga-Stina. "The Fiend-Like Queen: A Note on *Macbeth* and Seneca's *Medea.*" *ShS* 19 (1966):82–94.

3311 FERGUSSON, James. *The Man behind Macbeth, and Other Studies.* London: Faber & Faber, 1969.

3312 FREUD, Sigmund. "Those Wrecked by Success." *The Standard Edition of the Complete Psychological Works of Sigmund Freud.* Trans. James STRACHEY, et al. Vol. 14 (1914–16). London: Hogarth, 1957, pp. 316–31.*

3313 HEILMAN, Robert B. "The Criminal as Tragic Hero: Dramatic Methods." *ShS* 19 (1966):12–24.*

3314 JAARSMA, Richard J. "The Tragedy of Banquo." *L&P* 17 (1967):87–94.

3315 JEKELS, Ludwig. "The Riddle of Shakespeare's *Macbeth.*" *Selected Papers.* New York: International U.P., 1953. Rpt. in *Psychoanalysis and Literature.* Ed. H. M. RUITENBECK. New York: Dutton, 1964.

3316 KIRSCHBAUM, Leo. "Banquo and Edgar: Character or Function?" *EIC* 7 (1957):1–21.

3317 KNIGHTS, L. C. "How Many Children Had Lady Macbeth? An Essay in the Theory and Practice of Shakespeare Criticism." In **1228.***

3318 MERCHANT, W. Moelwyn. " 'His Fiend-Like Queen.' " *ShS* 19 (1966):75–81.

3319 RAMA MOORTHY, P. "Fear in *Macbeth.*" *EIC* 23 (1973):154–66.

3320 RAMSEY, Jarold W. "The Perversion of Manliness in *Macbeth.*" *SEL* 13 (1973): 285–300.

3321 SADLER, Lynn Veach. "The Three Guises of Lady Macbeth." *CLAJ* 19 (1975): 10–19.

3322 SMIDT, Kristian. "Two Aspects of Ambition in Elizabethan Tragedy: *Doctor Faustus* and *Macbeth.*" *ES* 50 (1969):235–48.

3323 TAYLOR, Michael. "Ideals of Manhood in *Macbeth.*" *EA* 21 (1968):337–48.

3324 THUMBOO, Edwin. "Macbeth and the Generous Duncan." *SQ* 22 (1971):181–86.

3325 TOPPEN, W. H. *Conscience in Shakespeare's "Macbeth."* Groningen: Wolters, 1962.

3326 VESZY-WAGNER, L. "*Macbeth:* 'Fair is Foul and Foul is Fair.' " *AI* 25 (1968): 242–57. A psychoanalytic study of Lady Macbeth as woman-mother and seductress of Macbeth.

3327 WAITH, Eugene M. "Manhood and Valor in Two Shakespearean Tragedies." See **2212.**

Particular Scenes or Passages

3328 ALLEN, Michael J. B. "Macbeth's Genial Porter." *ELR* 4 (1974):326–36.

3329 AMNÉUS, Daniel A. "The Cawdor Episode in *Macbeth.*" *JEGP* 63 (1964): 185–90.

3330 AMNÉUS, Daniel A. "Macbeth's 'Greater Honor.'" *ShakS* 6 (1972 for 1970): 223–30. Argues that the "greater honor" mentioned in I, iii originally referred to the Princedom of Cumberland.

3331 AMNÉUS, Daniel A. "A Missing Scene in *Macbeth.*" *JEGP* 60 (1961):435–40.

3332 ARNOLD, Aerol. "The Recapitulation Dream in *Richard III* and *Macbeth.*" *SQ* 6 (1955):51–62. Focuses in part on Lady Macbeth's sleepwalking scene.

3333 BREUER, Horst. "Disintegration of Time in Macbeth's Soliloquy 'Tomorrow, and Tomorrow, and Tomorrow.'" *MLR* 71 (1976):256–71.

3334 DE QUINCEY, Thomas. "On the Knocking at the Gate in *Macbeth.*" *London Magazine* (October, 1823). Rpt. in **946.***

3335 DYSON, J. P. "The Structural Function of the Banquet Scene in *Macbeth.*" *SQ* 14 (1963):369–78.

3336 FLATTER, Richard. "Who Wrote the Hecate-Scene?" *SJ* 93 (1957):196–210. Argues that the scene was by Shakespeare. For a rejoinder, see John P. CUTTS, "Who Wrote the Hecate-Scene?" *SJ* 94 (1958):200–02.

3337 FLATTER, Richard. "Hecate, 'The Other Three Witches,' and Their Songs." *SJ* 95 (1959):225–37. A counter-rejoinder to CUTTS in the above item.

3338 HARCOURT, John B. "'I Pray You, Remember the Porter.'" *SQ* 12 (1961): 393–402.

3339 HUNTLEY, Frank L. "*Macbeth* and the Background of Jesuitical Equivocation." *PMLA* 79 (1964):390–400.

3340 KOCHER, Paul H. "Lady Macbeth and the Doctor." *SQ* 5 (1954):341–49.

3341 MARTIN, Graham. "William Shakespeare: *Macbeth,* Act I, Scene vii, Lines 1 to 28." *Interpretations.* Ed. John WAIN. London: Routledge & K. Paul, 1955.

3342 NOSWORTHY, J. M. "The Bleeding Captain Scene in *Macbeth.*" *RES* 22 (1946):126–30.

3343 SPARGO, John Webster. "The Knocking at the Gate in *Macbeth:* An Essay in Interpretation." In **1154.**

3344 TROMLY, Frederic B. "Macbeth and His Porter." *SQ* 26 (1975):151–56. Argues that the Porter scene is integral to the play and comments on Macbeth himself.

3345 WICKHAM, Glynne. "Hell-Castle and Its Door-Keeper." *ShS* 19 (1966):68–74.

3346 ZENDER, Karl F. "The Death of Young Siward: Providential Order and Tragic Loss in *Macbeth.*" *TSLL* 17 (1975):415–25.

Staging and Stage History

See also **729, 763, 788, 790, 795, 806, 819–20, 835, 847, 855, 895,** and **922.**

3347 BARTHOLOMEUSZ, Dennis. *Macbeth and the Players.* Cambridge: Cambridge U.P., 1969.

3348 DAVID, Richard. "The Tragic Curve." *ShS* 9 (1956):122–31. A review of two productions of *Macbeth* at Stratford-upon-Avon in 1954 and 1955.

3349 MULLIN, Michael. "*Macbeth* at Stratford-upon-Avon, 1955." *ShakS* 9 (1976): 269–82.

3350 MULLIN, Michael. "Strange Images of Death: Sir Herbert Beerbohm Tree's *Macbeth*, 1911." *Theatre Survey* 17 (1976):125–42.

3351 MULLIN, Michael, ed. *"Macbeth" Onstage: An Annotated Facsimile of Glen Byam Shaw's 1955 Promptbook.* Columbia: U. of Missouri P., 1976.

3352 NIELSEN, Elizabeth. *"Macbeth:*The Nemesis of the Post-Shakespearian Actor." *SQ* 16 (1965):193–99.

3353 SCRAGG, Leah. "Macbeth on Horseback." *ShS* 26 (1973):81–88. A reply to **3347** above.

3354 WAITH, Eugene M. *"Macbeth:* Interpretation Versus Adaptation." In **1161.**

Language and Imagery

See also **475, 539, 541, 555, 572,** and **3286.**

3355 BERRY, Francis. *"Macbeth:* Tense and Mood." *Poet's Grammar: Person, Time, and Mood in Poetry.* London: Routledge & K. Paul, 1958. Rpt. in **1125.***

3356 BIGGINS, Dennis. "Scorpions, Serpents, and Treachery in *Macbeth.*" *ShakS* 1 (1965):29–36. On the connection between images of scorpions and treacherous behavior.

3357 BROOKS, Cleanth. "The Naked Babe and the Cloak of Manliness." *The Well-Wrought Urn.* New York: Harcourt, Brace, and World; Reynal & Hitchcock, 1947. Rpt., London: Methuen, 1968. Rpt. in **1163.***

3358 FOSSE, Jean J. "The Lord's Anointed Temple: A Study of Some Symbolic Patterns in *Macbeth.*" *CahiersE* 6 (1974):15–22.

3359 KANTAK, V. Y. "An Approach to Shakespearian Tragedy: The 'Actor' Image in *Macbeth.*" *ShS* 16 (1963):42–52.

3360 LAWLOR, John. "Mind and Hand: Some Reflections on the Study of Shakespeare's Imagery." *SQ* 8 (1957):179–93. Contains illustrations from *Macbeth.* Rpt., rev., in **1953.**

3361 MUIR, Kenneth. "Image and Symbol in *Macbeth.*" *ShS* 19 (1966):45–54.

3362 MURRAY, W. A. "Why Was Duncan's Blood Golden?" *ShS* 19 (1966):34–44.

3363 PARKER, Barbara L. *"Macbeth:* The Great Illusion." *SR* 78 (1970):476–87. On images of time, planting, and harvesting, especially as set forth in the opening scene.

3364 RISSANEN, Matti. " 'Nature's Copy,' 'Great Bond,' and 'Lease of Nature' in *Macbeth.*" *NM* 70 (1969):714–23.

3365 SMITH, Grover. "The Naked New-Born Babe in *Macbeth:* Some Iconographical Evidence." *RenP 1964* (1965):21–27.

3366 STAMM, Rudolf. "Word-Scenery in *Macbeth* and Some Other Plays." In **1255.**

3367 STEIN, Arnold. "Macbeth and Word-Magic." *SR* 59 (1951):271–84. Focuses on Macbeth's speeches to the Weird Sisters and on his soliloquies.

Measure for Measure

Textual Commentary and Sources

See also **134** and **3411**.

3368 BALL, Robert Hamilton. "Cinthio's *Epitia* and *Measure for Measure.*" In **1172**.

3369 BULLOUGH, Geoffrey. "Another Analogue of *Measure for Measure.*" In **1143**.

3370 KAULA, David. "*Measure for Measure* and John Mush's Dialogue." *ShakS* 6 (1972 for 1970):185–95. Concerns a pamphlet involved in the so-called "Archpriest Controversy," as a possible source.

3371 MUSGROVE, Sydney. "Some Composite Scenes in *Measure for Measure.*" *SQ* 15.1 (1964):67–74. A textual study.

3372 PROUTY, Charles Tyler. "George Whetstone and the Sources of *Measure for Measure.*" *SQ* 15.2 (1964):131–45. Also in **1153**.

General Studies

See also **945, 1201–02, 1211, 1221, 1247, 1559, 1628, 1631, 1637, 1780–97**, and **3522**.

3373 ALEXANDER, Nigel. *Shakespeare: "Measure for Measure."* London: Arnold, 1975.

3374 ALTIERI, Joanne. "Style and Social Disorder in *Measure for Measure.*" *SQ* 25 (1974):6–16.

3375 BACHE, William B. *"Measure for Measure" as Dialectical Art.* Lafayette, Ind.: Purdue U. Studies, 1969.

3376 BECKERMAN, Bernard. "A Shakespearean Experiment: The Dramaturgy of *Measure for Measure.*" In **607**, vol. 2 (1970 for 1969).

3377 BLACK, James. "The Unfolding of *Measure for Measure.*" *ShS* 26 (1973):119–28.

3378 CAPUTI, Anthony. "Scenic Design in *Measure for Measure.*" *JEGP* 60 (1961): 423–34.

3379 CHAMBERS, R. W. "The Jacobean Shakespeare and *Measure for Measure.*" *PBA* 23 (1938 for 1937):135–92. Rpt., rev., in *Man's Unconquerable Mind;* see **4666**. Rpt. in **1660**.*

3380 COGHILL, Nevill. "Comic Form in *Measure for Measure.*" *ShS* 8 (1955):14–27.

3381 CRAIG, David. "Love and Society: *Measure for Measure* and Our Own Time." In **1148**.

3382 DURHAM, W. H. *"Measure for Measure* as Measure for Critics." *UCPE* 1 (1929):113–32.

3383 DURRANT, Geoffrey. *"Measure for Measure:* A Comedy." In **1145** (1972 for 1968–69).

3384 EMPSON, William. "Sense in *Measure for Measure.*" In **530.**

3385 FERGUSSON, Francis. "Philosophy and Theatre in *Measure for Measure.*" *KR* 14 (1952):103–20.

3386 GECKLE, George L. "Poetic Justice and *Measure for Measure.*" *Costerus,* n.s. 1 (1974):95–111.

3387 GECKLE, George L., ed. *Twentieth Century Interpretations of "Measure for Measure."* Englewood Cliffs, N.J.: Prentice-Hall, 1970.

3388 GELB, Hal. "Duke Vincentio and the Illusion of Comedy; or All's Not Well That Ends Well." *SQ* 22 (1971):25–34. Discusses how the play's experimental structure is used for dramatic effect.

3389 GILBERT, Allan H. "The More Shakespeare He: *Measure for Measure.*" In **1171.**

3390 GODSHALK, William Leigh. "*Measure for Measure:* Freedom and Restraint." *ShakS* 6 (1972 for 1970):137–50. Studies the dramatic conflicts between mercy and justice, freedom and restraint. Rpt. in **1215.**

3391 HALL, Lawrence Sargent. "Isabella's Angry Ape." *SQ* 15.3 (1964):157–65. On Isabella's speech to Angelo in II, ii.

3392 HARRISON, John L. "The Convention of 'Heart and Tongue' and the Meaning of *Measure for Measure.*" *SQ* 5 (1954):1–10.

3393 HETHMON, Robert H. "The Theatrical Design of *Measure for Measure.*" *Drama Survey* 1 (1962):261–77.

3394 HYMAN, Lawrence W. "The Unity of *Measure for Measure.*" *MLQ* 36 (1975): 3–20.

3395 KAUFMANN, R. J. "Bond Slaves and Counterfeits: Shakespeare's *Measure for Measure.*" *ShakS* 3 (1968 for 1967):85–97.

3396 KIRSCH, Arthur C. "The Integrity of *Measure for Measure.*" *ShS* 28 (1975): 89–105.*

3397 KNIGHTS, L. C. "The Ambiguity of *Measure for Measure.*" *Scrutiny* 10 (1942): 222–33.*

3398 KRIEGER, Murray. "*Measure for Measure* and Elizabethan Comedy." *PMLA* 66 (1951):775–84.

3399 LASCELLES, Mary. *Shakespeare's "Measure for Measure."* London: Athlone Press of the U. of London, 1953. Rpt., Folcroft, Pa.: Folcroft, 1974.

3400 LAVIN, J. A. "*Measure for Measure.*" In **1145** (1972 for 1968–69).

3401 LEAVIS, F. R. "The Greatness of *Measure for Measure.*" *Scrutiny* 10 (1942): 234–47. Rpt. in **1232.***

3402 LEECH, Clifford. "The 'Meaning' of *Measure for Measure.*" *ShS* 3 (1950):66–73. Rpt. in **1660.***

3403 LEVER, J. W. "The Date of *Measure for Measure.*" *SQ* 10 (1959):381–88.

3404 LEVER, J. W., ed. *Measure for Measure.* In the Arden Shakespeare. See **350.**

3405 MACKAY, Eileen. "*Measure for Measure.*" *SQ* 14 (1963):109–13.

3406 MANSELL, Darrel, Jr. " 'Seemers' in *Measure for Measure.*" *MLQ* 27 (1966): 270–84.

3407 MARSH, D. R. C. "The Mood of *Measure for Measure.*" *SQ* 14 (1963):31–38.

3408 MAXWELL, J. C. *"Measure for Measure:* The Play and the Themes." *PBA* 60 (1974):199–218.

3409 MILES, Rosalind. *The Problem of "Measure for Measure."* New York: Barnes & Noble, 1976.

3410 MILLET, Stanton. "The Structure of *Measure for Measure." BUSE* 2 (1956): 207–17.

3411 MINCOFF, Marco. *"Measure for Measure:* A Question of Approach." *ShakS* 2 (1967 for 1966):141–52. Argues that a play with so many different meanings can have no single "meaning."

3412 MÜLLER, Heiner. "Implizierte Satire in *Mass für Mass." SJW* 106 (1970): 100–26.

3413 NUTTALL, A. D. *"Measure for Measure:* Quid Pro Quo?" *ShakS* 4 (1969 for 1968):231–51.

3414 ORNSTEIN, Robert. "The Human Comedy: *Measure for Measure." UKCR* 24 (1957):15–22.

3415 PARTEE, Morriss Henry. "The Comic Unity of *Measure for Measure." Genre* 6 (1973):274–97.

3416 POWELL, Jocelyn. "Theatrical 'trompe l'oeil' in *Measure for Measure."* In **1722.**

3417 PRICE, Jonathan R. *"Measure for Measure* and the Critics: Towards a New Approach." *SQ* 20 (1969):179–204.

3418 ROSENBERG, Marvin. "Shakespeare's Fantastic Trick: *Measure for Measure." SR* 80 (1972):51–72.

3419 ROSSITER, A. P. *"Measure for Measure."* In **1245.**

3420 SALE, Roger. "The Comic Mode of *Measure for Measure." SQ* 19 (1968):55–61.

3421 SCOUTEN, A. H. "An Historical Approach to *Measure for Measure." PQ* 54 (1975):68–84.*

3422 SIEGEL, Paul N. *"Measure for Measure:* The Significance of the Title." *SQ* 4 (1953):317–20.

3423 SKULSKY, Harold. "Pain, Law, and Conscience in *Measure for Measure." JHI* 25 (1964):147–68. Rpt., rev., in **1251.**

3424 SMITH, Robert M. "Interpretations of *Measure for Measure." SQ* 1 (1950): 208–18.

3425 SMITH, Warren D. "More Light on *Measure for Measure." MLQ* 23 (1962): 309–22.

3426 SOELLNER, Rolf, and Samuel BERTSCHE, eds. *"Measure for Measure": Text, Source, and Criticism.* Boston: Houghton Mifflin, 1966.

3427 STEAD, C. K., ed. *Shakespeare, "Measure for Measure": A Casebook.* London: Macmillan, 1971.

3428 STEVENSON, David Lloyd. *The Achievement of Shakespeare's "Measure for Measure."* Ithaca: Cornell U.P., 1966.

3429 SYPHER, Wylie. "Shakespeare as Casuist: *Measure for Measure." SR* 58 (1950): 262–80. Rpt. in **1125.***

3430 TRAVERSI, Derek. *"Measure for Measure." Scrutiny* 11 (1942):40–58.

3431 TROMBETTA, James. "Versions of Dying in *Measure for Measure.*" *ELR* 6 (1976):60–76.

3432 WEIL, Herbert, Jr. "Form and Contexts in *Measure for Measure.*" *CritQ* 12 (1970):55–72.

3433 WILSON, Harold S. "Action and Symbol in *Measure for Measure* and *The Tempest.*" *SQ* 4 (1953):375–84. Rpt. in **1132.***

Some Essays in Christian Interpretation

See also **1411, 1419,** and **1651.**

3434 BATTENHOUSE, Roy W. "*Measure for Measure* and Christian Doctrine of the Atonement." *PMLA* 61 (1946):1029–59.

3435 COLE, Howard C. "The 'Christian' Context of *Measure for Measure.*" *JEGP* 64 (1965):425–51.

3436 DIFFEY, Carole T. "The Last Judgment in *Measure for Measure.*" *DUJ* 66, n.s. 35 (1974):232–37.

3437 KNIGHT, G. Wilson. "*Measure for Measure* and the Gospels." In **1951.***

3438 MCBRIDE, Tom. "*Measure for Measure* and the Unreconciled Virtues." *CompD* 8 (1974):264–74. Argues that the play's central action mirrors a great medieval and Renaissance allegory.

3439 MCGINN, Donald Joseph. "The Precise Angelo." In **1154.** On possible references to Puritanism.

3440 SOUTHALL, Raymond. "*Measure for Measure* and the Protestant Ethic." *EIC* 11 (1961):10–33.

3441 VELZ, Sarah C. "Man's Need and God's Plan in *Measure for Measure* and Mark iv." *ShS* 25 (1972):37–44.

The Political Background and James I

See also **1474.**

3442 BENNETT, Josephine Waters. *"Measure for Measure" as Royal Entertainment.* New York and London: Columbia U.P., 1966.

3443 GROSS, Von Manfred. *Shakespeares "Measure for Measure" und die Politik Jacobs I.* Neumünster: Karl Wachholtz, 1965.

3444 HOWARTH, Herbert. "Shakespeare's Flattery in *Measure for Measure.*" *SQ* 16 (1965):29–37. Rpt., rev., in **1221.**

3445 LEVIN, Richard. "The King James·Version of *Measure for Measure.*" *ClioW* 3 (1974):129–63. A critique of topical political analysis.

3446 POPE, Elizabeth Marie. "The Renaissance Background of *Measure for Measure.*" *ShS* 2 (1949):66–82.

3447 STEVENSON, David Lloyd. "The Role of James I in Shakespeare's *Measure for Measure.*" *ELH* 26 (1959):188–208. Rpt., rev., in **3428.**

3448 WASSON, John. "*Measure for Measure:* A Text for Court Performance?" *SQ* 21 (1970):17–24.

Law and Equity; The Bed Trick and Elizabethan Marriage Contracts

See also **1283, 1911,** and **3468.**

3449 BERMAN, Ronald. "Shakespeare and the Law." *SQ* 18 (1967):141–50.

3450 BIRJE-PATIL, J. "Marriage Contracts in *Measure for Measure.*" *ShakS* 5 (1970 for 1969):106–11.

3451 BRADBROOK, M. C. "Authority, Truth, and Justice in *Measure for Measure.*" *RES* 17 (1941):385–99. Rpt. in **1790.***

3452 DICKINSON, John W. "Renaissance Equity and *Measure for Measure.*" *SQ* 13 (1962):287–97.

3453 DUNKEL, Wilbur D. "Law and Equity in *Measure for Measure.*" *SQ* 13 (1962): 275–85.

3454 HARDING, Davis P. "Elizabethan Betrothals and *Measure for Measure.*" *JEGP* 49 (1950):139–58.

3455 HYMAN, Lawrence W. "Mariana and Shakespeare's Theme in *Measure for Measure.*" *UR* 31 (1964):123–27.

3456 MCCORD, Howard. "Law and Equity in *Measure for Measure.*" *RS* 30 (1962): 64–70.

3457 NAGARAJAN, S. "*Measure for Measure* and Elizabethan Betrothals." *SQ* 14 (1963):115–19.

3458 NUTTALL, A. D. "*Measure for Measure:* The Bed-Trick." *ShS* 28 (1975):51–56.

3459 ROSCELLI, William John. "Isabella, Sin, and Civil Law." *UR* 28 (1962):215–27.

3460 SCHANZER, Ernest. "The Marriage-Contracts in *Measure for Measure.*" *ShS* 13 (1960):81–89. Rpt., rev., in **1792.**

3461 WILSON, Robert H. "The Mariana Plot of *Measure for Measure.*" *PQ* 9 (1930): 341–50.

Character Studies

See also **1405, 1699, 1705,** and **1711.**

3462 DODDS, Winifred M. T. "The Character of Angelo in *Measure for Measure.*" *MLR* 41 (1946):246–55. Rpt. in **1790.***

3463 FAIRCHILD, Hoxie N. "The Two Angelo's." *ShAB* 6 (1931):53–59.

3464 GECKLE, George L. "Shakespeare's Isabella." *SQ* 22 (1971):163–68.

3465 GRECO, Anne. "A Due Sincerity." *ShakS* 6 (1972 for 1970):151–73. On Isabella.

3466 HAMBURGER, Michael P. "Besonderheiten der Herzogsfigur in *Measure for Measure.*" *SJW* 105 (1969):158–67.

3467 HAMILTON, Donna B. "The Duke in *Measure for Measure:* 'I Find an Apt Remission in Myself.'" *ShakS* 6 (1972 for 1970):175–83.

3468 HAPGOOD, Robert. "The Provost and Equity in *Measure for Measure.*" *SQ* 15.1 (1964):114–15.

3469 LAWRENCE, W. W. "*Measure for Measure* and Lucio." *SQ* 9 (1958):443–53.

3470 LAWSON, Reginald. "Lucio in *Measure for Measure.*" *ES* 19 (1937):259–64.

3471 OWEN, Lucy. "Mode and Character in *Measure for Measure.*" *SQ* 25 (1974): 17–32.

3472 REID, Stephen A. "A Psychoanalytic Reading of *Troilus and Cressida* and *Measure for Measure.*" *PsyR* 57 (1970):263–82.

3473 SMITH, Gordon Ross. "Isabella and Elbow in Varying Contexts of Interpretation." *JGE* 17 (1965):63–78.

3474 WASSON, John. "*Measure for Measure:* A Play of Incontinence." *ELH* 27 (1960):262–75. Argues that Angelo is to be viewed as inconstant rather than as vicious.

The Merchant of Venice

General Studies

See also **555, 812, 1035, 1177, 1187, 1218, 1221, 1234, 1256, 1454, 1484, 1580, 1585, 1628, 1631, 1637, 1689, 1700, 1717, 1719–33, 3768, 3785,** and **4241.**

3475 AUDEN, W. H. "Brothers and Others." In **1179.** Rpt. in **1656** and **3505.***

3476 BARNET, Sylvan. "Prodigality and Time in *The Merchant of Venice.*" *PMLA* 87 (1972):26–30.*

3477 BARNET, Sylvan, ed. *Twentieth Century Interpretations of "The Merchant of Venice."* Englewood Cliffs, N.J.: Prentice-Hall, 1970. A collection of essays.

3478 BRYANT, J. A., Jr. "*The Merchant of Venice* and the Common Flaw." *SR* 81 (1973):606–22.

3479 CARDOZO, Jacob Lopes. "The Background of Shakespeare's *The Merchant of Venice.*" *ES* 14 (1932):177–86.

3480 COOLIDGE, John S. "Law and Love in *The Merchant of Venice.*" *SQ* 27 (1976):243–63.

3481 DESHPANDE, M. G. "'Loneliness' in *The Merchant of Venice.*" *EIC* 11 (1961): 368–69. A reply to **3495.**

3482 DOBBINS, Austin C., and Roy W. BATTENHOUSE. "Jessica's Morals: A Theological View." *ShakS* 9 (1976):107–20.

3483 DONOW, Herbert S. "Shakespeare's Caskets: Unity in *The Merchant of Venice.*" *ShakS* 4 (1969 for 1968):86–93.

3484 FELHEIM, Marvin. "The Merchant of Venice." *ShakS* 4 (1969 for 1968):94–108.

3485 FREUD, Sigmund. "The Theme of the Three Caskets." *The Standard Edition of the Complete Psychological Works of Sigmund Freud.* Trans. James STRACHEY, et al. Vol. 12 (1911–13). London: Hogarth, 1958, pp. 291–301.*

3486 FUJIMURA, Thomas H. "Mode and Structure in *The Merchant of Venice.*" *PMLA* 81 (1966):499–511.

3487 GRAHAM, Cary B. "Standards of Value in *The Merchant of Venice.*" *SQ* 4 (1953):145–51.

3488 HILL, R. F. "*The Merchant of Venice* and the Pattern of Romantic Comedy." *ShS* 28 (1975):75–87.

3489 HUMPHREYS, A. R. *The Merchant of Venice.* Oxford: Blackwell, 1973.

3490 HURRELL, John D. "Love and Friendship in *The Merchant of Venice.*" *TSLL* 3 (1961):328–41.

3491 HYMAN, Lawrence W. "The Rival Lovers in *The Merchant of Venice.*" *SQ* 21 (1970):109–16. About the struggle between Portia and Antonio for Bassanio's love.

3492 LEWALSKI, Barbara K. "Biblical Allusion and Allegory in *The Merchant of Venice.*" *SQ* 13 (1962):327–43.*

3493 LINK, Franz H. "Die Zeit in Shakespeares *Midsummer Night's Dream* und *The Merchant of Venice.*" *SJH* (1975):121–36.

3494 MACKAY, Maxine. "*The Merchant of Venice:* A Reflection of the Early Conflict Between Courts of Law and Courts of Equity." *SQ* 15.4 (1964):371–75.

3495 MIDGLEY, Graham. "*The Merchant of Venice:* A Reconsideration." *EIC* 10 (1960):119–33.

3496 MOODY, A. D. *Shakespeare: "The Merchant of Venice."* London: Arnold, 1964.

3497 NATHAN, Norman. "Three Notes on *The Merchant of Venice.*" *ShAB* 23 (1948):152–73.

3498 PALMER, D. J. "*The Merchant of Venice,* or the Importance of Being Earnest." In **1722.**

3499 RABKIN, Norman. "Meaning and Shakespeare." In **1151.** Uses *The Merchant of Venice* as a chief instance in an examination of current critical methods.*

3500 ROCKAS, Leo. " 'A Dish of Doves': *The Merchant of Venice.*" *ELH* 40 (1973): 339–51. Argues that the focus of the play is on harmony, marriage, and feasting.

3501 SCHLÖSSER, Anselm. "Dialectic in *The Merchant of Venice.*" *ZAA* 23 (1975): 5–11.

3502 SIS, John P. "Bondage and Release in *The Merchant of Venice.*" *SQ* 20 (1969): 217–23.

3503 TUCKER, E. F. J. "The Letter of the Law in *The Merchant of Venice.*" *ShS* 29 (1976):93–102.

3504 WEST, E. J. "The Use of Contrast in *The Merchant of Venice.*" *ShAB* 21 (1946): 172–76.

3505 WILDERS, John. *Shakespeare, "The Merchant of Venice": A Casebook.* London: Macmillan, 1969.

3506 WITHINGTON, Robert. "Shakespeare and Race Prejudice." In **1172.**

Shylock

See also **1576, 1689, 1708, 1711,** and **3542.**

3507 BABULA, William. "Shylock's Dramatic Function." *DR* 53 (1973):30–38.

3508 BRONSTEIN, Herbert. "Shakespeare, the Jews, and *The Merchant of Venice.*" *SQ* 20 (1969):3–10.

3509 BROWN, John Russell. "The Realization of Shylock: A Theatrical Criticism." In **1582.**

3510 CARDOZO, Jacob Lopes. *The Contemporary Jew in the Elizabethan Drama.* Amsterdam: H. J. Paris, 1925.

3511 CARNOVSKY, Morris. "Mirror of Shylock." *TDR* 3.1 (1958):35–45.

3512 COLEMAN, Edward D., comp. *The Jew in English Drama: An Annotated Bibliography.* New York: New York Public Library and KTAV, 1970. Orig. *Bulletin of the New York Public Library* 42 (1938):827–50, 919–32, and continuation in vols. 43 and 44.

3513 COOPER, John R. "Shylock's Humanity." *SQ* 21 (1970):117–24.

3514 DESSEN, Alan C. "The Elizabethan Stage Jew and Christian Example: Gerontus, Barabas, and Shylock." *MLQ* 35 (1974):231–45.

3515 ECHERUO, Michael J. C. "Shylock and the 'Conditioned Imagination': A Reinterpretation." *SQ* 22 (1971):3–15.

3516 GREBANIER, Bernard. *The Truth about Shylock.* New York: Random House, 1962.

3517 HENZE, Richard. " 'Which Is the Merchant Here? And Which the Jew?' " *Criticism* 16 (1974):287–300.

3518 LANDA, M. J. *The Shylock Myth.* London: Allen, 1942.

3519 LELYVELD, Toby. *Shylock on the Stage.* Cleveland: Press of Western Reserve U., 1960.

3520 LEVITSKY, Ruth M. "Shylock as Unregenerate Man." *SQ* 28 (1977):58–64.

3521 NATHAN, Norman. "Shylock, Jacob, and God's Judgment." *SQ* 1 (1950):255–59.

3522 PEARLMAN, E. "Shakespeare, Freud, and the Two Usuries, or, Money's a Meddler." *ELR* 2 (1972):217–36. A comment on **3485.**

3523 PETTET, E. C. "*The Merchant of Venice* and the Problem of Usury." *E&S* 31 (1946 for 1945):19–33.

3524 REA, John D. "Shylock and the Processus Belial." *PQ* 8 (1929):311–13. Sees the trial scene as based on medieval accounts of the "court of heaven," where the devil appears to demand the soul of Mankind.

3525 ROTH, Cecil. "The Background of Shylock." *RES* 9 (1933):148–56.

3526 SIEGEL, Paul N. "Shylock, the Elizabethan Puritan and Our Own World." In **1249.**

3527 SIEGEL, Paul N. "Shylock the Puritan." *CUF* 5.4 (1962):14–19.

3528 SINSHEIMER, Hermann. *Shylock, the History of a Character, or The Myth of the Jew.* London: Gollancz, 1947. Rpt., New York: Blom.

3529 SMITH, John Hazel. "Shylock: 'Devil Incarnation' or 'Poor Man . . . Wronged'?" *JEGP* 60 (1961):1–21.

3530 SMITH, Warren D. "Shakespeare's Shylock." *SQ* 15.3 (1964):193–99.

3531 STOLL, Elmer Edgar. "Shylock." *JEGP* 10 (1911):236–79. Rpt. in **1261.**

3532 STONEX, Arthur Bivins. "The Usurer in Elizabethan Drama." *PMLA* 31 (1916): 190–210.

3533 WERTHEIM, Albert. "The Treatment of Shylock and Thematic Integrity in *The Merchant of Venice.*" *ShakS* 6 (1972 for 1970):75–87.

Other Characters

See also **1721** and **3491.**

3534 BIGGS, Murray. "A Neurotic Portia." *ShS* 25 (1972):153–59.

3535 FODOR, A. "Shakespeare's Portia." *AI* 16 (1959):49–64.

3536 FORTIN, René E. "Launcelot and the Uses of Allegory in *The Merchant of Venice.*" *SEL* 14 (1974):259–70.

3537 HAPGOOD, Robert. "Portia and *The Merchant of Venice:* The Gentle Bond." *MLQ* 28 (1967):19–32.

3538 HASSEL, R. Chris, Jr. "Antonio and the Ironic Festivity of *The Merchant of Venice.*" *ShakS* 6 (1972 for 1970):67–74.

3539 HENNEDY, John F. "Launcelot Gobbo and Shylock's Forced Conversion." *TSLL* 15 (1973):405–10.

3540 HOLADAY, Allan. "Antonio and the Allegory of Salvation." *ShakS* 4 (1969 for 1968):109–18.

3541 JIJI, Vera M. "Portia Revisited: The Influence of Unconscious Factors upon Theme and Characterization in *The Merchant of Venice.*" *L&P* 26 (1976):5–15.

3542 LEVER, J. W. "Shylock, Portia, and the Values of Shakespearian Comedy." *SQ* 3 (1952):383–86. For a reply, see Norman NATHAN, "Rejoinder." *SQ* 3 (1952): 386–88.

3543 MITCHELL, Charles. "The Conscience of Venice: Shakespeare's Merchant." *JEGP* 63 (1964):214–25.

3544 PETTIGREW, Helen Purinton. "Bassanio, The Elizabethan Lover." *PQ* 16 (1937):296–306.

Particular Scenes or Passages

3545 ANDREWS, Mark Edwin. *Law versus Equity in "The Merchant of Venice": A Legalization of Act IV, Scene I, with Foreword Judicial Precedents, and Notes.* Boulder: U. of Colorado P., 1965.

3546 BRATCHER, James T. "The Lorenzo-Jessica Subplot and *Genesis* xxxiv." In **1128.**

3547 MILLS, Lloyd L. "Shakespearean Impudence: *The Merchant of Venice,* V. i. 273–279." *NM* 74 (1973):510–14.

3548 SIEMON, James Edward. "*The Merchant of Venice:* Act V as Ritual Reiteration." *SP* 67 (1970):201–09.

3549 TILLYARD, E. M. W. "The Trial Scene in *The Merchant of Venice.*" *REL* 2.4 (1961):51–59. Rpt. in **1266.**

3550 TRAVER, Hope. "I Will Try Confusions with Him." *ShAB* 13 (1938):108–20.

3551 WILLIAMSON, Marilyn L. "The Ring Episode in *The Merchant of Venice.*" *SAQ* 71 (1972):587–94.

The Merry Wives of Windsor

See also **175, 382, 1183, 1213, 1637, 1704, 1721, 1733, 1781, 2718, 2738–72** (esp. **2740, 2742, 2744, 2749–50,** and **2763**), and **2784.**

3552 BENNETT, A. L. "The Sources of Shakespeare's *Merry Wives.*" *RenQ* 23 (1970): 429–33.

3553 BRUCE, Dorothy Hart. "*The Merry Wives* and Two Brethren." *SP* 39 (1942): 265–78. On a fabliau source for the play, by Barnabe Riche.

3554 BRYANT, J. A., Jr. "Falstaff and the Renewal of Windsor." *PMLA* 89 (1974): 296–301.

3555 CAMPBELL, Oscar James. "The Italianate Background of *The Merry Wives of Windsor.*" *Essays and Studies in English and Comparative Literature by Members of the English Department of the University of Michigan* 8 (1932):81–117.

3556 GODSHALK, William Leigh. "An Apology for *The Merry Wives of Windsor.*" *RenP 1973* (1974):97–108.

3557 GOLDSTEIN, Leonard. "Some Aspects of Marriage and Inheritance in Shakespeare's *The Merry Wives of Windsor* and Chapman's *All Fools.*" *ZAA* 12 (1964): 375–86.

3558 GREEN, William. *Shakespeare's "Merry Wives of Windsor."* Princeton: Princeton U.P., 1962.*

3559 LEGGATT, Alexander. *Citizen Comedy in the Age of Shakespeare.* Toronto: U. of Toronto P., 1973.*

3560 LONG, John H. "Another Masque for *The Merry Wives of Windsor.*" *SQ* 3 (1952):39–43.

3561 OLIVER, H. J., ed. *The Merry Wives of Windsor.* In the Arden Shakespeare. See **350.**

3562 ROBERTS, Jeanne Addison. "Falstaff in Windsor Forest: Villain or Victim?" *SQ* 26 (1975):8–15.

3563 ROBERTS, Jeanne Addison. "*The Merry Wives of Windsor* as a Hallowe'en Play." *ShS* 25 (1972):107–12.

3564 ROBERTS, Jeanne Addison. "*The Merry Wives* Q and F: The Vagaries of Progress." *ShakS* 8 (1975):143–75.

3565 ROBERTS, Jeanne Addison. "*The Merry Wives:* Suitably Shallow, But Neither Simple Nor Slender." *ShakS* 6 (1972 for 1970):109–23.

3566 ROBERTS, Jeanne Addison. "The Windsor Falstaff." *PLL* 9 (1973):202–30. A survey of critical attitudes toward the Falstaff of *Merry Wives* from the seventeenth century to the present.

3567 ROSENBERG, S. L. Millard. "Duke Friedrich of Württemberg." *ShAB* 8 (1933): 92–93.

3568 SEWELL, Sallie. "The Relation between *The Merry Wives of Windsor* and Jonson's *Every Man In His Humour.*" *ShAB* 16 (1941):175–89.

3569 STEADMAN, John M. "Falstaff as Actaeon: A Dramatic Emblem." *SQ* 14 (1963):231–44.

3570 WHITE, David M. "An Explanation of the *Brooke-Broome* Question in Shakespeare's *Merry Wives.*" *PQ* 25 (1946):280–83.

A Midsummer Night's Dream

See also **810, 922, 1189, 1217, 1231, 1358, 1580, 1628, 1631, 1633, 1637, 1666, 1689, 1708–09, 1714,** and **1719–33.**

3571 ALLEN, John A. "Bottom and Titania." *SQ* 18 (1967):107–17.

3572 BETHURUM, Dorothy. "Shakespeare's Comment on Mediaeval Romance in *Midsummer-Night's Dream.*" *MLN* 60 (1945):85–94.

3573 BONNARD, Georges A. "Shakespeare's Purpose in *Midsummer-Night's Dream.*" *SJ* 92 (1956):268–79.

3574 BRIGGS, K. M. *The Anatomy of Puck: An Examination of Fairy Beliefs Among Shakespeare's Contemporaries and Successors.* London: Routledge & K. Paul, 1959.

3575 BRIGGS, K. M. *Pale Hecate's Team: An Examination of the Beliefs on Witchcraft and Magic Among Shakespeare's Contemporaries and His Immediate Successors.* London: Routledge & K. Paul, 1962.

3576 CLAYTON, Thomas. " 'Fie What a Question's That If Thou Wert Near a Lewd Interpreter': The Wall Scene in *A Midsummer Night's Dream.*" *ShakS* 7 (1974): 101–13.

3577 DENT, R. W. "Imagination in *A Midsummer Night's Dream.*" *SQ* 15.2 (1964): 115–29. Also in **1153.***

3578 DORAN, Madeleine. "*A Midsummer Night's Dream:* A Metamorphosis." *RIP* 46.4 (1960):113–35.

3579 DORAN, Madeleine. "Pyramus and Thisbe Once More." In **1144.**

3580 DORAN, Madeleine. "Titania's Wood." *Rice U. Studies* 60.2 (1974):55–70.

3581 EDDY, Darlene Mathis. "The Poet's Eye: Some Shakespearean Reflections." *BSUF* 16.3 (1975):3–11. About the imagination as a shaping principle in *A Midsummer Night's Dream* and *Hamlet.*

3582 FABER, M. D. "Hermia's Dream: Royal Road to *A Midsummer Night's Dream.*" *L&P* 22 (1972):179–90.

3583 FENDER, Stephen. *Shakespeare: "A Midsummer Night's Dream."* London: Arnold, 1968.

3584 FISHER, Peter F. "The Argument of *A Midsummer Night's Dream.*" *SQ* 8 (1957):307–10.

3585 FOSTER, Leslie D. "The Relation of Act Five to the Structure of *A Midsummer Night's Dream.*" *MichA* 8 (1975):191–206.

3586 GOLDSTEIN, Melvin. "Identity Crises in a Midsummer Nightmare: Comedy as Terror in Disguise." *PsyR* 60 (1973):169–204.

3587 GREEN, Roger Lancelyn. "Shakespeare and the Fairies." *Folklore* 73 (1962): 89–103.

3588 GREENFIELD, Thelma N. "*A Midsummer Night's Dream* and *The Praise of Folly.*" *CL* 20 (1968):236–44.

3589 GUI, Weston A. "Bottom's Dream." *AI* 9 (1952):251–305.

3590 GUILHAMET, Leon. "*A Midsummer-Night's Dream* as the Imitation of an Action." *SEL* 15 (1975):257–71.

3591 HAWKINS, Harriett. "Fabulous Counterfeits: Dramatic Construction and Dramatic Perspectives in *The Spanish Tragedy, A Midsummer Night's Dream,* and *The Tempest.*" *ShakS* 6 (1972 for 1970):51–65.

3592 HEMINGWAY, Samuel B. "The Relation of *A Midsummer Night's Dream* to *Romeo and Juliet.*" *MLN* 26 (1911):78–80.

3593 HENZE, Richard. "*A Midsummer Night's Dream:* Analogous Image." *ShakS* 7 (1974):115–23.

3594 HERBERT, T. Walter. "Dislocation and the Modest Demand in *A Midsummer Night's Dream.*" *RenP 1961* (1962):31–36.

3595 HERBERT, T. Walter. "Invitations to Cosmic Laughter in *A Midsummer Night's Dream.*" In **1171.**

3596 HOMAN, Sidney R. "The Single World of *A Midsummer Night's Dream.*" *BuR* 17.1 (1969):72–84.

3597 HUSTON, J. Dennis. "Bottom Waking: Shakespeare's 'Most Rare Vision.' " *SEL* 13 (1973):208–22.

3598 ISAACS, Neil D., and Jack E. REESE. "Dithyramb and Paean in *A Midsummer Night's Dream.*" *ES* 55 (1974):351–57.

3599 KERSTEN, Dorelies. "Shakespeares Puck." *SJ* 98 (1962):189–200.

3600 LATHAM, Minor White. *The Elizabethan Fairies: The Fairies of Folklore and the Fairies of Shakespeare.* New York: Columbia U.P., 1930. Rpt., New York: Octagon.

3601 LINK, Franz H. "Die Zeit in Shakespeares *Midsummer Night's Dream* und *The Merchant of Venice.*" *SJH* (1975):121–36.

3602 MCPEEK, James A. S. "The Psyche Myth and *A Midsummer Night's Dream.*" *SQ* 23 (1972):69–79.

3603 MERCHANT, W. Moelwyn. "*A Midsummer Night's Dream:* A Visual Re-creation." In **1582.**

3604 MILLER, Donald C. "Titania and the Changeling." *ES* 22 (1940):66–70.

3605 MILLER, Raeburn. "The Persons of Moonshine: *A Midsummer Night's Dream* and the 'Disfigurement' of Realities." *Explorations of Literature.* Ed. Rima Drell RECK. Baton Rouge: Louisiana State U.P., 1966.

3606 MILLER, Ronald F. "*A Midsummer Night's Dream:* The Fairies, Bottom, and the Mystery of Things." *SQ* 26 (1975):254–68.

3607 MUIR, Kenneth. "Pyramus and Thisbe: A Study in Shakespeare's Method." *SQ* 5 (1954):141–53.

3608 MUIR, Kenneth. "Shakespeare as Parodist." *N&Q* 199 (1954):467–68.

3609 NEMEROV, Howard. "The Marriage of Theseus and Hippolyta." *KR* 18 (1956): 633–41.

3610 OLSON, Paul A. "*A Midsummer Night's Dream* and the Meaning of Court Marriage." *ELH* 24 (1957):95–119. Rpt. in **1656.***

3611 PEARSON, D'Orsay W. " 'Vnkinde' Theseus: A Study in Renaissance Mythography." *ELR* 4 (1974):276–98.

3612 REYNOLDS, Lou Agnes, and Paul SAWYER. "Folk Medicine and the Four Fairies of *A Midsummer-Night's Dream.*" *SQ* 10 (1959):513–21.

3613 ROBINSON, J. W. "Palpable Hot Ice: Dramatic Burlesque in *A Midsummer Night's Dream.*" *SP* 61 (1964):192–204.

3614 ROBINSON, James E. "The Ritual and Rhetoric of *A Midsummer Night's Dream.*" *PMLA* 83 (1968):380–91.

3615 SCHANZER, Ernest. "The Central Theme of *A Midsummer Night's Dream.*" *UTQ* 20 (1951):233–38.*

3616 SCHANZER, Ernest. "*A Midsummer-Night's Dream.*" In **1660.**

3617 SCHANZER, Ernest. "The Moon and the Fairies in *A Midsummer Night's Dream.*" *UTQ* 24 (1955):234–46.

3618 SIEGEL, Paul N. "*A Midsummer Night's Dream* and the Wedding Guests." *SQ* 4 (1953):139–44. Rpt. in **1249.**

3619 STATON, Walter F., Jr. "Ovidian Elements in *A Midsummer Night's Dream.*" *HLQ* 26 (1963):165–78.

3620 TAYLOR, Michael. "The Darker Purpose of *A Midsummer Night's Dream.*" *SEL* 9 (1969):259–73.

3621 TURNER, Robert K., Jr. "Printing Methods and Textual Problems in *A Midsummer Night's Dream* Q1." *SB* 15 (1962):33–55.

3622 WEINER, Andrew D. " 'Multiformitie Uniforme': *A Midsummer Night's Dream.*" *ELH* 38 (1971):329–49.

3623 WILLSON, Robert F., Jr. "The Plays within *A Midsummer Night's Dream* and *The Tempest.*" *SJW* 110 (1974):101–11.

3624 YOUNG, David. *Something of Great Constancy: The Art of "A Midsummer Night's Dream.*" New Haven: Yale U.P., 1966.*

3625 ZIMBARDO, Rose A. "Regeneration and Reconciliation in *A Midsummer Night's Dream.*" *ShakS* 6 (1972 for 1970):35–50.

3626 ZITNER, Sheldon P. "The Worlds of *A Midsummer Night's Dream.*" *SAQ* 59 (1960):397–403.

Much Ado About Nothing

See also **106, 514, 1249, 1261, 1580, 1585, 1628, 1632, 1637, 1646, 1651, 1666, 1682, 1699, 1708, 1710, 1719–33, and 1999.**

3627 ALLEN, John A. "Dogberry." *SQ* 24 (1973):35–53.

3628 BARISH, Jonas A. "Pattern and Purpose in the Prose of *Much Ado About Nothing.*" *Rice U. Studies* 60.2 (1974):19–30.

3629 BERRY, Ralph. "*Much Ado About Nothing:* Structure and Texture." *ES* 52 (1971):211–23. Rpt. in **1721.**

3630 CRAIK, T. W. "*Much Ado About Nothing.*" *Scrutiny* 19 (1953):297–316.

3631 CRICHTON, Andrew B. "Hercules Shaven: A Centering Mythic Metaphor in *Much Ado About Nothing.*" *TSLL* 16 (1975):619–26.

3632 DAVIS, Walter R., ed. *Twentieth Century Interpretations of "Much Ado About Nothing."* Englewood Cliffs, N.J.: Prentice-Hall, 1969. A collection of essays.

3633 DENNIS, Carl. "Wit and Wisdom in *Much Ado About Nothing.*" *SEL* 13 (1973): 223–37.

3634 DRAPER, John W. "Dogberry's Due Process of Law." *JEGP* 42 (1943):563–76. Rpt. in **1585.**

3635 EVERETT, Barbara. "*Much Ado About Nothing.*" *CritQ* 3 (1961):319–35. Rpt. in **1125.***

3636 FELHEIM, Marvin. "Comic Realism in *Much Ado About Nothing.*" *PP* 7 (1964):213–25.

3637 FERGUSSON, Francis. "Two Comedies: *The Comedy of Errors* and *Much Ado About Nothing.*" See **2269.***

3638 GILBERT, Allan H. "Two Margarets: The Composition of *Much Ado About Nothing.*" *PQ* 41 (1962):61–71. Also in **1174.**

3639 HARTLEY, Lodwick. "Claudio and the Unmerry War." *CE* 26 (1965):609–14.

3640 HENZE, Richard. "Deception in *Much Ado About Nothing.*" *SEL* 11 (1971): 187–201.

3641 HOCKEY, Dorothy C. "Notes, Notes, Forsooth . . ." *SQ* 8 (1957):353–58. Sees the key to the play in a pun on "nothing" and "noting," or observing.

3642 JORGENSEN, Paul A. "Much Ado About *Nothing.*" *SQ* 5 (1954):287–95. Rpt. in **538.**

3643 KING, Walter N. "Much Ado About *Something.*" *SQ* 15.3 (1964):143–55.

3644 LEWALSKI, Barbara K. "Love, Appearance, and Reality: Much Ado About Something." *SEL* 8 (1968):235–51.

3645 MCCOLLOM, William G. "The Role of Wit in *Much Ado About Nothing.*" *SQ* 19 (1968):165–74. Rpt., rev., in *The Divine Average: A View of Comedy.* Cleveland and London: The Press of Case Western Reserve U., 1971.

3646 MCPEEK, James A. S. "The Thief 'Deformed' and Much Ado About 'Noting.' " *BUSE* 4 (1960):65–84.

3647 MUESCHKE, Paul, and Miriam MUESCHKE. "Illusion and Metamorphosis in *Much Ado About Nothing.*" *SQ* 18 (1967):53–65.

3648 MULRYNE, J. R. *Shakespeare: "Much Ado About Nothing."* London: Arnold, 1965.

3649 NEILL, Kerby. "More Ado About Claudio: An Acquittal for the Slandered Groom." *SQ* 3 (1952):91–107.

3650 ORMEROD, David. "Faith and Fashion in *Much Ado About Nothing.*" *ShS* 25 (1972):93–105.

3651 OWEN, Charles A., Jr. "Comic Awareness, Style, and Dramatic Technique in *Much Ado About Nothing.*" *BUSE* 5 (1961):193–207.

3652 PAGE, Nadine. "Beatrice: 'My Lady Disdain.' " *MLN* 50 (1935):494–99.

3653 PAGE, Nadine. "The Public Repudiation of Hero." *PMLA* 50 (1935):739–44.

3654 PROUTY, Charles Tyler. *The Sources of "Much Ado About Nothing."* New Haven: Yale U.P., 1950.*

3655 ROSE, Steven. "Love and Self-Love in *Much Ado About Nothing.*" *EIC* 20 (1970):143–50.

3656 ROSS, Thomas W. "Maimed Rites in *Much Ado About Nothing.*" *Costerus* 5 (1972):125–34.

3657 ROSSITER, A. P. *"Much Ado About Nothing."* In **1245.** Rpt. in **1660.***

3658 SCHOFF, Francis G. "Claudio, Bertram, and a Note on Interpretation." *SQ* 10 (1959):11–23.

3659 SEXTON, Joyce Hengerer. "The Theme of Slander in *Much Ado About Nothing* and Garter's *Susanna.*" *PQ* 54 (1975):419–33.

3660 SMITH, James. *"Much Ado About Nothing."* *Scrutiny* 13 (1946):242–57.

3661 SMITH, John Hazel. "The Composition of the Quarto of *Much Ado About Nothing.*" *SB* 16 (1963):9–26.

3662 STOREY, Graham. "The Success of *Much Ado About Nothing.*" In **1138.** Rpt. in **1731.***

3663 SYPHER, Wylie. "Nietzsche and Socrates in Messina." *PR* 16 (1949):702–13.

3664 TAYLOR, Michael. *"Much Ado About Nothing:* The Individual in Society." *EIC* 23 (1973):146–53.

3665 THALER, Alwin. "Spenser and *Much Ado About Nothing.*" *SP* 37 (1940):225–35.

3666 WAIN, John. "The Shakespearean Lie-Detector: Thoughts on *Much Ado About Nothing.*" *CritQ* 9 (1967):27–42.

3667 WEY, James J. " 'To Grace Harmony': Musical Design in *Much Ado About Nothing.*" *BUSE* 4 (1960):181–88.

Othello

Textual Commentary and Sources

See also **106** and **389**.

3668 ADAMS, Maurianne S. " 'Ocular Proof' in *Othello* and Its Source." *PMLA* 79 (1964):234–41.

3669 ENGLER, Balz. "How Shakespeare Revised *Othello.*" *ES* 57 (1976):515–21.

3670 GRAVES, Wallace. "Plutarch's *Life of Cato Utican* as a Major Source of *Othello.*" *SQ* 24 (1973):181–87.

3671 HINMAN, Charlton. "The 'Copy' for the Second Quarto of *Othello.*" In **1154.**

3672 KAULA, David. "Othello Possessed: Notes on Shakespeare's Use of Magic and Witchcraft." *ShakS* 2 (1967 for 1966):112–32. Comments on the play's sources.

3673 MUIR, Kenneth. "The Text of *Othello.*" *ShakS* 1 (1965):227–39.

General Studies

See also **339, 348, 889, 1008, 1213, 1218, 1251, 1260, 1263, 1268, 1306, 1413, 1448, 1454, 1646, 1911, 1927–28, 1933, 1937, 1947, 1951, 1953, 1957, 1976, 1978, 1981, 2011–31,** and **2059.**

3674 ALEXANDER, Nigel. "Thomas Rymer and *Othello.*" *ShS* 21 (1968):67–77.

3675 ALLEN, Ned B. "The Two Parts of *Othello.*" *ShS* 21 (1968):13–29.

3676 ANDREWS, Michael C. "Honest Othello: The Handkerchief Once More." *SEL* 13 (1973):273–84.

3677 BAYLEY, John. "Love and Identity: *Othello.*" *The Characters of Love.* London: Constable, 1960.

3678 BERRY, Ralph. "Pattern in *Othello.*" *SQ* 23 (1972):3–19.

3679 BÖHM, Rudolf. "Die Verleumdungsszene bei Shakespeare." *SJH* (1967):221–36.

3680 BOOSE, Lynda E. "Othello's Handkerchief: 'The Recognizance and Pledge of Love.' " *ELR* 5 (1975):360–74.

3681 BRADLEY, A. C. *Shakespearean Tragedy.* See **2011.***

3682 BURKE, Kenneth. "*Othello:* An Essay to Illustrate a Method." *HudR* 4 (1951): 165–203. Rpt. in *Perspectives by Incongruity.* Ed. Stanley Edgar HYMAN. Bloomington: Indiana U.P., 1964.* For a reply, see Neal J. OSBORN, "Kenneth Burke's Dilemma: A Courtship of Clio?" *HudR* 19 (1966):267–75.

3683 CHAMPION, Larry S. "Tragic Perspective in *Othello.*" *ES* 54 (1973):447–60. Rpt., rev., in **1926.**

3684 CURTIS, Jared R. "The 'Speculative and Offic'd Instrument': Reason and Love in *Othello.*" *SQ* 24 (1973):188–97.

3685 DAVIDSON, Clifford. "Structure and Theme in *Othello.*" *Discourse* 12 (1969): 30–53.

3686 DEAN, Leonard F., ed. *A Casebook on "Othello."* New York: Crowell, 1961.

3687 DOEBLER, Bettie Anne. "Othello's Angels: The *Ars Moriendi.*" *ELH* 34 (1967): 156–72. Argues that the final act examines the theme of holy dying, in contrast with Othello's despairing and violent death.

3688 DORAN, Madeleine. "Good Name in *Othello.*" *SEL* 7 (1967):195–217.

3689 DRAPER, John W. *The "Othello" of Shakespeare's Audience.* Paris: Didier, 1952. Rpt., New York: Octagon, 1966.

3690 ELLIOTT, G. R. *Flaming Minister: A Study of "Othello" as Tragedy of Love and Hate.* Durham, N.C.: Duke U.P., 1953. Rpt., New York: AMS.

3691 GARDNER, Helen. "*Othello:* A Retrospect, 1900–67." *ShS* 21 (1968):1–11.

3692 GODFREY, D. R. "Shakespeare and the Green-Eyed Monster." *Neophil* 56 (1972):207–20.

3693 HALIO, Jay L. "Anxiety in *Othello.*" *Costerus* 1 (1972):123–31.

3694 HALLSTEAD, R. N. "Idolatrous Love: A New Approach to *Othello.*" *SQ* 19 (1968):107–24.

3695 HALSTEAD, William L. "Artifice and Artistry in *Richard II* and *Othello.*" In **1150.**

3696 HAPGOOD, Robert. "The Trials of Othello." In **1156.**

3697 HEILMAN, Robert B. *Magic in the Web: Action and Language in "Othello."* Lexington: U. of Kentucky P., 1956.*

3698 HIBBARD, G. R. "*Othello* and the Pattern of Shakespearian Tragedy." *ShS* 21 (1968):39–46.

3699 JEFFREY, David L., and Patrick GRANT. "Reputation in *Othello.*" *ShakS* 6 (1972 for 1970):197–208.

3700 JORDAN, Hoover H. "Dramatic Illusion in *Othello.*" *SQ* 1 (1950):146–52.

3701 JORGENSEN, Paul A. " 'Perplex'd in the Extreme': The Role of Thought in *Othello.*" *SQ* 15.2 (1964):265–75. Also in **1153.***

3702 KLENE, Jean. "Othello: 'A Fixed Figure for the Time of Scorn.' " *SQ* 26 (1975): 139–50. About reputation and honor.

3703 LEVITSKY, Ruth M. "Prudence Versus Wisdom in *Othello.*" *DR* 54 (1974): 281–88.

3704 MCGUIRE, Philip C. "*Othello* as an 'Assay of Reason.' " *SQ* 24 (1973):198–209.

3705 MCLAUCHLAN, Juliet. *Shakespeare: "Othello."* London: Arnold, 1971.

3706 MCPEEK, James A. S. "The 'Arts Inhibited' and the Meaning of *Othello.*" *BUSE* 1 (1955):129–47.

3707 MENDONÇA, Barbara Heliodora Carneiro de. "*Othello:* A Tragedy Built on a Comic Structure." *ShS* 21 (1968):31–38.

3708 MERCER, Peter. "*Othello* and the Form of Heroic Tragedy." *CritQ* 11 (1969): 45–61.

3709 MORRIS, Harry. "No Amount of Prayer Can Possibly Matter." *SR* 77 (1969): 8–24. Sees *Othello* as a play about damnation and the "four last things."

3710 MUIR, Kenneth, and Philip EDWARDS. *Aspects of "Othello."* London and New York: Cambridge U.P., 1977.

3711 NOWOTTNY, Winifred M. T. "Justice and Love in *Othello.*" *UTQ* 21 (1952): 330–44. Rpt. in **1125.***

3712 POIRIER, Michel. "Le 'Double Temps' dans *Othello.*" *EA* 5 (1952):107–16.

3713 PRYSE, Marjorie. "Lust for Audience: An Interpretation of *Othello.*" *ELH* 43 (1976):461–78.

3714 RICHMOND, Hugh M. "Love and Justice: *Othello*'s Shakespearean Context." In **1156.**

3715 RIDLEY, M. R., ed. *Othello.* In the Arden Shakespeare. See **350.**

3716 ROBESON, Paul. "Some Reflections on *Othello* and the Nature of Our Time." *American Scholar* 14 (1945):391–92.

3717 ROGERS, Stephen. "*Othello:* Comedy in Reverse." *SQ* 24 (1973):210–20.

3718 ROSS, Lawrence J. "Shakespeare's 'Dull Clown' and Symbolic Music." *SQ* 17 (1966):107–28.

3719 ROSSITER, A. P. "*Othello:* A Moral Essay." In **1245.**

3720 SEDGEWICK, G. G. "Irony as Dramatic Preparation: *Othello.*" In **1336.**

3721 *Shakespeare Survey* 21 (1968). Chiefly about *Othello.**

3722 SHAW, John. " 'What Is the Matter?' in *Othello.*" *SQ* 17 (1966):157–61.

3723 SNYDER, Susan. "*Othello* and the Conventions of Romantic Comedy." *RenD,* n.s. 5 (1972):123–41.*

3724 SPROULE, Albert Frederick. "A Time Scheme for *Othello.*" *SQ* 7 (1956):217–26.

3725 STEWART, Douglas J. "*Othello:* Roman Comedy as Nightmare." *EUQ* 22 (1967):252–76.

3726 STOCKHOLDER, Katherine. "Egregiously an Ass: Chance and Accident in *Othello.*" *SEL* 13 (1973):256–72.

3727 STOLL, Elmer Edgar. *"Othello": An Historical and Comparative Study.* Minneapolis: U. of Minnesota, 1915. Rpt., New York: Haskell House, 1964.

3728 STOLL, Elmer Edgar. "Slander in Drama." *SQ* 4 (1953):433–50.

3729 STOLL, Elmer Edgar. "Source and Motive in *Macbeth* and *Othello.*" *RES* 19 (1943):25–32. Rpt. in **1258.**

3730 WAIN, John, ed. *Shakespeare, "Othello": A Casebook.* London: Macmillan, 1971.

3731 WALTON, J. K. " 'Strength's Abundance': A View of *Othello.*" *RES,* n.s. 11 (1960):8–17.

3732 WATTS, H. H. "*Othello* and the Issue of Multiplicity." *Costerus* 2 (1972):213–24.

3733 WATTS, Robert A. "The Comic Scenes in *Othello.*" *SQ* 19 (1968):349–54.

3734 WEBB, Henry J. "The Military Background in *Othello.*" *PQ* 30 (1951):40–52.

3735 WEEDIN, E. K., Jr. "Love's Reason in *Othello.*" *SEL* 15 (1975):293–308.

3736 YODER, R. A. "The Two Worlds of *Othello.*" *SAQ* 72 (1973):213–25.

Iago

See also **1012, 1026, 1077, 1372, 1440, 1576, 1986, 1989, 1999, 3794, 3802, 3815, and 3818.**

3737 AUDEN, W. H. "The Joker in the Pack." In **1179.***

3738 BABCOCK, Weston. "Iago—An Extraordinary Honest Man." *SQ* 16 (1965): 297–301.

3739 BODKIN, Maud. "The Images of the Devil, of the Hero, and of God." *Archetypal Patterns in Poetry.* London: Oxford U.P., 1934.

3740 CAMDEN, Carroll. "Iago on Women." *JEGP* 48 (1949):57–71.

3741 GÉRARD, Albert. "Alack, Poor Iago! Intellect and Action in *Othello.*" *SJ* 94 (1958):218–32.

3742 GLAZ, A. André. "Iago or Moral Sadism." *AI* 19 (1962):323–46.

3743 HAWKES, Terence. "Iago's Use of Reason." *SP* 58 (1961):160–69. Rpt., rev., in **2016.**

3744 HOMAN, Sidney R. "Iago's Aesthetics: *Othello* and Shakespeare's Portrait of an Artist." *ShakS* 5 (1970 for 1969):141–48.

3745 HYMAN, Stanley Edgar. *Iago: Some Approaches to the Illusion of His Motivation.* New York: Atheneum, 1970. Sees Iago as a latent homosexual.

3746 LERNER, Laurence. "The Machiavel and the Moor." *EIC* 9 (1959):339–60.

3747 MAUROCORDATO, Alexandre. "Autopsie de Iago." *EA* 26 (1973):12–21.

3748 MUIR, Kenneth. "The Jealousy of Iago." *EM* 2 (1951):65–83.

3749 ORGEL, Shelley. "Iago." *AI* 25 (1968):258–73.

3750 RAND, Frank Prentice. "The Over Garrulous Iago." *SQ* 1 (1950):155–61.

3751 SCRAGG, Leah. "Iago—Vice or Devil?" *ShS* 21 (1968):53–65.

3752 SMITH, Gordon Ross. "Iago the Paranoiac." *AI* 16 (1959):155–67. Rpt. in **1401.**

3753 STAEBLER, Warren. "The Sexual Nihilism of Iago." *SR* 83 (1975):284–304.

3754 STEMPEL, Daniel. "The Silence of Iago." *PMLA* 84 (1969):252–63.

3755 WANGH, Martin. "*Othello:* The Tragedy of Iago." *PsyQ* 19 (1950):202–12.

3756 WARNKEN, Henry L. "Iago as a Projection of Othello." In **1160.**

3757 WATSON, Thomas L. "The Detractor-Backbiter: Iago and the Tradition." *TSLL* 5 (1964):546–54.

3758 WEISINGER, Herbert. "Iago's Iago." *UKCR* 20 (1953):83–90.

3759 WEST, Robert H. "Iago and the Mystery of Iniquity." *RenP 1961* (1962):63–69. Rpt. in **1448.**

3760 ZACHA, Richard B. "Iago and the *Commedia dell'Arte.*" *ArlQ* 2 (1969):98–116.

Other Characters

See also **1247, 1402, 1406, 1988, 1995, 2017, 3506, 3693, 3696, and 4241.**

3761 ADAMOWSKI, T. H. "The Aesthetic Attitude and Narcissism in *Othello.*" *L&P* 18 (1968):73–81.

3762 ALEXANDER, Peter. "Under Which King, Bezonian?" In **1131.** On the death of Othello.

3763 ARNOLD, Aerol. "The Function of Brabantio in *Othello.*" *SQ* 8 (1957):51–56.

3764 ARTHOS, John. "The Fall of Othello." *SQ* 9 (1958):93–104.

3765 BONNARD, Georges A. "Are Othello and Desdemona Innocent or Guilty?" *ES* 30 (1949):175–84.

3766 COHEN, Eileen Z. "Mirror of Virtue: The Role of Cassio in *Othello.*" *ES* 57 (1976):115–27.

3767 DICKES, Robert. "Desdemona: An Innocent Victim?" *AI* 27 (1970):279–97.

3768 DRAPER, John W. "Shakespeare and the Doge of Venice." *JEGP* 46 (1947): 75–81.

3769 EASTMAN, Arthur M. "Othello as Ironist." In **1118.**

3770 EVANS, K. W. "The Racial Factor in *Othello.*" *ShakS* 5 (1970 for 1969):124–40.

3771 EVERETT, Barbara. "Reflections on the Sentimentalist's *Othello.*" *CritQ* 3 (1961):127–39. A comment on **3788.***

3772 FABER, M. D. "*Othello:* The Justice of It Pleases." *AI* 28 (1971):228–46.

3773 FABER, M. D. "Othello: Symbolic Action, Ritual, and Myth." *AI* 31 (1974): 159–205.

3774 FABER, M. D. "Two Studies in Self-Aggression in Shakespearean Tragedy." *L&P* 14 (1964):80–96. On *Othello* and *Hamlet.*

3775 FELDMAN, Abraham Bronson. "Othello's Obsessions." *AI* 9 (1952):147–64.

3776 FLATTER, Richard. *The Moor of Venice.* London: Heinemann, 1950.

3777 GARDNER, Helen. "The Noble Moor." *PBA* 41 (1956 for 1955):189–205. Rpt. in **1061.***

3778 GARNER, S. N. "Shakespeare's Desdemona." *ShakS* 9 (1976):233–52.

3779 GÉRARD, Albert. " 'Egregiously an Ass': The Dark Side of the Moor. A View of Othello's Mind." *ShS* 10 (1957):98–106.

3780 HAGOPIAN, John V. "Psychology and the Coherent Form of Shakespeare's *Othello.*" *PMASAL* 45 (1960):373–80.

3781 HUBLER, Edward. "The Damnation of Othello: Some Limitations on the Christian View of the Play." *SQ* 9 (1958):295–300.

3782 HUNTER, G. K. "Othello and Colour Prejudice." *PBA* 53 (1968 for 1967): 139–63.*

3783 JANTON, Pierre. "Othello's *Weak Function.*" *CahiersE* 7 (1975):43–50. About Othello's inability to cope with the force of Desdemona's eroticism.

3784 JOHNSON, Robert Carl. "Roderigo, That 'Poor Trash of Venice.' " *UR* 35 (1969):213–18.

3785 JONES, Eldred. *Othello's Countrymen: The African in English Renaissance Drama.* London: Oxford U.P., 1965.*

3786 KIRSCHBAUM, Leo. "The Modern Othello." *ELH* 11 (1944):283–96. Rpt. in **1377** and **3686.**

3787 KLIGER, Samuel. "Othello: The Man of Judgment." *MP* 48 (1951):221–24.

3788 LEAVIS, F. R. "Diabolic Intellect and the Noble Hero: A Note on *Othello.*" *Scrutiny* 6 (1937):259–83. Rpt. as "Diabolic Intellect and the Noble Hero: or The Sentimentalist's Othello" in **1232**. A rejoinder to Bradley and Stoll; see **2011** and **3727.***

3789 LEVIN, Harry. "*Othello* and the Motive-Hunters." *CentR* 8 (1964):1–16. Rpt. in **1233**.

3790 LEVITSKY, Ruth. "All-In-All Sufficiency in Othello." *ShakS* 6 (1972 for 1970): 209–21.

3791 MCGEE, Arthur R. "Othello's Motive for Murder." *SQ* 15.1 (1964):45–54.

3792 MARIENSTRAS, R. "La dégradation des vertus héroïques dans *Othello* et dans *Coriolan.*" *EA* 17 (1964):372–89.

3793 MATTHEWS, G. M. "Othello and the Dignity of Man." In **1148**.

3794 MOORE, John Robert. "Othello, Iago, and Cassio as Soldiers." *PQ* 31 (1952): 189–94.

3795 PRIOR, Moody E. "Character in Relation to Action in *Othello.*" *MP* 44 (1947): 225–37.

3796 RABKIN, Leslie Y., and Jeffrey BROWN. "Some Monster in His Thought: Sadism and Tragedy in *Othello.*" *L&P* 23 (1973):59–67.

3797 RANALD, Margaret Loftus. "The Indiscretions of Desdemona." *SQ* 14 (1963): 127–39.

3798 RAYMOND, William O. "Motivation and Character Portrayal in *Othello.*" *UTQ* 17 (1947):80–96.

3799 REID, Stephen A. "Desdemona's Guilt." *AI* 27 (1970):245–62.

3800 REID, Stephen A. "Othello's Jealousy." *AI* 25 (1968):274–93.

3801 RICE, Julian C. "Desdemona Unpinned: Universal Guilt in *Othello.*" *ShakS* 7 (1974):209–26.

3802 ROGERS, Robert. "Endopsychic Drama in *Othello.*" *SQ* 20 (1969):205–15. A psychoanalytic interpretation of endopsychic conflict, in which Othello and Iago are seen as decomposed parts of a single self, Othello.

3803 SHAPIRO, Stephen A. "Othello's Desdemona." *L&P* 14 (1964):56–61.

3804 SIEGEL, Paul N. "The Damnation of Othello." *PMLA* 68 (1953):1068–78.

3805 STIRLING, Brents. "Psychology in *Othello.*" *ShAB* 19 (1944):135–44.

3806 WAIN, John. "A Note on Characterization in *Othello.*" *Essays and Poems Presented to Lord David Cecil.* Ed. W. W. ROBSON. London: Constable, 1970.

3807 WEST, Robert H. "The Christianness of *Othello.*" *SQ* 15.4 (1964):333–43. Rpt. in **1448**.

3808 WILCOX, John. "Othello's Crucial Moment." *ShAB* 24 (1949):181–92. Focuses on III, ii and iii.

Staging and Stage History

See also **763, 805, 838,** and **895.**

3809 HOSLEY, Richard. "The Staging of Desdemona's Bed." *SQ* 14 (1963):57–65.

3810 ROSENBERG, Marvin. *The Masks of "Othello."* Berkeley and Los Angeles: U. of California P., 1961.*

3811 ROSS, Lawrence J. "The Use of a 'Fit-Up' Booth in *Othello." SQ* 12 (1961): 359–70.

3812 SELTZER, Daniel. "Elizabethan Acting in *Othello." SQ* 10 (1959):201–10.

3813 STANISLAVSKY [Alekseev, Konstantin S.] *Stanislavsky Produces "Othello."* Trans. Helen NOWAK. London: Bles, 1948.

Language and Imagery

See also **457, 475, 554, 572,** and **3697.**

3814 BETHELL, S. L. "Shakespeare's Imagery: The Diabolic Images in *Othello." ShS* 5 (1952):62–80.

3815 DORAN, Madeleine. "Iago's 'if': An Essay on the Syntax of *Othello."* In **1120.***

3816 EMPSON, William. " 'Honest' in *Othello."* In **530.**

3817 JORGENSON, Paul A. " 'Honesty' in *Othello." SP* 47 (1950):557–67. Rpt. in **538.**

3818 MCCULLEN, Joseph T., Jr. "Iago's Use of Proverbs for Persuasion." *SEL* 4 (1964):247–62.

3819 MONEY, John. "Othello's 'It Is the Cause . . . ': An Analysis." *ShS* 6 (1953): 95–105.

3820 NASH, Walter. "Paired Words in *Othello:* Shakespeare's Use of a Stylistic Device." *ES* 39 (1958):62–67. For a further comment, see pp. 212–16.

3821 SCHWARTZ, Elias. "Stylistic 'Impurity' and the Meaning of *Othello." SEL* 10 (1970):297–313.

3822 STAFFORD, Tony J. " 'Water,' 'Stone,' and 'Willow' Song: An Imagistic Motif in *Othello."* In **1149.**

3823 WILLIAMSON, Karina. " 'Honest' and 'False' in *Othello." SN* 35 (1963):211–20.

Pericles

See also **1177, 1226, 1599, 1600, 1603–15, 1637, 1740–77,** and **4661.**

3824 ARTHOS, John. *"Pericles, Prince of Tyre:* A Study in the Dramatic Use of Romantic Narrative." *SQ* 4 (1953):257–70.

3825 BARBER, C. L. " 'Thou That Beget'st Him That Did Thee Beget': Transformation in *Pericles* and *The Winter's Tale." ShS* 22 (1969):59–67.*

3826 BARKER, Gerard A. "Themes and Variations in Shakespeare's *Pericles.*" *ES* 44 (1963):401–14. Rpt. in **1766.***

3827 BECKER, Marvin. "A Historian's View of Another Pericles." *MQR* 15 (1976): 197–211.

3828 BROCKBANK, J. Philip. "*Pericles* and the Dream of Immortality." *ShS* 24 (1971):105–16.*

3829 CRAIG, Hardin. "*Pericles* and *The Painfull Adventures.*" *SP* 45 (1948):600–05.

3830 CUTTS, John P. "Pericles' 'Downright Violence.'" *ShakS* 4 (1969 for 1968): 275–93. Rpt. in **1744.**

3831 EDWARDS, Philip. "An Approach to the Problem of *Pericles.*" *ShS* 5 (1952): 25–49.

3832 EGGERS, Walter F., Jr. "Shakespeare's Gower and the Role of the Authorial Presenter." *PQ* 54 (1975):434–43.

3833 FLOWER, Annette C. "Disguise and Identity in *Pericles, Prince of Tyre.*" *SQ* 26 (1975):30–41.

3834 GOOLDEN, P. "Antiochus's Riddle in Gower and Shakespeare." *RES,* n.s. 6 (1955):245–51.

3835 GORFAIN, Phyllis. "Puzzle and Artifice: The Riddle as Metapoetry in *Pericles.*" *ShS* 29 (1976):11–20.

3836 GREENFIELD, Thelma N. "A Re-Examination of the 'Patient' Pericles." *ShakS* 3 (1968 for 1967):51–61.

3837 HOENIGER, F. David, ed. *Pericles.* In the Arden Shakespeare. See **350.**

3838 KNAPP, Peggy Ann. "The Orphic Vision of *Pericles.*" *TSLL* 15 (1974):615–26.

3839 MCINTOSH, William A. "Musical Design in *Pericles.*" *ELN* 11 (1973):100–06.

3840 MAXWELL, J. C., ed. *Pericles, Prince of Tyre.* In the New Cambridge Shakespeare. See **363.**

3841 PARROTT, Thomas Marc. "*Pericles:* The Play and the Novel." *ShAB* 23 (1948): 105–13.

3842 PRIOR, Roger. "George Wilkins and the Young Heir." *ShS* 29 (1976):33–40.

3843 SCHRICKX, Willem. "*Pericles* in a Book-List of 1619 from the English Jesuit Mission and Some of the Play's Special Problems." *ShS* 29 (1976):21–32.

3844 SEMON, Kenneth J. "*Pericles:* An Order Beyond Reason." *Essays in Literature* 1 (1974):17–27.

3845 THORNE, William Barry. "*Pericles* and the 'Incest-Fertility' Opposition." *SQ* 22 (1971):43–56.

3846 TOMPKINS, J. M. S. "Why *Pericles?*" *RES,* n.s. 3 (1952):315–24.

3847 WELSH, Andrew. "Heritage in *Pericles.*" In **1613.**

3848 WOOD, James O. "The Running Image in *Pericles.*" *ShakS* 5 (1970 for 1969): 240–52.

3849 WOOD, James O. "Shakespeare and the Belching Whale." *ELN* 11 (1973):40–44.

Richard II

Textual Commentary and Sources

See also **1849**, **1871**, and **3897**.

3850 BERGERON, David M. "The Deposition Scene in *Richard II.*" *RenP 1974* (1975):31–37.

3851 BLACK, Matthew W. "The Sources of Shakespeare's *Richard II.*" In **1154.**

3852 DODSON, Sarah Clara. "The Northumberland of Shakespeare and Holinshed." *UTSE* 19 (1939):74–85.

3853 HASKER, Richard E. "The Copy for the First Folio *Richard II.*" *SB* 5 (1952–53):53–72.

3854 LAW, Robert Adger. "Deviations from Holinshed in *Richard II.*" *UTSE* 29 (1950):91–101.

3855 LOGAN, George M. "Lucan—Daniel—Shakespeare: New Light on the Relation Between *The Civil Wars* and *Richard II.*" *ShakS* 9 (1976):121–40.

3856 TILLOTSON, Kathleen. "Drayton and Richard II: 1597–1600." *RES* 15 (1939): 172–79.

General Studies

See also **541, 779, 815, 1189, 1234, 1246, 1263, 1413, 1481, 1486, 1494, 1799, 1802, 1822, 1828–29, 1833–34, 1836, 1843, 1863–77, 1928, 1959, 1980,** and **2005–10.**

3857 BATTENHOUSE, Roy W. "Tudor Doctrine and the Tragedy of *Richard II.*" *Rice U. Studies* 60.2 (1974):31–53.

3858 BERMAN, Ronald. "*Richard II:* The Shapes of Love." *Moderna Språk* 58 (1964):1–8.

3859 BOGARD, Travis. "Shakespeare's Second Richard." *PMLA* 70 (1955):192–209.

3860 BONHEIM, Helmut, and Jean BONHEIM. "The Two Kings in Shakespeare's *Richard II.*" *SJH* (1971):169–79.

3861 BONNARD, Georges A. "The Actor in *Richard II.*" *SJ* 87–88 (1951–52):87–101.

3862 BORNSTEIN, Diane. "Trial by Combat and Official Irresponsibility in *Richard II.*" *ShakS* 8 (1975):131–41.

3863 BRERETON, J. Le Gay. "Shakespeare's *Richard the Second.*" *Writings on Elizabethan Drama.* Collected by R. G. HOWARTH. Carlton, Victoria: Melbourne U.P., 1948. Rpt., New York: AMS.

3864 BROOKE, Nicholas, ed. *Shakespeare, "Richard II": A Casebook.* London: Macmillan, 1973.

3865 CHAMPION, Larry S. "The Function of Mowbray: Shakespeare's Maturing Artistry in *Richard II.*" *SQ* 26 (1975):3–7.

3866 CUBETA, Paul M., ed. *Twentieth Century Interpretations of "Richard II."* Englewood Cliffs, N.J.: Prentice-Hall, 1971. A collection of essays.

3867 DORIUS, R. J. "A Little More Than a Little." *SQ* 11 (1960):13–26. Rpt. in **1845.** Rpt. as "Prudence and Excess in *Richard II* and the Histories," in **1865.***

3868 ELLIOTT, John R., Jr. "History and Tragedy in *Richard II." SEL* 8 (1968): 253–71.

3869 ELLIOTT, John R., Jr. *"Richard II* and the Medieval." *RenP 1965* (1966): 25–34.

3870 FOLLAND, Harold F. "King Richard's Pallid Victory." *SQ* 24 (1973):390–99.

3871 FRENCH, A. L. *"Richard II* and the Woodstock Murder." *SQ* 22 (1971): 337–44.

3872 GRABES, Herbert. *"The Tragedie of King Richard the Second." Poetica* (Munich), 2 (1968):196–215.

3873 GRIVELET, Michel. "Shakespeare's 'War with Time': The Sonnets and *Richard II." ShS* 23 (1970):69–78.

3874 HALSTEAD, William L. "Artifice and Artistry in *Richard II* and *Othello."* In **1150.**

3875 HAPGOOD, Robert. "Three Eras in *Richard II." SQ* 14 (1963):281–83.

3876 HILL, R. F. "Dramatic Techniques and Interpretation in *Richard II."* In **1582.**

3877 HOMAN, Sidney R. *"Richard II:* The Aesthetics of Judgment." *SLitI* 5.1 (1972): 65–71.

3878 HUMPHREYS, A. R. *Shakespeare: "Richard II."* London: Arnold, 1967.

3879 HUMPHREYS, A. R. "Shakespeare's Political Justice in *Richard II* and *Henry IV."* In **1145** (1965 for 1964).

3880 JEFFARES, A. Norman. "In One Person Many People: *King Richard the Second."* In **1146.**

3881 KANTOROWICZ, Ernst H. *The King's Two Bodies: A Study in Mediaeval Political Theology.* Princeton: Princeton U.P., 1957, pp. 24–41.*

3882 KELLY, Michael F. "The Function of York in *Richard II." SHR* 6 (1972): 257–67.

3883 MACISAAC, Warren J. "The Three Cousins in *Richard II." SQ* 22 (1971): 137–46.

3884 MCNEIR, Waldo F. "The Comic Scenes in *Richard II." NM* 73 (1972):815–22.

3885 MCPEEK, James A. S. "Richard and His Shadow World." *AI* 15 (1958):195–212. Rpt. in **1401.**

3886 MONTGOMERY, Robert L., Jr. "The Dimensions of Time in *Richard II." ShakS* 4 (1969 for 1968):73–85.

3887 PHIALAS, Peter G. "The Medieval in *Richard II." SQ* 12 (1961):305–10.

3888 PHIALAS, Peter G. *"Richard II* and Shakespeare's Tragic Mode." *TSLL* 5 (1963):344–55.

3889 POTTER, Lois. "The Antic Disposition of Richard II." *ShS* 27 (1974):33–41.

3890 PROVOST, Foster. "On Justice and the Music in *Richard II* and *King Lear." Annuale Mediaevale* 2 (1961):55–71.

3891 PROVOST, Foster. "The Sorrows of Shakespeare's Richard II." In **1155.**

3892 QUINN, Michael. " 'The King Is Not Himself': The Personal Tragedy of Richard II." *SP* 56 (1959):169–86.

3893 REED, Robert R., Jr. *Richard II: From Mask to Prophet.* University Park: Pennsylvania State U., 1968.

3894 REIMAN, Donald H. "Appearance, Reality, and Moral Order in *Richard II.*" *MLQ* 25 (1964):34–45.

3895 RIBNER, Irving. "Bolingbroke, A True Machiavellian." *MLQ* 9 (1948):177–84.*

3896 ROSSITER, A. P. *"Richard II."* In **1245**. Rpt. in **1125**.*

3897 ROSSITER, A. P., ed. *Woodstock, a Moral History.* London: Chatto & Windus, 1946.

3898 SCHOENBAUM, S. *"Richard II* and the Realities of Power." *ShS* 28 (1975): 1–13.

3899 SEEHASE, Georg. "Shakespeares Publikumsnähe in *König Richard II.*" *SJW* 108 (1972):53–63.

3900 SPEAIGHT, Robert. "Shakespeare and the Political Spectrum: As Illustrated by *Richard II.*" In **1145** (1965 for 1964).

3901 STIRLING, Brents. "Bolingbroke's 'Decision.' " *SQ* 2 (1951):27–34.*

3902 TAYLOR, John. "Richard II's Views on Kingship." *PLPLS-LHS* 14 (1971): 189–205.

3903 THOMPSON, Karl F. "Richard II, Martyr." *SQ* 8 (1957):159–66.

3904 TRAVERSI, Derek. "Richard II." In **1145** (1965 for 1964).

3905 URE, Peter, ed. *King Richard II.* In the Arden Shakespeare. See **350**.

3906 WILSON, J. Dover. "The Political Background of Shakespeare's *Richard II* and *Henry IV.*" *SJ* 75 (1939):36–51.

3907 YEATS, William Butler. "At Stratford-upon-Avon." *Ideas of Good and Evil* (Orig. pub. in 1903), collected in *Essays and Introductions.* London and New York: Macmillan, 1961. Rpt. in **1865**.*

3908 ZITNER, Sheldon P. "Aumerle's Conspiracy." *SEL* 14 (1974):239–57.

Language and Imagery

See also **475, 554–55**, and **3874**.

3909 ALTICK, Richard D. "Symphonic Imagery in *Richard II.*" *PMLA* 62 (1947): 339–65.*

3910 BRYANT, J. A., Jr. "The Linked Analogies of *Richard II.*" *SR* 65 (1957): 420–33. On Christian imagery. Rpt., rev., in **1413**.

3911 CUTTS, John P. "Christian and Classical Imagery in *Richard II.*" *Universitas* (Detroit) 2 (1964):70–76.

3912 DEAN, Leonard F. *"Richard II:* The State and the Image of the Theater." *PMLA* 67 (1952):211–18.*

3913 DORAN, Madeleine. "Imagery in *Richard II* and in *Henry IV.*" *MLR* 37 (1942): 113–22. Rpt. in **2702**.*

3914 FRIEDMAN, Donald M. "John of Gaunt and the Rhetoric of Frustration." *ELH* 43 (1976):279–99. An analysis of II, i.

3915 HARRIS, Kathryn Montgomery. "Sun and Water Imagery in *Richard II:* Its Dramatic Function." *SQ* 21 (1970):157–65.

3916 HAWKES, Terence. "The Word against the Word: The Role of Language in *Richard II.*" *Lang&S* 2 (1969):296–322. Rpt., rev., in **465.**

3917 HENINGER, S. K., Jr. "The Sun-King Analogy in *Richard II.*" *SQ* 11 (1960): 319–27.

3918 HOCKEY, Dorothy C. "A World of Rhetoric in *Richard II.*" *SQ* 15.3 (1964): 179–91.

3919 JORGENSEN, Paul A. "Vertical Patterns in *Richard II.*" *ShAB* 23 (1948): 119–34.

3920 KLIGER, Samuel. "The Sun Imagery in *Richard II.*" *SP* 45 (1948):196–202.

3921 MAVEETY, Stanley R. "A Second Fall of Cursed Man: The Bold Metaphor in *Richard II.*" *JEGP* 72 (1973):175–93.

3922 ROTHSCHILD, Herbert B., Jr. "Language and Social Reality in *Richard II.*" In **1149.**

3923 SUZMAN, Arthur. "Imagery and Symbolism in *Richard II.*" *SQ* 7 (1956): 355–70.

3924 URE, Peter. "The Looking-Glass of *Richard II.*" *PQ* 34 (1955):219–24.

3925 YAMAMOTO, Tadao. "The Verbal Structure of *Richard II.*" *ZAA* 12 (1964): 163–72.

Richard III

Textual Commentary and Sources

See also **389, 1849,** and **3953–54.**

3926 ALEXANDER, Peter. *Shakespeare's "Henry VI" and "Richard III."* See **1850.**

3927 BEGG, Edleen. "Shakespeare's Debt to Hall and to Holinshed in *Richard III.*" *SP* 32 (1935):189–96.

3928 BOWERS, Fredson. "The Copy for the Folio *Richard III.*" *SQ* 10 (1959):541–44.

3929 CAIRNCROSS, Andrew S. "The Quartos and the Folio Text of *Richard III.*" *RES,* n.s. 8 (1957):225–33.

3930 CHURCHILL, George B. *Richard the Third up to Shakespeare.* Palaestra 10. Berlin: Mayer & Müller, 1900. Rpt., New York: Johnson Reprint; Totowa, N.J.: Roman & Littlefield, 1976.

3931 HANHAM, Alison. *Richard III and His Early Historians: 1483–1535.* London: Oxford U.P., 1975.*

3932 HONIGMANN, E. A. J. "The Text of *Richard III.*" *ThR* 7 (1965):48–55.

3933 PATRICK, David Lyall. *The Textual History of "Richard III."* Stanford: Stanford U.P.; London: Oxford U.P., 1936.

3934 SMIDT, Kristian. *Injurious Impostors and "Richard III."* Oslo: Norwegian U.P.; New York: Humanities P., 1964.

3935 SMIDT, Kristian. *Memorial Transmission and Quarto Copy in "Richard III": A Reassessment.* Oslo: Universitetsforlaget; New York: Humanities P., 1970.

3936 SMIDT, Kristian, ed. *The Tragedy of King Richard the Third: Parallel Texts of the First Quarto and the First Folio with Variants of the Early Quartos.* Oslo: Universitetsforlaget; New York: Humanities P., 1969.

3937 WALTON, J. K. *The Copy for the Folio Text of "Richard III."* Auckland, N.Z.: Pilgrim, 1955.

General Studies

See also **554, 1246, 1261, 1358, 1451–52, 1481, 1486, 1508, 1779, 1799, 1802, 1813–14, 1826, 1829, 1833–36, 1843, 1850–62, 1980, 1985,** and **1999.**

3938 ARNOLD, Aerol. "The Recapitulation Dream in *Richard III* and *Macbeth.*" *SQ* 6 (1955):51–62.

3939 AYCOCK, Roy E. "Dual Progression in *Richard III.*" *SAB* 38.4 (1973):70–78. Focuses on Queen Margaret's curses and on Richard's self-destruction.

3940 BERMAN, Ronald. "Anarchy and Order in *Richard III* and *King John.*" *ShS* 20 (1967):51–59.

3941 BROOKE, Nicholas. "Reflecting Gems and Dead Bones: Tragedy Versus History in *Richard III.*" *CritQ* 7 (1965):123–34. Rpt., rev., in **2005.***

3942 CLEMEN, Wolfgang. *A Commentary on Shakespeare's "Richard III."* Trans. Jean BONHEIM. London: Methuen, 1968. A somewhat shortened version of the German original, published as *Kommentar zu Shakespeares "Richard III."* Göttingen: Vandenhoeck & Ruprecht, 1957. Rev. ed., 1969.*

3943 CLEMEN, Wolfgang. "Tradition and Originality in Shakespeare's *Richard III.*" *SQ* 5 (1954):247–57.

3944 DEAN, Leonard F. "Shakespeare's Richard III." *Studies in Language, Literature, and Culture of the Middle Ages and Later.* Eds. E. Bagby ATWOOD and Archibald A. HILL. Austin: U. of Texas, 1969.

3945 DOEBLER, Bettie Anne. " 'Despaire and Dye': The Ultimate Temptation of Richard III." *ShakS* 7 (1974):75–85.

3946 FAURE, François. "Langage religieux et langage pétrarquiste dans *Richard III* de Shakespeare." *EA* 23 (1970):23–37.

3947 FRENCH, A. L. "The World of *Richard III.*" *ShakS* 4 (1969 for 1968):25–39.

3948 GERBER, Richard. "Elizabethan Convention and Psychological Realism in the Dream and Last Soliloquy of *Richard III.*" *ES* 40 (1959):294–300.

3949 GURR, Andrew. "Richard III and the Democratic Process." *EIC* 24 (1974): 39–47.

3950 HAEFFNER, Paul. *A Critical Commentary on Shakespeare's "Richard III."* London: Macmillan, 1966.

3951 HARCOURT, John B. " 'Odde Old Ends, Stolne . . .': King Richard and Saint Paul." *ShakS* 7 (1974):87–100.

3952 HEILMAN, Robert B. "Satiety and Conscience: Aspects of *Richard III.*" *AR* 24 (1964):57–73. Rpt. in **1125.***

3953 KENDALL, Paul Murray. *Richard the Third.* New York: Norton, 1956; Double-day Anchor, 1965. A biographical and historical study.*

3954 KENDALL, Paul Murray, ed. *Richard III: The Great Debate.* New York: Norton; London: Folio Society, 1965.

3955 KRIEGER, Murray. "The Dark Generations of *Richard III.*" *Criticism* 1 (1959): 32–48. Rpt. in *The Play and Place of Criticism.* Baltimore: The Johns Hopkins P., 1967. Rpt. also in **1401.***

3956 MCNEIR, Waldo F. "The Masks of Richard the Third." *SEL* 11 (1971):167–86.

3957 MOMOSE, Izumi. "The Temporal Awareness in *Richard III.*" *ShStud* 3 (1964): 42–72.

3958 NEILL, Michael. "Shakespeare's Halle of Mirrors: Play, Politics, and Psychology in *Richard III.*" *ShakS* 8 (1975):99–129.

3959 ROSSITER, A. P. "Angel with Horns: The Unity of *Richard III.*" In **1245.** Rpt. in **1798.***

3960 SAHEL, Pierre. "Les Voies des hommes dans *Richard III.*" *EA* 25 (1972): 91–103.

3961 SHERIFF, William E. "The Grotesque Comedy of *Richard III.*" *SLitI* 5.1 (1972):51–64.

3962 SMITH, Denzell S. "The Credibility of the Wooing of Anne in *Richard III.*" *PLL* 7 (1971):199–202.

3963 SMITH, Fred Manning. "The Relation of *Macbeth* to *Richard the Third.*" *PMLA* 60 (1945):1003–20.

3964 STRAUSS, Jennifer. "Determined to Prove a Villain: Character, Action, and Irony in *Richard III.*" *Komos* 1 (1967):115–20.

3965 TANNER, Stephen L. "Richard III Versus Elizabeth: An Interpretation." *SQ* 24 (1973):468–72. On the confrontation of Richard and Elizabeth in IV, iv.

3966 TOOLE, William B. "The Motif of Psychic Division in *Richard III.*" *ShS* 27 (1974):21–32.

3967 WHEELER, Richard P. "History, Character, and Conscience in *Richard III.*" *CompD* 5 (1971–72):301–21.*

3968 WILLIAMS, Philip. "*Richard the Third:* The Battle Orations." *English Studies in Honor of James Southall Wilson.* Ed. Fredson BOWERS. Charlottesville: U.P. of Virginia, 1951.

Staging and Stage History

See also **779** and **819.**

3969 PARKER, Brian. "*Richard III* and the Modernizing of Shakespeare." *MD* 15 (1972):321–29.

3970 STONE, George Winchester, Jr. "Bloody, Cold, and Complex Richard: David Garrick's Interpretation." See **803.**

3971 WOOD, Alice I. Perry. *The Stage History of Shakespeare's "King Richard the Third."* New York: Columbia U.P.; London: Oxford U.P., 1909. Rpt., New York: AMS.

Romeo and Juliet

Textual Commentary and Sources

See also **4021.**

3972 CANTRELL, Paul L., and George Walton WILLIAMS. "The Printing of the Second Quarto of *Romeo and Juliet* (1599)." *SB* 9 (1957):107–28.

3973 DUTHIE, George Ian. "The Text of Shakespeare's *Romeo and Juliet.*" *SB* 4 (1951–52):3–29.

3974 GRAY, J. C. "Remnants of Earlier Time Schemes in *Romeo and Juliet.*" *PLL* 2 (1966):253–58.

3975 HOPPE, Harry R. *The Bad Quarto of "Romeo and Juliet": A Bibliographical and Textual Study.* Ithaca: Cornell U.P., 1948.

3976 HOSLEY, Richard. "The Corrupting Influence of the Bad Quarto on the Received Text of *Romeo and Juliet.*" *SQ* 4 (1953):11–33.

3977 HOSLEY, Richard. "Quarto Copy for Q2 *Romeo and Juliet.*" *SB* 9 (1957): 129–41.

3978 LAW, Robert Adger. "On Shakespeare's Changes of His Source Material in *Romeo and Juliet.*" *UTSE* 9 (1929):86–102.

3979 MCCOWN, Gary M. " 'Runnawayes Eyes' and Juliet's Epithalamium." *SQ* 27 (1976):150–70. On Shakespeare's indebtedness to the epithalamium tradition.

3980 MOORE, Olin H. *The Legend of "Romeo and Juliet."* Columbus: Ohio State U.P., 1950. A source study.

3981 NOSWORTHY, J. M. "The Two Angry Families of Verona." *SQ* 3 (1952): 219–26. A source study.

3982 WILLIAMS, George Walton, ed. *The Most Excellent and Lamentable Tragedie of Romeo and Juliet: A Critical Edition.* Durham, N.C.: Duke U.P., 1964.

General Studies

See also **905, 1189, 1202, 1216, 1218, 1289, 1326, 1358, 1419, 1522, 1526–27, 1580, 1585–86, 1589, 1594, 1941, 1965, 1981, 2005–10, 2056–61,** and **3592.**

3983 ADAMS, Barry B. "The Prudence of Prince Escalus." *ELH* 35 (1968):32–50.

3984 ANDREWS, John F. "The Catharsis of *Romeo and Juliet." Contibuti dell' Istituto di filologia moderna.* Serie inglese, I (ed. Sergio ROSSI, Milan: Università Cattolica del Sacro Cuore, 1974), pp. 142–75.

3985 BERMAN, Ronald. "The Two Orders of *Romeo and Juliet." Moderna Språk* 64 (1970):244–52.

3986 BLACK, James. "The Visual Artistry of *Romeo and Juliet." SEL* 15 (1975): 245–56.

3987 BONNARD, Georges A. "*Romeo and Juliet:* A Possible Significance?" *RES,* n.s. 2 (1951):319–27.

3988 BOWLING, Lawrence Edward. "The Thematic Framework of *Romeo and Juliet." PMLA* 64 (1949):208–20.

3989 BRYANT, James C. "The Problematic Friar in *Romeo and Juliet." ES* 55 (1974):340–50.

3990 CAIN, H. Edward. " 'Parting' and Justice in *Romeo and Juliet." TSL* 7 (1962): 99–104.

3991 CAIN, H. Edward. "*Romeo and Juliet:* A Reinterpretation." *ShAB* 22 (1947): 163–92.

3992 CHARLTON, H. B. "*Romeo and Juliet* as an Experimental Tragedy." *PBA* 25 (1940 for 1939):143–85. Rpt., rev., in **1927.**

3993 COLE, Douglas, ed. *Twentieth Century Interpretations of "Romeo and Juliet."* Englewood Cliffs, N.J.: Prentice-Hall, 1970.

3994 DRAPER, John W. "Shakespeare's 'Star-Crossed Lovers.' " *RES* 15 (1939): 16–34.

3995 DRIVER, Tom F. "The Shakespearian Clock: Time and the Vision of Reality in *Romeo and Juliet* and *The Tempest." SQ* 15.4 (1964):363–70.

3996 EVANS, Bertrand. "The Brevity of Friar Laurence." *PMLA* 65 (1950):841–65. On the final scene.*

3997 FABER, M. D. "The Adolescent Suicides of Romeo and Juliet." *PsyR* 59 (1972): 169–81.

3998 GRAY, J. C. "*Romeo and Juliet,* and Some Renaissance Notions of Love, Time, and Death." *DR* 48 (1968):58–69.

3999 HARTLEY, Lodwick. " 'Mercy but Murders': A Subtheme in *Romeo and Juliet." PLL* 1 (1965):259–64.

4000 HOLLAND, Norman N. "Romeo's Dream and the Paradox of Literary Realism." *L&P* 13 (1963):97–103. Rpt. in **1401.**

4001 HUNTER, G. K. "Shakespeare's Earliest Tragedies: *Titus Andronicus* and *Romeo and Juliet." ShS* 27 (1974):1–9.

4002 JOHNSON, Robert Carl. "Four Young Men." *UR* 36 (1969):141–47. On Benvolio, Tybalt, Paris, and Mercutio, and their contributions to the workings of "fate."

4003 LAWLOR, John. "*Romeo and Juliet.* " In **1582.**

4004 LEECH, Clifford. "The Moral Tragedy of *Romeo and Juliet.* " In **1143.**

4005 LEIMBERG, Inge. *Shakespeares "Romeo und Julia": Von der Sonettdichtung zur Liebestragödie.* Munich: Fink, 1968.

4006 LEVIN, Harry. "Form and Formality in *Romeo and Juliet.*" *SQ* 11 (1960):3–11. Rpt. in **1147, 1233,** and **3993.***

4007 LINK, Frederick M. "*Romeo and Juliet:* Character and Tragedy." *BUSE* 1 (1955):9–19.

4008 PEARCE, T. M. "*Romeo and Juliet* as Situation Ethics." In **1169.**

4009 PETERSON, Douglas L. "*Romeo and Juliet* and the Art of Moral Navigation." In **1156.***

4010 PETRONELLA, Vincent F. "The Musicians' Scene in *Romeo and Juliet.*" *HAB* 23.2 (1972):54–56.

4011 RABKIN, Norman. "Eros and Death." In **1243.***

4012 RIBNER, Irving. " 'Then I Denie You Starres': A Reading of *Romeo and Juliet.*" In **1119.** Rpt., rev., in **1968.**

4013 SCHLÖSSER, Anselm. "Komplexe Wirklichkeit und Dialektik in *Romeo und Julia.*" *SJW* 108 (1972):35–52.

4014 SEWARD, James H. *Tragic Vision in "Romeo and Juliet."* Washington, D.C.: Consortium P., 1973.

4015 SIEGEL, Paul N. "Christianity and the Religion of Love in *Romeo and Juliet.*" *SQ* 12 (1961):371–92. Rpt. in **1249.**

4016 SMITH, Gordon Ross. "The Balance of Themes in *Romeo and Juliet.*" In **1167.**

4017 SMITH, Warren D. "Romeo's Final Dream." *MLR* 62 (1967):579–83.

4018 SNYDER, Susan. "*Romeo and Juliet:* Comedy into Tragedy." *EIC* 20 (1970): 391–402.

4019 STEWART, Stanley. "Romeo and Necessity." In **1156.**

4020 TANSELLE, G. Thomas. "Time in *Romeo and Juliet.*" *SQ* 15.4 (1964):349–61.

4021 TRACI, Philip J. "Religious Controversy in *Romeo and Juliet:* The Play and Its Historical Context." *MichA* 8 (1976):319–25.

4022 ZEISEL, Hans. "In Defense of Shakespeare's *Romeo and Juliet.*" *ShStud* 6 (1967–68):37–61.

Mercutio and the Nurse

See also **1211** and **4002.**

4023 EVERETT, Barbara. "*Romeo and Juliet:* The Nurse's Story." *CritQ* 14 (1972): 129–39.***

4024 GUIDO, Angelina. "The Humor of Juliet's Nurse." *Bulletin of the History of Medicine* 17 (1945):297–303.

4025 HOLLAND, Norman N. "Mercutio, Mine Own Son the Dentist." In **1167.**

4026 MCARTHUR, Herbert. "Romeo's Loquacious Friend." *SQ* 10 (1959):35–44.

4027 STEVENS, Martin. "Juliet's Nurse: Love's Herald." *PLL* 2 (1966):195–206.

4028 UTTERBACK, Raymond V. "The Death of Mercutio." *SQ* 24 (1973):105–16.

Staging and Stage History

See also **800** and **895.**

4029 BROWN, John Russell. "S. Franco Zeffirelli's *Romeo and Juliet.*" *ShS* 15 (1962): 147–55.

4030 GOLDBERG, M. A. "The Multiple Masks of Romeo: Toward a New Shakespearean Production." *AR* 28 (1968–69):405–26.

4031 HOSLEY, Richard. "The Use of the Upper Stage in *Romeo and Juliet.*" *SQ* 5 (1954):371–79.

4032 LOWER, Charles B. "*Romeo and Juliet,* IV. v: A Stage Direction and Purposeful Comedy." *ShakS* 8 (1975):177–94.

4033 STONE, George Winchester, Jr. "*Romeo and Juliet:* The Source of Its Modern Stage Career." *SQ* 15.2 (1964):191–206. Also in **1153.**

Language and Imagery

See also **541, 578,** and **1256.**

4034 CHANG, Joseph S. M. J. "The Language of Paradox in *Romeo and Juliet.*" *ShakS* 3 (1968 for 1967):22–42.

4035 EVANS, Robert O. *The Osier Cage: Rhetorical Devices in "Romeo & Juliet."* Lexington: U. of Kentucky P., 1966.

4036 LAIRD, David. "The Generation of Style in *Romeo and Juliet.*" *JEGP* 63 (1964): 204–13. On the shift from a conventional poetic form to a new mastery of style.

4037 MCLUSKIE, Kathleen E. "Shakespeare's 'Earth-Treading Stars': The Image of the Masque in *Romeo and Juliet.*" *ShS* 24 (1971):63–69.

4038 MUIR, Kenneth. "The Imagery of *Romeo and Juliet.*" *Literary Half-Yearly* 9 (1968):71–82. Rpt., rev., in **1238.**

4039 PARKER, Douglas H. "Light and Dark Imagery in *Romeo and Juliet.*" *QQ* 75 (1968):663–74.

4040 PETTET, E. C. "The Imagery of *Romeo and Juliet.*" *English* 8 (1950):121–26.

4041 THOMAS, Sidney. "The Queen Mab Speech in *Romeo and Juliet.*" *ShS* 25 (1972):73–80.

4042 TRACI, Philip J. "Suggestions About the Bawdry in *Romeo and Juliet.*" *SAQ* 71 (1972):573–86.

The Taming of the Shrew

See also **1226, 1358, 1525–26, 1578, 1580, 1582, 1586, 1594–95, 1631, 1637, 1665–66, 1682, 1689, 1697, 1712–18, 1721,** and **1727.**

4043 ALEXANDER, Peter. "The Original Ending of *The Taming of the Shrew.*" *SQ* 20 (1969):111–16.

4044 BERGERON, David M. "The Wife of Bath and Shakespeare's *The Taming of the Shrew.*" *UR* 35 (1969):279–86.

4045 BRADBROOK, M. C. "Dramatic Role as Social Image: A Study of *The Taming of the Shrew.*" *SJ* 94 (1958):132–50.

4046 BRUNVAND, Jan Harold. "The Folktale Origin of *The Taming of the Shrew.*" *SQ* 17 (1966):345–59.

4047 DUTHIE, George Ian. "*The Taming of A Shrew* and *The Taming of the Shrew.*" *RES* 19 (1943):337–56.

4048 GREENFIELD, Thelma N. *The Induction in Elizabethan Drama.* Eugene: U. of Oregon P., 1969.

4049 GREENFIELD, Thelma N. "The Transformation of Christopher Sly." *PQ* 33 (1954):34–42.

4050 HARROLD, William E. "Shakespeare's Use of *Mostellaria* in *The Taming of the Shrew.*" *SJH* (1970):188–94.

4051 HEILMAN, Robert B. "The *Taming* Untamed, or, The Return of the Shrew." *MLQ* 27 (1966):147–61.

4052 HENZE, Richard. "Role Playing in *The Taming of the Shrew.*" *SHR* 4 (1970): 231–40.*

4053 HIBBARD, G. R. "*The Taming of the Shrew:* A Social Comedy." In **1171.**

4054 HOSLEY, Richard. "Sources and Analogues of *The Taming of the Shrew.*" *HLQ* 27 (1964):289–308.*

4055 HOSLEY, Richard. "Was There a 'Dramatic Epilogue' to *The Taming of the Shrew?*" *SEL* 1.2 (1961):17–34.*

4056 HOUK, Raymond A. "The Evolution of *The Taming of the Shrew.*" *PMLA* 57 (1942):1009–38.

4057 HOUK, Raymond A. "The Integrity of Shakespeare's *The Taming of the Shrew.*" *JEGP* 39 (1940):222–29.

4058 HOUK, Raymond A. "Shakespeare's Heroic Shrew." *ShAB* 18 (1943):121–32, 175–86.

4059 HOUK, Raymond A. "Strata in *The Taming of the Shrew.*" *SP* 39 (1942): 291–302.

4060 HUSTON, J. Dennis. " 'To Make a Puppet': Play and Play-Making in *The Taming of the Shrew.*" *ShakS* 9 (1976):73–87.

4061 JAYNE, Sears. "The Dreaming of *The Shrew.*" *SQ* 17 (1966):41–56.

4062 MURPHY, G. N. "Christopher Sly and the Pronoun-Game in *The Taming of the Shrew.*" *PLL* 2 (1966):67–70.

4063 ORANGE, L. E. "The Punning of *The Shrew.*" *SoQ* 3 (1965):295–305.

4064 RANALD, Margaret Loftus. "The Meaning of the Haggard; or *The Taming of the Shrew.*" *Essays in Literature* 1 (1975):149–65.

4065 RIBNER, Irving. "The Morality of Farce: *The Taming of the Shrew.*" *Essays in American and English Literature Presented to Bruce Robert McElderry, Jr.* Ed. Max F. SCHULZ, et al. Athens: Ohio U.P., 1967.

4066 SANDERS, Norman. "Themes and Imagery in *The Taming of the Shrew.*" *RenP 1963* (1964):63–72.

4067 SERONSY, Cecil C. " 'Supposes' as the Unifying Theme in *The Taming of the Shrew.*" *SQ* 14 (1963):15–30.

4068 SHROEDER, John W. "*The Taming of a Shrew* and *The Taming of the Shrew:* A Case Reopened." *JEGP* 57 (1958):424–43.

4069 STETNER, S. C. V. "Baptista and His Daughters." *PsyR* 60 (1973):223–37.

4070 THORNE, William Barry. "Folk Elements in *The Taming of the Shrew.*" *QQ* 75 (1968):482–96.

4071 TILLYARD, E. M. W. "The Fairy-Tale Element in *The Taming of the Shrew.*" In **1121.**

4072 WALDO, Tommy Ruth, and T. Walter HERBERT. "Musical Terms in *The Taming of the Shrew:* Evidence of Single Authorship." *SQ* 10 (1959):185–99.

4073 WENTERSDORF, Karl P. "The Authenticity of *The Taming of the Shrew.*" *SQ* 5 (1954):11–32.

4074 WEST, Michael. "The Folk Background of Petruchio's Wooing Dance: Male Supremacy in *The Taming of the Shrew.*" *ShakS* 7 (1974):65–73.

The Tempest

Sources

See also **117, 120,** and **138.**

4075 BARBER, Lester E. "*The Tempest* and New Comedy." *SQ* 21 (1970):207–11.

4076 KNOX, Bernard. "*The Tempest* and the Ancient Comic Tradition." *EIE 1954* (1955):52–73.

4077 LATHAM, Jacqueline E. "*The Tempest* and King James's *Daemonologie.*" *ShS* 28 (1975):117–23.

4078 NOSWORTHY, J. M. "The Narrative Sources of *The Tempest.*" *RES* 24 (1948): 281–94.

4079 SLATER, Ann Pasternak. "Variations within a Source: From Isaiah XXIX to *The Tempest.*" *ShS* 25 (1972):125–35.

General Studies

See also **326, 555, 1023, 1191, 1216, 1226, 1242, 1358, 1598–1615, 1620, 1633, 1637, 1642, 1646, 1651, 1666, 1680, 1687, 1735, 1738–39, 1740–77, 1904, 1928,** and **1976.**

4080 ALLEN, Don Cameron. *"The Tempest." Image and Meaning: Metaphoric Traditions in Renaissance Poetry.* Baltimore: The Johns Hopkins P., 1960. Rev. and enl. ed., 1968.

4081 AUDEN, W. H. "The Sea and the Mirror: A Commentary on Shakespeare's *The Tempest." The Collected Poetry of W. H. Auden.* New York: Random House, 1945. Also in *Collected Longer Poems.* London: Faber & Faber, 1968, and in *For the Time Being.* New York: Random House, 1944.*

4082 BACK, Guy. "Dramatic Convention in the First Scene of *The Tempest." EIC* 21 (1971):74–85.

4083 BAREHAM, T. *"The Tempest:* The Substantial Pageant Unfaded." *DUJ* 63, n.s. 32 (1971):213–22.

4084 BERGER, Harry, Jr. "Miraculous Harp: A Reading of Shakespeare's *Tempest." ShakS* 5 (1970 for 1969):253–83.*

4085 BOUGHNER, Daniel C. "Jonsonian Structure in *The Tempest." SQ* 21 (1970): 3–10.

4086 BRADBROOK, M. C. "Romance, Farewell! *The Tempest." ELR* 1 (1971): 239–49.

4087 BROCKBANK, J. Philip. *"The Tempest:* Conventions of Art and Empire." In **1599.**

4088 BROWER, Reuben A. "The Heresy of Plot." *EIE 1951* (1952):44–69. An evaluation of Aristotelian formal criticism in terms of *The Tempest.*

4089 BROWER, Reuben A. "The Mirror of Analogy: *The Tempest." The Fields of Light: An Experiment in Critical Reading.* New York: Oxford U.P., 1951.*

4090 BROWN, John Russell. *Shakespeare: "The Tempest."* London: Arnold, 1969.

4091 CARNES, Valerie. "Renaissance Conceptions of Mind, Imagination, and Art in Shakespeare's *The Tempest." NDQ* 35 (1967):93–103.

4092 COLETTI, Theresa. "Music and *The Tempest."* In **1613.**

4093 COLLINS, J. Churton. "Poetry and Symbolism: A Study of *The Tempest." ContempR* 93 (1908):65–83.

4094 CRAIG, Hardin. "Magic in *The Tempest." PQ* 47 (1968):8–15.

4095 CURRY, Walter Clyde. "Sacerdotal Science in Shakespeare's *The Tempest."* In **3258.**

4096 CUTTS, John P. "Music and the Supernatural in *The Tempest:* A Study in Interpretation." *M&L* 39 (1958):347–58.

4097 DAVIDSON, Frank. *"The Tempest:* An Interpretation." *JEGP* 62 (1963):501–17.

4098 DEVEREUX, E. J. "Sacramental Imagery in *The Tempest." HAB* 19.1 (1968): 50–62.

4099 DOBRÉE, Bonamy. *"The Tempest." E&S,* n.s. 5 (1952):13–25. Rpt. in **1660** and **4143.***

4100 DRIVER, Tom F. "The Shakespearian Clock: Time and the Vision of Reality in *Romeo and Juliet* and *The Tempest." SQ* 15.4 (1964):363–70.

4101 EBNER, Dean. *"The Tempest:* Rebellion and the Ideal State." *SQ* 16 (1965): 161–73.

4102 EDDY, Darlene Mathis. "The Brave Diligence: The Harmonies of *The Tempest.*" *BSUF* 16.3 (1975):12–25.

4103 EPSTEIN, Harry. "The Divine Comedy of *The Tempest.*" *ShakS* 8 (1975): 279–96.

4104 FITZ, L. T. "The Vocabulary of the Environment in *The Tempest.*" *SQ* 26 (1975):42–47.

4105 FRANK, Mike. "Shakespeare's Existential Comedy." In **1613.**

4106 FRYE, Northrop, ed. *The Tempest.* In the Pelican Shakespeare. See **356.***

4107 GESNER, Carol. "*The Tempest* as Pastoral Romance." *SQ* 10 (1959):531–39. Rpt., rev., in **1645.**

4108 GILBERT, Allan H. "*The Tempest:* Parallelism in Characters and Situations." *JEGP* 14 (1915):63–74.

4109 GOHN, Ernest. "*The Tempest:* Theme and Structure." *ES* 45 (1964):116–25.

4110 HAWKINS, Harriett. "Fabulous Counterfeits: Dramatic Construction and Dramatic Perspectives in *The Spanish Tragedy, A Midsummer Night's Dream,* and *The Tempest.*" *ShakS* 6 (1972 for 1970):51–65.

4111 HENZE, Richard. "*The Tempest:* Rejection of a Vanity." *SQ* 23 (1972):420–34.

4112 HEUER, Hermann. "Traumwelt und Wirklichkeit in der Sprache des *Tempest.*" *SJ* 90 (1954):210–28.

4113 HIGGS, Elton D. "Post-Creation Freedom in *The Tempest.*" In **1613.**

4114 HOFLING, Charles K. "Psychological Aspects of Shakespeare's *Tempest.*" *PsyR* 61 (1974):375–95.

4115 HOMAN, Sidney R. "*The Tempest* and Shakespeare's Last Plays: The Aesthetic Dimensions." *SQ* 24 (1973):69–76.

4116 HUNT, John Dixon. *A Critical Commentary on Shakespeare's "The Tempest."* London: Macmillan, 1968.

4117 HUTCHENS, Eleanor N. "The Transfer of Power in *King Lear* and *The Tempest.*" *REL* 4.2 (1963):82–93.

4118 JEWKES, Wilfred T. " 'Excellent Dumb Discourse': The Limits of the Language in *The Tempest.*" In **1167.**

4119 KERMODE, Frank, ed. *The Tempest.* In the Arden Shakespeare. See **350.***

4120 KNIGHTS, L. C. "*The Tempest.*" In **1613.** Rpt. in *Explorations 3;* see **1229.**

4121 KUHL, E. P. "Shakespeare and the Founders of America: *The Tempest.*" *PQ* 41 (1962):123–46. Also in **1174.**

4122 LEVIN, Harry. "Two Magian Comedies: *The Tempest* and *The Alchemist.*" *ShS* 22 (1969):47–58. Rpt. in **1233.**

4123 LURIA, Maxwell S. "Standing Water and Sloth in *The Tempest.*" *ES* 49 (1968): 328–31.

4124 MCNEIR, Waldo F. "*The Tempest:* Space-Time and Spectacle-Theme." *ArlQ* 2 (1970):29–58.

4125 MAJOR, John M. "*Comus* and *The Tempest.*" *SQ* 10 (1959):177–83.

4126 MARX, Leo. "Shakespeare's American Fable." *The Machine in the Garden: Technology and the Pastoral Ideal in America.* London and New York: Oxford U.P., 1964.

4127 MILWARD, Peter. "Gonzalo's 'Merry Fooling.'" *ShStud* 11 (1975 for 1972–73):28–36.

4128 NEILSON, Francis. *Shakespeare and "The Tempest."* Rindge, N.H.: R. Smith, 1956.

4129 NUTTALL, A. D. *Two Concepts of Allegory: A Study of Shakespeare's "The Tempest" and the Logic of Allegorical Expression.* London: Routledge & K. Paul; New York: Barnes & Noble, 1967.*

4130 ORGEL, Stephen. *The Illusion of Power: Political Theater in the English Renaissance.* Berkeley and Los Angeles: U. of California P., 1975.

4131 ORGEL, Stephen. "New Uses of Adversity: Tragic Experience in *The Tempest.*" In **1123.** Rpt. in **1125.***

4132 PALMER, D. J., ed. *Shakespeare, "The Tempest": A Casebook.* London: Macmillan, 1968.

4133 PEARSON, D'Orsay W. "'Unless I Be Reliev'd by Prayer': *The Tempest* in Perspective." *ShakS* 7 (1974):253–82.

4134 PHILLIPS, James Emerson, Jr. "*The Tempest* and the Renaissance Idea of Man." *SQ* 15.2 (1964):147–59. Also in **1153.**

4135 ROBINSON, James E. "Time and *The Tempest.*" *JEGP* 63 (1964):255–67.

4136 ROCKETT, William. "Labor and Virtue in *The Tempest.*" *SQ* 24 (1973):77–84.

4137 RYKEN, Leland. "The Temptation Theme in *The Tempest* and the Question of Dramatic Suspense." *TSL* 14 (1969):119–27.

4138 SCHORIN, Gerald. "Approaching the Genre of *The Tempest.*" In **1613.**

4139 SEIDEN, Melvin. "Utopianism in *The Tempest.*" *MLQ* 31 (1970):3–21.

4140 SEMON, Kenneth J. "Shakespeare's *Tempest:* Beyond a Common Joy." *ELH* 40 (1973):24–43.

4141 SHERWOOD, H. C. *The Tempest.* Oxford: Blackwell, 1973.

4142 SILHOL, Robert. "Magie et Utopie dans *La Tempête.*" EA 17 (1964):447–56.

4143 SMITH, Hallett, ed. *Twentieth Century Interpretations of "The Tempest."* Englewood Cliffs, N.J.: Prentice-Hall, 1969. A collection of essays.

4144 SOLOMON, Andrew. "A Reading of *The Tempest.*" In **1613.**

4145 STILL, Colin. *The Timeless Theme.* London: Nicholson & Watson, 1936. A shorter version was originally published as *Shakespeare's Mystery Play: A Study of "The Tempest."* London: Palmer, 1921.

4146 STOLL, Elmer Edgar. "*The Tempest.*" *PMLA* 47 (1932):699–726. Rpt., rev., in **1260.** Rpt. in **4143.**

4147 TEYTAUD, Jean-Paul. "Catharsis comique et reconnaissance dramatique dans *La Tempête.*" *EA* 21 (1968):113–24.

4148 TRAVERSI, Derek. "*The Tempest.*" *Scrutiny* 16 (1949):127–57.

4149 WEST, Robert H. "Ceremonial Magic in *The Tempest.*" In **1171.** Rpt. in **1448.**

4150 WILLSON, Robert F., Jr. "The Plays within *A Midsummer Night's Dream* and *The Tempest.*" *SJW* 110 (1974):101–11.

4151 WILSON, Harold S. "Action and Symbol in *Measure for Measure* and *The Tempest.*" *SQ* 4 (1953):375–84. Rpt. in **1132.***

4152 WILSON, J. Dover. *The Meaning of "The Tempest."* Newcastle upon Tyne: Literary and Philosophical Society, 1936.

4153 ZIMBARDO, Rose A. "Form and Disorder in *The Tempest.*" *SQ* 14 (1963): 49–56.

Prospero, Ariel, and Caliban

See also **343, 1372, 1707,** and **4177.**

4154 BARTENSCHLAGER, Klaus. "Shakespeares *The Tempest:* Der ideale Traum und Prosperos Magie." *SJH* (1970):170–87.

4155 CLARK, John Pepper. "The Legacy of Caliban." *The Example of Shakespeare.* Evanston, Ill.: Northwestern U.P., 1970.

4156 COURSEN, Herbert R., Jr. "Prospero and the Drama of the Soul." *ShakS* 4 (1969 for 1968):316–33.

4157 FYLER, Anson C., Jr. "Self-Unification: An Archetypal Analysis of Prospero in Shakespeare's *The Tempest.*" *HSL* 3 (1971):45–50.

4158 GOLDSMITH, Robert Hillis. "The Wild Man on the English Stage." *MLR* 53 (1958):481–91.

4159 GRANT, Patrick. "The Magic of Charity: A Background to Prospero." *RES,* n.s. 27 (1976):1–16.

4160 HANKINS, John E. "Caliban the Bestial Man." *PMLA* 62 (1947):793–801.

4161 HART, Jeffrey P. "Prospero and Faustus." *BUSE* 2 (1956):197–206.

4162 HOENIGER, F. David. "Prospero's Storm and Miracle." *SQ* 7 (1956):33–38.

4163 JAMES, D. G. *The Dream of Prospero.* Oxford: Clarendon, 1967.

4164 JOHNSON, W. Stacy. "The Genesis of Ariel." *SQ* 2 (1951):205–10.

4165 KOSZUL, A. "Ariel." *ES* 19 (1937):200–04.

4166 MCPEEK, James A. S. "The Genesis of Caliban." *PQ* 25 (1946):378–81.

4167 MANNONI, O. *Prospero and Caliban: The Psychology of Colonization.* Trans. Pamela POWESLAND. 2nd ed., New York: Praeger, 1964. Orig. pub. in Paris in 1950.

4168 REED, Robert R., Jr. "The Probable Origin of Ariel." *SQ* 11 (1960):61–65. Argues the probable origin is Munday's *John a Kent.*

4169 RICKEY, Mary Ellen. "Prospero's Living Drolleries." *RenP 1964* (1965):35–42.

4170 SISSON, Charles J. "The Magic of Prospero." *ShS* 11 (1958):70–77.

4171 SUMMERS, Joseph H. "The Anger of Prospero." *MQR* 12 (1973):116–35.

4172 WEIMANN, Robert. "Puck und Ariel: Mythos und Poetische Phantasie." *SJW* 104 (1968):17–33.

4173 WEST, Robert H. "Ariel and the Outer Mystery." In **1121.** Rpt. in **1448.**

The Masque and Staging

See also **827** and **847**.

4174 BÜCHLER, Klaus. "Explizite und implizite Bühnen- und Spielanweisungen in Shakespeares *Tempest.*" *SJH* (1975):174–78.

4175 GRUDIN, Robert. "Prospero's Masque and the Structure of *The Tempest.*" *SAQ* 71 (1972):401–09.

4176 SHRIMPTON, Nick. "Directing *The Tempest.*" *ShS* 29 (1976):63–67.

4177 SMITH, Irwin. "Ariel and the Masque in *The Tempest.*" *SQ* 21 (1970):213–22.

4178 WICKHAM, Glynne. "Masque and Anti-Masque in *The Tempest.*" *E&S,* n.s. 28 (1975):1–14.

4179 WILLIAM, David. "*The Tempest* on the Stage." *Jacobean Theatre.* Eds. John Russell BROWN and Bernard HARRIS. Stratford-upon-Avon Studies 1. London: Arnold, 1960. Rpt., New York: Capricorn, 1967.

Timon of Athens

See also **1211, 1256, 1380, 1621, 1779, 1781, 1787, 1797, 1975, 1981–82, 2032–35, 2045,** and **2052.**

4180 BERGERON, David M. "Alchemy and *Timon of Athens.*" *CLAJ* 13 (1970): 364–73.

4181 BIZLEY, W. H. "Language and Currency in *Timon of Athens.*" *Theoria* 44 (1975):21–42.

4182 BRADBROOK, M. C. "*The Comedy of Timon:* A Reveling Play of the Inner Temple." *RenD* 9 (1966):83–103.

4183 BRADBROOK, M. C. *The Tragic Pageant of "Timon of Athens."* Cambridge: Cambridge U.P., 1966. Rpt. in **1183** with the title, "Blackfriars: The Pageant of *Timon of Athens.*"

4184 BULMAN, James C., Jr. "The Date and Production of *Timon* Reconsidered." *ShS* 27 (1974):111–27.

4185 BULMAN, James C., Jr. "Shakespeare's Use of the *Timon* Comedy." *ShS* 29 (1976):103–16.

4186 BURKE, Kenneth. "*Timon of Athens* and Misanthropic Gold." In **1188.***

4187 BUTLER, Francelia. *The Strange Critical Fortunes of Shakespeare's "Timon of Athens."* Ames: Iowa State U.P., 1966.

4188 COLLINS, A. S. "*Timon of Athens:* A Reconsideration." *RES* 22 (1946):96–108.

4189 COOK, David. "*Timon of Athens.*" *ShS* 16 (1963):83–94.

4190 DRAPER, R. P. "Timon of Athens." *SQ* 8 (1957):195–200.

4191 ELLIS-FERMOR, Una. "*Timon of Athens:* An Unfinished Play." *RES* 18 (1942):270–83. Rpt. in **1203.**

4192 EMPSON, William. "Timon's Dog." In **530.***

4193 FARNHAM, Willard. "The Beast Theme in Shakespeare's *Timon.*" *UCPE* 14 (1943):49–56.

4194 FLY, Richard D. "The Ending of *Timon of Athens:* A Reconsideration." *Criticism* 15 (1973):242–52.***

4195 FULTON, Robert C., III. "Timon, Cupid, and the Amazons." *ShakS* 9 (1976): 283–99.

4196 GOLDSMITH, Robert Hillis. "Did Shakespeare Use the Old Timon Comedy?" *SQ* 9 (1958):31–38.

4197 GOLDSTEIN, Leonard. "Alcibiades' Revolt in *Timon of Athens.*" *ZAA* 15 (1967):256–78.

4198 GOMME, Andor. *"Timon of Athens." EIC* 9 (1959):107–25.

4199 HONIGMANN, E. A. J. *"Timon of Athens." SQ* 12 (1961):3–20.

4200 KNIGHT, G. Wilson. "The Pilgrimage of Hate." In **1951.**

4201 KNIGHT, G. Wilson. "*Timon of Athens* and Its Dramatic Descendants." *REL* 2.4 (1961):9–18. Rpt. in **1145** (1964 for 1963).

4202 KNIGHTS, L. C. *"Timon of Athens."* In **1146.** Rpt. in *Explorations 3;* see **1229.**

4203 KUCKHOFF, Armin-Gerd. "*Timon von Athen:* Konzeption und Aufführunsspraxis." *SJW* 100–01 (1964–65):135–59.

4204 LANCASHIRE, Anne. *"Timon of Athens:* Shakespeare's *Dr. Faustus." SQ* 21 (1970):35–44.

4205 LEVIN, Harry. "Shakespeare's Misanthrope." *ShS* 26 (1973):89–94. Rpt. in **1233.**

4206 MARTIN, Walther. "Shakespeares *Timon von Athen* im Lichte der Widerspiegelungstheorie." *SJW* 100–01 (1964–65):227–52. Also in *ZAA* 12 (1964): 142–62.

4207 MAXWELL, J. C. *"Timon of Athens." Scrutiny* 15 (1948):195–208.

4208 MAXWELL, J. C., ed. *The Life of Timon of Athens.* In the New Cambridge Shakespeare. See **363.**

4209 MERCHANT, W. Moelwyn. *"Timon of Athens* and the Visual Conceit." In **1559.** An amplified version of an article in *SQ* 6 (1955):249–57.

4210 MORSBERGER, Robert E. *"Timon of Athens:* Tragedy or Satire?" In **1169.**

4211 MUIR, Kenneth. *"Timon of Athens* and the Cash-Nexus." *Modern Quarterly Miscellany* 1 (1947):57–76.

4212 NICHOLS, Marianna da Vinci. *"Timon of Athens* and the Rhetoric of *No."* *CahiersE* 9 (1976):29–40. Argues that the play is not unequivocally tragic or heroic because the play's rhetoric is designed not to move an audience deeply.

4213 NOWOTTNY, Winifred M. T. "Acts IV and V of *Timon of Athens." SQ* 10 (1959):493–97.

4214 OLIVER, H. J., ed. *Timon of Athens.* In the Arden Shakespeare. See **350.**

4215 PAULIN, Bernard. "La Mort de Timon d'Athènes." *EA* 17 (1964):1–8.

4216 PETTET, E. C. *"Timon of Athens:* The Disruption of Feudal Morality." *RES* 23 (1947):321–36.

4217 RAMSEY, Jarold W. "Timon's Imitation of Christ." *ShakS* 2 (1967 for 1966): 162–73.

4218 REID, Stephen A. " 'I Am Misanthropos'—A Psychoanalytic Reading of Shakespeare's *Timon of Athens.*" *PsyR* 56 (1969):442–52.

4219 SPENCER, T. J. B. " 'Greeks' and 'Merrygreeks': A Background to *Timon of Athens* and *Troilus and Cressida.*" In **1144.**

4220 SPENCER, T. J. B. "Shakespeare Learns the Value of Money: The Dramatist at Work on *Timon of Athens.*" *ShS* 6 (1953):75–78.

4221 SWIGG, R. "*Timon of Athens* and the Growth of Discrimination." *MLR* 62 (1967):387–94. Sees the play as asserting the need for a discriminating judgment, enabling man to discern true value amidst confusion and impure motives.

4222 TINKER, Michael. "Theme in *Timon of Athens.*" In **1613.**

4223 WAGGONER, George R. "*Timon of Athens* and the Jacobean Duel." *SQ* 16 (1965):303–11. Argues that the subplot of Alcibiades demonstrates a timely attitude toward duelling.

4224 WALKER, Lewis. "Fortune and Friendship in *Timon of Athens.*" *TSLL* 18 (1977):577–600.

4225 WILLIAMS, Stanley T. "Some Versions of *Timon of Athens* on the Stage." *MP* 18 (1920):269–85.

4226 WOODS, Andrew H. "Syphilis in Shakespeare's Tragedy of *Timon of Athens.*" *American Journal of Psychiatry* 91 (1934):95–107.

Titus Andronicus

See also **149, 539, 554, 584, 1189, 1315, 1580, 1582, 1592–93, 1892, 1927, 1968, 1980, 1999, 2005–10, 2036–55,** and **3785.**

4227 ADAMS, John Cranford. "Shakespeare's Revisions in *Titus Andronicus.*" *SQ* 15.2 (1964):177–90. Also in **1153.**

4228 BAKER, Howard. *Induction to Tragedy: A Study in a Development of Form in "Gorboduc," "The Spanish Tragedy," and "Titus Andronicus."* Baton Rouge: Louisiana State U.P., 1939. Rpt., New York: Russell & Russell.*

4229 BOLTON, Joseph S. G. "*Titus Andronicus:* Shakespeare at Thirty." *SP* 30 (1933):208–24.

4230 BRAEKMAN, W. *Shakespeare's "Titus Andronicus": Its Relationship to the German Play of 1620 and to Jan Vos's "Aran en Titus."* Ghent: Blandijnberg, 1969.

4231 BROUDE, Ronald. "Roman and Goth in *Titus Andronicus.*" *ShakS* 6 (1972 for 1970):27–34.

4232 CANTRELL, Paul L., and George Walton WILLIAMS. "Roberts' Compositors in *Titus Andronicus* Q2." *SB* 8 (1956):27–38.

4233 CUTTS, John P. "Shadow and Substance: Structural Unity in *Titus Andronicus.*" *CompD* 2 (1968):161–72.

4234 DANSON, Lawrence. "The Device of Wonder: *Titus Andronicus* and Revenge Tragedies." *TSLL* 16 (1974):27–43. Rpt., rev., in **1931.***

4235 DESMONDE, William H. "The Ritual Origin of Shakespeare's *Titus Andronicus.*" *International Journal of Psycho-Analysis* 36 (1955):61–65.

4236 DESSEN, Alan C. "Two Falls and a Trap: Shakespeare and the Spectacles of Realism." *ELR* 5 (1975):291–307. Discusses particular scenes in *Titus Andronicus* and *King Lear.* Rpt., rev., in **1296.**

4237 ETTIN, Andrew V. "Shakespeare's First Roman Tragedy." *ELH* 37 (1970): 325–41.

4238 FINDLATER, Richard. "Shakespearean Atrocities." *Twentieth Century* 158 (1955):364–72. A review of Olivier's production of the play at Stratford-upon-Avon.

4239 HAAKER, Ann. "*Non sine causa:* The Use of Emblematic Method and Iconology in the Thematic Structure of *Titus Andronicus.*" *RORD* 13–14 (1970–71):143–68.

4240 HAMILTON, A. C. "*Titus Andronicus:* The Form of Shakespearian Tragedy." *SQ* 14 (1963):201–13. Rpt., rev., in **1586.**

4241 HARRIS, Bernard. "A Portrait of a Moor." *ShS* 11 (1958):89–97.

4242 HARRISON, Thomas P. "*Titus Andronicus* and *King Lear:* A Study in Continuity." In **1171.**

4243 HASTINGS, William T. "The Hardboiled Shakespeare." *ShAB* 17 (1942):114–25.

4244 HILL, R. F. "The Composition of *Titus Andronicus.*" *ShS* 10 (1957):60–70.

4245 HUFFMAN, Clifford Chalmers. "*Titus Andronicus:* Metamorphosis and Renewal." *MLR* 67 (1972):730–41.

4246 HUNTER, G. K. "Shakespeare's Earliest Tragedies: *Titus Andronicus* and *Romeo and Juliet.*" *ShS* 27 (1974):1–9.

4247 KISTNER, A. L., and M. K. KISTNER. "The Senecan Background of Despair in *The Spanish Tragedy* and *Titus Andronicus.*" *ShakS* 7 (1974):1–9.

4248 KRAMER, Joseph E. "*Titus Andronicus:* The 'Fly-Killing' Incident." *ShakS* 5 (1970 for 1969):9–19.

4249 LAW, Robert Adger. "The Roman Background of *Titus Andronicus.*" *SP* 40 (1943):145–53.

4250 MAXWELL, J. C., ed. *Titus Andronicus.* In the Arden Shakespeare. See **350.**

4251 OPPEL, Horst. "*Titus Andronicus*": *Studien zur dramengeschichtlichen Stellung von Shakespeares früher Tragödie.* Heidelberg: Quelle & Meyer, 1961.

4252 PALMER, D. J. "The Unspeakable in Pursuit of the Uneatable: Language and Action in *Titus Andronicus.*" *CritQ* 14 (1972):320–39.

4253 PRICE, Hereward T. "The Authorship of *Titus Andronicus.*" *JEGP* 42 (1943): 55–81. Rpt. in part in **1942.**

4254 PRICE, Hereward T. "The First Quarto of *Titus Andronicus.*" *EIE 1947* (1948): 137–68.

4255 PRICE, Hereward T. "The Language of *Titus Andronicus.*" *PMASAL* 21 (1935): 501–07.

4256 REESE, Jack E. "The Formalization of Horror in *Titus Andronicus.*" *SQ* 21 (1970):77–84.

4257 SARGENT, Ralph M. "The Source of *Titus Andronicus.*" *SP* 46 (1949):167–83.

4258 SCHLÖSSER, Anselm. *"Titus Andronicus."* *SJW* 104 (1968):75–84.

4259 SHADOIAN, Jack. *"Titus Andronicus."* *Discourse* 13 (1970):152–75.

4260 SOMMERS, Alan. " 'Wilderness of Tigers': Structure and Symbolism in *Titus Andronicus.*" *EIC* 10 (1960):275–89.

4261 STAMM, Rudolf. "The Alphabet of Speechless Complaint: A Study of the Mangled Daughter in *Titus Andronicus.*" *ES* 55 (1974):325–39.

4262 STAMM, Rudolf. "Der Gebrauch der Spiegeltechnik in *Titus Andronicus:* Ein Blick in das Regiebuch Shakespeares." *Sprachkunst* 1 (1970):331–57.

4263 STAMM, Rudolf. "Die Gesten des Bösen in Shakespeares *Titus Andronicus.*" *SJH* (1974):48–83.

4264 TOOLE, William B. "The Collision of Action and Character Patterns in *Titus Andronicus:* A Failure in Dramatic Strategy." *RenP 1971* (1972):25–39.

4265 TRICOMI, Albert H. "The Aesthetics of Mutilation in *Titus Andronicus.*" *ShS* 27 (1974):11–19.

4266 TRICOMI, Albert H. "The Mutilated Garden in *Titus Andronicus.*" *ShakS* 9 (1976):89–105.

4267 WAITH, Eugene M. "The Metamorphosis of Violence in *Titus Andronicus.*" *ShS* 10 (1957):39–49.*

4268 WILSON, J. Dover. *"Titus Andronicus* on the Stage in 1595." *ShS* 1 (1948): 17–22.

4269 WILSON, J. Dover, ed. *Titus Andronicus.* In the New Cambridge Shakespeare. See **363.**

Troilus and Cressida

Textual Commentary and Sources

See Also **389** and **4293.**

4270 ALEXANDER, Peter. *"Troilus and Cressida,* 1609." *Library,* 4th ser. 9 (1928): 267–86.

4271 BRADBROOK, M. C. "What Shakespeare Did to Chaucer's *Troilus and Criseyde.*" *SQ* 9 (1958):311–19.

4272 DAWSON, Giles E. "A Bibliographical Problem in the First Folio of Shakespeare." *Library,* 4th ser. 22 (1941–42):25–33.

4273 ELTON, William R. "Textual Transmission and Genre of Shakespeare's *Troilus.*" *Literatur als Kritik des Lebens: Festschrift zum 65. Geburtstag von Ludwig Borinski.* Eds. Rudolf HAAS, Heinz-Joachim MÜLLENBROCK, and Claus UHLIG. Heidelberg: Quelle & Meyer, 1975.

4274 GREG, W. W. "The Printing of Shakespeare's *Troilus and Cressida* in the First Folio." *PBSA* 45 (1951):273–82.

4275 MISKIMIN, Alice S. *The Renaissance Chaucer.* New Haven and London: Yale U.P., 1975, Chap. VII.

4276 PRESSON, Robert K. *Shakespeare's "Troilus and Cressida" and the Legends of Troy.* Madison: U. of Wisconsin P., 1953.

4277 RICHARDS, I. A. "*Troilus and Cressida* and Plato." *HudR* 1 (1948):362–76.

4278 ROLLINS, Hyder E. "The Troilus-Cressida Story from Chaucer to Shakespeare." *PMLA* 32 (1917):383–429.*

4279 RÜEGG, August. "Homerisches und Unhomerisches in Shakespeares *Troilus and Cressida.*" *SJH* (1968):28–42.

4280 SACHAROFF, Mark. "The Traditions of the Troy-Story Heroes and the Problem of Satire in *Troilus and Cressida.*" *ShakS* 6 (1972 for 1970):125–35.

4281 SPENCER, T. J. B. " 'Greeks' and 'Merrygreeks': A Background to *Timon of Athens* and *Troilus and Cressida.*" In **1144.**

4282 TATLOCK, John S. P. "The Siege of Troy in Elizabethan Literature, Especially in Shakespeare and Heywood." *PMLA* 30 (1915):673–770.

4283 WHITAKER, Virgil K. "Still Another Source for *Troilus and Cressida.*" In **1143.**

4284 WILLIAMS, Philip. "The 'Second Issue' of Shakespeare's *Troilus and Cressida,* 1609." *SB* 2 (1949–50):25–33.

4285 WILLIAMS, Philip. "Shakespeare's *Troilus and Cressida:* The Relationship of Quarto and Folio." *SB* 3 (1950–51):131–43.

General Studies

See also **339, 382, 1177, 1201–02, 1268, 1279, 1292, 1459, 1477, 1621, 1628, 1637, 1682, 1779–97, 1911, 1924, 1951, 1981, 2045, 2052, 2057,** and **2346.**

4286 ALMEIDA, Barbara Heliodora C. de M. F. de. "*Troilus and Cressida:* Romantic Love Revisited." *SQ* 15.4 (1964):327–32.

4287 ASP, Carolyn. "Th' Expense of Spirit in a Waste of Shame." *SQ* 22 (1971): 345–57.

4288 BAYLEY, John. "Time and the Trojans." *EIC* 25 (1975):55–73.

4289 BERGER, Harry, Jr. "*Troilus and Cressida:* The Observer as Basilisk." *CompD* 2 (1968):122–36.

4290 BOWDEN, William R. "The Human Shakespeare and *Troilus and Cressida.*" *SQ* 8 (1957):167–77.

4291 BROOKE, C. F. Tucker. "Shakespeare's Study in Culture and Anarchy." *YR* 17 (1928):571–77. Rpt. in **1186.**

4292 CAMPBELL, Oscar James. *Comicall Satyre and Shakespeare's "Troilus and Cressida."* San Marino, Calif.: Huntington Library, 1938.*

4293 COX, John D. "The Error of Our Eye in *Troilus and Cressida.*" *CompD* 10 (1976):147–71.

4294 ELLIS-FERMOR, Una. " 'Discord in the Spheres': The Universe of *Troilus and Cressida.*" *The Frontiers of Drama.* 2nd ed., London: Methuen, 1946.

4295 EMPSON, William. "Double Plots." In **2659.**

4296 ENCK, John J. "The Peace of the Poetomachia." *PMLA* 77 (1962):386–96.

4297 FLY, Richard D. " 'I Cannot Come to Cressid But by Pandar': Mediation in the Theme and Structure of *Troilus and Cressida.*" *ELR* 3 (1973):145–65. Rpt., rev., in **1211.***

4298 FLY, Richard D. " 'Suited in Like Conditions as Our Argument': Imitative Form in Shakespeare's *Troilus and Cressida.*" *SEL* 15 (1975):273–92.*

4299 FOAKES, R. A. "*Troilus and Cressida* Reconsidered." *UTQ* 32 (1963):142–54.

4300 GÉRARD, Albert. "Meaning and Structure in *Troilus and Cressida.*" *ES* 40 (1959):144–57.

4301 GRUDIN, Robert. "The Soul of State: Ulyssean Irony in *Troilus and Cressida.*" *Anglia* 93 (1975):55–69.

4302 HARGREAVES, H. A. "An Essentially Tragic *Troilus and Cressida.*" *HAB* 18.2 (1967):49–60.

4303 HOUSER, David J. "Armor and Motive in *Troilus and Cressida.*" *RenD,* n.s. 4 (1971):121–34.

4304 JONES-DAVIES, M. T. "Discord in Shakespeare's *Troilus and Cressida;* or, The Conflict between 'Angry Mars and Venus Queen of Love.' " *SQ* 25 (1974):33–41.

4305 KAUFMANN, R. J. "Ceremonies for Chaos: The Status of *Troilus and Cressida.*" *ELH* 32 (1965):139–59.

4306 KAULA, David. "Will and Reason in *Troilus and Cressida.*" *SQ* 12 (1961):271–83.

4307 KENDALL, Paul Murray. "Inaction and Ambivalence in *Troilus and Cressida.*" *English Studies in Honor of James Southall Wilson.* Ed. Fredson BOWERS. Charlottesville: U.P. of Virginia, 1951.

4308 KERMODE, Frank. "Opinion, Truth, and Value." *EIC* 5 (1955):181–87. A reply to **4318.**

4309 KIMBROUGH, Robert. *Shakespeare's "Troilus and Cressida" and Its Setting.* Cambridge, Mass.: Harvard U.P., 1964.*

4310 KNIGHTS, L. C. "The Theme of Appearance and Reality in *Troilus and Cressida.*" In **1230.***

4311 KNIGHTS, L. C. "*Troilus and Cressida* Again." *Scrutiny* 18 (1951):144–57.

4312 KNOWLAND, A. S. "*Troilus and Cressida.*" *SQ* 10 (1959):353–65.

4313 LYONS, Charles. "Cressida, Achilles, and the Finite Deed." *EA* 20 (1967):233–42. On Cressida's and Achilles' inability to hold on to what they desire in a changing world.

4314 MARSH, D. R. C. "Interpretation and Misinterpretation: The Problem of *Troilus and Cressida.*" *ShakS* 1 (1965):182–98.

4315 MORRIS, Brian. "The Tragic Structure of *Troilus and Cressida.*" *SQ* 10 (1959):481–91.

4316 MUIR, Kenneth. "*Troilus and Cressida.*" *ShS* 8 (1955):28–39.

4317 NEWLIN, Jeanne T. "The Modernity of *Troilus and Cressida:* The Case for Theatrical Criticism." *Harvard Lib. Bull.* 17 (1969):353–73.

4318 NOWOTTNY, Winifred M. T. " 'Opinion' and 'Value' in *Troilus and Cressida.*" *EIC* 4 (1954):282–96.

4319 OATES, Joyce Carol. "The Ambiguity of *Troilus and Cressida.*" *SQ* 17 (1966): 141–50.

4320 POTTS, Abbie Findlay. *"Cynthia's Revels, Poetaster,* and *Troilus and Cressida.*" *SQ* 5 (1954):297–302.

4321 RABKIN, Norman. *"Troilus and Cressida:* The Uses of the Double Plot." *ShakS* 1 (1965):265–82. Rpt., rev., in **1243,** as "Self Against Self." Rpt. also in **1125.** *

4322 RAMSEY, Jarold W. "The Provenance of *Troilus and Cressida.*" *SQ* 21 (1970): 223–40. Investigates the sort of theater and audience for which Shakespeare evidently wrote the play, and asks whether it was staged at all.

4323 REYNOLDS, George F. *"Troilus and Cressida* on the Elizabethan Stage." In **1154.**

4324 RICKEY, Mary Ellen. " 'Twixt the Dangerous Shores: *Troilus and Cressida* Again." *SQ* 15.1 (1964):3–13.

4325 ROSSITER, A. P. *"Troilus and Cressida."* In **1245.**

4326 ROY, Emil. "War and Manliness in Shakespeare's *Troilus and Cressida.*" *CompD* 7 (1973):107–20.

4327 SCHWARTZ, Elias. "Tonal Equivocation and the Meaning of *Troilus and Cressida.*" *SP* 69 (1972):304–19.

4328 SEEHASE, Georg. "William Shakespeares *Troilus und Cressida*—Originalität und Bearbeitung." *SJW* 110 (1974):62–77.

4329 SLIGHTS, Camille. "The Parallel Structure of *Troilus and Cressida.*" *SQ* 25 (1974):42–51.

4330 SMITH, J. Oates. "Essence and Existence in Shakespeare's *Troilus and Cressida.*" *PQ* 46 (1967):167–85.

4331 SOUTHALL, Raymond. *"Troilus and Cressida* and the Spirit of Capitalism." In **1148.**

4332 STAMM, Rudolf. "The Glass of Pandar's Praise: The Word-Scenery, Mirror Passages, and Reported Scenes in Shakespeare's *Troilus and Cressida.*" *E&S,* n.s. 17 (1964):55–77. Rpt. in **1255.**

4333 STEIN, Arnold. *"Troilus and Cressida:* The Disjunctive Imagination." *ELH* 36 (1969):145–67.

4334 STOCKHOLDER, Katherine. "Power and Pleasure in *Troilus and Cressida,* or Rhetoric and Structure of the Anti-Tragic." *CE* 30 (1969):539–54.

4335 SWANSTON, Hamish F. G. "The Baroque Element in *Troilus and Cressida.*" *DUJ* 50, n.s. 19 (1957):14–23.

4336 TAYLOR, George Coffin. "Shakespeare's Attitude towards Love and Honor in *Troilus and Cressida.*" *PMLA* 45 (1930):781–86.

4337 TRAVERSI, Derek. *"Troilus and Cressida."* *Scrutiny* 7 (1938):301–19.

4338 YODER, R. A. " 'Sons and Daughters of the Game': An Essay on Shakespeare's *Troilus and Cressida.*" *ShS* 25 (1972):11–25.

Character Studies

See also **1211, 1372,** and **1380.**

4339 BONNEY, James. "Shakespeare's Heroic Warriors." *Discourse* 11 (1968):257–68.

4340 DUNKEL, Wilbur D. "Shakespeare's Troilus." *SQ* 2 (1951):331–34.

4341 DYER, Frederick B., Jr. "The Destruction of Pandare." In **1160.**

4342 ELTON, William R. "Shakespeare's Portrait of Ajax in *Troilus and Cressida.*" *PMLA* 63 (1948):744–48.

4343 ELTON, William R. "Shakespeare's Ulysses and the Problem of Value." *ShakS* 2 (1967 for 1966):95–111. Also published in German in *SJW* 104 (1968):49–74.

4344 FARNHAM, Willard. "Troilus in Shapes of Infinite Desire." *SQ* 15.2 (1964): 257–64. Also in **1153.**

4345 FRIEDMAN, Lester D. "Shakespeare's Ambiguous Hero: A Re-examination of Hector." *Thoth* 12.2 (1972):50–58.

4346 GAGEN, Jean. "Hector's Honor." *SQ* 19 (1968):129–37.

4347 HARRIER, Richard C. "Troilus Divided." In **1119.**

4348 KENNY, Hamill. "Shakespeare's Cressida." *Anglia* 61 (1937):163–76.

4349 KIMBROUGH, Robert. "The Problem of Thersites." *MLR* 59 (1964):173–76.

4350 LAWRENCE, W. W. "Troilus, Cressida, and Thersites." *MLR* 37 (1942):422–37.

4351 MAIN, William W. "Character Amalgams in Shakespeare's *Troilus and Cressida.*" *SP* 58 (1961):170–78.

4352 REID, Stephen A. "A Psychoanalytic Reading of *Troilus and Cressida* and *Measure for Measure.*" *PsyR* 57 (1970):263–82.

4353 SACHAROFF, Mark. "Thersites as Crucial Figure in Shakespeare's *Troilus and Cressida.*" *HAB* 21.4 (1970):3–9.

4354 THOMPSON, Karl F. "The Unknown Ulysses." *SQ* 19 (1968):125–28.

4355 VOTH, Grant L., and Oliver H. EVANS. "Cressida and the World of the Play." *ShakS* 8 (1975):231–39.

Particular Scenes or Passages

4356 ARNOLD, Aerol. "The Hector-Andromache Scene in Shakespeare's *Troilus and Cressida.*" *MLQ* 14 (1953):335–40.

4357 BONJOUR, Adrien. "Hector and the 'One in Sumptuous Armour.'" *ES* 45 (1964):104–08.

4358 DANIELS, F. Quinland. "Order and Confusion in *Troilus and Cressida* I. iii." *SQ* 12 (1961):285–91.

4359 KLEINSTÜCK, Johannes. "Ulysses' Speech on Degree as Related to the Play of *Troilus and Cressida.*" *Neophil* 43 (1959):58–63.

4360 LYONS, Clifford P. "The Trysting Scenes in *Troilus and Cressida.*" In **1171.**

4361 SACHAROFF, Mark. "The Orations of Agamemnon and Nestor in Shake-speare's *Troilus and Cressida.*" *TSLL* 14 (1972):223–34.

4362 SACHAROFF, Mark. "Tragic vs. Satiric: Hector's Conduct in II, ii of Shake-speare's *Troilus and Cressida.*" *SP* 67 (1970):517–31.

4363 SOELLNER, Rolf. "Prudence and the Price of Helen: The Debate of the Trojans in *Troilus and Cressida.*" *SQ* 20 (1969):255–63.

Language and Imagery

4364 FLY, Richard D. "Cassandra and the Language of Prophecy in *Troilus and Cressida.*" *SQ* 26 (1975):157–71.

4365 KAULA, David. " 'Mad Idolatry' in Shakespeare's *Troilus and Cressida.*" *TSLL* 15 (1973):25–38. On biblical analogies.

4366 MCALINDON, T. "Language, Style, and Meaning in *Troilus and Cressida.*" *PMLA* 84 (1969):29–43. See also response by Mark SACHAROFF. *PMLA* 87 (1972):90–93.

4367 SCHMIDT DI SIMONI, Karen. *Shakespeares "Troilus and Cressida": Eine sprachlich-stilistische Untersuchung.* Heidelberg: Quelle & Meyer, 1960.

4368 SHALVI, Alice. " 'Honor' in *Troilus and Cressida.*" *SEL* 5 (1965):283–302.

4369 STAFFORD, Tony J. "Mercantile Imagery in *Troilus and Cressida.*" In **1169.**

4370 THOMSON, Patricia. "Rant and Cant in *Troilus and Cressida.*" *E&S,* n.s. 22 (1969):33–56.

Twelfth Night

Sources

See also **87.**

4371 KAUFMAN, Helen Andrews. "Nicolò Secchi as a Source of *Twelfth Night.*" *SQ* 5 (1954):271–80.

4372 KING, Walter N. "Shakespeare and Parmenides: The Metaphysics of *Twelfth Night.*" *SEL* 8 (1968):284–306.

4373 MELZI, Robert C. "From Lelia to Viola." *RenD* 9 (1966):67–81.

4374 PRUVOST, René. "*The Two Gentlemen of Verona, Twelfth Night,* et *Gl'Ingan-nati.*" *EA* 13 (1960):1–9.

4375 PYLE, Fitzroy. "*Twelfth Night, King Lear,* and *Arcadia.*" *MLR* 43 (1948): 449–55.

4376 SIMMONS, J. L. "A Source for Shakespeare's Malvolio: The Elizabethan Contro-versy with the Puritans." *HLQ* 36 (1973):181–201.

General Studies

See also **510, 526, 1183, 1221, 1226, 1234, 1289, 1628, 1631, 1637, 1666, 1671,** and **1719–33.**

4377 BARTON, Anne. "*As You Like It* and *Twelfth Night:* Shakespeare's Sense of an Ending." In **1722.**

4378 BENNETT, Josephine Waters. "Topicality and the Date of the Court Production of *Twelfth Night.*" *SAQ* 71 (1972):473–79.

4379 BROWN, John Russell. "Directions for *Twelfth Night,* or What You Will." *TDR* 5.4 (1961):77–88. Rpt. in **905.**

4380 CRANE, Milton. "*Twelfth Night* and Shakespearian Comedy." *SQ* 6 (1955):1–8.

4381 DENNIS, Carl. "The Vision of *Twelfth Night.*" *TSL* 18 (1973):63–74.

4382 DRAPER, John W. *The "Twelfth Night" of Shakespeare's Audience.* Stanford: Stanford U.P.; London: Oxford U.P., 1950. Rpt., New York: Octagon, 1975. For a response, see Norman A. BRITTIN, "The *Twelfth Night* of Shakespeare and of Professor Draper." *SQ* 7 (1956):211–16.

4383 EAGLETON, Terence. "Language and Reality in *Twelfth Night.*" *CritQ* 9 (1967):217–28.

4384 FORBES, Lydia. "What You Will?" *SQ* 13 (1962):475–85.

4385 FORTIN, René E. "*Twelfth Night:* Shakespeare's Drama of Initiation." *PLL* 8 (1972):135–46.

4386 GÉRARD, Albert. "Shipload of Fools: A Note on *Twelfth Night.*" *ES* 45 (1964): 109–15.

4387 GREG, W. W. "When Was Twelfth Night?" In **1131.**

4388 HARDY, Barbara. *Twelfth Night.* Oxford: Blackwell, 1962.

4389 HARTWIG, Joan. "Feste's 'Whirligig' and the Comic Providence of *Twelfth Night.*" *ELH* 40 (1973):501–13.

4390 HENZE, Richard. "*Twelfth Night:* Free Disposition on the Sea of Love." *SR* 83 (1975):267–83.

4391 HOLLAND, Norman N. "Cuckold or Counsellor in *Twelfth Night,* I. v. 56." *SQ* 8 (1957):127–29.

4392 HOLLANDER, John. "*Musica Mundana* and *Twelfth Night.*" *EIE 1956* (1957): 55–82.

4393 HOLLANDER, John. "*Twelfth Night* and the Morality of Indulgence." *SR* 67 (1959):220–38. Rpt. in **1125** and **1731.***

4394 HOTSON, Leslie. *The First Night of "Twelfth Night."* London: Hart-Davis; New York: Macmillan, 1954.

4395 HUSTON, J. Dennis. " 'When I Came to Man's Estate': *Twelfth Night* and Problems of Identity." *MLQ* 33 (1972):274–88.

4396 JENKINS, Harold. "Shakespeare's *Twelfth Night.*" *RIP* 45.4 (1959):19–42. Rpt. in **1660.***

4397 KING, Walter N., ed. *Twentieth Century Interpretations of "Twelfth Night."* Englewood Cliffs, N.J.: Prentice-Hall, 1968. A collection of essays.

4398 LAWRY, Jon S. "*Twelfth Night* and 'Salt Waves Fresh in Love.' " *ShakS* 6 (1972 for 1970):89–108.

4399 LEECH, Clifford. *"Twelfth Night" and Shakespearian Comedy.* Toronto: U. of Toronto P., 1965.*

4400 LEVIN, Harry. "The Underplot of *Twelfth Night.*" *De Shakespeare à T. S. Eliot: Mélanges offerts à Henri Fluchère.* Eds. M. J. DURRY, Robert ELLRODT, and M. T. JONES-DAVIES. Paris: Librairie Marcel Didier, 1975. Rpt. in **1233.**

4401 LEWALSKI, Barbara K. "Thematic Patterns in *Twelfth Night.*" *ShakS* 1 (1965): 168–81.

4402 LOTHIAN, John M., and T. W. CRAIK, eds. *Twelfth Night.* In the Arden Shakespeare. See **350.**

4403 MANHEIM, Leonard F. "The Mythical Joys of Shakespeare: Or, What You Will." In **1160.** Rpt. in **1401.**

4404 MARKELS, Julian. "Shakespeare's Confluence of Tragedy and Comedy: *Twelfth Night* and *King Lear.*" *SQ* 15.2 (1964):75–88. Also in **1153.**

4405 MINCOFF, Marco. "*Twelfth Night:* An End and a Beginning." *Filoloski Pregled* (Beograd) 1–2 (1964):117–29.

4406 MUESCHKE, Paul, and Jeannette FLEISHER. "Jonsonian Elements in the Comic Underplot of *Twelfth Night.*" *PMLA* 48 (1933):722–40.

4407 NAGARAJAN, S. " 'What You Will': A Suggestion." *SQ* 10 (1959):61–67.

4408 PALMER, D. J. "Art and Nature in *Twelfth Night.*" *CritQ* 9 (1967):201–12.

4409 PALMER, D. J., ed. *Shakespeare, "Twelfth Night": A Casebook.* London: Macmillan, 1972.

4410 PROUTY, Charles Tyler. *"Twelfth Night."* In **1145** (1969 for 1965–67).

4411 SALINGAR, Leo. "The Design of *Twelfth Night.*" *SQ* 9 (1958):117–39. Rpt. in **1731.***

4412 SCHWARTZ, Elias. "*Twelfth Night* and the Meaning of Shakespearean Comedy." *CE* 28 (1967):508–19.

4413 SUMMERS, Joseph H. "The Masks of *Twelfth Night.*" *UR* 22 (1955):25–32. Rpt. in **1132** and **1731.***

4414 TAYLOR, Michael. "*Twelfth Night* and *What You Will.*" *CritQ* 16 (1974): 71–80.

4415 TILLEY, Morris Palmer. "The Organic Unity of *Twelfth Night.*" *PMLA* 29 (1914):550–66.

4416 WEAVER, John J. W. "The Other Twin: Sebastian's Relationship to Viola and the Theme of *Twelfth Night.*" In **1149.**

4417 WILLIAMS, Porter, Jr. "Mistakes in *Twelfth Night* and Their Resolution: A Study in Some Relationships of Plot and Theme." *PMLA* 76 (1961):193–99.

Character Studies

See also **1370, 1374, 1387, 1396, 1696, 1706,** and **1709.**

4418 BARNET, Sylvan. "Charles Lamb and the Tragic Malvolio." *PQ* 33 (1954): 178–88.

4419 BRADLEY, A. C. "Feste the Jester." In **1141**. Rpt. in **1184**.

4420 DOWNER, Alan S. "Feste's Night." *CE* 13 (1952):258–65. Argues that Feste sounds the play's theme of disguise and foolery.*

4421 MARES, F. H. "Viola and Other Transvestite Heroines in Shakespeare's Comedies." In **1145** (1969 for 1965–67).

4422 MOGLEN, Helene. "Disguise and Development: The Self and Society in *Twelfth Night.*" *L&P* 23 (1973):13–20.

4423 PRESTON, Dennis R. "The Minor Characters in *Twelfth Night.*" *SQ* 21 (1970): 167–76.

4424 SEIDEN, Melvin. "Malvolio Reconsidered." *UKCR* 28 (1961):105–14.

4425 SISSON, Charles J. "Tudor Intelligence Tests: Malvolio and Real Life." In **1144.**

The Two Gentlemen of Verona

See also **118, 1578–96, 1631, 1637, 1640, 1651, 1666, 1700, 1712–18, 1721, 1727, 1729–30,** and **1733.**

4426 ATKINSON, Dorothy F. "The Source of *The Two Gentlemen of Verona.*" *SP* 41 (1944):223–34.

4427 BROOKS, Harold F. "Two Clowns in a Comedy (to Say Nothing of the Dog): Speed, Launce (and Crab) in *The Two Gentlemen of Verona.*" *E&S*, n.s. 16 (1963):91–100.

4428 CAMPBELL, Oscar James. "*The Two Gentlemen of Verona* and Italian Comedy." In *Studies in Shakespeare, Milton, and Donne;* see **3210.**

4429 DANBY, John F. "Shakespeare Criticism and *Two Gentlemen of Verona.*" *CritQ* 2 (1960):309–21.

4430 EWBANK, Inga-Stina. " 'Were Man But Constant, He Were Perfect': Constancy and Consistency in *The Two Gentlemen of Verona.*" In **1722.***

4431 GODSHALK, William Leigh. "The Structural Unity of *Two Gentlemen of Verona.*" *SP* 66 (1969):168–81.

4432 JAARSMA, Richard J. "The 'Lear Complex' in *The Two Gentlemen of Verona.*" *L&P* 22 (1972):199–202.

4433 KNORR, Friedrich. *"Die Beiden Veroneser."* Donum Autumnale III-V. Coburg: Coburger Dienstagsgesellschaft, 1957–59.

4434 LINDENBAUM, Peter. "Education in *The Two Gentlemen of Verona.*" *SEL* 15 (1975):229–44.*

4435 PARKS, George B. "The Development of *The Two Gentlemen of Verona.*" *Huntington Lib. Bull.* 11 (1937):1–11.

4436 PERRY, Thomas A. "Proteus, Wry-Transformed Traveller." *SQ* 5 (1954):33–40.

4437 PRUVOST, René. "*The Two Gentlemen of Verona, Twelfth Night*, et *Gl'Ingannati.*" *EA* 13 (1960):1–9.

4438 SARGENT, Ralph M. "Sir Thomas Elyot and the Integrity of *The Two Gentlemen of Verona.*" *PMLA* 65 (1950):1166–80.

4439 SCHEYE, Thomas E. "Two Gentlemen of Milan." *ShakS* 7 (1974):11–23.

4440 SCHLÖSSER, Anselm. "Betrachtungen über *Die beiden Veroneser.*" *SJW* 103 (1967):145–55.

4441 SCOTT, William O. "Proteus in Spenser and Shakespeare: The Lover's Identity." *ShakS* 1 (1965):283–93.

4442 SMALL, Samuel Asa. "The Ending of *The Two Gentlemen of Verona.*" *PMLA* 48 (1933):767–76.

4443 STEPHENSON, William E. "The Adolescent Dream-World of *The Two Gentlemen of Verona.*" *SQ* 17 (1966):165–68.

4444 WEIMANN, Robert. "Laughing with the Audience: *The Two Gentlemen of Verona* and the Popular Tradition of Comedy." *ShS* 22 (1969):35–42. Pub. also in German in *SJW* 106 (1970):85–99.

4445 WELLS, Stanley. "The Failure of *The Two Gentlemen of Verona.*" *SJ* 99 (1963): 161–73.

The Winter's Tale

General Studies

See also **1035, 1177, 1201, 1204, 1216, 1226, 1358, 1419, 1508, 1559, 1598–1615, 1637, 1651, 1666, 1687, 1735–77,** and **2241.**

4446 BARBER, C. L. " 'Thou That Beget'st Him That Did Thee Beget': Transformation in *Pericles* and *The Winter's Tale.*" *ShS* 22 (1969):59–67.*

4447 BARBER, Charles. "*The Winter's Tale* and Jacobean Society." In **1148.**

4448 BETHELL, S. L. "*The Winter's Tale*": *A Study*. London: Staples, 1947. Rpt., Folcroft, Pa.: Folcroft, 1974.

4449 BIGGINS, Dennis. " 'Exit Pursued by a Beare': A Problem in *The Winter's Tale.*" *SQ* 13 (1962):3–13.

4450 BLISSETT, William. "This Wide Gap of Time: *The Winter's Tale.*" *ELR* 1 (1971):52–70.

4451 BONJOUR, Adrien. "The Final Scene of *The Winter's Tale.*" *ES* 33 (1952): 193–208.

4452 BRYANT, J. A., Jr. "Shakespeare's Allegory: *The Winter's Tale.*" *SR* 63 (1955): 202–22. Rpt., rev., in **1413.**

4453 BRYANT, Jerry H. "*The Winter's Tale* and the Pastoral Tradition." *SQ* 14 (1963):387–98.

4454 CLUBB, Louise George. "The Tragicomic Bear." *CLS* 9 (1972):17–30.

4455 COGHILL, Nevill. "Six Points of Stage-Craft in *The Winter's Tale.*" *ShS* 11 (1958):31–41.

4456 EWBANK, Inga-Stina. "The Triumph of Time in *The Winter's Tale.*" *REL* 5.2 (1964):83–100. Rpt. in **1766.**

4457 FRYE, Northrop. "Recognition in *The Winter's Tale.*" In **1144.** Rpt. in **1125.***

4458 HARTWIG, Joan. "The Tragicomic Perspective of *The Winter's Tale.*" *ELH* 37 (1970):12–36. Rpt., rev., in **1752.**

4459 HELLENGA, Robert R. "The Scandal of *The Winter's Tale.*" *ES* 57 (1976): 11–18.

4460 HOENIGER, F. David. "The Meaning of *The Winter's Tale.*" *UTQ* 20 (1950): 11–26.*

4461 KAULA, David. "Autolycus' Trumpery." *SEL* 16 (1976):287–303. On Anti-Catholic allusions in *The Winter's Tale.*

4462 KNIGHT, G. Wilson. "Great Creating Nature." In **1605.**

4463 LANCASTER, H. Carrington. "Hermione's Statue." *SP* 29 (1932):233–38.

4464 LAROQUE, François. "Feasts and Festivity in *The Winter's Tale:* A Study of the 'Sheep-Shearing' Scenes." *CahiersE* 6 (1974):8–14.

4465 LAWLOR, John. "*Pandosto* and the Nature of Dramatic Romance." *PQ* 41 (1962):96–113. Also in **1174.**

4466 LINDENBAUM, Peter. "Time, Sexual Love, and the Uses of Pastoral in *The Winter's Tale.*" *MLQ* 33 (1972):3–22.*

4467 LIVINGSTON, Mary L. "The Natural Art of *The Winter's Tale.*" *MLQ* 30 (1969):340–55.

4468 MARTINET, Marie-Madeleine. "*The Winter's Tale* et 'Julio Romano.'" *EA* 28 (1975):257–68.

4469 MATCHETT, William H. "Some Dramatic Techniques in *The Winter's Tale.*" *ShS* 22 (1969):93–107.

4470 MAVEETY, Stanley R. "What Shakespeare Did with *Pandosto:* An Interpretation of *The Winter's Tale.*" In **1156.**

4471 MELDRUM, Ronald M. "Dramatic Intention in *The Winter's Tale.*" *HAB* 19.2 (1968):52–60.

4472 MOWAT, Barbara A. "A Tale of Sprights and Goblins." *SQ* 20 (1969):37–46. Argues that Leontes is not a tragic hero, but a type appropriate to comedy. Rpt., rev., in **1761.**

4473 MUELLER, Martin. "Hermione's Wrinkles, or, Ovid Transformed: An Essay on *The Winter's Tale.*" *CompD* 5 (1971):226–39.

4474 MUIR, Kenneth. "The Conclusion of *The Winter's Tale.*" In **1146.**

4475 MUIR, Kenneth, ed. *Shakespeare, "The Winter's Tale": A Casebook.* London: Macmillan, 1968.

4476 NUTTALL, A. D. *William Shakespeare: "The Winter's Tale."* London: Arnold, 1966.

4477 PAFFORD, J. H. P. "Music, and the Songs in *The Winter's Tale.*" *SQ* 10 (1959):161–75.

4478 PAFFORD, J. H. P., ed. *The Winter's Tale.* In the Arden Shakespeare. See **350.**

4479 PYLE, Fitzroy. *"The Winter's Tale": A Commentary on the Structure.* London: Routledge & K. Paul; New York: Barnes & Noble, 1969.

4480 RAVENSCROFT, Arthur. "Monstrous to Our Human Reason: The Limits of Knowledge in *The Winter's Tale.*" *Seven Studies in English for Dorothy Cavers.* Ed. Gildas ROBERTS. Cape Town and London: Purnell, 1971.

4481 SCHANZER, Ernest. "The Structural Pattern of *The Winter's Tale.*" *REL* 5.2 (1964):72–82.*

4482 SCOTT, William O. "Seasons and Flowers in *The Winter's Tale.*" *SQ* 14 (1963): 411–17.

4483 SIEMON, James Edward. " 'But It Appears She Lives': Iteration in *The Winter's Tale.*" *PMLA* 89 (1974):10–16.

4484 STUDING, Richard. "Spectacle and Masque in *The Winter's Tale.*" *EM* 21 (1970):55–80.

4485 TAYLER, Edward William. *"The Winter's Tale." Nature and Art in Renaissance Literature.* New York: Columbia U.P., 1964.

4486 TAYLOR, John. "The Patience of *The Winter's Tale.*" *EIC* 23 (1973):333–56.

4487 TAYLOR, Michael. "Shakespeare's *The Winter's Tale:* Speaking in the Freedom of Knowledge." *CritQ* 14 (1972):49–56.

4488 THORNE, William Barry. " 'Things Newborn': A Study of the Rebirth Motif in *The Winter's Tale.*" *HAB* 19.1 (1968):34–43.

4489 TINKLER, F. C. *"The Winter's Tale." Scrutiny* 5 (1937):344–64.

4490 WEINSTEIN, Philip M. "An Interpretation of Pastoral in *The Winter's Tale.*" *SQ* 22 (1971):97–109.

4491 WICKHAM, Glynne. "Romance and Emblem: A Study in the Dramatic Structure of *The Winter's Tale.*" In **607,** vol. 3 (1973 for 1970).

4492 WILLIAMS, John Anthony. *The Natural Work of Art: The Experience of Romance in Shakespeare's "Winter's Tale."* Cambridge, Mass.: Harvard U.P.; London: Oxford U.P., 1967.*

Character Studies

See also **1376, 1391, 1711,** and **4472.**

4493 BONJOUR, Adrien. "Polixenes and the Winter of His Discontent." *ES* 50 (1969):206–12.

4494 COX, Lee Sheridan. "The Role of Autolycus in *The Winter's Tale.*" *SEL* 9 (1969):283–301.

4495 FOAKES, R. A. "Character and Dramatic Technique in *Cymbeline* and *The Winter's Tale.*" See **2367.**

4496 HOFLING, Charles K. "Notes on Shakespeare's *The Winter's Tale.*" *PsyR* 58 (1971):90–110.

4497 HUGHES, Merritt Y. "A Classical vs. a Social Approach to Shakespeare's Autolycus." *ShAB* 15 (1940):219–26.

4498 NATHAN, Norman. "Leontes' Provocation." *SQ* 19 (1968):19–24.

4499 REID, Stephen A. *"The Winter's Tale."* *AI* 27 (1970):263–78.

4500 SCHWARTZ, Murray M. "Leontes' Jealousy in *The Winter's Tale.*" *AI* 30 (1973):250–73.

4501 SCHWARTZ, Murray M. *"The Winter's Tale:* Loss and Transformation." *AI* 32 (1975):145–99. An elaboration on the above item.

4502 SIEGEL, Paul N. "Leontes a Jealous Tyrant." *RES,* n.s. 1 (1950):302–07.

4503 SMITH, Hallett. "Leontes' 'Affectio.' " *SQ* 14 (1963):163–66.

4504 SMITH, Jonathan. "The Language of Leontes." *SQ* 19 (1968):317–27.

4505 TRIENENS, Roger J. "The Inception of Leontes' Jealousy in *The Winter's Tale.*" *SQ* 4 (1953):321–26.

Language and Imagery

See also **541, 1358, 4488,** and **4504.**

4506 GOURLAY, Patricia Southard. " 'O My Most Sacred Lady': Female Metaphor in *The Winter's Tale.*" *ELR* 5 (1975):375–95.

4507 NEELY, Carol Thomas. *"The Winter's Tale:* The Triumph of Speech." *SEL* 15 (1975):321–38.

4508 PROUDFOOT, G. Richard. "Verbal Reminiscence and the Two-Part Structure of *The Winter's Tale.*" *ShS* 29 (1976):67–78.

4509 TROUSDALE, Marion. "Style in *The Winter's Tale.*" *CritQ* 18 (1976):25–32.

4510 WILSON, Harold S. " 'Nature and Art' in *Winter's Tale* (IV, iv, 86 ff)." *ShAB* 18 (1943):114–20.

Shakespeare's Poems

General Studies of the Sonnets and the Other Poems

See also **316, 1356,** and **1580.**

4511 ALPERS, Paul J., ed. *Elizabethan Poetry: Modern Essays in Criticism.* New York: Oxford U.P., 1967.

4512 BROWN, John Russell, and Bernard HARRIS, eds. *Elizabethan Poetry.* Stratford-upon-Avon Studies 2. London: Arnold, 1960.

4513 PRINCE, F. T. *William Shakespeare: The Poems.* London: Longmans, Green, 1963. Includes discussion of the Sonnets and the other poems.

4514 *Shakespeare Survey* 15 (1962). Devoted chiefly to the poems and music, including the Sonnets.

4515 SMITH, Hallett. *Elizabethan Poetry*. Cambridge, Mass.: Harvard U.P., 1952, chaps. 2 and 3.

The Sonnets

See also **64, 316, 377, 385, 474, 541, 1025, 1191, 1202, 1447, 1526, 2105,** and **4515.**

4516 AKRIGG, G. P. V. "The Shakespeare of the Sonnets." *QQ* 72 (1965):78–90.

4517 BARBER, C. L. "An Essay on the Sonnets." *The Laurel Shakespeare: The Sonnets.* Western Printing & Lithograph, 1960. Rpt. in **4511.***

4518 BATES, Paul A. "Shakespeare's Sonnets and Pastoral Poetry." *SJW* 103 (1967): 81–96.

4519 BATESON, F. W. "Elementary, My Dear Hotson! A Caveat for Literary Detectives." *EIC* 1 (1951):81–88. A reply to **4538.** Rpt. in **4535.***

4520 BEECHING, H. C., ed. *The Sonnets of Shakespeare.* Boston and London: Ginn, 1904.

4521 BERRY, Francis. " 'Thou' and 'You' in Shakespeare's *Sonnets.* " *EIC* 8 (1958): 138–46.

4522 BOOTH, Stephen. *An Essay on Shakespeare's Sonnets.* New Haven and London: Yale U.P., 1969.*

4523 BOYETTE, Purvis E. "Shakespeare's Sonnets: Homosexuality and the Critics." *TSE* 21 (1974):35–46.

4524 FERRY, Anne. *All in War with Time: Love Poetry of Shakespeare, Donne, Jonson, Marvell.* Cambridge, Mass., and London: Harvard U.P., 1975. Chap. I, "Shakespeare," pp. 3–63.*

4525 GOLDSMITH, Ulrich K. "Words Out of a Hat? Alliteration and Assonance in Shakespeare's Sonnets." *JEGP* 49 (1950):33–48.

4526 GOLDSTIEN, Neal L. "Money and Love in Shakespeare's Sonnets." *BuR* 17.3 (1969):91–106.

4527 GRAVES, Robert, and Laura RIDING. "A Study in Original Punctuation and Spelling." *The Common Asphodel: Collected Essays on Poetry, 1922–1949.* London: H. Hamilton, 1949.

4528 GREEN, A. Wigfall. "Significant Words in Shakespeare's Sonnets." *UMSE* 3 (1962):95–113.

4529 GREEN, Martin. *The Labyrinth of Shakespeare's Sonnets: An Examination of Sexual Elements in Shakespeare's Language.* London: C. Skilton, 1974.

4530 GRIVELET, Michel. "Shakespeare's 'War with Time': The Sonnets and *Richard II.*" *ShS* 23 (1970):69–78.

4531 GRUNDY, Joan. "Shakespeare's Sonnets and the Elizabethan Sonneteers." *ShS* 15 (1962):41–49.

4532 GURR, Andrew. "Shakespeare's First Poem: Sonnet 145." *EIC* 21 (1971):221–26.

4533 HARBAGE, Alfred. "Dating Shakespeare's Sonnets." *SQ* 1 (1950):57–63.

4534 HAYASHI, Tetsumaro. *Shakespeare's Sonnets: A Record of 20th-Century Criticism.* Metuchen, N.J.: Scarecrow, 1972.

IMPORTANT MESSAGE

FOR _____

DATE _____ TIME _____ A.M.
P.M.

M _____

OF _____

PHONE _____
AREA CODE   NUMBER   EXTENSION

TELEPHONED		PLEASE CALL	
CAME TO SEE YOU		WILL CALL AGAIN	
WANTS TO SEE YOU		RUSH	
RETURNED YOUR CALL		SPECIAL ATTENTION	

MESSAGE _____

_____

_____

_____

_____

_____

SIGNED _____

LITHO IN U.S.A.

71100

4535 HERRNSTEIN, Barbara, ed. *Discussions of Shakespeare's Sonnets.* Boston: Heath, 1964. A collection of essays.

4536 HOBDAY, C. H. "Shakespeare's Venus and Adonis Sonnets." *ShS* 26 (1973): 103–09.

4537 HOTSON, Leslie. *Mr. W. H.* See **174.**

4538 HOTSON, Leslie. *Shakespeare's Sonnets Dated and Other Essays.* London: Hart-Davis; New York: Oxford U.P., 1949.

4539 HUBLER, Edward. *The Sense of Shakespeare's Sonnets.* Princeton: Princeton U.P., 1952; New York: Hill & Wang, 1962.*

4540 HUBLER, Edward, Northrop FRYE, Leslie A. FIEDLER, Stephen SPENDER, and R. P. BLACKMUR. *The Riddle of Shakespeare's Sonnets.* New York: Basic Books, 1962.*

4541 HUNTER, G. K. "The Dramatic Technique of Shakespeare's Sonnets." *EIC* 3 (1953):152–64.*

4542 INGRAM, W. G., and Theodore REDPATH, eds. *Shakespeare's Sonnets.* London: U. of London P., 1964; New York: Barnes & Noble, 1965.

4543 JAKOBSON, Roman, and Lawrence G. JONES. *Shakespeare's Verbal Art in "Th' Expense of Spirit."* The Hague and Paris: Mouton, 1970.

4544 KAULA, David. " 'In War with Time': Temporal Perspectives in Shakespeare's Sonnets." *SEL* 3 (1963):45–57.

4545 KNIGHT, G. Wilson. *The Mutual Flame.* See **4602.**

4546 KNIGHTS, L. C. "Shakespeare's Sonnets." *Scrutiny* 3 (1934):133–60. Rpt. in **1228** and **4511.***

4547 KNIGHTS, L. C. "Time's Subjects: The Sonnets and *King Henry IV, Part II.*" In **1230.***

4548 KRIEGER, Murray. "The Innocent Insinuations of Wit: The Strategy of Language in Shakespeare's *Sonnets.*" *The Play and Place of Criticism.* Baltimore: The Johns Hopkins P., 1967.

4549 KRIEGER, Murray. *A Window to Criticism: Shakespeare's "Sonnets" and Modern Poetics.* Princeton: Princeton U.P., 1964.

4550 LANDRY, Hilton. *Interpretations in Shakespeare's Sonnets.* Berkeley and Los Angeles: U. of California P., 1963.

4551 LANDRY, Hilton. "The Marriage of True Minds: Truth and Error in Sonnet 116." *ShakS* 3 (1968 for 1967):98–110.

4552 LANDRY, Hilton, ed. *New Essays on Shakespeare's Sonnets.* New York: AMS, 1976.

4553 LEE, Sidney. "Ovid and Shakespeare's Sonnets." *QR* 210 (1909):455–76. Rpt. in *Elizabethan and Other Essays.* Ed. Frederick S. BOAS. Oxford: Clarendon, 1929.

4554 LEISHMAN, J. B. *Themes and Variations in Shakespeare's Sonnets.* London: Hutchinson; New York: Hillary House, 1961.*

4555 LEVER, J. W. *The Elizabethan Love Sonnet.* London: Methuen, 1956; 2nd ed., 1966.*

4556 MCCANLES, Michael. " 'Increasing Store with Loss': Some Themes of Shakespeare's Sonnets." *TSLL* 13 (1971):391–406.

4557 MAHOOD, M. M. "Love's Confined Doom." *ShS* 15 (1962):50–61.

4558 MARTIN, Philip. *Shakespeare's Sonnets: Self, Love, and Art.* Cambridge: Cambridge U.P., 1972.

4559 MELCHIORI, Giorgio. *Shakespeare's Dramatic Meditations: An Experiment in Criticism.* Oxford: Clarendon, 1976.

4560 MIZENER, Arthur. "The Structure of Figurative Language in Shakespeare's Sonnets." *SoR* 5 (1940):730–47. Rpt. in **1125** and **4535.***

4561 NEELY, Carol Thomas. "Detachment and Engagement in Shakespeare's Sonnets: 94, 116, and 129." *PMLA* 92 (1977):83–95.

4562 NEJGEBAUER, A. "Twentieth-Century Studies in Shakespeare's Songs, Sonnets, and Poems: 2. The Sonnets." *ShS* 15 (1962):10–18.

4563 NOSWORTHY, J. M. "All Too Short a Date: Internal Evidence in Shakespeare's Sonnets." *EIC* 2 (1952):311–24.

4564 NOWOTTNY, Winifred M. T. "Formal Elements in Shakespeare's Sonnets: Sonnets I–VI." *EIC* 2 (1952):76–84. Rpt. in **4535.***

4565 OSHIO, Toshiko. "*The Sonnets:* From the Poems to the Poet." *ShStud* 12 (1973–74):46–71.

4566 PARKER, David. "Verbal Moods in Shakespeare's Sonnets." *MLQ* 30 (1969): 331–39.

4567 PETERSON, Douglas L. "Shakespeare's Sonnets." *The English Lyric from Wyatt to Donne.* Princeton: Princeton U.P., 1967.

4568 PIRKHOFER, Anton M. " 'Pretty Pleasing Pricket'—On the Use of Alliteration in Shakespeare's Sonnets." *SQ* 14 (1963):3–14.

4569 PRINCE, F. T. "The Sonnet from Wyatt to Shakespeare." In **4512.**

4570 RANSOM, John Crowe. "Shakespeare at Sonnets." *SoR* 3 (1938):531–53. Rpt. in *The World's Body.* Baton Rouge: Louisiana State U.P.; New York: Scribner's, 1938. Rpt. by Louisiana State U.P. in 1968. Rpt. in **4535.*** See also "A Postscript on Shakespeare's Sonnets." *KR* 30 (1968):523–31.

4571 ROLLINS, Hyder E., ed. *A New Variorum Edition of Shakespeare: The Sonnets.* 2 vols. Philadelphia: Lippincott, 1944.

4572 SCHARR, Claes. *Elizabethan Sonnet Themes and the Dating of Shakespeare's "Sonnets."* Lund: C. W. K. Gleerup; Copenhagen: Ejnar Munksgaard, 1962.

4573 STIRLING, Brents. *The Shakespeare Sonnet Order: Poems and Groups.* Berkeley and Los Angeles: U. of California P., 1968.

4574 WAIT, R. J. C. *The Background to Shakespeare's Sonnets,* London: Chatto & Windus; New York: Schocken, 1972.

4575 WHEELER, Richard P. "Poetry and Fantasy in Shakespeare's Sonnets 88–96." *L&P* 22 (1972):151–62.

4576 WILDE, Oscar. *The Portrait of Mr. W. H.* Ed. Vyvyan HOLLAND. London: Methuen, 1921. New ed., 1958. Rpt. in **4540.**

4577 WILLEN, Gerald, and Victor B. REED, eds. *A Casebook on Shakespeare's Sonnets.* New York: Crowell, 1964.

4578 WILLIAMSON, C. F. "Themes and Patterns in Shakespeare's Sonnets." *EIC* 26 (1976):191–208.

4579 WILSON, J. Dover. *An Introduction to the Sonnets of Shakespeare for the Use of Historians and Others.* Cambridge: Cambridge U.P., 1963. Printed as introduction to the New Cambridge Shakespeare edition of the Sonnets, 1963.

4580 WILSON, Katharine M. *Shakespeare's Sugared Sonnets.* London: Allen & Unwin; New York: Barnes & Noble, 1974.

4581 WINNY, James. *The Master-Mistress: A Study of Shakespeare's Sonnets.* London: Chatto & Windus; New York: Barnes & Noble, 1968.

4582 WINTERS, Yvor. "Poetic Styles, Old and New." *Four Poets on Poetry.* Ed. Don Cameron ALLEN. Baltimore: The Johns Hopkins P., 1959. Rpt. in **4535.***

General Studies of the Other Poems

See also **385.**

4583 GRIFFIN, Robert J. " 'These Contrarieties Such Unity Do Hold': Patterned Imagery in Shakespeare's Narrative Poems." *SEL* 4 (1964):43–55.

4584 LEVER, J. W. "Shakespeare's Narrative Poems." In **55.**

4585 LEVER, J. W. "Twentieth-Century Studies in Shakespeare's Songs, Sonnets, and Poems: 3. The Poems." *ShS* 15 (1962):18–30.

4586 MAXWELL, J. C., ed. *The Poems.* In the New Cambridge Shakespeare. See **363.**

4587 PRINCE, F. T., ed. *The Poems.* In the Arden Shakespeare. See **350.**

4588 ROLLINS, Hyder E., ed. *A New Variorum Edition of Shakespeare: The Poems.* Philadelphia: Lippincott, 1938.

A Lover's Complaint

4589 JACKSON, MacD. P. *Shakespeare's "A Lover's Complaint": Its Date and Authenticity.* Auckland, N.Z.: Dobbie, 1965.

4590 MACKAIL, J. W. " 'A Lover's Complaint.' " *E&S* 3 (1912):51–70.

4591 MUIR, Kenneth. " 'A Lover's Complaint': A Reconsideration." In **1121.** Rpt. in **1238.**

The Phoenix and the Turtle

4592 ALVAREZ, A. "William Shakespeare: *The Phoenix and the Turtle.*" *Interpretations.* Ed. John WAIN. London: Routledge & K. Paul, 1955.*

4593 BATES, Ronald. "Shakespeare's *The Phoenix and the Turtle.*" *SQ* 6 (1955): 19–30.

4594 BRADBROOK, M. C. "*The Phoenix and the Turtle.*" *SQ* 6 (1955):356–58.

4595 CAMPBELL, K. T. S. "*The Phoenix and the Turtle* as a Signpost of Shakespeare's Development." *BJA* 10 (1970):169–79.

4596 COPLAND, Murray. "The Dead Phoenix." *EIC* 15 (1965):279–87.

4597 CUNNINGHAM, J. V. " 'Essence' and the *Phoenix and Turtle.*" *ELH* 19 (1952):265–76. See also **1197.***

4598 DRONKE, Peter. *"The Phoenix and the Turtle."* OL 23 (1968):199–220.

4599 ELLRODT, Robert. "An Anatomy of *The Phoenix and the Turtle."* ShS 15 (1962):99–110.

4600 EMPSON, William. *"The Phoenix and the Turtle."* EIC 16 (1966):147–53.

4601 GREEN, Roger Lancelyn. "The Phoenix and the Tree." *English* 7 (1948):11–15.

4602 KNIGHT, G. Wilson. *The Mutual Flame: On Shakespeare's "Sonnets" and "The Phoenix and the Turtle."* London: Methuen; New York: Macmillan, 1955. Rpt., New York: Barnes & Noble.

4603 MATCHETT, William H. *"The Phoenix and the Turtle": Shakespeare's Poem and Chester's "Loues Martyr."* The Hague and Paris: Mouton; New York: Humanities P., 1965.

4604 OAKESHOTT, Walter. *"Loves Martyr."* HLQ 39 (1975):29–49.

4605 ONG, Walter J. "Metaphor and the Twinned Vision (*The Phoenix and the Turtle*)." SR 63 (1955):193–201.*

4606 PETRONELLA, Vincent F. "Shakespeare's *The Phoenix and the Turtle* and the Defunctive Music of Ecstasy." *ShakS* 8 (1975):311–31.

4607 RICHARDS, I. A. "The Sense of Poetry: Shakespeare's *The Phoenix and the Turtle."* Daedalus 87.3 (1958):86–94.*

4608 SCHWARTZ, Elias. "Shakespeare's Dead Phoenix." *ELN* 7 (1969):25–32.

4609 SELTZER, Daniel. " 'Their Tragic Scene': *The Phoenix and Turtle* and Shakespeare's Love Tragedies." *SQ* 12 (1961):91–101.

4610 UNDERWOOD, Richard A. *Shakespeare's "The Phoenix and Turtle": A Survey of Scholarship.* Salzburg: Institut für Englische Sprache und Literatur, 1974.

The Rape of Lucrece

See also **474.**

4611 ALLEN, Don Cameron. "Some Observations on *The Rape of Lucrece."* ShS 15 (1962):89–98. Rpt. in *Image and Meaning: Metaphoric Traditions in Renaissance Poetry.* 2nd ed., Baltimore: The Johns Hopkins P., 1968.

4612 BUSH, Douglas. *"Venus and Adonis* and *Lucrece." Mythology and the Renaissance Tradition in English Poetry.* Minneapolis: U. of Minnesota P., 1932. Rev. ed., New York: Norton, 1963.

4613 FRYE, Roland Mushat. "Shakespeare's Composition of *Lucrece:* New Evidence." *SQ* 16 (1965):289–96.

4614 KAHN, Coppélia. "The Rape in Shakespeare's *Lucrece." ShakS* 9 (1976):45–72.

4615 KUHL, E. P. "Shakespeare's *Rape of Lucrece." PQ* 20 (1941):352–60.

4616 MAJORS, G. W. "Shakespeare's First Brutus: His Role in *Lucrece." MLQ* 35 (1974):339–51.

4617 MONTGOMERY, Robert L., Jr. "Shakespeare's Gaudy: The Method of *The Rape of Lucrece."* In **1142.**

4618 MUIR, Kenneth. *"The Rape of Lucrece."* Anglica 5.4 (1964):25–40.

4619 PLATT, Michael. *"The Rape of Lucrece* and the Republic for Which It Stands." *CentR* 19 (1975):59–79. Rpt. in **2046.**

4620 SIMONE, R. Thomas. *Shakespeare and "Lucrece": A Study of the Poem and Its Relation to the Plays.* Salzburg: Institut für Englische Sprache und Literatur, 1974.

4621 SYLVESTER, Bickford. "Natural Mutability and Human Responsibility: Form in Shakespeare's *Lucrece.*" *CE* 26 (1965):505–11.

4622 TOLBERT, James M. "The Argument of Shakespeare's *Lucrece:* Its Sources and Authorship." *UTSE* 29 (1950):77–90.

4623 WALLEY, Harold R. *"The Rape of Lucrece* and Shakespearean Tragedy." *PMLA* 76 (1961):480–87.

4624 WATKINS, W. B. C. "Shakespeare's Banquet of Sense." In **4511.** On *Venus and Adonis* and *Lucrece.*

Venus and Adonis

See also **474, 1216,** and **4515.**

4625 ALLEN, Don Cameron. "On *Venus and Adonis.*" In **1131.** Also rpt. in *Image and Meaning,* 2nd ed.; see **4611.**

4626 ALLEN, Michael J. B. "The Chase: The Development of a Renaissance Theme." *CL* 20 (1968):301–12.

4627 ASALS, Heather. *"Venus and Adonis:* The Education of a Goddess." *SEL* 13 (1973):31–51.

4628 BEAUREGARD, David N. *"Venus and Adonis:* Shakespeare's Representation of the Passion." *ShakS* 8 (1975):83–98.

4629 BONJOUR, Adrien. "From Shakespeare's Venus to Cleopatra's Cupids." *ShS* 15 (1962):73–80.

4630 BOWERS, R. H. "Anagnorisis, or the Shock of Recognition, in Shakespeare's *Venus and Adonis.*" *RenP 1962* (1963):3–8.

4631 BRADBROOK, M. C. "Beasts and Gods: Greene's *Groats-worth of Witte* and the Social Purpose of *Venus and Adonis.*" *ShS* 15 (1962):62–72.

4632 BROWN, Huntington. *"Venus and Adonis:* The Action, the Narrator, and the Critics." *MichA* 2.2 (1969):73–87.

4633 BUSH, Douglas. *"Venus and Adonis* and *Lucrece.*" See **4612.**

4634 CANTELUPE, Eugene B. "An Iconographical Interpretation of *Venus and Adonis,* Shakespeare's Ovidian Comedy." *SQ* 14 (1963):141–51.

4635 GENT, Lucy. *"Venus and Adonis:* The Triumph of Rhetoric." *MLR* 69 (1974):721–29.

4636 HAMILTON, A. C. *"Venus and Adonis.*" *SEL* 1.1 (1961):1–15. Rpt., rev., in **1586.**

4637 HATTO, A. T. *"Venus and Adonis*—and the Boar." *MLR* 41 (1946):353–61.

4638 JACKSON, Robert Sumner. "Narrative and Imagery in Shakespeare's *Venus and Adonis.*" *PMASAL* 43 (1958):315–20.

4639 JAHN, J. D. "The Lamb of Lust: The Role of Adonis in Shakespeare's *Venus and Adonis.*" *ShakS* 6 (1972 for 1970):11–25.

4640 LAKE, James H. "Shakespeare's Venus: An Experiment in Tragedy." *SQ* 25 (1974):351–55.

4641 LEECH, Clifford. "Venus and Her Nun: Portraits of Women in Love by Shakespeare and Marlowe." *SEL* 5 (1965):247–68.

4642 LEVER, J. W. "Venus and the Second Chance." *ShS* 15 (1962):81–88.

4643 MILLER, Robert P. "The Myth of Mars's Hot Minion in *Venus and Adonis.*" *ELH* 26 (1959):470–81.

4644 MILLER, Robert P. "Venus, Adonis, and the Horses." *ELH* 19 (1952):249–64.

4645 MUIR, Kenneth. "*Venus and Adonis:* Comedy or Tragedy?" In **1171**. Rpt. in **1238**.

4646 PEGG, Barry. "Generation and Corruption in Shakespeare's *Venus and Adonis.*" *MichA* 8 (1975):105–15.

4647 PRICE, Hereward T. "Function of Imagery in *Venus and Adonis.*" *PMASAL* 31 (1945):275–97.

4648 PUTNEY, Rufus. "Venus Agonistes." *UCSLL* 4 (1953):52–66.

4649 PUTNEY, Rufus. "*Venus and Adonis:* Amour with Humor." *PQ* 20 (1941): 533–48.

4650 RABKIN, Norman. "*Venus and Adonis* and the Myth of Love." In **1156**.*

4651 ROTHENBERG, Alan B. "The Oral Rape Fantasy and Rejection of Mother in the Imagery of Shakespeare's *Venus and Adonis.*" *PsyQ* 40 (1971):447–68.

4652 SHEIDLEY, William E. " 'Unless It Be a Boar': Love and Wisdom in Shakespeare's *Venus and Adonis.*" *MLQ* 35 (1974):3–15.

4653 SMITH, Gordon Ross. "Mannerist Frivolity and Shakespeare's *Venus and Adonis.*" *HSL* 3 (1971):1–11.

4654 STREITBERGER, W. R. "Ideal Conduct in *Venus and Adonis.*" *SQ* 26 (1975): 285–91.

4655 WATKINS, W. B. C. "Shakespeare's Banquet of Sense." In **4511**. On *Venus and Adonis* and *Lucrece.*

Plays of Doubtful or Composite Authorship

General Studies

See also **583**.

4556 BRADBROOK, M. C. "Shakespeare and His Collaborators." In **1151**.

4657 BROOKE, C. F. Tucker, ed. *The Shakespeare Apocrypha.* See **349**. A new edition of the Shakespeare Apocrypha by G. Richard Proudfoot is forthcoming.

4658 ERDMAN, David V., and Ephim G. FOGEL, eds. *Evidence for Authorship: Essays on Problems of Attribution.* Ithaca: Cornell U.P., 1966.

4659 EVERITT, Ephraim B., and Ray L. ARMSTRONG, eds. *Six Early Plays Related to the Shakespeare Canon.* Anglistica 14. Copenhagen: Rosenkilde & Bagger, 1965. Includes *Leir, The Weakest Goeth to the Wall, Edmund Ironsides, The Troublesome Reign of King John, Edward III,* and *Woodstock.*

4660 KOZLENKO, William, ed. *Disputed Plays of William Shakespeare.* New York: Hawthorne, 1974.

4661 MUIR, Kenneth. *Shakespeare as Collaborator.* London: Methuen; New York: Barnes & Noble, 1960.*

4662 NOSWORTHY, J. M. *Shakespeare's Occasional Plays: Their Origin and Transmission.* See **382.***

4663 PRIOR, Moody E. "Imagery as a Test of Authorship." *SQ* 6 (1955):381–86.

4664 SCHOENBAUM, S. *Internal Evidence and Elizabethan Dramatic Authorship: An Essay in Literary History and Method.* Evanston, Ill.: Northwestern U.P., 1966.*

The Book of Sir Thomas More

See also **1576.**

4665 BALD, R. C. "*The Booke of Sir Thomas More* and Its Problems." *ShS* 2 (1949): 44–61. Rpt. in **4658.***

4666 CHAMBERS, R. W. "Shakespeare and the Play of *More.*" *Man's Unconquerable Mind.* London: Cape, 1939. Rpt., Philadelphia: Saifer, 1953; New York: Haskell House, 1967.

4667 COLLINS, D. C. "On the Date of *Sir Thomas More.*" *RES* 10 (1934):401–11.

4668 HAYS, Michael L. "Shakespeare's Hand in *Sir Thomas More:* Some Aspects of the Paleographic Argument." *ShakS* 8 (1975):241–53.*

4669 MCMILLIN, Scott. "*The Book of Sir Thomas More:* A Theatrical View." *MP* 68 (1970):10–24.

4670 NOSWORTHY, J. M. "Shakespeare and *Sir Thomas More.*" *RES,* n.s. 6 (1955): 12–25.

4671 POLLARD, Alfred W., et al. *Shakespeare's Hand in "The Play of Sir Thomas More."* Cambridge: Cambridge U.P., 1923.*

4672 SPURGEON, Caroline F. E. "Imagery in the *Sir Thomas More* Fragment." *RES* 6 (1930):257–70.

4673 WENTERSDORF, Karl P. "Linkages of Thought and Imagery in Shakespeare and *More.*" *MLQ* 34 (1973):384–405.

Cardenio

4674 FRAZIER, Harriet C. *A Babble of Ancestral Voices: Shakespeare, Cervantes, and Theobald.* The Hague: Mouton, 1974. On the origin of Shakespeare's *Cardenio* and Theobald's *The Double Falsehood.*

4675 FREEHAFER, John. "*Cardenio,* by Shakespeare and Fletcher." *PMLA* 84 (1969):501–13.

Edward III

See also **4661.**

4676 HART, Alfred. "The Vocabulary of *Edward III.*" In **119.**

4677 KOSKENNIEMI, Inna. "Themes and Imagery in *Edward III.*" *NM* 65 (1964): 446–80.

4678 WENTERSDORF, Karl P. "The Date of *Edward III.*" *SQ* 16 (1965):227–31.

The Two Noble Kinsmen

See also **1756, 4656,** and **4661.**

For discussions of composite authorship in *Henry VIII,* see under *Henry VIII.* On the question of composite authorship in *Pericles,* see under *Pericles* and also **4661.**

4679 BERTRAM, Paul. *Shakespeare and "The Two Noble Kinsmen."* New Brunswick, N.J.: Rutgers U.P., 1965.*

4680 BRADLEY, A. C. "Scene Endings in Shakespeare and in *The Two Noble Kinsmen.*" In **1184.**

4681 EDWARDS, Philip. "On the Design of *The Two Noble Kinsmen.*" *REL* 5.4 (1964):89–105.*

4682 ELLIS-FERMOR, Una. *"The Two Noble Kinsmen."* In **1203.**

4683 HART, Alfred. "Shakespeare and the Vocabulary of *The Two Noble Kinsmen.*" *RES* 10 (1934):274–87. Rpt. in **119.**

4684 LEECH, Clifford. *The John Fletcher Plays.* Cambridge, Mass.: Harvard U.P., 1962, pp. 144–68.

4685 MINCOFF, Marco. "The Authorship of *The Two Noble Kinsmen.*" *ES* 33 (1952):97–115.

4686 PETRONELLA, Vincent F. "Stylistic Logic in Shakespeare's Part of *The Two Noble Kinsmen.*" *HAB* 25 (1974):38–40.

4687 PROUDFOOT, G. Richard. "Shakespeare and the New Dramatists of the King's Men, 1606–1613." In **1599.**

4688 SPENCER, Theodore. *"The Two Noble Kinsmen."* *MP* 36 (1939):255–76.

4689 WALLER, Frederick O. "Printer's Copy for *The Two Noble Kinsmen.*" *SB* 11 (1958):61–84.

INDEX

INDEX

INDEX

INDEX

INDEX

INDEX

INDEX

INDEX

INDEX

INDEX

INDEX

INDEX

INDEX

INDEX

INDEX

INDEX

INDEX

INDEX

NOTES